OKANAGAN UNIV/COLLEGE LIBRARY
K

`152`

D0871961

RC 489 .R3 E437
The essential Albert Ellis
Ellis, Albert
169615

DATE DUE

FEB 01 1994	
APR 1 1 1994	
JUL 2 8 1994	
FEB 1 1995	
MAR 2 4 1995	
FEB 0 7 1997	
APR 2 1 1997	
JAN	
JUN 8 2000	

BRODART   Cat. No. 23-221

The Essential Albert Ellis
Seminal Writings on Psychotherapy

ALBERT ELLIS

OKANAGAN UNIVERSITY COLLEGE
LIBRARY
BRITISH COLUMBIA

The Essential Albert Ellis
Seminal Writings on Psychotherapy

Windy Dryden, Ph.D.
Editor

SPRINGER PUBLISHING COMPANY
New York

Copyright © 1990 by Springer Publishing Company, Inc.

All rights reserved

No part of this publication may be reproduced, stored in a
retrieval system, or transmitted in any form or by any means,
electronic, mechanical, photocopying, recording, or otherwise,
without the prior permission of Springer Publishing Company,
Inc.

Springer Publishing Company, Inc.
536 Broadway
New York, NY 10012

90 91 92 93 94 / 5 4 3 2 1

Library of Congress Cataloging-in-Publication Data

Ellis, Albert.
   The essential Albert Ellis: seminal papers on psychotherapy /
Windy Dryden, editor.
      p. cm.
   Includes bibliographical references.
   ISBN 0-8261-6940-6
   1. Rational-emotive psychotherapy. I. Dryden, Windy. II. Title.
RC489.R3E437 1990
616.89'14--dc20   89-26338
                                                              CIP

Printed in the United States of America

Contents

Introduction

Albert Ellis founded rational–emotive therapy (RET) in 1955. His influence in the field of psychology is now such that in a survey of APA clinical and counseling psychologists published in 1982 (Smith, 1982) he was ranked the second most influential psychotherapist (behind Carl Rogers, but ahead of Sigmund Freud). In another study (Heesacker, Hepper, & Rogers, 1982) he was the most-cited contributor of works published since 1957 in three major counseling psychology journals over a 27-year period.

The influence of RET has also been profound. In its 35 years of existence it has been practiced in various therapeutic modalities (individual, group, marital, and family), by many kinds of helping professionals (e.g., psychologists, psychiatrists, social workers), and with a variety of client populations (e.g., adults, children, the elderly) suffering from a wide range of psychological disorders. Apart from their use in counseling and psychotherapy, rational-emotive principles have been applied in educational, industrial, and commercial settings. A very recent development has been the application of RET to public education in the form of 9-hour intensive workshops. In this respect it is playing a significant role in the field of preventive psychology. RET is practiced throughout the world, and there are RET "institutes" in the United States, Italy, West Germany, Holland, Australia, England, and Mexico. Ellis has had and continues to have an international influence on the field of psychology.

Ellis has been extremely prolific in writing about RET. He has published over 50 books and over 600 articles and book chapters. Such is the immense quantity of Ellis's publications on RET that there is a distinct need for a brief collection of his seminal articles on psychotherapy. This volume seeks to meet that need by bringing together Albert Ellis's most important writings on RET. It thus serves both as a handy reference for knowledgeable professionals and as a helpful guide for the beginner who wants to know where to start with Ellis's work. The balance of this introduction will briefly review the origins of RET and its major influences and will place each of the seminal papers that follow within the overall context of Ellis's thought.

ORIGINS OF RET

As a result of research he was doing in the early 1940s for a massive theoretical work, to be entitled "The Case for Sexual Liberty," Albert Ellis decided to pursue formal training in clinical psychology after he had gained a local reputation as an authority on sexual and marital relationships. He had been consulted by his friends on their sexual and relationship problems and discovered that he could help them with such problems in a short period of time. There were no formal training possibilities then offered in sex and marital counseling. After getting a PhD degree in clinical psychology, Ellis chose to be trained in psychoanalysis, believing then that it was the deepest and most effective form of psychotherapy available. He decided on this course of action because his experiences as an informal sex and marital counselor had taught him that disturbed relationships were really a product of disturbed persons "and that if people were truly to be helped to live happily with each other they first had better be shown how they could live peacefully with themselves" (Ellis, 1962, p. 3).

Ellis initially enjoyed working as a psychoanalyst partly because it allowed him to express both his helping and problem-solving interests. However, he became increasingly dissatisfied with psychoanalysis as an effective and efficient form of treatment. In the early 1950s he began to experiment with different forms of therapy, including psychoanalytically oriented psychotherapy and eclectic-analytic therapy. But although he became more effective with his clients, he remained dissatisfied about the efficiency of these methods. During this period of experimentation he returned to his lifelong hobby of reading philosophy to help him with his search for an effective and efficient form of therapy. One of the major influences on his thought at that time was the work of the Greek and Roman Stoic philosophers (e.g., Epictetus and Marcus Aurelius). They emphasized the primacy of philosophic causation in psychological disturbances—a viewpoint that was not popular in America in the 1950s—and de-emphasized the part played by psychoanalytic psychodynamic factors. In essence, the Stoic viewpoint, which stated that people are disturbed not by things but by their view of things, became the foundation of RET.

Ellis first called his new approach to psychotherapy Rational Psychotherapy, in 1955, to emphasize two facts: (a) that it focused on clients' illogical or irrational thinking, which he deemed to be at the core of much psychological disturbance, and (b) that the major task of rational therapists was to help clients think more rationally about themselves, other people, and the world. However, from the outset Ellis claimed that thoughts, feelings, and behaviors are interdependent psychological processes and that, as a consequence, he encouraged his clients to change their irrational thoughts by using emotive and behavioral techniques as well as cognitive methods. Despite this threefold emphasis, Rational Psychotherapy was wrongly criticized for neglecting clients' emotions and behaviors. As a result Ellis soon changed the name of his therapeutic approach to Rational–Emotive Therapy to stress that it did not, in particular, neglect clients' feelings. Raymond Corsini urged Ellis to retitle his method Rational–Emotive–Behavior Therapy to emphasize that it also stressed behavioral change, but Ellis found that term too cumbersome.

Ellis has always been keen on promulgating his views widely, and in 1959 he established the Institute for Rational Living, a nonprofit educational foundation, a major function of which was to promote RET to the general public through books, tapes, and other publications. In 1968 Ellis founded the Institute for the Advanced Study of Rational Psychotherapy, primarily to offer clinical services to the public and training for professionals. These two institutes were later merged to form the Institute for Rational–Emotive Therapy, of which Ellis is now the president, having been its executive director for many years.

MAJOR INFLUENCES ON ELLIS'S THOUGHT

Philosophical Influences

Apart from Stoicism, Ellis owes a philosophical debt to a number of other sources that have influenced his development of RET. Immanuel Kant's writings on the power (and limitations) of cognition and ideation strongly impressed Ellis, and the works of Spinoza and Schopenhauer also were important in this respect. Philosophers of science, such as Popper, Reichenbach, and Bertrand Russell, were influential in helping Ellis to see that all humans develop hypotheses about the nature of the world. Moreover, these philosophers stressed the importance of testing the validity of such hypotheses rather than assuming that they are necessarily correct. Indeed, the practice of RET has become synonymous, in many respects, with the logico-empirical methods of science. Following these philosophers of science, Ellis stresses the flexibility and antidogmatism of the scientific method. He opposes all dogmas, just as science does, and holds that rigid absolutism is the very core of human disturbance.

Although the philosophy of RET is at variance with devout religiosity, in one respect Christian philosophy has influenced Ellis. RET's theory of human value (see Chapter 4) is similar to the Christian viewpoint of condemning the sin but forgiving the sinner. Similarly, in accord with his stand on self-acceptance and his opposition to all forms of human rating, Ellis allies himself with the philosophy of ethical humanism, which opposes the deification and devil-ification of humans. Because RET considers that humans are at the center of their universe (but not of *the* universe) and have the power of choice (but not of unlimited choice) with regard to their emotional realm, it has roots in the existential philosophies of Heidegger and Tillich. Indeed, RET has a pronounced humanistic existential outlook.

Ellis was also influenced, particularly in the 1960s, by the work of the general semanticists, such as Alfred Korzybski. These theorists outlined the powerful effect that language has on thought and the fact that our emotional processes are heavily dependent on the way we, as humans, structure our thought by the language we employ.

Psychological Influences

In developing RET, Ellis has similarly been influenced by the work of a number of psychologists. He received a training analysis from an analyst of the Karen Horney school, and Horney's concept of the "tyranny of the shoulds" was certainly an early influence, leading to his emphasis on the primacy of absolute, dogmatic evaluative thought in the development and maintenance of much psychological disturbance.

The work of Alfred Adler was important to the development of Ellis's ideas in several respects. Adler was the first therapist to emphasize inferiority feelings; RET similarly stresses self-rating and the ego anxiety to which it leads (see Chapter 4). Like Adler's Individual Psychology, RET also emphasizes people's goals, purposes, values, and meanings. In addition, RET follows Adler in regard to the use of active–directive teaching, the stress placed on social interest, the use of a holistic and humanistic outlook, and the employment of a highly cognitive–persuasive form of psychological treatment.

As stated above, although Ellis originally termed his therapeutic approach Rational Psychotherapy, he always advocated the use of behavioral methods as well as cognitive and emotive techniques in the practice of therapy. Indeed, he utilized many of the methods advocated by some of the earliest pioneers in behavior therapy (such as John B. Watson and Mary Cover Jones), first in overcoming his own early fears of speaking in public and of approaching women and second in the active–directive form of sex therapy that he practiced in the early 1950s. This behavioral active–directive emphasis remains prominent in present-day RET.

Ellis's Major Contributions to Psychotherapy

For this book, I have endeavored to select Ellis's most seminal writings on the theory (Part I) and practice (Part II) of psychotherapy, which demonstrate his unique contribution to the field.

Ellis is perhaps best known for emphasizing the role of cognitions—in particular, dogmatic "musturbatory" cognitions (irrational beliefs)—in the development and maintenance of psychological disturbance (see Chapter 1). However, Ellis has not only put forward a theory of psychopathology; he also expounded, in 1978, a theory of personality that underpins his ideas about therapeutic practice (Chapter 2).

An interesting feature of this personality theory is the emphasis Ellis places on the role of biological factors in the development of personality. This view is paralleled by Ellis's position that human beings are biologically predisposed to think irrationally (see Chapter 3). Although at first glance this seems like a pessimistic view, Ellis is quick to stress that we also have the ability to think about and change our irrational thinking, and thereby our emotional problems, through hard work and practice. This viewpoint, which is at variance with the environmentalist position taken by psychoanalytic therapists and radical behaviorists, was first published by Ellis in 1976.

Whereas Ellis argues that there is a biological *basis* for human irrationality and hence psychopathology, he argues that the *content* of much psychological distress is expressed through two major types of disturbance. First, we make ourselves disturbed by the demands we make on ourselves. A central part of this *ego disturbance* is our tendency to make exaggerated global negative ratings of the self; this view was originally articulated in Ellis's (1962) first book, *Reason and Emotion in Psychotherapy* and developed, in 1972, in the seminal article presented in this volume (Chapter 4).

The second major type of psychological disturbance is what Ellis calls *discomfort disturbance*, which relates to our tendency to make demands about experiencing a sense of comfort. This form of disturbance is less dramatic than ego disturbance but is, as Ellis argues, often more prevalent and is a major component of many psychological disorders, particularly anxiety, a view that Ellis first articulated in 1979 and 1980 (Chapter 5).

The final chapter in the theoretical part of this volume concerns an important debate that is currently going on in the field of cognitive psychotherapy. In an important article, Michael Mahoney (1988) has argued that cognitive approaches to psychotherapy can be divided into two camps, rationalist and constructivist. Mahoney places RET firmly in the rationalist camp, a position challenged by Ellis who holds that, on the contrary, it is clearly constructivist in its theoretical concepts. This view was first articulated by Ellis in a keynote address at the first World Congress on Cognitive Therapy in Oxford, June 1989. Chapter 6 shows that 35 years after he founded RET, Ellis is still writing seminal articles on this approach.

The second part of the volume deals with Ellis's contributions to the practice of psychotherapy. In Chapter 7, Ellis presents an overview of the practice of RET, showing clearly how it is an active–directive approach that freely utilizes cognitive, imaginal, emotive–evocative, and behavioral methods. The remaining chapters in Part II each address a key element of RET practice.

Many authorities on psychotherapy have argued that psychotherapeutic change is predicated on the close bond that develops between therapist and client. Ellis's position on that point is to caution therapists against being overly warm toward their clients, noting that undue therapist warmth may well reinforce clients' dire needs for love and approval. This and Ellis's other views of the therapeutic relationship are presented in Chapter 8, and as such the piece is the most complete statement Ellis has made on this topic.

Another unique contribution that Ellis has made to the practice of psychotherapy concerns his use of rational humorous songs. Ellis has often argued that one way of conceptualizing psychological disturbance is to consider it the result of taking oneself, others, and the world *too* seriously. Ellis suggests that one method of overcoming psychological problems is to take an ironic, humorous attitude toward them. Chapter 9 deals with this issue and includes some of the rational songs written by Ellis himself.

Ever since he originated RET, Ellis has argued that clients need to "work and practice" repeatedly at changing their irrational beliefs if they are to effect meaningful and long-lasting therapeutic change. In particular, because clients make themselves disturbed by clinging devoutly and powerfully to their irrational beliefs, if they are to counteract this process, they are called upon to challenge and change these beliefs forcefully and energetically. Chapter 10, which was first published in 1979, presents Ellis's fullest statement on this issue, although the ideas expressed within it were present in embryonic form in Ellis's earliest writings on RET.

In addition to Ellis's many continuing writing projects, he works over 12 hours a day conducting therapy and training and supervising other therapists. Ellis has claimed that the reason that he is able to get so much done is that he has a "gene for efficiency." It is not surprising, then, that Ellis is concerned with efficiency in psychotherapy; in 1980 he published an important article outlining several significant dimensions of psychotherapeutic efficiency (see Chapter 11).

Ellis has a nonutopian view of the potential of psychotherapy, and in recent years he has turned his attention to writing about treatment failures (Chapter 12) and about helping clients (Chapter 13) and their therapists (Chapter 14) overcome resistance to change. These articles (all published in 1983) reflect Ellis's biologically based views on disturbance and change. These views are that we very easily block ourselves from changing even when we understand how we make ourselves disturbed and how we can tackle our disturbances. However, we can overcome these resistances by repeatedly identifying, challenging, and changing the irrational beliefs that underpin the resistance process.

A NOTE ON THE EDITORIAL PROCESS

These seminal writings, taken together, provide a comprehensive overview of Ellis's work on the theory and practice of RET. Although I worked closely with him on the selection of this work, the final choice of the 14 chapters was ultimately mine. Each piece contains a brief introduction outlining the paper's importance and in some cases the circumstances in which it was written. Each appears as it was originally published, with two exceptions. First, in some papers I deleted sections that appear in other chapters in order to avoid unnecessary duplication. Second, I have updated references that appeared in the bibliography of the original paper as "in press."

The reader should bear in mind that sexism in language was not an issue when these papers was originally written. The language has not been changed here but I recognize that were these papers written today Ellis would not have used sexist language.

It is my hope that this volume will serve as a comprehensive guide to Albert Ellis's seminal ideas on the theory and practice of psychotherapy or, as the title makes clear, "The Essential Albert Ellis."

REFERENCES

Ellis, A. (1962). *Reason and emotion in psychotherapy*. New York: Lyle Stuart.

Heesacker, M., Hepper, P. P., & Rogers, M. E. (1982). Classics and emerging classics in counseling psychology. *Journal of Counseling Psychology, 29*, 400–405.

Mahoney, M. J. (1988). The cognitive sciences and psychotherapy: Patterns in a developing relationship. In K. S. Dobson (Ed.), *Handbook of cognitive-behavioral therapies* (pp. 357–386). New York: Guilford.

Smith, D. (1982). Trends in counseling and psychotherapy. *American Psychologist, 37*, 802–809.

Theory

I

The General Theory of RET

1

INTRODUCTION

Originally, Ellis's general theory of RET was quite simple (e.g., Ellis 1958, 1962). But in the late 1960s and 1970s, Ellis made several important additions to RET. These included clearly distinguishing between appropriate and inappropriate negative emotions, using dramatic and forceful methods to dispute irrational beliefs, emphasizing the primacy of dogmatic "shoulds" and "musts," and stressing the importance of discomfort disturbance, or low frustration tolerance.

Ellis has since spoken about these changes in many of his talks, workshops, and supervision sessions with therapists and mentioned them in a number of his writings (e.g., Ellis & Whiteley, 1979). This chapter, written with Windy Dryden (Ellis & Dryden, 1987), provides an up-to-date summary of the basic theory of RET.

REFERENCES

Ellis, A. (1958). Rational psychotherapy. *Journal of General Psychology, 59*, 35–49.

Ellis, A. (1962). *Reason and emotion in psychotherapy*. Secaucus, NJ: Lyle Stuart.

Ellis, A., & Dryden, W. (1987). *The practice of rational–emotive therapy*. New York: Springer Publishing Co.

Ellis, A., & Whiteley, J. M. (Eds.). (1979). *Theoretical and empirical foundations of rational–emotive therapy*. Monterey, CA: Brooks/Cole.

Parts of this chapter were adapted from Dryden and Ellis (1986) and W. Dryden and A. Ellis, "Rational–Emotive Therapy," in K. S. Dobson (Ed.), *Handbook of Cognitive–Behavioral Therapies*. New York: Guilford, 1987 (Used by permission.) and have been previously published in *The Nurse Practitioner: The American Journal of Primary Health Care, 12*(7), July 1987.

In this chapter we discuss the general theory underpinning the practice of RET. First, we outline RET's major theoretical concepts. Second, we put forward an expanded version of RET's well-known ABC framework. Third, we consider RET's perspective on the nature of psychological disturbance and health. Fourth, we elaborate this theme by detailing RET's viewpoint on how psychological disturbance is acquired and perpetuated. Finally, we outline the RET general theory of therapeutic change.

MAJOR THEORETICAL CONCEPTS

RET is based on a set of assumptions that stress the complexity and fluidity of human beings. Given this fundamental view of human nature, RET rests on the following theoretical concepts.

Goals, Purposes, and Rationality

According to RET theory, humans are happiest when they establish important life goals and purposes and actively strive to attain these. It is argued that, in establishing and pursuing these goals and purposes, human beings had better mind the fact that they live in a social world and that a philosophy of self-interest, where a person places him or herself first, also implies putting others a close second. This is in contrast to a philosophy of selfishness where the desires of others are neither respected nor regarded. Given that humans will tend to be goal-directed, *rational* in RET theory means "that which helps people to achieve their basic goals and purposes, whereas 'irrational' means that which prevents them from achieving these goals and purposes" (Dryden, 1984, p. 238). Thus, rationality is not defined in any absolute sense, but is relative in nature.

Humanistic Emphasis

RET does not pretend to be "purely" objective, scientific, or technique-centered, but takes a definite humanistic–existential approach to human problems and their basic solutions. It primarily deals with disturbed human evaluations, emotions, and behaviors. It is highly rational and scientific but uses rationality and science in the service of humans in an attempt to enable them to live and be happy. It is hedonistic, but it espouses long-range instead of short-range hedonism so that people may achieve the pleasure of the moment and that of the future and may arrive at maximum freedom *and* discipline. It hypothesizes that nothing superhuman probably exists and that devout belief in superhuman agencies tends to foster dependency and increase emotional disturbance. It assumes that no humans, whatever their antisocial or obnoxious behavior, are damnable nor subhuman. It particularly emphasizes the importance of will and choice in human affairs, even though it accepts the likelihood that some human behavior is partially determined by biological, social, and other forces (Bandura, 1977; Ellis, 1973, 1984a).

The Interaction of Psychological Processes and the Place of Cognition

RET theory has from its inception stressed an interactive view of human psychological processes. Cognitions, emotions, and behaviors are not experienced in isolation and often, particularly in the realm of psychological disturbance, overlap to a significant degree. Recently RET has stressed the inferential nature of activating events and has shown how events (or, more correctly, how we perceive events) again interact with our cognitive evaluations, emotions, and behaviors (Ellis, 1984a). This point will be amplified in the section entitled "The ABC's of RET: An Expanded Framework."

Given this interactional view, it is true, however, that RET is most noted for the special place it has accorded cognition in human psychological procesess, particularly the role that evaluative thought plays in psychological health and disturbance. One of RET's unique contributions to the field of cognitive–behavior therapy lies in its distinction between rational and irrational Beliefs. Rational Beliefs are evaluative cognitions of personal significance that are preferential (i.e., nonabsolute) in nature. They are expressed in the form of "desires," "preferences," "wishes," "likes," and "dislikes." Positive feelings of pleasure and satisfaction are experienced when humans get what they desire, whereas negative feelings of displeasure and dissatisfaction (e.g., sadness, concern, regret, annoyance) are experienced when they do not get what they desire. These negative feelings (the strength of which is closely related to the importance of the desire) are regarded as appropriate responses to negative events and do not significantly interfere with the pursuit of established or new goals and purposes. These Beliefs, then, are "rational" in two respects. First, they are relative, and second, they do not impede the attainment of basic goals and purposes.

Irrational Beliefs, on the other hand, differ in two respects from rational beliefs. First, they are absolute (or dogmatic) in nature and are expressed in the form of "musts," "shoulds," "oughts," "have-to's," etc. Second, as such they lead to negative emotions that largely interfere with goal pursuit and attainment (e.g., depression, anxiety, guilt, anger). Rational Beliefs strongly tend to underlie functional behaviors, whereas irrational Beliefs underpin dysfunctional behaviors such as withdrawal, procrastination, alcoholism, and substance abuse (Ellis, 1982).

TWO BASIC BIOLOGICAL TENDENCIES

Unlike most other theories of therapy, which stress the impact of significant life events on the development of psychological disturbance, RET theory hypothesizes that the biological tendency of humans to think irrationally has a notable impact on such disturbance. Its view that irrational thinking is heavily determined by biological factors (always interacting with influential environmental conditions) rests on the seeming ease with which humans think crookedly and the prevalence of such thinking even among people who have been rationally raised (Ellis, 1976). While I (AE) have acknowledged that there are social influences operating here, I have also noted "even if everybody had had the most rational upbringing, virtually all humans would often irrationally escalate their individual and social preferences into absolutistic demands on (a) themselves, (b) other people, and (c) the universe around them" (Ellis, 1984a, p. 20).

Evidence in favor of RET's hypothesis of the biological basis of human irrationality is presented in Chapter 3.

However, RET holds that humans have a second basic biological tendency, namely, to exercise the power of human choice and to work toward changing their irrational thinking. Thus, they have (1) the ability to see that they make themselves disturbed by the irrational views they bring to situations, (2) the ability to see that they can change their thinking, and, most importantly, (3) the ability to actively and continually work toward changing this thinking by the application of cognitive, emotive, and behavioral methods. While RET theory asserts that humans have a strong biological tendency to think irrationally (as well as rationally), it holds that they are by no means slaves to this tendency and can transcend (although not fully) its effects. In the final analysis, then, the RET image of the person is quite an optimistic one (Ellis, 1973; Ellis & Bernard, 1983, 1985).

Two Fundamental Human Disturbances

According to RET, humans can make absolute demands on self, other people, and the world (Ellis, 1984a). However, if these demands are more closely investigated they can be seen to fall into two major categories of psychological disturbance: ego disturbance and discomfort disturbance (Ellis, 1979a, 1980).

In ego disturbance a person makes demands on self, others, and the world, and if these demands are not met in the past, present, or future, the person becomes disturbed by damning "self." As I (WD) have shown, self-damnation involves (1) the process of giving my "self" a global negative rating and (2) "devil-ifying" my "self" as being bad or less worthy (Dryden, 1984). The rational and healthy alternative to self-damnation is self-acceptance, which involves refusing to give one's "self" a single rating (because it is an impossible task, due to one's complexity and fluidity, and because it normally interferes with attaining one's basic goals and purposes) and acknowledging one's fallibility.

In discomfort disturbance the person again makes demands on self, others, and the world, which are related to dogmatic commands that comfort and comfortable life conditions must exist. When these demands are not met in the past, present, or future, the person becomes disturbed. Tolerating discomfort in order to aid goal attainment and long-range happiness is the healthy and rational alternative to demands for immediate gratification.

Thus, as will be shown later, self-acceptance and a high level of frustration tolerance are two of the main cornerstones of the rational–emotive image of the psychologically healthy human being (Ellis, 1979b).

THE ABC's OF RET: AN EXPANDED FRAMEWORK

When RET was originally established I (AE) employed a simple ABC assessment framework to conceptualize clients' psychological problems (Ellis, 1962). In this schema, "A" stood for the Activating event, "B" represented a person's Belief about that event, and "C" denoted the person's emotional and behavioral responses or Consequences to holding the particular Beliefs at "B." The major advantage of the ABC framework lay in its simplicity. However, its simplicity was also a disadvantage in that important distinctions between different types of cognitive activity were glossed over (Wessler & Wessler, 1980). It is important to note that different

RET therapists use different expanded versions of the original ABC framework (cf., Ellis, 1985; Wessler & Wessler, 1980). There is thus no absolutely correct way of conceptualizing clients' problems according to such an expanded schema. What is presented below is one version of the expanded ABC framework.

Activating Events or Activators (A's) of Cognitive, Emotional, and Behavioral Consequences (C's)

The RET theory of personality and personality disturbances begins with people trying to fulfill their Goals (G's) in some kind of environment and encountering a set of Activating events or Activators (A's) that tend to help them achieve or block these Goals. The A's they encounter usually are present or current events or their own thoughts, feelings, or behaviors about these events, but they may be imbedded in memories or thoughts (conscious or unconscious) about past experiences. People are prone to seek out and respond to these A's because of (1) their biological or genetic predispositions, (2) their constitutional history, (3) their prior interpersonal and social learning, and (4) their innately predisposed and acquired habit patterns (Ellis, 1976, 1979b, 1983).

A's (Activating events) virtually never exist in a pure or monolithic state; they almost always interact with and partly include B's and C's. People bring themselves (their goals, thoughts, desires, and physiological propensities) to A's.

Beliefs (B's) about Activating Events (A's)

According to RET theory, people have almost innumerable Beliefs (B's)—cognitions, thoughts, or ideas—about their Activating events (A's); and these B's importantly and directly tend to exert strong influences on their cognitive, emotional, and behavioral Consequences (C's). Although A's often seem to directly "cause" or contribute to C's, this is rarely true, because B's normally serve as important mediators between A's and C's and therefore more directly "cause" or "create" C's (Bard, 1980; Ellis, 1962; Goldfried & Davison, 1976; Grieger & Boyd, 1980; Wessler & Wessler, 1980). People largely bring their Beliefs to A; and they prejudicially view or experience A's in the light of these biased Beliefs (expectations, evaluations) and also in the light of their emotional Consequences (C's). Therefore, humans virtually never experience A without B and C; but they also rarely experience B and C without A.

B's take many different forms because people have many kinds of cognitions. In RET, however, we are mainly interested in their rational Beliefs (rB's), which we hypothesize lead to their self-helping behaviors, and in their irrational Beliefs (iB's), which we theorize lead to their self-defeating (and social-defeating) behaviors. We can list some of the main (but not the only) kinds of B's as follows:

Nonevaluative Observations

Example: "(I see) . . . the man is walking." Such observations do not go beyond the available data. They are nonevaluative because they are not relevant to our goals. When such observations are relevant to our goals they become evaluative; for example, when the man walking is my father who has just recovered from a car accident. The evaluative aspects of such "evaluative observations" are often implicit—for example, "(I am pleased that) . . . the man is walking."

Nonevaluative Inferences

Example: "The man who is walking is going to the post office." Such cognitions are called "inferences" because they go beyond the available data. All we are able to observe in this example is a man walking in a certain direction. Although he is proceeding in the direction of the post office, he may or may not be "going to the post office." As such, inferences may be viewed as hypotheses about our observations that may or may not be correct. These inferences are nonevaluative when they are not relevant to our goals. When such inferences are relevant to our goals, they become evaluative; for example, when the man who may be going to the post office will bring us back our birthday parcels (if indeed he does make such a visit). The evaluative aspects of such "evaluative inferences" are again often implicit—for example, "(it is good that) . . . the man who is walking is going to the post office."

It is helpful to realize for assessment purposes that inferences are frequently chained together (Moore, 1983) and that it is often important to find the most relevant inference in the chain, that is, the one that overlaps with the person's musturbatory evaluations (i.e., events that are dogmatic in nature and couched in the form of musts, shoulds, oughts, and have-to's, etc.) Thus, if a client reports experiencing anger at his wife for forgetting the shopping, shopping may not actually be the "event" that triggers his anger-producing evaluations. The inference chain may be revealed thus: wife forgets shopping → I will mention this to her → she will nag me → I won't be able to watch the football game on TV in peace. Any of these inferences may trigger anger-creating evaluations and it is often important to involve clients as fully as possible in the assessment process by asking questions to help them provide reliable information concerning their most relevant inferences in particular chains.

Positive Preferential Evaluations

Example: "I prefer people to approve of me" or "I like people to approve of me . . . (but they do not have to)." These cognitions are termed "positive preferential evaluations" because (1) they are relative and nonabsolute (statements like "but they do not have to" are rarely stated but are implicit in such cognitions); and (2) they refer to what the person evaluates as positive—"people approving of me." They are often termed "rational" in RET theory since they tend to aid and abet a person's basic goals and purposes.

Let us assume that a man who holds the Belief "I prefer people to approve of me" observes a group of people laughing and infers that they are laughing *with* him. This person may conclude the following based on the positive preferential evaluation that he likes approval and the inference that they are laughing with him:

"(I presume) . . . they think I am funny."
"(I presume) . . . they like me."
"(I presume) . . . their liking me has real advantages."

These cognitions are all positive nonabsolute inferences since (1) they go beyond the available data, (2) they are relevant to the person's goal (he is getting what he values), and (3) they are not held with absolute conviction.

"My ability to make them laugh is good."
"It's pleasant to hear them enjoy themselves."

The latter are both positive nonabsolute evaluations since this man is appraising his ability to make them laugh and their pleasure at laughing in a positive but relative manner.

Positive Musturbatory Evaluations

Example: "I must have people approve of me." Such cognitions are termed "positive musturbatory evaluations" because they are absolute and dogmatic and they refer to what the person evaluates as positive in a devout manner. They are often termed "irrational" in RET theory in that they tend to impede and inhibit a person from achieving his or her other basic goals and purposes.

Let us again assume that a group of people are laughing with a man and presumably like him. He may conclude the following based on his positive musturbatory evaluations—thinking errors are categorized in parentheses:

"I am a great, noble person!" (overgeneralization)
"My life will be completely wonderful!" (overgeneralization)
"I deserve to have only fine and wonderful things happen to me!" (demandingness and deification)

These are all positive absolute evaluations. The evaluations of "I" and the world are positive and grossly exaggerated.

"I am sure they will always like me." (delusions of certainty)
"I am convinced that I will always please them." (delusions of certainty)

The latter are both positive absolute inferences since (1) they go beyond the data at hand, (2) are positively relevant to the person's goal, and (3) are held with absolute conviction.

Negative Preferential Evaluations

Example: "I prefer people not to disapprove of me . . . " or "I dislike people disapproving of me . . . (but there's no reason why they must not disapprove of me)." These cognitions are termed "negative preferential evaluations" because, once again, (1) they are relative and nonabsolute (statements like "but there's no reason why they must not . . . " are also rarely stated but are again implicit in such Beliefs); and (2) they refer to what the person evaluates as negative—"people disapproving of me." They are also termed "rational" in RET theory since they again tend to aid and abet a person's basic goals and purposes.

This time let us assume that a man who holds the Belief "I prefer people not to disapprove of me" observes a group of people laughing but infers that they are laughing *at* him. This man may conclude the following based on the negative preferential evaluations:

"(I presume) . . . they think I am stupid."
"(I presume) . . . they don't like me."
"(I presume) . . . that their not liking me has real disadvantages."

These are all negative nonabsolute inferences since (1) they go beyond the data at hand; (2) they are relevant to the person's goal (he is getting what he dislikes); and (3) they are not held with absolute conviction.

This man may further conclude:

"It's unfortunate that they are laughing at me."
"It would be bad if I have some unfortunate trait."

These are both negative nonabsolute evaluations. The evaluations of his "situation" and of his "unfortunate trait" are negative and nondevout (i.e., not absolutistic).

Negative Musturbatory Evaluations

Example: "I must not have people disapprove of me." Such cognitions are termed "negative musturbatory evalutations" because (1) they are absolute and dogmatic and (2) they refer to what the person evaluates as negative in a devout manner. They are further examples of "irrational" Beliefs in that they tend to impede the achievement of a person's basic goals and purposes.

If we assume again that a group of people are laughing at a man and presumably disapprove of him, he may conclude the following based on the above negative musturbatory evaluations—again, the categories of thinking errors are listed in parentheses.

"I am an incompetent, rotten person!" (overgeneralization, self-downing)
"My life will be completely miserable!" (overgeneralization, awfulizing)
"The world is a totally crummy place!" (overgeneralization, awfulizing)
"I deserve to have only bad or good things happen to me!" (demandingness and damnation)
"This is awful, horrible, and terrible!" (awfulizing, catastrophizing)
"I can't bear it!" (I-can't-stand-it-itis)

These are all examples of negative absolute evaluations. The prople and things appraised are all evaluated in a negative and grossly exaggerated manner.

"I will always act incompetently and have significant people disapprove of me." (overgeneralization)
"They know that I am no good and will always be incompetent." (non sequitur, jumping to conclusions, mind reading)

"They will keep laughing at me and will always despise me."
(non sequitur, jumping to conclusions, fortune-telling)
"They only despise me and see nothing good in me." (focusing on
the negative, overgeneralization)
"When they laugh with me and see me favorably that is only
because they are in a good mood and do not see that I am
fooling them." (disqualifying the positive, non sequitur, phonyism)
"Their laughing at me and disliking me will definitely make me
lose my job and lose all my friends." (catastrophizing, magnification)
"They could only be laughing because of some foolish thing I
have done and could not possibly be laughing for any other
reason." (personalizing, non sequitur, overgeneralization)

The above seven are all examples of negative absolute inferences
since (1) they go beyond the data at hand, (2) they tend to sabotage the person's goal, and (3) they are held with absolute conviction.

Consequences (C's) of Activating Events (A's) and Beliefs (B's) about A's

C's (cognitive, affective, and behavioral Consequences) follow
from the interaction of A's and B's. We can say, mathematically,
that $A \times B = C$, but this formula may actually be too simple and
we may require a more complex one to express the relationship
adequately. C is almost always significantly affected or influenced
but not exactly "caused" by A, because humans naturally to some
degree react to stimuli in their environments. Moreover, when A is
powerful (e.g., a set of starvation conditions or an earthquake) it
tends to affect C profoundly.

When C consists of emotional disturbance (e.g., severe feelings of
anxiety, depression, hostility, self-deprecation, and self-pity), B
usually (but not always) mainly or more directly creates or
"causes" C. Emotional disturbance, however, may at times stem
from powerful A's—for example, from environmental disasters
such as floods or wars. Emotional disturbance may also follow
from factors in the organism—for example, hormonal or disease
factors—that are somewhat independent of yet may actually
"cause" Consequences (C's).

When strong or unusual A's significantly contribute to or "cause"
C's, or when physiological factors "create" C's, they are usually

accompanied by contributory B's too. Thus, if people are caught in an earthquake or if they experience powerful hormonal changes and they "therefore" become depressed, their A's and their physiological processes probably are strongly influencing them to create irrational Beliefs (iB's), such as, "This earthquake shouldn't have occurred! Isn't it awful! I can't stand it!" These iB's, in turn, add to or help create their feelings of depression at C.

C's usually consist of feelings and behaviors but may also consist of thoughts (e.g., obsessions). C's (Consequences) that follow from As and Bs are virtually never pure or monolithic but also partially include and inevitably interact with A and B. Thus if A is an obnoxious event (e.g., a job refusal) and B is, first, a rational Belief (e.g., "I hope I don't get rejected for this job!") as well as, second, an irrational Belief (e.g., "I must have this job! I'm no good if I don't get it!"), C tends to be, first, healthy feelings of frustration and disappointment and, second, unhealthy feelings of severe anxiety, inadequacy, and depression.

So A $\times$ B = C. But people also *bring* feelings (as well as hopes, goals, and purposes) to A. They would not keep a job unless they desired or favorably evaluated it or unless they enjoyed some aspect of it. Their A therefore partially includes their B and C. The three, from the beginning, are related rather than completely disparate.

At the same time, people's Beliefs (B's) also partly or intrinsically relate to and include their A's and their C's. Thus, if they tell themselves, at B, "I want to get a good job," they partly create the Activating event at A (going for a job interview), and they partly create their emotional and behavioral Consequences at C (feeling disappointed when they encounter a job rejection). Without their evaluating a job as good they would not try for it nor have any particular feeling about being rejected.

A, B, and C, then, are all closely related, and none of them tends to exist without the other.

THE NATURE OF PSYCHOLOGICAL DISTURBANCE AND HEALTH

Psychological Disturbance

Rational–emotive theory, then, posits that at the heart of psychological disturbance lies the tendency of humans to make devout, absolutistic evaluations of the perceived events in their lives. As has been shown, these evaluations are couched in the form of dogmatic "musts," "shoulds," "have to's," "got to's," and "oughts." We hypothesize that these absolutistic cognitions are at the core of a philosophy of religiosity that is the central feature of human emotional and behavioral disturbance (cf., Ellis, 1983). These Beliefs are deemed to be irrational in RET theory in that they usually (but not invariably) impede and obstruct people in the pursuit of their basic goals and purposes. Absolute musts do not invariably lead to psychological disturbance because it is possible for a person to devoutly believe "I must succeed at all important projects," have confidence that he or she will be successful in these respects, and actually succeed in them and thereby not experience psychological disturbance. However, the person remains vulnerable in this respect because there is always the possibility that he or she may fail in the future. So while on probabilistic grounds RET theory argues that an absolutistic philosophy will frequently lead to such disturbance, it does not claim that this is absolutely so. Thus, even with respect to its view of the nature of human disturbance RET adopts an antiabsolutistic position.

RET theory goes on to posit that if humans adhere to a philosophy of "musturbation" they will strongly tend to make a number of core irrational conclusions that are deemed to be derivatives of these "musts." These major derivatives are viewed as irrational because they too tend to sabotage a person's basic goals and purposes.

The first major derivative is known as *"awfulizing."* This occurs when a perceived event is rated as being more than 100% bad—a truly exaggerated and magical conclusion that stems from the Belief: "This must not be as bad as it is."

The second major derivative is known as *"I-can't-stand-it-itis."* This means believing that one cannot experience virtually any happiness at all, under any conditions, if an event that "must" not happen actually occurs or threatens to occur.

The third major derivative, known as *"damnation,"* represents a tendency for humans to rate themselves and other people as "subhuman" or "undeserving" if self or other does something that they "must" not do or fail to do something that they "must" do. "Damnation" can also be applied to world or life conditions that are rated as being "rotten" for failing to give the person what he or she must have.

While RET holds that "awfulizing," "I-can't-stand-it-itis," and "damnation" are secondary irrational processes in that they stem from the philosophy of "musts," these processes can sometimes be primary (Ellis, 1984a). Indeed, Wessler (1984) has argued that they are more likely to be primary and that "musts" are derived from them. However, the philosophy of "musts," on the one hand, and those of "awfulizing," "I-can't-stand-it-itis," and "damnation," on the other, are, in all probability, interdependent processes and often seem to be different sides of the same "cognitive" coin.

RET notes that humans also make numerous kinds of illogicalities when they are disturbed (Ellis, 1984a, 1985). In this respect RET agrees with cognitive therapists (Beck, Rush, Shaw, & Emery, 1979; Burns, 1980) that such cognitive distortions are a feature of psychological disturbance. However, RET theory holds that such distortions almost always stem from the "musts." Some of the most frequent of them are

1. *All-or-none thinking*: "If I fail at any important task, as I *must* not, I'm a *total* failure and *completely* unlovable!"
2. *Jumping to conclusions and negative non sequiturs*: "Since they have seen me dismally fail, as I *should* not have done, they will view me as an incompetent worm."
3. *Fortune-telling*: "Because they are laughing at me for failing, they know that I *should* have succeeded, and they will despise me forever."
4. *Focusing on the negative*: "Because I *can't stand* things going wrong, as they *must* not, I can't see any good that is happening in my life."
5. *Disqualifying the positive*: "When they compliment me on the good things I have done, they are only being kind to me and forgetting the foolish things that I *should* not have done."
6. *Allness and neverness*: "Because conditions of living ought to be good and actually are so bad and so intolerable, they'll *always* be this way and I'll *never* have any happiness."
7. *Minimization*: "My good shots in this game were lucky and unimportant. But my bad shots, which I *should* never have made, were as bad as could be and were totally unforgivable."
8. *Emotional reasoning*: "Because I have performed so poorly, as I *should* not have done, I feel like a total nincompoop, and my strong feeling proves that I *am* no damned good!"
9. *Labeling and overgeneralization*: "Because I *must* not fail at important work and have done so, I am a complete loser and failure!"
10. *Personalizing*: "Since I am acting far worse than I *should* act and they are laughing, I am sure they are only laughing at me, and that is *awful!*"
11. *Phonyism*: "When I don't do as well as I *ought* to do and they still praise and accept me, I am a real phony and will soon fall on my face and show them how despicable I am!"

12. *Perfectionism*: "I realize that I did fairly well, but I *should* have done perfectly well on a task like this and am therefore really an incompetent!"

Although RET clinicians at times discover all the illogicalities just listed—and a number of others that are less frequently found with clients—they particularly focus on the unconditional "shoulds," "oughts," and "musts" that seem to constitute the philosophic core of irrational Beliefs that lead to emotional disturbance. They hold that if they do not get to and help clients surrender these core Beliefs, the clients will most probably keep holding them and create new irrational derivatives from them.

RET practitioners also particularly look for "awfulizing," "I-can't-stand-it-itis," and "damnation," and they show clients how these almost invariably stem from their "musts" and can be surrendered if they give up their absolutistic demands on themselves, or other people, and on the universe. At the same time, rational–emotive therapists usually encourage their clients to have strong and persistent desires, wishes, and preferences, and to avoid feelings of detachment, withdrawal, and lack of involvement (Ellis, 1972, 1973, 1984a).

More importantly, RET holds that unrealistic and illogical Beliefs do not *in themselves* create emotional disturbance. Why? Because it is quite possible for people to unrealistically believe, "Because I frequently fail, I always do" and it is possible for them also to believe illogically, "Because I have frequently failed, I always will." But they can, in both these instances, rationally conclude, "Too bad! Even though I always fail, there is no reason why I *must* succeed. I would *prefer to* but I never *have to* do well. So I'll manage to be as happy as I can be even *with* my constantly failing." They would then rarely be emotionally disturbed.

To reiterate, the essence of human emotional disturbance, according to RET, consists of the absolutistic "musts" and "must nots" that people think *about* their failure, *about* their rejections, *about* their poor treatment by others, and *about* life's frustrations and losses. RET therefore differs from other cognitive–behavioral therapies—such as those of Bandura (1969, 1977), Beck (1967, 1976), Goldfried and Davision (1976), Janis (1983), Lazarus (1981), Mahoney (1977), Maultsby (1984), and Meichenbaum (1977)—in that it particularly stresses therapists looking for clients' dogmatic, unconditional "musts," differentiating them from their preferences, and teaching them how to surrender the former and retain the latter (Bard, 1980; Ellis, 1962, 1984a, 1985; Ellis & Becker, 1982; Ellis & Harper, 1975; Grieger & Boyd, 1980; Grieger

& Grieger, 1982; Phadke, 1982; Walen, DiGiuseppe, & Wessler, 1980; Wessler & Wessler, 1980).

Psychological Health

If the philosophy of musturbation is at the core of much psychological disturbance, then what philosophy is characteristic of psychological health? RET theory argues that a philosophy of relativism or "desiring" is a central feature of psychologically healthy humans. This philosophy acknowledges that humans have a large variety of desires, wishes, wants, preferences, etc.; but if they refuse to escalate these nonabsolute values into grandiose dogmas and demands, they will not become psychologically disturbed. They will, however, experience appropriate negative emotions (e.g., sadness, regret, disappointment, annoyance) whenever their desires are not fulfilled. These emotions are considered to have constructive motivational properties in that they both help people to remove obstacles to goal attainment and help them to make constructive adjustments when their desires cannot be met.

Three major derivatives of the philosophy of desiring are postulated by rational–emotive theory. They are deemed to be rational in that they tend to help people reach their goals or formulate new goals if their old ones cannot be realized.

The first major derivative, known as "*rating or evaluating badness*," is the rational alternative to "awfulizing." Here, if a person does not get what she wants, she acknowledges that this is bad. However, because she does not believe "I have to get what I want," she contains her evaluation along a 0–100% continuum of badness and does not therefore rate this situation as "awful"—a magical rating that is placed on a nonsensical 101%–infinity continuum. In general, when the person adheres to the desiring philosphy, the stronger her desire, the greater her rating of badness will be when she does not get what she wants.

The second major derivative is known as "*tolerance*" and is the rational alternative to "I-can't-stand-it-itis." Here the person (1) acknowledges that an undesirable event has happened (or may happen), (2) believes that the event should empirically occur if it does, (3) rates the event along the badness continuum, (4) attempts to change the undesired event or accepts the "grim" reality if it cannot be modified, and (5) actively pursues other goals even though the situation cannot be altered.

The third major derivative, known as "*acceptance*," is the rational alternative to "damnation." Here the person accepts herself and others as fallible human beings who do not have to act other than they do and as too complex and fluid to be given any legitimate or global rating. In addition, life conditions are accepted as they exist. People who have the philosophy of acceptance fully acknowledge that the world is highly complex and exists according to laws that are often outside their personal control. It is important to emphasize here that acceptance does not imply resignation. A rational philosophy of acceptance means that the person acknowledges that whatever exists empirically should exist but does not absolutely have to exist forever. This prompts the person to make active attempts to change reality. The person who is resigned to a situation usually does not attempt to modify it.

RET theory also puts forward 13 criteria of psychological health. These are

1. *Self-interest*: Sensible and emotionally healthy people tend to be first or primarily interested in themselves and to put their own interests at least a little above the interests of others. They sacrifice themselves to some degree for those for whom they care, but not overwhelmingly or completely.

2. *Social interest*: Social interest is usually rational and self-helping because most people choose to live and enjoy themselves in a social group or community; if they do not act morally, protect the rights of others, and abet social survival, it is unlikely that they will create the kind of world in which they themselves can live comfortably and happily.

3. *Self-direction*: Healthy people tend to mainly assume responsibility for their own lives while simultaneously preferring to cooperate with others. They do not need or demand considerable support or succoring from others.

4. *High frustration tolerance*: Rational individuals give both themselves and others the right to be wrong. Even when they intensely dislike their own and others' behavior, they refrain for damning themselves or others, as persons, for unacceptable or obnoxious behavior. People who are not plagued with debilitating emotional distress tend to go along with St. Francis and Reinhold Niebuhr by changing obnoxious conditions they can change, accepting those they cannot, and having the wisdom to know the difference between the two.

5. *Flexibility*: Healthy and mature individuals tend to be flexible in their thinking, open to change, and unbigoted and pluralistic in their view of other people. They do not make rigid, invariant rules for themselves and others.

6. *Acceptance of uncertainty*: Healthy men and women tend to acknowledge and accept the idea that we seem to live in a world

of probability and chance where absolute certainties do not, and probably never will, exist. They realize that it is often fascinating and exciting, and definitely not horrible, to live in this kind of probabilistic and uncertain world. They enjoy a good degree of order but do not demand to know exactly what the future will bring or what will happen to them.

7. *Commitment to creative pursuits*: Most people tend to be healthier and happier when they are vitally absorbed in something outside themselves and preferably have at least one powerful creative interest, as well as some major human involvement, that they consider so important that they structure a good part of their daily existence around it.

8. *Scientific thinking*: Nondisturbed individuals tend to be more objective, rational, and scientific than more disturbed ones. They are able to feel deeply and act concertedly, but they tend to regulate their emotions and actions by reflecting on them and evaluating their consequences in terms of the extent to which they lead to the attainment of short-term and long-term goals.

9. *Self-acceptance*: Healthy people are usually glad to be alive and accept themselves just because they are alive and have some capacity to enjoy themselves. They refuse to measure their intrinsic worth by their extrinsic achievements or by what others think of them. They frankly choose to accept themselves unconditionally, and they try to completely avoid rating themselves—their totality or their being. They attempt to enjoy rather than to prove themselves (Ellis, 1973, 1984b; Ellis & Harper, 1975).

10. *Risk-taking*: Emotionally healthy people tend to take a fair amount of risk and to try to do what they want to do, even when there is a good chance that they may fail. They tend to be adventurous but not foolhardy.

11. *Long-range hedonism*: Well-adjusted people tend to seek both the pleasures of the moment and those of the future and do not often court future pain for present gain. They are hedonistic, that is, happiness-seeking and pain-avoidant, but they assume that they will probably live for quite a few years and that they had therefore better think of both today and tomorrow, and not be obsessed with immediate gratification.

12. *Nonutopianism:* Healthy people accept the fact that utopias are probably unachievable and that they are never likely to get everything they want and to avoid all pain. They refuse to strive unrealistically for total joy, happiness, or perfection, or for total lack of anxiety, depression, self-downing, and hostility.

13. *Self-responsibility for own emotional disturbance:* Healthy individuals tend to accept a great deal of responsibility for their own

disturbance rather than defensively blaming others or social conditions for their self-defeating thoughts, feelings, and behaviors.

Distinction between Appropriate and Inappropriate Negative Emotions

Rational–emotive theory argues that people can hold rational and irrational Beliefs at the same time. They can easily escalate their desires into demands. Thus, I may rationally believe, "I want you to love me" and simultaneously believe that "since I want you to love me, you must do so." Thus, it is important for therapists to discriminate between their clients' rational and irrational Beliefs. When such distinctions are made it is easier to distinguish between appropriate and inappropriate negative emotions. Appropriate negative emotions are deemed to be associated with rational Beliefs and inappropriate negative emotions with irrational Beliefs. In the following, the appropriate negative emotion is listed first.

1. *Concern vs. anxiety.* Concern is an emotion that is associated with the Belief, "I hope that this threat does not happen, but if it does, it would be unfortunate," whereas anxiety occurs when the person believes, "This threat must not happen, and it would be awful if it does."

2. *Sadness vs. depression.* Sadness is deemed to occur when the person believes, "It is very unfortunate that I have experienced this loss but there is no reason why it should not have happened." Depression, on the other hand, is associated with the Belief, "This loss should not have occurred, and it is terrible that it did." Here, when the person feels responsible for the loss, he or she will tend to damn himself: "*I* am no good," whereas if the loss is outside the person's control he or she will tend to damn the world/life conditions: "*It* is terrible." As shown earlier, RET theory holds that it is the philosophy of musturbation implicit in such evaluations that leads the person to consider that he or she will never get what he wants, an inference that leads to feelings of hopelessness. Example: "Because I must always get the things I really want and did not get it this time, I'll never get it at all. It's hopeless!"

3. *Regret vs. guilt.* Feelings of regret or remorse occur when a person acknowledges that he has done something bad in public or private but accepts himself as a fallible human being for doing so. The person feels bad about the act or deed but not about himself because he holds the Belief, "I prefer not to act badly, but if I do, too bad!" Guilt occurs when the person damns himself as bad,

wicked, or rotten for acting badly. Here, the person feels bad both about the act and his "self" because he holds the Belief, "I must not act badly, and if I do it's *awful* and I am a *rotten* person!"

4. *Disappointment vs. shame/embarrassment.* Feelings of disappointment occur when a person acts "stupidly" in public, acknowledges the stupid act, but accepts herself in the process. The person feels disappointed about her action but not with herself because she prefers but does not demand that she act well. Shame and embarrassment occur when the person again recognizes that she has acted "stupidly" in public and then condemns herself for acting in a way that she should not have done. People who experience shame and embarrassment often predict that the watching audience will think badly of them, in which case they tend to agree with these perceived judgments. Thus, they often believe that they absolutely need the approval of these others. Shame can sometimes be distinguished from embarrassment in that the public "pratfall" is regarded by the person as more serious in shame. However, both emotions involve self-denigration.

5. *Annoyance vs. anger.* Annoyance occurs when another person disregards an individual's rule of living. The annoyed person does not like what the other has done but does not damn him or her for doing it. Such a person tends to believe, "I wish the other person did not do that and I don't like what he/she did, but it does not follow that he/she must not break my rule." In anger, however, the person does believe that the other absolutely must not break the rule and thus damns the other for doing so.

It should be noted that rational–emotive therapists do not generally target appropriate negative emotions for change during therapy since they are deemed to be Consequences of rational thinking.

ACQUISITION AND PERPETUATION OF PSYCHOLOGICAL DISTURBANCE

Rational–emotive theory does not put forward an elaborate view concerning the acquisition of psychological disturbance. This partly follows from the hypothesis that humans have a distinct biological tendency to think and act irrationally, but it also reflects the RET viewpoint that theories of acquisition do not necessarily suggest therapeutic interventions. While RET holds that humans' tendencies toward irrational thinking are biologically rooted, it also acknowledges that environmental variables do contribute to psychological disturbance and thus encourage people to make their biologically based demands (Ellis, 1976, 1979b). Thus, I (AE) have said, "Parents and culture usually teach children *which* superstitions, taboos and prejudices to abide by, but they do not originate their basic tendency to superstitiousness, ritualism and bigotry" (Ellis, 1984b, p. 209).

Rational–emotive theory also posits that humans vary in their disturbability. Some people emerge relatively unscathed psychologically from being raised by uncaring or overprotective parents, while others emerge emotionally damaged from more "healthy" child-rearing regimens (Werner & Smith, 1982). In this respect, RET claims that "individuals with serious aberrations are more innately predisposed to have rigid and crooked thinking than those with lesser aberrations, and that consequently they are likely to make lesser advances" (Ellis, 1984b, p. 223). Thus, the RET theory of acquisition can be summed up in the view that as humans we are not made disturbed simly by our experiences; rather, we bring our ability to disturb ourselves to our experiences.

While rational–emotive theory does not posit an elaborate view to explain the acquisition of psychological disturbance, it does deal more extensively with how such disturbance is perpetuated. First, people tend to maintain their psychological problems by their own "naive" theories concerning the nature of these problems and to what can be attributed. They lack what RET calls "RET Insight No. 1": that psychological disturbance is primarily determined by the absolutistic Beliefs that people hold about negative life events (B determines C). Rather, they consider that their disturbances are caused by these situations (A causes C). Since people make incorrect hypotheses about the major determinants of their problems, they consequently attempt to change A rather than B. Second, people may have Insight No. 1 but lack "RET Insight No. 2": that people remain disturbed by reindoctrinating themselves *in the present* with their absolutistic Beliefs. While they may see that their problems are determined by their Beliefs, they may distract themselves and thus perpetuate their problems by searching for the historical antecedents of these Beliefs instead of directing themselves to change them as currently held. Third, people may have Insights No. 1 and No. 2 but still sustain their disturbance because they lack "RET Insight No. 3": that only if people diligently work and practice in the present as well as in the future to think, feel, and act against their irrational Beliefs are they likely to change them and make themselves significantly less disturbed. People who have all three insights clearly see that they had better persistently and strongly challenge their Beliefs cognitively, emo-

tively, and behaviorally to break the perpetuation of the disturbance cycle. Merely acknowledging that a Belief is irrational is
usually insufficient to effect change (Ellis, 1979b).

RET contends that the major reason why people perpetuate
their psychological problems is that they adhere to a *philosophy of
low frustration tolerance* (LFT) (Ellis, 1979a, 1980). Such people
believe that they *must* be comfortable and thus do not work to
effect change because such work involves experiencing discomfort.
They are short-range hedonists in that they are motivated to avoid
short-term discomfort even though accepting and working against
their temporary uncomfortable feelings would probably help them
to reach their long-range goals. Such people rate cognitive and
behavioral therapeutic tasks as "too painful," even more painful
than the psychological disturbance to which they have achieved
some measure of habituation. They prefer to remain with their
"comfortable" discomfort rather than face the "change-related"
discomfort that they believe they must not experience. Maultsby
(1975) has argued that people often back away from change because they are afraid that they will not feel right about it. He calls
this the "neurotic fear of feeling a phony" and actively shows
clients that these feelings of "unnaturalness" are natural concomi-
tants of relearning. Another prevalent form of LFT is "anxiety
about anxiety." Here, individuals believe that they must not be
anxious and thus do not expose themselves to anxiety-provoking
situations because they might become anxious if they did so—an
experience they would rate as "awful." As such, they perpetuate
their problems and overly restrict their lives to avoid experiencing
anxiety.

"Anxiety about anxiety" constitutes an example of the clinical
fact that people often make themselves *disturbed about their disturbances*. Having created secondary (and sometimes tertiary)
disturbances about their original disturbance, they become preoccupied with these "problems about problems" and thus find it
difficult to get back to solving the original problem. Humans
are often very inventive in this respect. They can make themselves depressed about their depression, guilty about being angry
(as well as anxious about their anxiety), etc. Consequently, people often had better tackle their disturbances about their disturbances before they can successfully solve their original problems
(Ellis, 1979a, 1980).

RET theory endorses the Freudian view of human defensiveness
in explaining how people perpetuate their psychological problems
(Freud, 1937). Thus, people maintain their problems by employing

various defense mechanisms (e.g., rationalization, avoidance) that are designed to help deny the existence of these problems or to minimize their severity. The RET view is that these defenses are used to ward off self-damnation tendencies and that under such circumstances if these people were to honestly take responsibility for their problems, they would severely denigrate themselves for having them. In addition, these defense mechanisms are also employed to ward off discomfort anxiety, since if, again, such people admitted their problems they would rate them as "too hard to bear" or "too difficult to overcome."

I (AE) have noted that people sometimes experience a form of perceived payoff for their psychological problems other than avoidance of discomfort (Ellis, 1979b). The existence of these payoffs serves to perpetuate these problems. Thus, a woman who claims to want to overcome her procrastination may avoid tackling the problem because she is afraid that should she become successful she might then be criticized by others as being "too masculine," a situation she would evaluate as "awful." Her procrastination serves to protect her (in her mind) from this "terrible" state of affairs. I (WD) have noted that "rational–emotive therapists stress the phenomenological nature of these payoffs, i.e., it is the person's view of the payoff that is important in determining its impact, not the events delineated in the person's description" (Dryden, 1984, p. 244).

Finally, the well-documented "self-fulfilling prophecy" phenomenon helps to explain why people perpetuate their psychological problems (Jones, 1977; Wachtel, 1977). Here, people act according to their evaluations and consequent predictions and thus often elicit from themselves or from others responses that they then interpret in a manner that confirms their initial hypotheses. Thus, a socially anxious man may believe that other people would not want to get to know "a worthless individual such as I truly am." He then attends a social function and acts as if he were worthless, avoiding eye contact and keeping away from others. Unsurprisingly, such social behavior does not invite approaches from others, a lack of response that he interprets and evaluates thus: "You see, I was right. Other people don't want to know me. I really am no good."

In conclusion, RET theory holds that people "naturally tend to perpetuate their problems and have a strong innate tendency to cling to self-defeating, habitual patterns and therby resist basic change. Helping clients change, then, poses quite a challenge for RET practitioners" (Dryden, 1984, pp. 244–245).

THE THEORY OF THERAPEUTIC CHANGE

We have argued that the rational–emotive view of the person is basically an optimistic one, since although it posits that humans have a distinct biological tendency to think irrationally, it also holds that they have the capacity to *choose* to work toward changing this irrational thinking and its self-defeating effects.

There are various levels of change. Rational–emotive theory holds that the most elegant and long-lasting changes that humans can effect are ones that involve philosophic restructuring of irrational Beliefs. Change at this level can be specific or general. Specific philosophic change means that individuals change their irrational absolutistic demand ("musts," "shoulds") and *given* situations to rational relative preferences. General philosophic change involves people adopting a nondevout attitude toward life events in general.

To effect a philosophic change at either the specific or general level, people are advised to

1. First, realize that they create, to a large degree, their own psychological disturbances and that while environmental conditions can contribute to their problems they are in general of secondary consideration in the change process.
2. Fully recognize that they do have the ability to significantly change these disturbances.
3. Understand that emotional and behavioral disturbances stem largely from irrational, absolutistic dogmatic Beliefs.
4. Detect their irrational Beliefs and discriminate them from their rational alternatives.
5. Dispute these irrational Beliefs using the logico-empirical methods of science.
6. Work toward the internalization of their new rational Beliefs by employing cognitive, emotive, and behavioral methods of change.
7. Continue this process of challenging irrational Beliefs and using multimodal methods of change for the rest of their lives.

When people effect a philosophic change at B in the ABC model, they often are able to spontaneously correct their distorted inferences of reality (overgeneralizations, faulty attributions, etc.). However, they can often benefit from challenging these distorted inferences more directly, as RET has always emphasized (Ellis, 1962, 1971, 1973; Ellis & Harper, 1961a, 1961b) and as Beck (Beck et al., 1979) has also stressed.

While rational–emotive theory argues that irrational Beliefs are the breeding ground for the development and maintenance of inferential distortions, it is possible for people to effect inferentially based changes without making a profound philosophic change. Thus, they may regard their inferences as hunches about reality rather than facts, may generate alternative hypotheses, and may seek evidence and/or carry out experiments that test out each hypothesis. They may then accept the hypothesis that represents the "best bet" of those available.

Consider a man who thinks that his co-workers view him as a fool. To test this hypothesis he might first specify their negative reactions to him. These constitute the data from which he quickly draws the conclusion, "They think I'm a fool." He might then realize that what he has interpreted to be negative responses to him might not be negative. If they seem to be negative, he might then carry out an experiment to test out the meaning he attributes to their responses. Thus, he might enlist the help of a colleague whom he trusts to carry out a "secret ballot" of others' opinions of him. Or he could test his hunch more explicitly by directly asking them for their view of him. As a result of these strategies this person may conclude that his co-workers find some of his actions foolish rather than considering him to be a complete fool. His mood may lift because his inference of the situation has changed, but he may still believe, "If others think I'm a fool, they're right. I am a fool and that would be awful." Thus, he has made an inferential change but not a philosophic one. If this person were to attempt to make a philosophic change he would *first* assume that his inference was true, *then* address himself to his evaluations about this inference and hence challenge these if they were discovered to be irrational (i.e., musturbatory evaluations). Thus, he might conclude, "Even if I act foolishly, that makes me a *person with* foolish behavior, not a *foolish person*. And even if they deem me a total idiot, that is simply *their* view, with which I can choose to disagree." Rational–emotive therapists hypothesize that people are more likely to make a profound philosophic change if they first assume that their inferences are true and then challenge their irrational Beliefs, rather than if they first correct their inferential distortions and then challenge their underlying irrational Beliefs. However, this hypothesis awaits full empirical inquiry.

People can also make direct changes of the situation at A. Thus, in the example quoted above, the man could leave his job or distract himself from the reactions of his colleagues by taking on extra work and devoting himself to this. Or he might carry out relaxation exercises whenever he comes in contact with his co-workers and thus distract himself once again from their perceived reactions. Additionally, the man might have a word with his supervisor, who might then instruct the other workers to change their behavior toward the man.

When we use this model to consider behavioral change, it is apparent that a person can change his or her behavior to effect inferential and/or philosophic change. Thus, again using the above example, a man whose co-workers view him as a fool might change his own behavior toward them and thus elicit a different set of responses from them that would lead him to reinterpret his previous inference (behavior change to effect inferential change). However, if it could be determined that they did indeed consider him to be a fool, then the man could actively seek them out and show himself that he could stand the situation and that just because they think him a fool does not make him one; that is, he learns to accept himself in the face of their views while exposing himself to their negative reactions (behavior change to effect philosophic change).

While rational–emotive therapists prefer to help their clients make profound philosophic changes at B, they do not dogmatically insist that their clients make such changes. If it becomes apparent that clients are not able at any given time to change their irrational Beliefs, then RET therapists would endeavor to help them either to change A directly (by avoiding the troublesome situation or by behaving differently) or to change their distorted inferences about the situation.

REFERENCES

Bandura, A. (1969). *Principles of behavior modification.* New York: Holt, Rinehart, & Winston.

Bandura, A. (1977). *Social learning theory.* Englewood Cliffs, NJ: Prentice-Hall.

Bard, J. (1980). *Rational–emotive therapy in practice.* Champaign, IL: Research Press.

Beck, A. T. (1967). *Depression.* New York: Hoeber-Harper.

Beck, A. T. (1976). *Cognitive therapy and the emotional disorders.* New York: International Universities Press.

Beck, A. T., Rush, A. J., Shaw, B. F., & Emery, G. (1979). *Cognitive therapy of depression.* New York: Guilford.

Burns, D. D. (1980). *Feeling good: The new mood therapy.* New York: Morrow.

Dryden, W. (1984). Rational–emotive therapy. In W. Dryden (Ed.), *Individual therapy in Britain* (pp. 235–263). London: Harper & Row.

Ellis, A. (1962). *Reason and emotion in psychotherapy.* Secaucus, NJ: Lyle Stuart.

Ellis, A. (1971). *Growth through reason.* North Hollywood, CA: Wilshire Books.

Ellis, A. (1972). Helping people get better: Rather than merely feel better. *Rational Living,* 7(2), 2–9.

Ellis, A. (1973). *Humanistic psychotherapy: The rational–emotive approach.* New York: McGraw-Hill.

Ellis, A. (1976). The biological basis of human irrationality. *Journal of Individual Psychology,* 32, 145–168.

Ellis, A. (1979a). Discomfort anxiety: Part 1. A new cognitive behavioral construct. *Rational Living,* 14(2), 3–8.

Ellis, A. (1979b). The theory of rational–emotive therapy. In A. Ellis & J. M. Whiteley (Eds.), *Theoretical and empirical foundations of rational–emotive therapy* (pp. 33–60). Monterey, CA: Brooks/Cole.

Ellis, A. (1980). Discomfort anxiety: Part 2. A new cognitive behavioral construct. *Rational Living,* 15(1), 25–30.

Ellis, A. (1982). Rational–emotive family therapy. In A. M. Horne & M. M. Ohlsen (Eds.), *Family counseling and therapy* (pp. 302–328). Itasca, IL: Peacock.

Ellis, A. (1983). *The case against religiosity.* New York: Institute for Rational–Emotive Therapy.

Ellis, A. (1984a). The essence of RET—1984. *Journal of Rational–Emotive Therapy,* 2(1), 19–25.

Ellis, A. (1984b). Rational–emotive therapy. In R. J. Corsini (Ed.), *Current psychotherapies* (3rd ed.) (pp. 196–238). Itasca, IL: Peacock.

Ellis, A. (1985). *Overcoming resistance: Rational–emotive therapy with difficult clients.* New York: Springer Publishing Co.

Ellis, A., & Becker, I. (1982). *A guide to personal happiness.* North Hollywood, CA: Wilshire.

Ellis, A., & Bernard, M. E. (Eds.). (1983). *Rational–emotive approches to the problems of childhood.* New York: Plenum.

Ellis, A., & Bernard, M. E. (Eds.). (1985). *Clinical applications of rational–emotive therapy.* New York: Plenum.

Ellis, A., & Harper, R. A. (1961a). *A guide to rational living.* Englewood Cliffs, NJ: Prentice-Hall.

Ellis, A., & Harper, R. A. (1961b). *A guide to successful marriage.* North Hollywood, CA: Wilshire Books.

Ellis, A., & Harper, R. A. (1975). *A new guide to rational living.* North Hollywood, CA: Wilshire.

Freud, A. (1937). *The ego and the mechanisms of defense.* London: Hogarth.

Goldfried, M., & Davison, G. (1976). *Clinical behavior therapy.* New York: Holt, Rinehart, & Winston.

Grieger, R., & Boyd, J. (1980). *Rational–emotive therapy: A skills-based approach.* New York: Van Nostrand Reinhold.

Grieger, R., & Grieger, I. (Eds.). (1982). *Cognition and emotional disturbance.* New York: Human Sciences Press.

Janis, I. L. (1983). *Short-term counseling.* New Haven, CT: Yale University Press.

Jones, R. A. (1977). *Self-fulfilling prophecies: Social, psychological effects of expectancies*. Hillsdale, NJ: Lawrence Erlbaum.

Lazarus, A. A. (1981). *The practice of multimodal therapy*. New York: McGraw-Hill.

Mahoney, M. (1977). Personal science: A cognitive learning theory. In A. Ellis & R. Grieger (Eds.), *Handbook of rational–emotive therapy* vol. 1, pp. 352–366. New York: Springer Publishing Co.

Maultsby, M. C., Jr. (1975). *Help yourself to happiness: Through rational self-counseling*. New York: Institute for Rational–Emotive Therapy.

Maultsby, M. C., Jr. (1984). *Rational behavior therapy*. Englewood Cliffs, NJ: Prentice-Hall.

Meichenbaum, D. (1977). *Cognitive-behavior modification*. New York: Plenum.

Moore, R. H. (1983). Inference as "A" in RET. *British Journal of Cognitive Psychotherapy*, *1*(2), 17–23.

Perls, F. (1969). *Gestalt therapy verbatim*. Lafayette, CA: Real People Press.

Phadke, K. M. (1982). Some innovations in RET theory and practice. *Rational Living*, *17*(2), 25–30.

Wachtel, P. L. (1977). *Psychoanalysis and behavior therapy: Toward an integration*. New York: Basic Books.

Walen, S. R., DiGiuseppe, R., & Wessler, R. L. (1980). *A practitioner's guide to rational–emotive therapy*. New York: Oxford.

Werner, E. E., & Smith, R. S. (1982). *Vulnerable but invincible: A study of resilient children*. New York: McGraw-Hill.

Wessler, R. A., & Wessler R. L. (1980). *The principles and practice of rational–emotive therapy*. San Francisco: Jossey-Bass.

Wessler, R. L. (1984). Alternative conceptions of rational–emotive therapy: Toward a philosophically neutral psychotherapy. In M. A. Reda & M. J. Mahoney (Eds.), *Cognitive psychotherapies: Recent developments in theory, research and practice* (pp. 65–79). Cambridge, MA: Ballinger.

Toward a Theory of Personality

2

INTRODUCTION

RET has often been accused of having no *personality theory. It actually has one, though not fully developed, that stems from its theory of personality disturbance. For these reasons Ellis thought it a good idea to expand on his previous writings in this respect (Ellis, 1962, 1977) and outline some of its main aspects. Ellis wrote the following paper in response to a request from Raymond J. Corsini, who was editing a book,* Readings in Current Personality Theories, *and wanted to be sure that RET was properly represented.*

This is a seminal essay in RET personality theory for several reasons: (1) It presents a skeptical view of many other well-known personality theories; (2) it gives more details on the RET view of personality than any of Ellis's other writings; (3) it shows where RET stands on many vectors of personality that Corsini (1978), Coan (1968), and other theorists have considered important; and (4) it makes the point that RET is mainly a theory of personality disturbance and change but that, as such, it inevitably includes a fairly well developed theory of personality that can be applied to a number of nontherapeutic aspects of life. Thus, it has been applied to fields such as education; executive leadership and management; humor and fun; law and criminality; love, marriage, and sex; philosophy; parenting; religion; and sports psychology.

RET personality theory is far from complete. Among other things, it has yet to develop a detailed developmental theory. Ellis's guess is that humans develop ideas, expectations, and hypotheses about themselves and the world during the first year or two of their lives but that these are rather vague and do not lead to very consistent predictions. They become more specific about these ideas and guesses during their second to fifth years and still more specific in later childhood.

Reprinted from *Readings in Current Personality Theories* (pp. 298–311) by Raymond V. Corsini, 1978, Itasca, IL: F. E. Peacock Publishers.

Ellis's view is that, originally, infants have rational behaviors (e.g., sucking and crying out when pained), but these seem to be largely instinctive and have few rational ideas to spark them. As they become older and their cerebral cortex develops, they create more rational predictions, checks, and conclusions about their pleasant and unpleasant feelings; and from the age of 5 or 6 onward they probably develop a great many rational ideas—for example, "Pleasure is good, and I want more of it; pain is bad, and I want less of it. Therefore, let me try to seek out pleasure and avoid pain."

According to Ellis, the main irrational belief that young children probably first develop is that leading to discomfort disturbance, or low frustration tolerance (LFT)—for example, "Because pain and discomfort are so bad, I can't stand these feelings. They must *not exist, and it's awful when they do!" LFT may therefore be the first major irrationality of young children.*

The second major irrationality of children is their self-downing— for example, the idea "Because I must *do better than I am doing, I am a* bad *child who often deserves to be deprived or punished." As children develop their sense of self (ego), perhaps a year or two after they develop their sense of comfort and discomfort, and particularly as they develop language (with the help of their parents), they begin to see* themselves, *not merely their actions, as "good" and "bad," as "deserving" and "undeserving."*

Ellis holds that even the child's original irrational idea, "I must *be loved and approved, and it's* awful *if I'm not!" is probably at first a dire need for comfort—for being taken care of, soothed, and given goodies. Later, probably, the child adds the ego, self-downing irrationality, "If I'm not loved and catered to, as I* must *be, there must be something wrong with me, and therefore I am no good!"*

These are only some tentative hypotheses about the development of children's rationality and irrationality that Ellis has put forward, and research should be done to test their plausibility. Ellis notes that RET developmental theory is still in its infancy, but he believes that it could well lead to some fascinating growth and development.

REFERENCES

Coan, R. W. (1968). Dimensions of psychological theory. *American Psychologist, 23,* 715–722.

Corsini, R. J. (Ed.). (1978). *Readings in current personality theories.* Itasca, IL: Peacock.

Ellis, A. (1962). *Reason and emotion in psychotherapy.* New York: Lyle Stuart.

Ellis, A. (1977). RET as a personality theory, therapy approach, and philosophy of life. In J. L. Wolfe & E. Brand (Eds.), *Twenty years of rational therapy* (pp. 16–30). New York: Institute for Rational–Emotive Therapy.

During the past several years, I have begun to develop a theory of personality that significantly disagrees with the views of other personality theorists who have also originated schools of psychotherapy—such as Adler, Freud, Jung, Reich, and Rogers. In this paper I shall first state why virtually all existent personality theorists make wrong conclusions about how humans function; then I shall outline and defend my own theory, which is developing out of the practice of rational–emotive therapy (Ellis, 1962, 1973a, 1973b, 1977a; Ellis & Grieger, 1977; Morris & Kanitz, 1975).

WHY PERSONALITY THEORISTS OFTEN GO WRONG

Personality theorists almost invariably go wrong because, like most humans, they think crookedly. Their tendency to cognize irrationally leads them astray in various respects. They consequently come up with highly brilliant views of "human nature" which often include almost incredible errors of logic and antiempiricism. Examples of crooked thinking in personality theories include the following.

1. *Attribution of special reasons to events and behaviors.* Humans tend to attribute special (transpersonal) reasons to various non-human events. Because they then feel comfortable (in the Gestalt psychology sense of effecting "closure") with these "explanations," they then wrongly believe they have "proved" the validity of their assertions. Thus, primitives pray for rain; it eventually does rain, and they see their prayers as an explanation for the downpour. Sailors observe a certain kind of cloud formation before it rains, and they loosely see this formation "causing" a storm. The primitives clearly believe in magic, for their prayers have no connection whatever with the rain. But sailors also think crookedly; for cloud formations only constitute part of a worldwide pressure system of events, ranging from conditions at the North Pole to those at the Equator, all of which contribute to the downpour. Meteorologists know about these causes but often fail to explain them to laypeople when they talk about the "causation" of rain; and we laypeople buy the simple explanation of the rain clouds causing storms and do not bother with other complications that go with these causal connections.

And so with personality theories. If I murder someone, and you want to "explain" the "cause" of my act, you will likely focus upon some outstanding "influences"—for example, my mother taught me that hostility pays off, or my early religious teachings led me to embrace an eye-for-an-eye philosophy. Certainly, these influences *may* have affected me. But of a hundred children whose mothers or whose early religious teachings favored hostility, very few, if any, would murder someone later in life! Literally hundreds of influences may have contributed to my act, such as (*a*) my tendency to demand that things go my way, (*b*) my rebellion against social teachings, (*c*) my low frustration tolerance, (*d*) my vulnerability to feeling hurt, (*e*) my happening to have a gun when I experienced extreme hostility, and so on. Considering all these possible "causes," your simplistic, unitary "explanation" of my murderous act hardly seems accurate, even though it may show some mild degree of causality.

Rational–emotive therapy (RET) holds that any special, exclusive reason for a behavioral act or personality pattern rarely, if ever, exists. If I murder regularly (and thus have the "trait" of a murderer), I may do so for many reasons, none of which probably has exclusive importance. If I regularly kill people, probably simultaneously (*a*) I have a strong innate predisposition toward feeling hostile at "injustices," (*b*) I think murder is justified under certain conditions, (*c*) I believe I can get away with homicide, (*d*) I have somehow developed a low frustration tolerance, (*e*) I have problems, perhaps connected with my early interpersonal experiences, in relating to others, (*f*) I think in absolutistic, *must*urbatory ways, and so on. Any one of these tendencies or conditions could make me a confirmed murderer; and a combination of several of them would increase the probability of my turning into one. Your selecting one primary "cause" of my homicidal character merely shows that almost all humans frequently attribute "special," determining causes to the origin or development of personality traits, when the "real" causes probably arise out of multifaceted, often obscure, partly accidental conditions.

2. *Illogical thinking about special reasons for personality behaviors.* Once we attribute special causative reasons for personality behaviors, we usually tend to feel so convinced of their truth that we ignore evidence that contradicts our hypotheses. Such reasons seem to "fit" the observed facts of human functioning, and in perceiving this good fit we convince ourselves of their indubitable "truth." Even when we finally surrender these "explanations" for another set, we may do so because they jibe better with our preconceived aesthetic notions of good fit. They have greater "elegance." They "feel" better than the old ones. So we decide that (for now and for all time to come) they *are* better.

We can easily, then, convince ourselves of the validity of an elegant theory—by (*a*) ignoring data that do not fit, (*b*) falsifying data that fit poorly, or (*c*) failing to seek better theories that fit the data more accurately. When the "true" explanations for a given behavior remain truly multifaceted and complex, we have more temptation than usual to settle for special reasons for this behavior—simply because a simple explanation fits better and feels better.

3. *Environmentalist prejudices.* The great majority of psychologists remain do-gooders, hoping not merely to understand but also to help change dysfunctional behaviors. They believe that the basic way to do this consists of relearning, or behavior modification. They also know that some behaviors (e.g., obsessions and phobias) have such strong instinctive or overlearned factors that people have great difficulty in changing them.

Because of their essential altruism and hopefulness, some personality theorists who begin with the assumption, "We must help people change their disordered traits," go on to the empirical observation, "Humans find it very difficult to change solidly rooted inherited predispositions," and wind up with the illogical conclusion, "Therefore, such traits must have arisen from learning rather than hereditary tendencies."

Other forms of illogical thinking about environmental influences on personality include the following:

a. Because people have great difficulty in making certain personality changes, they find it impossible to change.
b. Because a behavior has learned elements, it has virtually no innate component, and one can fairly easily unlearn it.
c. If a personality trait involves a hereditary predisposition, one cannot change it.
d. Because one has learned to behave badly, one has no responsibility for continuing this behavior, or environmental conditions have to change before one can modify this behavior.
e. Because others have conditioned one to behave in a defeating manner, helpers must recondition one to behave differently.
f. Because the environment significantly contributes to dysfunctioning, only through someone's significantly changing the environment will one have the ability to act less dysfunction ally.
g. Because virtually all human behavior includes learning, learning constitutes the main element in this behavior, and one must use external forces to modify it.

Due to do-goodism and cognitive slippage, the importance of environmental factors in the formation and changing of personality tends to get enormously exaggerated; almost all systematic views of psychotherapy fall victim to this kind of exaggeration.

4. *Overemphasis on dramatic incidents from the past.* We humans tend to dramatize so-called traumatic incidents and to remember them vividly. Thus, you may vividly recall how you wet yourself at age four and made a fool of yourself in class at age six. Because these remembrances leave dramatic effects, people make erroneous conclusions such as

a. The original occurrence *caused* negative self-ratings.
b. Having no memory or bad feelings about them results from the mechanism of repression.
c. Recalling such "traumatic" memories and the accompanying feelings has curative effects.
d. That particular happening and one's original reaction to it invariably "caused" one's present lifestyle and tells the therapist a great deal about one's personality.
e. If one reacted dysfunctionally to an early remembered incident, one must react the same way in similar circumstances today and for the rest of one's life.

Dramatic early events in people's lives may well tell us something about them personalitywise. But theorists tend to overemphasize this phenomenon and to make all-encompassing, and often false, conclusions about it. Just as people make false "observations" and conclusions about contemporary dramatic events (e.g., accidents), so too do they and their psychological observers easily make misleading "observations" and conclusions about past dramatic events. Such events probably had *some* importance, but we tend to make them *all*-important. Since most people experience satisfaction in reviewing their past histories, they foolishly expend much time and energy talking to therapists about their past when they would do themselves more good by thinking about their present and future. For this reason, woefully inefficient psychotherapies, such as psychoanalysis, continue to have immense popularity (Ellis, 1962; Ellis & Harper, 1975).

5. *Overgeneralization.* People have an exceptionally strong tendency to overgeneralization, as Aaron Beck (1976), Albert Ellis (1962, 1977a), George Kelly (1955), and Alfred Korzybski (1933) have pointed out. Because of this tendency, personality theorists seem to make certain valid observations about human personality

and then go on to make certain overgeneralized, hence partly false, conclusions about these observations. Here are some examples:

a. Because humans desire certain things—such as approval and success—they *must* have them to achieve any significant degree of happiness.
b. Because dreams to some degree show people's underlying wishes and anxieties, virtually all dreams consist of wish fulfillments or indicate deep-seated fears.
c. Because dreams and free associations sometimes reveal material of which the individual has little awareness, they constitute the royal road to the unconscious and give highly accurate information.
d. Because people sometimes symbolize sex organs in their dreams by objects such as guns or keyholes, every time they dream about such objects they really mean sex organs.
e. Because some individuals feel inferior due to physical or other deficiencies, such deficiencies always lead to feelings of inferiority.
f. Because feelings of love frequently enhance happiness, everyone requires a fine one-to-one relationship to exist in a "normal" or "healthy" manner.

Hundreds of such overgeneralizations contribute to false views of personality. The human tendency to jump from "Some people do this some of the time" to "Virtually everyone does this all of the time" and from "A minority of individuals under certain conditions act this way" to "The majority of people always act this way" leads to misleading, and virtually pandemic, views of personality.

6. *Hereditarian biases.* Many psychologists have hereditarian biases and consequently overemphasize the importance of innate influences on personality (Pastore, 1949). Cyril Burt, for example, for many years seems to have faked data to support his theories about the importance of genetic factors in intelligence (Evans, 1976). Typical hereditarian mistakes include such conclusions as the following:

a. Because heredity represents a strong element in virtually all behavior, it almost exclusively determines that behavior.
b. If certain individuals have an innate tendency to act in a certain way, virtually all the members of their groups act that way because of their genetic differences from other groups.

   c. If a personality trait has strong hereditarian influences, peo-
      ple with that trait find it virtually impossible to change it
      significantly.
   d. If one personality trait has strong heredity determinants,
      other traits must have equally strong innate determinants.

Hereditarian overgeneralizations lead to many false conclusions
about personality. Proenvironmentalist theorists overemphasize the
significance of learned factors, while prohereditarians overemphasize innate factors. Environmentalists tend to forget that social
learning rests on an inherited tendency to learn or to adopt social
"conditioning" (Ellis, 1976). Hereditarians tend to forget that no
matter what their genetic background, humans start learning immediately after birth. Both sets of theorists, failing to look at the
other side of the fence, overlook the fact that all behaviors include
a combination of learned and innate factors, and both tend to
present a one-sided view of personality.

   7. *Human autism and grandiosity.* Humans often take an autistic,
grandiose, cosmological view. They conceptualize that the universe
revolves around them and runs in accordance with their wishes
and goals. They will not accept that the world seems to have no
intrinsic purpose and that it has no interest, concern, or love for
them. They exist and it exists; and their existence, of course, depends on an outside world in which they live. But individuals and
the world have no necessary connection. The universe existed
without humans probably for billions of years and may well do so
for billions of future years. We have no evidence that it exists *just*
for us.

   People seem loath to accept the great influence of accident, pur-
poselessness, and unintentionality in cosmology. They consequently
tend to invent special reasons for personality behaviors, and they
frequently come up with semimystical, transpersonal, religiously
oriented views that have nothing to do with reality.

   8. *Self-rating influences.* Humans value life and happiness and,
reasonably enough, rate their performances with how well these
permit them to enjoy life. But then they jump to rating their total
selves, and this has no sensible basis (Ellis, 1962, 1972, 1975; Ellis
& Harper, 1975). That doesn't stop humans from continuing to rate
their essences as well as their deeds!

   Personality theorists tend to make the same error. They talk in
favor of self-esteem, self-confidence, and self-regard, not realizing
that even if we do achieve self-esteem we harm ourselves thereby
if we remain preoccupied with our own ratings rather than simply

changing our dysfunctional behaviors. If we rate ourselves as "good," we imply that we can also be rated as "bad"—and as a consequence we live on the verge of anxiety, due to these self-determined "report cards."

Personality theory includes an enormous "self-worth" literature—most of it quite misleading! For humans, as such, do not actually have differential worth. They merely have aliveness. Intrinsic worth or value differs little from other mythical entities, such as "spirit" and "soul" (Ellis, 1972).

9. *Absolutistic and musturbatory thinking.* People tend to take proper probabilistic views (e.g., "I like others' approval") and then escalate them into absolutes and musts (e.g., "I must have others' approval"). This kind of thinking also leads personality theorists astray, who promulgate *musts* by the dozen instead of more realistic it-would-seem-better-ifs (Ellis, 1973a, 1973b, 1977a; Ellis & Grieger, 1977). Some of the *musts* that theorists uphold include

a. You must have a happy, secure childhood to achieve a happy adult life.
b. If you have an emotional problem, you must have prolonged intensive therapy.
c. To change your behavior, you must have specific reinforcers, such as money or love.
d. Self-defeating behavior must result from irrational ideas.
e. You must feel terribly anxious about the possibility of eventually dying.
f. When people treat you unfairly, you must feel real hostility toward them.

10. *Defensiveness and resistance to change.* Personality theorists generally tend to resist change in their thinking, and they construct defenses against acknowledging defects in their theories. They consequently ignore evidence that contradicts their views. They claim their theories explain practically all aspects of personality. They give specious answers to the objections of critics. They avoid probing new areas that might uncover evidence that confutes their hypotheses. They neglect to even read other personality theorists. They come to conclusions that do not jibe with the evidence they themselves turn up. They cling to views that have long outlived their usefulness. They see flaws in their own theories but refuse to acknowledge these flaws publicly.

Possibly for ego-bolstering and grandiose reasons, personality scientists hold to and promulgate views that never had, or at least no longer have, a high degree of validity. Let me see, therefore, if I can do at least a little better!

TOWARD A NEW THEORY OF PERSONALITY

Assuming, as claimed above, that many contemporary theories of personality have woeful inadequacies and little likelihood of verification, can a more valid theory arise out of clinical data?

The A-B-C Theory of Personality

Rational–emotive therapy has implied from its very beginning a theory of personality, stemming from its theory of personality change. Scores of clinical reports have given evidence for the validity of this A-B-C theory by citing case histories of people who came for RET in a state of near despair and, after consultation, usually soon thereafter emerged as significantly improved—with their symptoms gone, with new understanding of how they created their problems, and with a readiness to face the world and make for themselves a better, more joyous existence (Ellis, 1977b; Murphy & Ellis, 1977). In addition to clinical evidence, the A-B-C theory has considerable experimental backing. DiGiuseppe, Miller, and Trexler (1977) and Murphy (Murphy & Ellis, 1977) have comprehensively reviewed clinical outcome studies in which some subjects experienced RET and others experienced no therapy or other forms of psychotherapy. When the researchers made statistical comparisons between experimental (RET) and control groups, in almost all these studies subjects given RET changed their behavior significantly better than did non-RET subjects (Ellis, 1977b).

We can state the essence of RET theory in this way: When people feel upset at point C (emotional Consequence), after they have undergone some unpleasant Activating Event (at point A), they almost always conclude that A caused C. They say, "No wonder I feel depressed; my mate has just left me," or "Of course I feel anxious in view of this exam that I may fail." For most people—including clients and personality theorists—the connection between A (Activating Experience) and C (emotional Consequence) seems evident and obvious.

RET rejects this "evident" explanation, and RET therapists have taught thousands of clients to reject it over the past two decades. The stimulus does not explain the reaction; S-R theorizing does not work. RET conceptualization, following Woodworth (Woodworth & Schlosberg, 1954) constitutes an S-O-R theory. RET makes B, the individual's Belief System, the crucial issue. A does not determine C—B does! Consequently, if two people get labeled "stupid," and one laughs at the statement and the other feels depressed, we cannot explain these radically different Consequences by A (the Activating Event) but rather by B (the Belief System) *about* A.

The salient points of RET have appeared in much detail elsewhere (Ellis, 1962, 1971, 1973a, 1973b, 1977a; Ellis & Grieger, 1977; Ellis & Harper, 1975; Maultsby, 1975). Now, the crucial issue arises: How do people obtain their Belief Systems—rational Beliefs (rBs) and irrational Beliefs (iBs)? Why does Johanna have such a healthy attitude and behave so sanely while her brother, John, has such an unhealthy view of life and acts so unsuccessfully?

Hereditarian Influences on Personality

Although almost all formal views of modern personality formation say otherwise, it seems probable that the main influence on human personality comes from heredity. It seems almost impossible to deny this, since if we humans do exhibit different personality traits as we react to environmental conditions, we obviously inherit this kind of teachability or conditionability. Thus, we seem unusually teachable compared to "lower" animals. Our teachability, mediated through our unusually large and specially wired cerebral cortex, comprises one of the main essences of our humanity. Subhuman animals remain much more driven by instincts, while humans largely have what Maslow (1954) called "instinctoid" tendencies—strong predispositions to act in certain ways that nonetheless can get radically modified by environmental and educational influences.

RET-oriented personality theory hypothesizes that probably 80% of the variance of human behavior rests on biological bases and about 20% on environmental training (Ellis, 1976). We find a good example of this in the iB's (irrational Beliefs) which spark people's disturbances. At first blush, these beliefs seem to stem primarily from cultural learning: from absorbing the standards that parents, schools, churches, and other institutions teach. Almost all of us largely subscribe to these standards, in spite of the fact that many of them appear insane and inane. Do not our personalities, then, get mainly set by culture?

Yes—and no! Our "normal" standards do seem to follow cultural prescriptions and proscriptions—so that most of us wear considerable clothing even when temperatures soar, permit ourselves to love intensely only one member of the other sex at a time, and try to win the approval of many people whom we hate or in whom we have little interest. We do these silly things to follow cultural conventions. But in addition, because we innately tend to elevate *preferences* into *musts*, we frequently convince ourselves that we *have to* do these preferable things; that we must find it awful and horrible (rather than merely damned annoying) if we do not; and that we rate as thoroughly *rotten persons* if we fall below cultural standards.

Just as we often take stupid cultural norms and make them into absolutistic *shoulds*, we do much the same thing with sensible rules. Thus, our culture teaches us that we had better wear warm clothes in winter—but we tend to add that we *must* wear the most fashionable clothes, no matter how uncomfortable or expensive we personally find them. Our culture tells us the advantages of falling in love; so we often insist that we *have to* love and gain the love of the most special person in the world, who will madly love us forever! Our culture informs us that we will benefit by having others approve of us (so that they will give us jobs, act companionably, do us favors, and so on). And then we demand that virtually everyone we meet, including perfect strangers we will rarely encounter again, *must* like us!

This kind of *must*urbation—admittedly encouraged but not demanded by our society—seems largely innate. Just about all humans in all cultures frequently *must*urbate—even though they soon note its pernicious results. We demand guarantees; we insist that we have to do well, others must treat us considerately, and world conditions have to arrange themselves so that we get almost everything we want immediately, easily. Just about all children frequently think this way, and virtually no adults fully surrender this kink of crazy thinking.

Personality consists not merely of our silly demandingness but perhaps even more of our wishing, wanting, and desiring. Wants give purpose to life. If we had no desires (as extreme Zen Buddhism strives for, in a state called Nirvana), we would hardly survive; and if we did, who would really want to? Desiring, seeking, striving, yearning seem the main essence of living.

But where do most of our desires originally come from? Almost certainly, from biological predispositions. We naturally enjoy eating. We innately enjoy and prefer certain odors, sights, and sounds. We fundamentally like to play, to build, to create. In all these pursuits, we learn cultural standards and generally follow them. In our society, for example, we eat beef but not grasshoppers; we copulate in private rather than in public; and we play tennis and golf more than we perform archery. But just about all our cultur-ally taught pursuits rest on a pronounced biological basis; as Karl Buehler (1965) stated, we inherently have a "function pleasure."

The RET emphasis on the importance of the biological bases of human behavior attempts to balance the environmentalist posi-tion, which has dominated personality and therapy theory for the last half century. Freud (1965) had strong biological leanings, but virtually all his main followers, including Fromm (1941, 1975), Horney (1965), Sullivan (1953), and Berne (1964) have overempha-sized so-called cultural and early childhood conditioning. Many good reasons exist for suspecting that self-defeating behavior basi-cally has innate (as well as acquired) causes. Since I have else-where (Ellis, 1976) reviewed these reasons in detail, I shall not repeat them here (see Chapter 3).

Multiplicity of Origins and Maintainers of Personality

The RET theory of personality posits a multiplicity of origins and maintainers of personality, often environmental as well as biologically based, such as (1) Interpersonal relations with other humans; (2) specific teachings by others; (3) teachings through impersonal communications, such as books and other forms of mass media; (4) group influences; (5) reinforcers or rewards, such as money, social approval, honors, medals, or compliments; (6) penalizers, such as disapproval, failures, fines, imprisonment, or threats; (7) self-ratings—evaluations of the self as "good" or "bad"; (8) self-observation—noting how one behaves and comprehending the usual consequences of such behavior; (9) modeling after others, particularly after outstanding individuals; (10) identifying with certain people or groups and going along with their behavior; (11) formulating goals, purposes, and ideals and striving to achieve them; (12) magical and mystical notions, such as belief in perfec-tion, in utopia, or in rewarding or punishing deities; (13) gullibil-ity and suggestibility to the teachings and persuasions of others; (14) urges favoring freedom and individuality; (15) innate tenden-cies to seek love, pleasure, and self-actualization; (16) emotional consequences of behavior considered "beneficial" by the individ-ual: feeling "good" about operating according to the "correct" norms of self or others, achieving success, and so on; feeling "bad" about violations of laws, ethics, customs, traditions, or mores, and specifically feeling anxious, guilty, and depressed about such viola-tions.

Because people have so many internal and external influences and because these significantly conflict with each other in many ways, human behavior displays both consistencies and inconsistencies. Consistencies ("personality traits") probably arise out of the strength and statistical prevalence of one influence over another. But no matter how much "evidence" we find for our "explanations" of personality, we never have all the facts; we can always think of an alternative "reason" that also connects with the known data; we can easily find five or more "answers" for the existence of the same trait; and we have no sure way of knowing which one, two, or all of these answers truly account for the personality factors we seek to explain. In view of this, a truly dynamic psychology had better include not only "vertical" factors—relate to past and future—but also "horizontal" considerations and concern itself with the organism's selection calculus relative to a decision for action considering the importance of all these and other influences of past and present, of near and far, of inner and outer factors.

Does theorizing about personality, then, seem a rather hopeless pursuit? To some extent, yes. For the present, and perhaps never, we probably will not arrive at precise, certain hypotheses that cover all or most of the observed data. Nonetheless, if we watch the kinds of errors outlined in the first part of this article, we can at least come up with some tentative (and I hope highly tentative!) conclusions.

RET's Stand on 10 Major Dimensions of Personality

Many personality analysts have come up with major dimensions of personality on which various theorists can take a stand. Coan (1968) outlined six dimensions, and Corsini (1977) has added four more. On these factors (as described in Corsini, 1977), RET makes the following choices:

1. *Objective–subjective.* Objective theories of personality feature explicit, observable, unequivocal behavior that one can count and number; subjective theories concern themselves with the inner personal life of an individual. In this respect, RET favors observing and counting behavior for research purposes. But it largely deals with inner personal life, with the ineffable individual, and sees the person as having *some* degree of choice or "free will" and a significant ability to change his or her traits (behavior patterns). Thus, RET mainly remains in the subjective camp.

2. *Elementaristic–holistic.* Elementaristic theory sees the person as composed of parts: organs, units, elements put together to make a whole. Holistic theories see the person as having a central unity and the parts as aspects of the total entity. While RET sees people

as having units or elements (e.g., high sexuality or low energy) that influence their whole lives, it also sees them as having interacting parts (including cognitions, emotions, and behaviors) that cannot really be separated, and it primarily sees them as having a holistic or central "consciousness" or "will" that tends to direct these various parts.

3. *Apersonal–personal.* Apersonal theories have impersonal, statistically based outlooks and consider generalities rather than individualities. Largely based on group norms, they differ from personal theories, which deal with the single individual in an idiographic manner. RET distinctly uses general laws of behavior, statistically based—e.g., the probability law that behind virtually every "emotional" disturbance lies an irrational idea, and this idea takes the form of some *should* or *must*. It claims unusual efficiency as a theory of personality and of personality change precisely because it has inducted these general laws from observations of many people and has clinically and experimentally tested them often. It therefore claims a scientific, partly nomothetic basis. But it also deals, especially in therapy, with individuals in their own right, emphasizes their uniqueness and their changeability, accords them personal responsibility for their own disturbance and change, and sees them idiographically. We can label RET as largely being a personal theory of personality.

4. *Quantitative–qualitative.* A quantitative theory makes it possible to measure units of behavior. A qualitative theory does not see behavior as exactly measurable, viewing it as too complex for such dealings. RET stresses quality rather than quantity, since (as noted in this article) personality seems infinitely complex in its origins and development, so that we can only partially and inaccurately quantify it. RET hypothesizes, however, that quantity frequently metamorphoses into quality in behavioral change. Forcing oneself *many times* to think and act differently finally helps one to "naturally" enjoy something one previously disliked—or vice versa.

5. *Static–dynamic.* Static theory sees the individual as a reactor, not a learner; filled with instincts, and based on generalizations presented by heredity. Dynamic theory concerns itself with the individual as a learner, with interactions between behavior and consciousness and between consciousness and unconsciousness. RET sees people as having instinctoid tendencies rather than fixed instincts—and as having, for example, the tendency to see their own behaviors (including their own disturbances) and to change these. In this sense, in spite of its strong emphasis on heredity, RET has an unusually powerful dynamic quality.

6. *Endogenistic–exogenistic.* Endogenous theories view the per-

son as biologically based. Exogenistic theories consist of social learning theories. RET supports both endogenistic *and* exogenistic views. It sees the person as biologically based, but it also strongly holds that people have the innate capacity to make themselves less conditionable, less suggestible, and more self-directing. RET also sees humans as inheriting strong tendencies toward gregariousness and social learning, so that they always remain highly affectable by both their heredity and their social environment.

7. *Deterministic–indeterministic.* Deterministic theories see individuals as not responsible for their behavior, as the pawns of society, heredity, or both. Indeterministic theories put emphasis on self-direction and place control within the person. RET stands mainly in the indeterministic camp. But it sees choice as *limited*. It hypothesizes that the more rationally people think and behave, the less deterministically they act. But rationality itself has its limits and hardly leads to completely free, healthy, or utopian existences!

8. *Past–future.* Some theories see the individual in terms of past influences, biological or social, and others see the person as explained by his or her anticipation of future goals. RET takes a two-headed-arrow stand in this respect, for it definitely sees people in terms of what they have inherited and learned in the past, but it also strongly sees them as able to think for themselves, make some free choices, and, by hard work and effort, carry out their goals. RET techniques emphasize the present and future and waste little time with the past.

9. *Cognitive–affective.* Cognitive theories include the so-called ego theories, which see people as essentially rational, with the emotions subserving the intellect. Conversely, affective theories of personality see them as operating on an emotional basis, with the intellect at the service of the emotions. Although RET has a reputation for cognitive therapy, its personality theory contains strong affective elements as well. It says that humans inextricably intertwine and cannot really separate their emotions and cognitions, and that what we call "emotion" largely consists of and results from powerful evaluations or cognitions. Secondly, RET places cognition or "intellect" squarely in the service of "affect" or emotion. It hypothesizes that people get born with a tendency to "value" or "feel" or "desire" in order to survive and to survive reasonably happily; and that the term "rational," as used in RET, only applies to thoughts, emotions, and acts that abet these basic affective goals. Although RET uses cognitive, emotive, and behavioral methods of treatment, and uses them on theoretical grounds and not merely because they work, its aim and philosophy remain exceptionally hedonistic.

10. *Unconsciousness–consciousness.* Theories that stress the unconscious see the person as having considerable investment below the level of awareness. Consciousness refers to awareness, and consciousness theories see the individual as basically rational. In this personality dimension RET leans toward the consciousness side, but it heavily emphasizes the role of "unconscious" automaticity and habituation in the formation of disturbance. It therefore advocates a great deal of behavior therapy, forced practice, throwing oneself into doing "risky" things whether one likes to do so or not, and *in vivo* homework assignments designed to bring about "nonthinking" habituation or dehabituation.

Other RET Hypotheses about Personality

RET posits many concepts about personality, some of them unique and some held by other systems, especially by other cognitive–behavior therapeutic formulations. Some of the main RET personality hypotheses that now have a large amount of clinical and experimental research data behind them (Ellis, 1977b) include the following:

1. Human thinking and emotion do not constitute two disparate or different processes, but significantly overlap. Cognition represents a mediating operation between stimuli and responses. Emotions and behaviors stem not merely from people's reactions to their environment but also from their thoughts, beliefs, and attitudes about that environment.

2. People self-reflexively "talk" to themselves, and the kinds of things they say, as well as the form in which they say them, significantly affect their emotions and behaviors and sometimes lead to emotional disturbance.

3. Humans have the ability not only to think (and generalize) but to think about their thinking and to think about thinking about their thinking. When disturbed, they often tend to think about their disturbances and thereby create additional anxiety or depression.

4. People cognize, emote, and behave interrelatedly. Cognition contributes to emotion and to action; emotion to cognition and to action; and action to cognition and to emotion. When people change one of these three modalities they concomitantly tend to change the other two.

5. When people expect something to happen they act significantly differently than when they have no such expectancies. Their

cognitive expectancy influences both their emotions and their behaviors.

6. Humans have powerful innate and/or acquired tendencies to construct basic values and to think and act rationally (to abet) and irrationally (to sabotage) such values. They frequently have irrational or absolutistic ideas that interfere with healthy thoughts, emotions, and behaviors.

7. People have strong tendencies not only to rate their acts, behaviors, performances, and traits as "good" or "bad" but to rate their *selves* or *essences* similarly, and these self-ratings constitute one of the main sources of their disturbances.

8. People have a strong tendency to do things that seem easier in the short run even though they may bring poor future results.

SUMMARY AND CONCLUSION

While a full theory of human personality would go beyond the here and now and would look backwards into history to seek out biological and environmental causes and forward into the anticipated future, a multiplicity of factors makes all theories partly fanciful. These factors include poor reporting, the crucial element of how theorists construe and misconstrue the facts of biology and social influence, and the existence of so many elements in personality that no theory can put them all together properly. This explains why we have so many competing theories, all plausible, none satisfactory. While theory making seems an interesting but harmless occupation, it would appear more useful if theorists and experimenters concentrated on (1) the here-and-now aspects of behavior rather than its "origins" or "development," and (2) effective methods of modifying dysfunctional behaviors more than the "whys" of how they arose.

With such a practical emphasis, social scientists would not only come to better conclusions about how people change, they would also tend to discover which elements of therapy prove most effective and elegant, would hasten their discarding of the many useless and iatrogenic therapies now prevalent, and would help more people live increasingly satisfying lives. As a model, RET has helped researchers in their efforts to discover efficient ways of helping humans overcome intractable pain, to discover some basic facts of the nervous system which have led to theories about the biological and sociological origins and development of pain (Cherry, 1977).

In psychotherapy, research on therapy procedures by Bandura

(1971), Beck (1976), Goldfried (Goldfried & Davison, 1976), Kanfer (1970), Mahoney (1974), Meichenbaum (1977), Mischel (1976), and many other experimenters has led to significant advances in personality theory. If this kind of research continues, we have a good prospect of looking more closely at the origins of human personality and disentangling (if possible) hereditarian from environmental influences. Without such research and the basic solid knowledge of behavior which it tends to give, the present confusing situation in which almost 100 separate theories of personality and personality change keep competing for attention (and the situation grows worse annually) will continue, and we may never come to any definitive conclusions.

As a basic issue, there is the question of whether personality theory shall be viewed as religion or science. If religion, then anyone can have a revelation and state that boys universally crave sexual intercourse with their mothers—or similar garbage. Given a beard and a doctoral degree, one can make any assertion without any proof, and obtain many devout listeners. If we read the 100 or so personality theories in existence, from the completely biological theory of William Sheldon (1942) to the almost completely psychological theories of George Kelly (1955), we can find literally tens of thousands of assertions made in good faith by honest people, few of which have any proven validity and, worse, many of which seem completely unprovable. Thus, we can have evidence that the moon does not consist of green cheese, but we seem to have no way of proving the existence or nonexistence of archetypes.

Personality theorists might do well to take some of the hypotheses in this article as the beginning of a truly scientific inquiry into personality. In this way we might finally determine the nature of people in the here and now, in their interactions in life and in therapy, and do so under controlled clinical and experimental conditions. Wouldn't this seem preferable to the continual creation of fanciful and intellectually *must*urbatory conceptionalizations that lead nowhere—as a reading of the latest issues of many journals devoted to personality theory will show?

REFERENCES

Bandura, A. (1971). *Psychological modeling: Conflicting theories.* Chicago: Aldine.

Beck, A. T. (1976). *Cognitive therapy and the emotional disorders.* New York: International Universities Press.

Berne, E. (1964). *Games people play.* New York: Grove Press.

Buehler, K. (1965). *Die krise der psychologie.* Stuttgart: Gustave Fisher.

Cherry, L. (1977, January 30). Solving the mysteries of pain. *New York Times Magazine*, pp. 12–13, 50–53.

Coan, R. W. (1968). *The optimal personality*. New York: Wiley.

Corsini, R. (1977). *Current personality theories*. Itasca, IL: F. E. Peacock.

DiGiuseppe, R., Miller, N., & Trexler, L. A review of rational–emotive psychotherapy outcome studies. *The Counseling Psychologist*, 7(1), 64–72.

Ellis, A. (1962). *Reason and emotion in psychotherapy*. New York: Lyle Stuart.

Ellis, A. (1971). *Growth through reason*. Palo Alto, CA: Science and Behavior Books; Hollywood, CA: Wilshire Books.

Ellis, A. (1972). Psychotherapy and the value of a human being. In J. W. Davis (Ed.), *Value and valuation* (pp. 117–139). Knoxville: University of Tennessee Press.

Ellis, A. (1973a). *Humanistic psychotherapy: The rational–emotive approach*. New York: Julian Press and McGraw-Hill Paperbacks.

Ellis, A. (1973b). Rational–emotive therapy. In R. J. Corsini (Ed.), *Current psychotherapies*. Itasca, IL: F. E. Peacock.

Ellis, A. (1975). *How to live with a "neurotic"* (rev. ed.). New York: Crown.

Ellis, A. (1976). The biological basis of human irrationality. *Journal of Individual Psychology, 32*, 145–168.

Ellis, A. (1977a). *How to live with—and without—anger*. New York: Reader's Digest Press.

Ellis, A. (1977b). Rational–emotive therapy: Research data that supports the clinical and personality hyotheses of RET and other modes of cognitive behavior therapy. *Counseling Psychologist, 7* (1), 2–42.

Ellis, A., & Grieger, R. (Eds.). (1977). *Handbook of rational–emotive therapy* (vol. 1). New York: Springer Publishing Co.

Ellis, A., & Harper, R. A. (1975). *A new guide to rational living*. Englewood Cliffs, NJ: Prentice-Hall; Hollywood, CA: Wilshire Books.

Evans, P. (1976). The Burt Affair . . . sleuthing in science. *APA Monitor, 1*, 4.

Freud, S. (1965). *Standard edition of the works of Sigmund Freud*. London: Hogarth Press.

Fromm, E. (1941). *Escape from freedom*. New York: Rinehart.

Fromm, E. (1975). *The anatomy of human destructiveness*. Greenwich, CT: Fawcett.

Goldfried, M. R., & Davison, G. C. (1976). *Clinical behavior therapy*. New York: Holt, Rinehart & Winston.

Horney, K. (1965). *Collected Writings*. New York: Norton.

Kanfer, F. (1970). Self-regulation: Research, issues and speculations. In C. Neuringer & J. L. Michael (Eds.), *Behavior modification in clinical psychology*. New York: Appleton-Century-Crofts.

Kelly, G. (1955). *The psychology of personal constructs*. New York: Norton.

Korzybski, A. (1933). *Science and sanity*. Lancaster, PA: Lancaster Press.

Mahoney, M. (1974). *Cognition and behavior modification*. Cambridge, MA: Ballinger.

Maslow, A. H. (1954). The instinctoid nature of basic needs. *Journal of Personality, 22*, 326–347.

Maultsby, M. C. Jr. (1975). *Help yourself to happiness.* New York: Institute for Rational Living.

Meichenbaum, D. H. (1977). *Cognitive behavior therapy.* New York: Plenum.

Mischel, W. (1976). The self as the person. In A. Wandersman (Ed.), *Behavioristic and humanistic approaches to personality change.* New York: Pergamon.

Morris, K. T., & Kanitz, J. M. (1975). *Rational–emotive therapy.* Boston: Houghton Mifflin.

Murphy, R., & Ellis, A. (1977). *A comprehensive bibliography of rational–emotive therapy and cognitive–behavior therapy.* New York: Institute for Rational Living.

Pastore, N. (1949). *The nature–nurture controversy.* New York: King's Crown Press.

Sheldon, W. (1942). *Varieties of human temperament.* New York: Harper.

Sullivan, H. S. (1953). *Conceptions of modern psychiatry.* New York: Norton.

Woodworth, R. S., & Schlosberg, H. (1954). *Experimental psychology.* New York: Holt.

The Biological Basis of Human Irrationality

3

INTRODUCTION

When Ellis first created RET in 1955, he was largely an environmentalist. He believed that human disturbance—or at least neurosis—was picked up from our parents and our culture during early childhood. His experiences as, first, a scientific psychologist and, second, a psychoanalyst predisposed him, though not rigidly, to this "observation." His extensive reading, however, as well as his early clinic and state hospital experience in the New Jersey Department of Institutions and Agencies soon convinced Ellis that psychotic, but not neurotic, individuals were usually biologically predisposed to disturbance, as were autistic and mentally deficient children.

This view was consolidated by Ellis's first 5 years of using RET with hundreds of clients, for he soon noticed several important facts: (1) His severely neurotic and borderline clients frequently had much less disturbed siblings who were treated much the same way as they were; (2) they almost always had close relatives, including uncles and aunts and cousins who had nothing to do with their upbringing, who were also emotionally nonfunctional; (3) many of them were adopted by nonrelatives who were sane, loving, and noncritical and who reared them quite sensibly; (4) many of them had adopted children who were much saner than they were; (5) no matter how well they understood RET and helped to teach it to others, they often had great trouble practicing it themselves; (6) when they used RET to help themselves considerably, they often stopped using it later (just as they stopped dieting) and then fell back to their own dysfunctional ways; (7) some RET therapists who first made considerable progress with their own problems later started acting neurotically again.

Ellis still felt that emotional disturbance, including neurosis, re-

*sulted from an interplay between environmental and hereditary fac-
tors. But around the beginning of 1960, as the clinical evidence
accumulated, Ellis became convinced that almost all severe neurotics,
as well as practically all borderline personalities, are born with a
strong tendency to become* easily *disturbed by environmental stresses
as well as with a powerful tendency to exaggerate those stresses and
creatively disturb themselves. As George Kelly (1955) pointed out, humans* construct *their emotional reactions and are not merely* conditioned *to have certain personality traits.*

*Going beyond Kelly, in the 1960s Ellis began to stress the exception-
ally important difference between people's acquiring* standards of
conduct *(goals, values, customs, mores, and rules), which they largely*
learn, *and their* creatively adding *to these standards dogmatic, absolutist* musts *(shoulds, oughts, demands, commands, necessities),
which they largely* invent. *As Ellis increasingly stressed in his talks
and workshops and with his psychotherapy clients, what we call*
learning and conditioning *are obviously biologically based because
humans are clearly born teachable, suggestible, and gullible. And even
our learned customs, such as our food and clothing habits, have
biological as well as environmental bases—what culture would teach
its members to go naked in winter and wear heavy furs in summer or
to put salt instead of sugar in their coffee?*

*By the same token, Ellis holds that most people are born easily
distur*bable. *They have an innate tendency to think that they* need
what they want *and that they* have to *be competent, be approved,
and be comfortable. Therefore, they are easily thrown by (or, better,
traumatize themselves by) unpleasant childhood (and adulthood) experiences. Because the vast majority of them, in Ellis's view, are quite*
predisposed *or* vulnerable *to upsetting themselves about negative
happenings (Activating Events, as they are called in RET), it is hardly
surprising that they see these happenings (as the psychoanalysts and
orthodox behaviorists especially do) as* causing *their emotional problems. But because almost any series of frustrations and disapprovals
would send them over the neurotic (and sometimes psychotic) brink,
Ellis asks, are we wise when we blame their environment rather than
their* natural *reactivity to this environment as the main "cause" of
their disturbances?*

*Ellis originally presented this paper on the biological basis of hu-
man irrationality at an American Psychological Association convention in 1975. It was rejected by several leading professional journals
before being published in the Adlerian* Journal of Individual Psychology. *It represents an important aspect of RET that Ellis has not
elucidated in depth elsewhere. Even though modern neuropsychologi-*

cal research has startlingly supported the biological underpinnings of severe emotional disturbance (Franklin, 1987), Ellis notes that psychotherapists are still very reluctant to accept their findings.

REFERENCES

Franklin, J. (1987). *Molecules of the mind*. New York: Delta.
Kelly, G. (1955). *The psychology of personal constructs* (2 vols.). New York: Norton.

Before stating any hypothesis about the basis of human irrationality, definitions of the main terms employed in this article, *biological basis* and *irrationality,* are presented. *Biological basis* means that a characteristic or trait has distinctly innate (as well as distinctly acquired) origins—that it partly arises from the organism's natural, easy predisposition to behave in certain stipulated ways. This does not mean that this characteristic or trait has a purely instinctive basis, that it cannot undergo major change, nor that the organism would perish, or at least live in abject misery, without it. It simply means that, because of its genetic and/or congenital nature, an individual easily develops this trait and has a difficult time modifying or eliminating it.

Irrationality means any thought, emotion, or behavior that leads to self-defeating or self-destructive consequences—that significantly interferes with the survival and happiness of the organism. More specifically, irrational behavior usually has several aspects: (1) The individual believes, often devoutly, that it accords with the tenets of reality although in some important respect it really does not; (2) people who adhere to it significantly denigrate or refuse to accept themselves; (3) it interferes with their getting along satisfactorily with members of their primary social groups; (4) it seriously blocks their achieving the kind of interpersonal relations

Reprinted from the *Journal of Individual Psychology*, 1976, *32*, 145–168. Adapted from a paper presented at the American Psychological Association annual convention, September 1975.

that they would like to achieve; (5) it hinders their working gainfully and joyfully at some kind of productive labor; and (6) it interferes with their own best interests in other important respects (Ellis, 1974, 1975; Maultsby, 1975).

The major hypothesis of this article is as follows: Humans ubiquitously and constantly act irrationally in many important respects. Just about all of them do so during all their lives, though some considerably more than others. There is, therefore, some reason to believe that they do so naturally and easily, often against the teachings of their families and their culture, frequently against their own conscious wish and determination. Although modifiable to a considerable extent, their irrational tendencies seem largely ineradicable and intrinsically go with their biological (as well as sociological) nature.

This hypothesis goes back to the statements of some of the earliest historians and philosophers and has received adequate documentation over the years by a host of authorities (Frazer, 1959; Hoffer, 1951; Levi-Strauss, 1970; Pitkin, 1932; Rachleff, 1973). Ellis (1962) and Parker (1973) agree with this documentation. The latter noted that "most people are self-destructive, they behave in ways that are obviously against their best interest" (Parker, 1973, p. 3). Nonetheless, whenever I address an audience of psychologists or psychotherapists and point out this fairly obvious conclusion and state or imply that it arises out of the biological tendency of humans to behave irrationally, a great many dyed-in-the-wool environmentalists almost always rise with horror, foam at the mouth, and call me a traitor to objective, scientific thinking.

Hence this paper. Following is a brief summary—for the amount of supporting evidence assumes overwhelming proportions and would literally take many volumes to summarize properly—of some of the main reasons behind the thesis that human irrationality roots itself in basic human nature. The summary is confined to outlining the multiplicity of major irrationalities and to giving some of the logical and psychological reasons why it seems almost certain that they have biological origins.

First are listed some of the outstanding irrationalities among the thousands collected over the years. The following manifestations of human behavior certainly do not appear completely irrational—for they also have (as what behavior has not?) some distinct advantages. Some people, such as those Eric Hoffer (1951) calls true believers, will even hold that many of them bring about much more good than harm. Almost any reasonably objective observer of human affairs, however, will probably tend to agree that they include a large amount of foolishness, unreality, and danger to our survival or happiness.

1. Custom and Conformity Irrationalities
    a. Outdated and rigid customs.
    b. Ever-changing, expensive fashions.
    c. Fads and popular crazes.
    d. Customs involving royalty and nobility.
    e. Customs involving holidays and festivals.
    f. Customary gifts and presentations.
    g. Customs in connection with social affairs and dating.
    h. Courtship, marriage, and wedding customs.
    i. Puberty rites, Bar Mitzvahs, etc.
    j. Academic rites and rituals.
    k. Hazings of schools, fraternal organizations, etc.
    l. Religious rites and rituals.
    m. Customs and rites regarding scientific papers.
    n. Circumcision conventions and rituals.
    o. Rigid rules of etiquette and manners.
    p. Blue laws.
    q. Strong disposition to obey authority, even when it makes
       unreasonable demands.
2. Ego-Related Irrationalities
    a. Tendency to deify oneself.
    b. Dire need to have superiority over others.
    c. Tendency to give oneself a global, total, all-inclusive rat-
       ing.
    d. Tendency to desperately seek for status.
    e. Tendency to prove oneself rather than enjoy oneself.
    f. Tendency to believe that one's value as a human depends
       on one's competency at an important performance or
       group of important performances.
    g. Tendency to value oneself or devalue oneself in regard to
       the performances of one's family.
    h. Tendency to value or devalue oneself in regard to the
       performances or status of one's school, neighborhood
       group, community, state, or country.
    i. Tendency to denigrate or devil-ify oneself.
3. Prejudice-Related Irrationalities
    a. Strong prejudice.
    b. Dogma.
    c. Racial prejudice.
    d. Sex prejudice.
    e. Political prejudice.
    f. Social and class prejudice.
    g. Religious prejudice.
    h. Appearance prejudice

4. Common Kinds of Illogical Thinking
   a. Overgeneralization.
   b. Magnification and exaggeration.
   c. Use of non sequiturs.
   d. Strong belief in antiempirical statements.
   e. Strong belief in absolutes.
   f. Gullibility and oversuggestibility.
   g. Strong belief in contradictory statements.
   h. Strong belief in utopianism.
   i. Strong adherence to unreality.
   j. Strong belief in unprovable statements.
   k. Shortsightedness.
   l. Overcautiousness.
   m. Giving up one extreme statement and going to the other extreme.
   n. Strong belief in shoulds, oughts, and musts.
   o. The dire need for certainty.
   p. Wishful thinking.
   q. Lack of self-perspective.
   r. Difficulty of learning.
   s. Difficulty of unlearning and relearning.
   t. Deep conviction that because one believes something strongly it must have objective reality and truth.
   u. Conviction that because one had better respect the rights of others to hold beliefs different from one's own, their beliefs have truth.

5. Experiential and Feeling Irrationalities
   a. Strong conviction that because one experiences something deeply and "feels" its truth, it must have objective reality and truth.
   b. Strong conviction that the more intensely one experiences something, the more objective reality and truth it has.
   c. Strong conviction that because one authentically and honestly feels something it must have objective truth and reality.
   d. Strong conviction that all authentic and deeply experienced feelings represent legitimate and healthy feelings.
   e. Strong conviction that when a powerful irrational thought or feeling exists (e.g., a mystical feeling that one understands everything in the universe) it constitutes a deeper, more important, and objectively truer idea or emotion than a rational thought or feeling.

6. Habit-Making Irrationalities
   a. The acquiring of nonproductive and self-defeating habits easily and unconsciously.
   b. The automatic retention and persistence of nonproductive and self-defeating habits in spite of one's conscious awareness of their irrationality.
   c. Failure to follow up on conscious determination and resolution to break a self-defeating habit.
   d. Inventing rationalizations and excuses for not giving up a self-defeating habit.
   e. Backsliding into self-defeating habits after one has temporarily overcome them.
7. Addictions to Self-Defeating Behaviors
   a. Addiction to overeating.
   b. Addiction to smoking.
   c. Addiction to alcohol.
   d. Addiction to drugs.
   e. Addiction to tranquilizers and other medicines.
   f. Addiction to work, at the expense of greater enjoyments.
   g. Addiction to approval and love.
8. Neurotic and Psychotic Symptoms
   a. Overweening and disruptive anxiety.
   b. Depression and despair.
   c. Hostility and rage.
   d. Extreme feelings of self-downing and hurt.
   e. Extreme feelings of self-pity.
   f. Childish grandiosity.
   g. Refusal to accept reality.
   h. Paranoid thinking.
   i. Delusions.
   j. Hallucinations.
   k. Psychopathy.
   l. Mania.
   m. Extreme withdrawal or catatonia.
9. Religious Irrationalities
   a. Devout faith unfounded in fact.
   b. Slavish adherence to religious dogma.
   c. Deep conviction that a supernatural force must exist.
   d. Deep conviction that a supernatural force or entity has special, personal interest in oneself.
   e. Deep conviction in Heaven and Hell.
   f. Religious bigotry.
   g. Persecution of other religious groups.
   h. Wars between religious groups.

    i. Scrupulous adherence to religious rules, rites, and taboos.
    j. Religious antisexuality and extreme puritanism.
    k. Religious conviction that all pleasure equates with sin.
    l. Complete conviction that some deity will heed one's prayers.
    m. Absolute conviction that one has a spirit or soul entirely divorced from one's material body.
    n. Absolute conviction that one's soul will live forever.
    o. Absolute conviction that no kind of superhuman force can possibly exist.

10. Population Irrationalities
    a. Population explosion in many parts of the world.
    b. Lack of education in contraceptive methods.
    c. Families having more children than they can afford to support.
    d. Restrictions on birth control and abortion for those who want to use them.
    e. Some nations deliberately fomenting a population explosion.

11. Health Irrationalities
    a. Air pollution.
    b. Noise pollution.
    c. Drug advertising and promotion.
    d. Poor health education.
    e. Harmful food additives.
    f. Uncontrolled medical costs and resultant poor health facilities.
    g. Unnecessary surgical procedures.
    h. Avoidance of physicians and dentists by people requiring diagnostic and medical procedures.
    i. Neglect of medical research.

12. Acceptance of Unreality
    a. Widespread acceptance and following of silly myths.
    b. Widespead acceptance and following of extreme romanticism.
    c. Widespread acceptance and following of foolish, inhumane fairy tales.
    d. Widespread acceptance and following of unrealistic movies.
    e. Widespread acceptance and following of unrealistic radio and TV dramas and serials.
    f. Widespread Pollyannaism.
    g. Widespread utopianism.

13. Political Irrationalities
    a. Wars.
    b. Undeclared wars and cold wars.
    c. Civil wars.
    d. Political corruption and graft.
    e. Foolish election and voting procedures.
    f. Political riots.
    g. Terrorism.
    h. Political persecution and torture.
    i. Extreme patriotism.
    j. Extreme nationalism.
    k. Constant international bickering.
    l. Sabotaging of attempts at world collaboration and coop-
       eration.
14. Economic Irrationalities
    a. Ecological waste and pollution.
    b. Poor use and development of natural resources.
    c. Economic boycotts and wars.
    d. Needless employer–employee bickering and strikes.
    e. Extreme profiteering.
    f. Business bribery, corruption, and theft.
    g. Extreme economic status-seeking.
    h. Union bribery, corruption, and graft.
    i. Misleading and false advertising.
    j. Foolish restrictions on business and labor.
    k. Inefficiency in business and industry.
    l. Addiction to foolish economic customs.
    m. Inequitable and ineffectual taxes.
    n. Gambling abuses.
    o. Foolish consumerism (e.g., expensive dog funerals, fu-
       nerals, weddings, alcohol consumption, etc.).
    p. Production of shoddy materials.
    q. Lack of intelligent consumerism information and control.
    r. Inefficiently run welfare system.
    s. Inefficiently run government agencies.
15. Avoidance Irrationalities
    a. Procrastination.
    b. Complete avoidance of important things; inertia.
    c. Refusal to face important realities.
    d. Oversleeping and avoidance of sufficient sleep.
    e. Refusal to get sufficient exercise.
    f. Lack of thought and preparation for the future.
    g. Needless suicide.

16. Dependency Irrationalities
    a. Need for approval and love of others.
    b. Need for authority figures to run one's life.
    c. Need for superhuman gods and devils.
    d. Need for parents when one has matured chronologically.
    e. Need for a helper, guru, or therapist.
    f. Need for a hero.
    g. Need for magical solutions to problems.
17. Hostility Irrationalities
    a. Condemning people totally because some of their acts appear undesirable or unfair.
    b. Demanding that people absolutely must do what one would like them to do and damning them when they don't.
    c. Setting up perfectionistic standards and insisting that people have to follow them.
    d. Commanding that justice and fairness must exist in the universe and making oneself quite incensed when they do not.
    e. Insisting that hassles and difficulties must not exist and that life turns absolutely awful when they do.
    f. Disliking unfortunate conditions and not merely working to overcome or remove them but overrebelliously hating the entire system that produced them and the people involved in this system.
    g. Remembering past injustices and vindictively feuding against the perpetrators of these injustices forever.
    h. Remembering past injustices in gory detail and obsessing about them and their perpetrators forever.
18. Excitement-Seeking Irrationalities
    a. Continuing to gamble compulsively in spite of serious losses.
    b. Leading a carousing, playboy or playgirl type of life at the expense of other more solid enjoyments.
    c. Engaging in dangerous sports or pastimes, such as mountain climbing, hunting, or skiing under hazardous conditions.
    d. Deliberately having sex without taking contraceptive or venereal disease precautions.
    e. Engaging in college hazing or other pranks of a hazardous nature.
    f. Turning in false fire alarms.
    g. Dangerous forms of dueling.

    h. Engaging in stealing or homicide for excitement–seeking.

    i. Engaging in serious forms of brawling, fighting, rioting, or warring for excitement-seeking.

    j. Engaging in cruel sports, such as clubbing baby seals or cockfighting for excitement-seeking.

19. Magic-Related Irrationalities

    a. Devout belief in magic, sorcery, witchcraft, etc.

    b. Devout belief in astrology.

    c. Devout belief in phrenology.

    d. Devout belief in mediums and ghosts.

    e. Devout belief in talking horses and other talking animals.

    f. Devout belief in extrasensory perception.

    g. Devout belief in demons and exorcism.

    h. Devout belief in the power of prayer.

    i. Devout belief in superhuman entities and gods.

    j. Devout belief in damnation and salvation.

    k. Devout belief that the universe really cares for humans.

    l. Devout belief that some force in the universe spies on humans and regulates their lives on the principle of deservingness and nondeservingness.

    m. Devout belief in the unity and union of all things in the world.

    n. Devout belief in immortality.

20. Immorality Irrationalities

    a. Engaging in immoral and criminal acts opposed to one's own strong moral code.

    b. Engaging in immoral or criminal acts for which one has a good chance of getting apprehended and severely penalized.

    c. Engaging in immoral and criminal acts when one would have a good chance of gaining more with less effort at noncriminal pursuits.

    d. Firmly believing that virtually no chance exists of one's getting caught at immoral and criminal acts when a good chance actually exists.

    e. Strong belief that because a good chance exists that one can get away with a single criminal act a good chance also exists that one can get away with repeated acts of that nature.

    f. Stubborn refusal to amend one's immoral ways even though one suffers severe penalties for engaging in them.

    g. Engaging in criminal, assaultive, or homicidal acts without any real sense of behaving irresponsibly or immorally.

21. Irrationalities Related to Low Frustration Tolerance or Short-Range Hedonism
    a. Strong insistence on going mainly or only for the pleasures of the moment instead of for those of the present and future.
    b. Obsession with immediate gratifications, whatever the cost.
    c. Whining and strongly pitying oneself when one finds it necessary to surrender short-range pleasures for other gains.
    d. Ignoring the dangers inherent in going for immediate pleasures.
    e. Striving for ease and comfort rather than for greater satisfactions that require some temporary discomfort.
    f. Refusing to work against a harmful addiction because of the immediate discomfort of giving it up.
    g. Refusing to continue with a beneficial or satisfying program of activity because one views its onerous aspects as too hard and devoutly believes that they should not exist.
    h. Champing at the bit impatiently when one has to wait for or work for a satisfying condition to occur.
    i. Procrastinating about doing activities that one knows would turn out beneficially and that one has promised oneself to do.
    j. Significantly contributing to the consumption of a scarce commodity that one knows one will very much want in the future.

22. Defensive Irrationalities
    a. Rationalizing about one's poor behavior instead of trying to honestly admit it and correct it.
    b. Denying that one has behaved poorly or stupidly when one clearly has.
    c. Avoiding facing some of one's serious problems and sweeping them under the rug.
    d. Unconsciously repressing some of one's "shameful" acts because one will savagely condemn oneself if one consciously admits them.
    e. Projecting one's poor behavior onto others and contending that they did it, in order to deny responsibility for it.
    f. Using the sour grapes mechanism, and claiming that you

really do not want something you do want, when you find it too difficult to face your not getting it.

g. Identifying with outstanding individuals and unrealistically believing that you have the same kinds of abilities or talents that they have.

h. Resorting to transference: confusing people who affected you seriously in your past life with those whom you have interests in today and assuming that the present individuals will act pretty much the same way as the past ones did.

i. Resorting to a reaction formation: expressing reverse feelings (such as love) for someone for whom you really have the opposite feeling (such as hate).

23. Attribution Irrationalities

a. Attributing to people feelings for you that they really do not have.

b. Attributing certain motives for people's behavior when they do not actually have those motives.

c. Attributing to people a special interest in you when they have no such interest.

d. Attributing certain characteristics or ideas to people because they have membership in a group whose constituents frequently have such characteristics or ideas.

24. Memory-Related Irrationalities

a. Forgetting painful experiences soon after they end, and not using them to avoid future pain.

b. Embellishing the facts about people's behavior and inventing exaggerations and rumors about them.

c. Focusing mainly or only on the immediate advantages or disadvantages of things and shortsightedly ignoring what will probably happen in connection with them in the future.

d. Repressing one's memory of important events, so as not to feel responsibility or shame about their occurring.

e. Remembering some things too well and thereby interfering with effective thought and behavior in other respects.

25. Demandingness-Related Irrationalities

a. Demanding that one must do well at certain goals in order to accept oneself as a human.

b. Demanding that one must win the approval or love of significant others.

c. Demanding that one must do perfectly well at practi-

cally everything and/or win the perfect approval of practically everyone.

d. Demanding that others must treat one fairly, justly, considerately, and lovingly.

e. Demanding that everyone must treat one perfectly fairly,
justly, considerately, and lovingly.

f. Demanding that the conditions of life must remain easy
and that one must get practically everything one wants
quickly, without any undue effort.

g. Demanding that one must have almost perfect enjoyment or ecstasy at all times.

26. Sex-Related Irrationalities

a. The belief that sex acts have intrinsic dirtiness, badness,
or wickedness.

b. The belief that sex acts prove absolutely bad or immoral
unless they go with love, marriage, or other nonsexual
relationships.

c. The belief that orgasm has a sacred quality and that sex
without it has no real joy or legitimacy.

d. The belief that intercourse has a sacred quality and that
orgasm must come about during penile-vaginal intromis-
sion.

e. The belief that one must have sex competence and that
one's worth as a person doesn't exist without it.

f. The belief that good sex must include simultaneous orgasm.

g. The belief that masturbation and petting to orgasm have
a shameful quality, not the legitimacy of intercourse.

h. The belief that men can legitimately and morally have
more sex or less restricted sex than can women.

i. The belief that sex competence should occur spontaneously and easily, without any particular kind of knowledge or practice.

j. The belief that women have little natural interest in sex,
remain naturally passive, and have inferior sexual abilities and capacities.

k. The belief that two people who love each other can have
little or no sexual interest in other individuals.

27. Science-Related Irrationalities

a. The belief that science provides a panacea for all human
problems.

b. The belief that the scientific method constitutes the only
method of advancing human knowledge.

   c. The belief that all technological inventions and advances prove good for humans.

   d. The belief that because the logico-empirical method of science does not give perfect solutions to all problems and has its limitations, it has little or no usefulness.

   e. The belief that because indeterminacy exists in scientific observation, the logico-empirical method has no validity.

   f. The belief that because science has found evidence and explanations for hypotheses that originally only existed in the human imagination (e.g., the theory of relativity), it has to and undoubtedly will find evidence and explanations for other imagined hypotheses (such as the existence of a soul or of God).

   g. The belief that because a scientist gets recognized as an authority in one area (e.g., Einstein as a physicist), he or she must have authoritative views in other areas (e.g., politics).

   h. The strong tendency of highly competent, exceptionally well trained scientists to act in a highly prejudiced, foolish manner in some important aspects of their scientific endeavors, and to behave even more foolishly in their personal lives.

   i. The strong tendency of applied social scientists—such as clinical psychologists, psychiatrists, social workers, counselors, and clergymen—to behave self-defeatingly and unscientifically in their personal and professional lives.

The foregoing list of human irrationalities, which in no way pretends to exhaust the field, includes 259 major happiness-sabotaging tendencies. Some of these, admittedly, overlap, so that the list includes repetitions. At the same time, it consists of only a bare outline; and under each of its headings we can easily subsume a large number of other irrationalities. Under heading 1.e., for example—irrationalities related to courtship, marriage, and wedding customs—we could easily include hundreds of idiocies, many of them historical, but many still extant.

Psychotherapy represents one of the most tragic examples in this respect. It is mentioned briefly, under heading 27.i.—science-related irrationalities—as "the strong tendency of applied social scientists—such as clinical psychologists, psychiatrists, social workers, counselors, and clergymen—to behave self-defeatingly and unscientifically in their personal and professional lives." This hardly tells the tale! For psychotherapy supposedly consists of a field of scientific inquiry and application whose practitioners remain strongly devoted to helping their clients eliminate or minimize their irrational, self-destructive thoughts, feelings, and behaviors. Actually, the opposite largely appears to hold true. For most therapists seem to have almost innumerable irrational ideas and to engage in ubiquitous antiscientific activities that help their clients maintain or even intensify their unreasonableness.

A few major irrationalities of psychotherapeutic "helpers": (1) Instead of taking a comprehensive multimodal, cognitive-emotive-behavioral approach to treatment, they fetishistically and obsessively-compulsively overemphasize some monolithic approach, such as awareness, insight, emotional release, understanding of the past, experiencing, rationality, or physical release (Lazarus, 1971). (2) They have their own dire needs for their clients' approval and frequently tie these clients to them in an extended dependency relationship. (3) They abjure scientific, empirically based analysis for farfetched conjectures that they rarely relate to factual data (Jurjevich, 1947; Leites, 1971). (4) They tend to focus on helping clients feel better rather than get better by learning specifically how they upset themselves and how they can stop doing so in the future. (5) They dogmatically assume that their own system or technique of therapy, and it alone, helps people; and they have a closed mind to other systems or techniques. (6) They promulgate therapeutic orthodoxies and excoriate and excommunicate deviates from their dogmas. (7) They confuse correlation with cause and effect and assume that if an individual hates, say, his mother, and later hates other women, his former feeling must have caused the latter feeling. (8) They mainly ignore the biological bases of human behavior and assume that *special* situational reasons for all disturbances must exist and, worse yet, that if one finds these special reasons the disturbances will almost automatically disappear. (9) They tend to look for (and "find"!) unique, clever, and "deep" explanations of behavior and ignore many obvious, "superficial," and truer explanations. (10) They either promulgate the need, on the part of their clients, for interminable therapy; or they promulgate the myth that easy, quick, miracle cures exist (LeShan, 1975). (11) They turn more and more to magic, faith healing, astrology, tarot cards, and other unscientific means of "transpersonal" psychotherapy (Ellis, 1973, 1977). (12) They strive for vaguely defined, utopian goals that mislead and harm clients (Watzlawick, Weakland, & Fisch, 1974). (13) They make irrational, unscientific attacks on experimentally inclined therapists (Hook, 1975; Strupp, 1975a, 1975b). (14) They apotheosize emotion and invent false dichotomies between reason and emotion (Frankel, 1973; Shibles, 1974; Strupp, 1975b).

To repeat the main point: virtually all the main headings and subheadings in the above list of major human irrationalities have a score or more further subdivisions; and for each subdivision a fairly massive amount of observational and experimental confirmatory evidence exists. For example, we have a massive amount of observational evidence that innumerable people overeat, procrastinate, think dogmatically, lose considerable amounts of money in foolish gambling, devoutly believe in astrology, and continually rationalize about their own inept behavior. And we have considerable experimental evidence that humans feel favorably biased in regard to those whom they consider attractive, that they backslide after giving up a habit like overeating, that they go for specious immediate gratifications instead of more enjoyable long-term satisfactions, that they repress memories of events they consider shameful, that they frequently attribute feelings to others that these others do not seem to have, and that they have an almost incredible degree of suggestibility in regard to an opinion of the majority of their fellows or of a presumed authority figure.

Granted that all the foregoing major human irrationalities—and many more like them!—exist, can one maintain the thesis that, in all probability, they have biological roots and stem from the fundamental nature of humans? Yes, on several important, convincing grounds, which follow:

1. All the major human irrationalities seem to exist, in one form or another, in virtually all humans. Not equally, of course! Some of us, on the whole, behave much less irrationally than others. But go find *any* individuals who do not fairly frequently in their lives subscribe to *all* of these major irrationalities. For example, using only the first ten main headings that apply to personal self-sabotaging, do you know of a single man or woman who has not often slavishly conformed to some asinine social custom, not given himself or herself global, total ratings, not held strong prejudices, not resorted to several kinds of illogical thinking, not fooled himself or herself into believing that his or her strong feelings represented something about objective reality, not acquired and persisted in self-defeating habits, not had any pernicious addictions, remained perfectly free of all neurotic symptoms, never subscribed to religious dogmas, and never surrendered to any foolish health habits? Is there a single such case?

2. Just about all the major irrationalities that now exist have held rampant sway in virtually all social and cultural groups that have been investigated historically and anthropologically. Although rules, laws, mores, and standards vary widely from group to

group, gullibility, absolutism, dogmas, religiosity, and demanding-ness *about* these standards remains surprisingly similar. Thus, your parents and your culture advise or educate you, in the Western civilized world, to wear one kind of clothes and, in the South Sea Islands, to wear another kind. But where they tend to inform you, "You had better dress in the right or proper way, so that people will accept your behavior and act advantageously toward you," you irrationally escalate this "proper" (and not too irratio-nal) standard into,"I *must* dress properly, because I absolutely *need* other people's approval. I *can't stand* their disapproval and the disadvantages that may thereby accrue to me; and if they do not like my behavior that means they do not like *me* and that I rate as a completely *rotten person!*" Although your parents and your teach-ers may encourage you to think in this absolutistic, self-downing manner, you seem to have the innate human propensity (a) to gullibly take them seriously; (b) to carry on their nonsense for the rest of your life; and (c) to invent it yourself if they happen to provide you with relatively little absolutism.

3. Many of the irrationalities that people profoundly follow go counter to almost all the teachings of their parents, peers, and mass media. Yet they refuse to give them up! Few parents encour-age you to overgeneralize, make antiempirical statements, or up-hold contradictory propositions; yet you tend to do this kind of thing continually. Your educational system strongly encourages you to learn, unlearn, and relearn; yet you have great difficulty doing so in many important respects. You encounter strong per-suasive efforts of others to get you to forego nonproductive and self-defeating habits, like overeating and smoking. But you largely tend to resist this constant teaching. You may literally go, at your own choosing, for years of psychotherapy to overcome your anxi-ety or tendencies toward depression. But look at the relatively little progress you often make!

You may have parents who raise you with extreme skepticism or antireligious tendencies. Yet, you easily can adopt some extreme religious orthodoxy in your adult years. You learn about the advis-ability of regularly visiting your physician and your dentist from grade school onward. But does this teaching make you go? Does widespread reading about the facts of life quiet your Pollyannaism or utopianism—or rid you of undue pessimism? Thousands of well-documented books and films have clearly exposed the inequi-ties of wars, riots, terrorism, and extreme nationalism. Have they really induced you to strongly oppose these forms of political irra-tionality?

Virtually no one encourages you to procrastinate and to avoid facing life's realities. Dangerous excitement-seeking rarely gets you the approval of others. Does that stop you from indulging in it? The vast majority of scientists oppose magical, unverifiable, absolutistic, devout thinking. Do you always heed them? You usually know perfectly well what moral and ethical rules you subscribe to; and almost everyone you know encourages you to subscribe to them. Do you? Low frustration tolerance and short-range hedonism rarely prove acceptable to your elders, your teachers, your clergymen, and your favorite writers. Does their disapproval stop you from frequently giving in to immediate gratification at the expense of future gains? Who teaches you to rationalize and reinforces you when you do so? What therapist, friend, or parent goes along with your other kinds of defensiveness? But does their almost universal opposition stop you? Do significant others in your life reward you for demanding perfection of yourself or of them, for whining and wailing that conditions *must* transpire the way you want them to turn out?

Certainly, a good many irrationalities have an important cultural component—or at least get significantly encouraged and exacerbated by the social group. But a good many seem minimally taught; and many others get severely discouraged, yet still ubiquitously flourish!

4. As mentioned before, practically all the irrationalities listed in this article hold true not only for ignorant, stupid, and severely disturbed individuals but also for highly intelligent, educated, and relatively little disturbed persons. PhD's in physics and psychology, for example, have racial and other prejudices, indulge in enormous amounts of wishful thinking, believe that if someone believes something strongly—or intensely experiences it—it must have objective reality and truth, fall prey to all kinds of pernicious habits (including additions like alcoholism), foolishly get themselves into debt, devoutly think that they must have others' approval, believe in the power of prayer, and invent rumors about others which they then strongly believe. Unusually bright and well-educated people probably hold fewer or less rigid irrationalities than average members of the populace, but they hardly have a monopoly on rational behavior!

5. So many humans hold highly irrational beliefs and participate in exceptionally self-defeating behaviors so often that we can only with great difficulty uphold the hypothesis that they entirely learn these ways of reacting. Even if we hypothesize that they largely or mainly learn how to behave so badly, the obvious question arises: Why do they allow themselves to get taken in so badly by the teachings of their culture, and if they do imbibe these

during their callow youth, why don't they teach themselves how to give up these inanities later? Almost all of us learn many significant political, social, and religious values from our parents and our institutions during our childhood, but we often give them up later, after we go to college, read some hardheaded books, or befriend people who subscribe to quite different values. Why don't we do this about many of our most idiotic and impractical views, which clearly do not accord with reality and which obviously do us considerable harm?

Take, for instance, the following ideas, which just a little reflection will show have little sense and which will almost always lead to bad results: (1) "If my sister did me in as a child, all women appear dangerous and I'd better not relate to them intimately." (2) "If I lack competency in an area, such as academic performance, I rate as a totally worthless individual and deserve no happiness." (3) "Because you have treated me unfairly, as you absolutely must not, you have to change your ways and treat me better in the future." (4) "Since I enjoy smoking very much, I can't give it up; and although others acquire serious disadvantages from continuing it, I can most probably get away with smoking without harming myself." (5) "Because blacks get arrested and convicted for more crimes than whites, they all rate as an immoral race and I'd better have nothing to do with them." (6) "If biological and hereditary factors play an important part in emotional disturbance, we can do nothing to help disturbed people, and their plight remains hopeless."

All of these irrational statements, and hundreds of similar ones, clearly make little or no sense and wreak immense social and individual harm. Yet we devoutly believe them in millions of cases; and even if we can show that some significant part of these beliefs stems from social learning (as it probably does), why do we so strongly imbibe and so persistently hang on to them? Clearly because we have a powerful biological predisposition to do so.

6. When bright and generally competent people give up many of their irrationalities, they frequently tend to adopt other inanities or to go to opposite irrational extremes. Devout religionists often turn into devout atheists. Political right-wing extremists wind up as left-wing extremists. Individuals who procrastinate mightily may later emerge as compulsive workers. People who surrender one irrational phobia frequently turn up with another equally irrational but quite different phobia. Extremism tends to remain as a natural human trait that takes one foolish form or another.

7. Humans who seem least afflicted by irrational thoughts and behaviors still revert to them, and sometimes seriously so, at cer-

tain times. A man who rarely gets angry at others may on occasion incense himself so thoroughly that he almost or actually murders someone. A woman who fearlessly studies difficult subjects and takes complicated examinations may feel that she can't bear rejection by a job interview and may fail to look for a suitable position. A therapist who objectively and dispassionately teaches his or her clients how to behave more rationally may, if one of them stubbornly resists, act quite irrationally and agitatedly dismiss that person from therapy. In cases like these, unusual environmental conditions often bring out silly behavior by normally sane individuals. But these individuals obviously react to these conditions because they have some basic disposition to go out of their heads under unusual kinds of stress—and that basic disposition probably has innate elements.

8. People highly opposed to various kinds of irrationalities often fall prey to them. Agnostics give in to devout, absolutistic thoughts and feelings. Highly religious individuals act quite immorally. Psychologists who believe that guilt or self-downing has no legitimacy make themselves guilty and self-downing.

9. Knowledge or insight into one's irrational behavior only partially, if at all, helps one change it. You may know full well about the harmfulness of smoking—and smoke more than ever! You may realize that you hate sex because your parents puritanically taught you to do so, but you may nonetheless keep hating it. You may have clearcut "intellectual" insight into your overweening egotism but have little "emotional" insight into how to change it. This largely arises from the basic human tendency to have two contradictory beliefs at the same time—an "intellectual" one, which you lightly and occasionally hold, and an "emotional" one, which you vigorously and consistently hold and which you therefore usually tend to act upon. This tendency to have simultaneous contradictory beliefs again seems part of the human condition.

10. No matter how hard and how long people work to overcome their irrational thoughts and behaviors, they usually find it exceptionally difficult to overcome or eradicate them; and to some degree they always remain exceptionally fallible in this respect (Ellis, 1962; Ellis & Harper, 1975; Hauck, 1973; Maultsby, 1975). We could hypothesize that because they overlearn their self-defeating behaviors at an early age, they therefore find it most difficult to recondition themselves. But it seems simpler and more logical to conclude that their fallibility has an inherent source—and that their early conditionability and proneness to accepting training in dysfunctional behavior *itself* represents a significant part of their innate fallibility! Certainly, they hardly acquired con-

ditionability solely through having someone condition them!

11. It appears reasonably clear that certain irrational ideas stem from personal, nonlearned (or even anti-learned) experiences; that we inventively, though crazily, *invent* them in a highly creative manner. Suppose, for instance, you fall in love with someone and you intensely feel, "know," and state, "I know I'll love you forever!" You certainly didn't *learn* that knowledge—since you not only read about Romeo and Juliet but also read lots of other information, such as divorce statistics, which show that people rarely romantically adore each other forever. You consequently *choose* your "knowledge" out of several other bits of data you could have chosen to "know." And you most probably did so because romantic love among humans frequently carries with it the intrinsic illusion that "because my feeling for you has such authenticity and intensity, I *know* it will last forever." You, at least for the most part, autistically *create* the false and irrational "knowledge" that goes with your genuine (and most probably temporary) feelings.

Again, you may get reared as a Jew or a Moslem and may convert yourself to Christianity and conclude, "I feel Jesus as my Savior, and I feel certain that He exists as the Son of God." Did your experience or your environmental upbringing lead to this feeling and belief? Or did you, for various reasons, invent it? The natural tendency of humans seems to consist of frequent dogmatic beliefs that their profound feelings prove something objectively exists in the universe, and this largely appears an innately based process of illusion.

12. If we look closely at some of the most popular irrational forms of thinking, it appears that humans figure them out. They start with a sensible or realistic observation, and they end up with a non sequitur type of conclusion. Thus, you start with "It would feel enjoyable and I would have advantages if Jane loved me." You then falsely conclude, "Therefore she *has* to love me, and I find it *awful* if she doesn't." If you begin with an even stronger observation, "I would find it *exceptionally* and *uniquely enjoyable if Jane loved me*," you have even more of a tendency to conclude, *"Therefore she must!"* But no matter how true the first part of your proposition proves, the second part remains a *non sequitur*, making no sense whatever.

Similarly, you tend to irrationally conclude, "Because I find order desirable, I *need* certainty." "Because I find failure most undesirable, (1) I *must* not fail; (2) I did not cause myself to fail—he made me do it; and (3) maybe I didn't really fail at all." "Because it would prove very hard for me to give up smoking, I find it *too* hard; and I *can't* do it." All these non sequiturs stem from autistic, grandiose thinking—you simply *command* that what you desire must exist and what you find obnoxious must not. This kind of autistic thinking largely appears innate.

13. Many types of irrational thinking largely consist of arrant overgeneralizations; and as Korzybski (1933) and his followers have shown, overgeneralizations seem a normal (though foolish) part of the human condition. Thus, you easily start with a sensible observation, again: "I failed at that test," and then you overgeneralize to "I will always fail; I have no ability to succeed at it." Or you start with, "They sometimes treat me unjustly," and you overgeneralize to "They always treat me unjustly, and I can't stand their continual unfair treatment!" Again: this seems the way that normal humans naturally think. Children, as Piaget (Piaget & Inhelder, 1974) has shown, lack good judgment until the age of seven or eight. Adults frequently lack it forever!

14. Human thinking not only significantly varies in relation to people's intelligence levels, but some forms of thinking stem largely from left-brain or right-brain functioning. Both intelligence and left-brain and right-brain functioning have a significant hereditary element and do not arise merely out of learned experiences (Austin, 1975; Sperry, 1975).

15. Some forms of irrationality, such as low frustration tolerance or the seeking of the specious rewards of immediate rather than long-term gratification, exist in many lower animals as well as in humans. Ainslie (1975) reviews the literature on specious reward and shows how a decline in the effectiveness of rewards occurs in both animals and humans as the rewards get delayed from the time of choice. Again, a fairly clear-cut physiological and hereditary element seems obvious here.

16. Some evidence exists that people often find it much easier to learn self-defeating than nondefeating behavior. Thus, they very easily overeat but have great trouble sticking to a sensible diet. They can learn, usually from their foolish peers, to smoke cigarettes; but if other peers or elders try to teach them to give up smoking or to act more self-disciplinedly in other ways, they resist this teaching to a faretheewell! They fairly easily pick up prejudices against blacks, Jews, Catholics, and Orientals; but they rarely heed the teachings of thoroughly tolerant leaders. They quickly condition themselves to feel anxious, depressed, hating, and self-downing; but they take an enormous amount of time and effort getting rid of these disturbed feelings. They don't seem exactly doomed to a lifetime of stupid, foolish, asinine behavior. But pretty nearly!

CONCLUSION

If we define irrationality as thought, emotion, or behavior that leads to self-defeating or self-destructive consequences or that significantly interferes with the survival and happiness of the organism, we find that literally hundreds of major irrationalities exist in all societies and in virtually all humans in those societies. These irrationalities persist despite peoples' conscious determination to change; many of them oppose almost all the teachings of the individuals who follow them; they persist among highly intelligent, educated, and relatively little disturbed individuals; when people give them up, they usually replace them with other, sometimes just as extreme—though opposite—irrationalities, people who strongly oppose them in principle nonetheless perpetuate them in practice; sharp insight into them or their origins hardly removes them; many of them appear to stem from autistic invention; they often seem to flow from deep-seated and almost ineradicable human tendencies toward fallibility, overgeneralization, wishful thinking, gullibility, prejudice, and short-range hedonism; and they appear at least in part tied up with physiological, hereditary, and constitutional processes.

Although we can as yet make no certain or unqualified claim for the biological basis of human irrationality, such a claim now has enough evidence behind it to merit serious consideration. People naturally and easily act rationally and self-fulfillingly (Friedman, 1975; Maslow, 1974; Rogers, 1974). Else they probably would not survive. But they also naturally and easily act against their own best interests. To some degree, their early and later environments encourage them to learn self-destructive behaviors. But how can we not conclude that they have powerful innate tendencies to listen to and agree with antihuman and inhumane teachings and—more importantly—to continue devoutly to believe in and idiotically carry on many of these obviously foolish, scientifically untenable teachings?

REFERENCES

Ainslie, G. (1975). Specious reward: A behavorial theory of impulsiveness and impulse control. *Psychological Bulletin, 82,* 463–496.

Austin, J. H. (1975, August 9) Eyes left! Eyes right! *Saturday Review,* p. 32.

Ellis, A. (1962). *Reason and emotion in psychotherapy.* New York: Lyle Stuart.

Ellis, A. (1973). What does transpersonal psychology have to offer the art and science of psychotherapy? *Rational Living, 8*(1), 20–28.

Ellis, A. (1974). *Humanistic psychotherapy: The rational–emotive approach.* New York: Julian Press and McGraw-Hill.

Ellis, A. (1975). *How to live with a "neurotic"* (rev. ed.). New York: Crown.

Ellis, A. (1977). Why "scientific" professionals believe mystical nonsense. *Psychiatric Opinion, 14*(2), 27–30.

Ellis, A. & Harper, R. A. (1975). *A new guide to rational living.* Englewood Cliffs, NJ: Prentice-Hall; Hollywood, CA: Wilshire Books.

Frankel, C. (1973). The nature and sources of irrationalism. *Science, 180,* 927–931.

Frazer, J. G. (1959). *The new golden bough.* New York: Criterion.

Friedman, M. (1975) *Rational behavior.* Columbia: University of South Carolina Press.

Hauck, P. A. (1973). *Overcoming depression.* Philadelphia: Westminster Press.

Hoffer, E. (1951). *The true believer.* New York: Harper.

Hook, S. (1975). The promise of humanism. *The Humanist, 35*(5), 41–43.

Jurjevich, R. M. (1974). *The hoax of Freudism.* Philadelphia: Dorrance.

Korzybski, A. (1933). *Science and sanity.* Lancaster, PA: Lancaster Press.

Lazarus, A. A. (1971). *Behavior therapy and beyond.* New York: McGraw-Hill.

Leites, N. (1971). *The new ego.* New York: Science House.

Le Shan, L. (1975, July). The achievement ethic and the human potential movement. *Association for Humanistic Psychology Newsletter,* pp. 13–14.

Levi-Strauss, C. (1970). *Savage mind.* Chicago: University of Chicago Press.

Maslow, A. H. (1974). *Toward a psychology of being* (2nd ed.). New York: Van Nostrand Reinhold.

Maultsby, M. C., Jr. (1975). *Help yourself to happiness.* New York: Institute for Rational Living.

Parker, R. S. (1973). *Emotional common sense.* New York: Harper.

Piaget, J., & Inhelder, B. (1974). *Psychology of the child.* New York: Basic Books.

Pitkin, W. B. (1932). *A short introduction to the history of human stupidity.* New York: Simon and Schuster.

Rachleff, O. (1973). *The occult conceit: A new look at astrology, witchcraft and sorcery.* New York: Bell.

Rogers, C. R. (1974). *On becoming a person.* Boston: Houghton Mifflin.

Shibles, W. (1974). *Emotion: The method of philosophical therapy.* Whitewater, WI: Language Press.

Sperry, R. W. (1975, Aug. 9) Left-brain, right-brain. *Saturday Review,* pp. 30–33.

Strupp, H. H. (1975a). The therapist's personal therapy: The influx of irrationalism. *Clinical Psychologist, 38*(3), 1–11.

Strupp, H. H. (1975b). Training the complete clinician. *Clinical Psychologist, 28*(4), 1–2.

Watzlawick, P., Weakland, J., & Fisch, R. (1974). *Change: Principles of problem formation and problem resolution.* New York: W. W. Norton.

Psychotherapy and the Value of a Human Being

4

INTRODUCTION

Ellis wrote the following article as a result of his friendship with Professor Robert Hartman. Ellis recollects that he was introduced to Hartman's writings by one of the early devotees of RET, probably in 1961. He corresponded with Hartman immediately and received from him a batch of articles and one of his books on the philosophy of value: The Measurement of Value *(Hartman, 1959).*

Ellis had already independently arrived at some of Hartman's views on unconditional self-acceptance, largely through the writings of Paul Tillich (1953) and other existentialists and from his own recent use of RET with his clients. So Ellis was happy that Hartman, partly through his authoritative study of Kant and partly through his work with several American business corporations, had come to similar views. Hartman also had some original ideas of his own on why people's intrinsic value (to themselves) was not dependent on their extrinsic value (to others) and why they could legitimately accept themselves whether or not they performed well and were approved of by others. Ellis used some of Hartman's arguments with his clients and in his writings, had a long talk with Hartman when the latter visited New York, and kept corresponding with Hartman until he died (c. 1975) in Mexico, where he spent the last 15 or so years of his life.

Ellis and Hartman differed on whether intrinsic value or worth actually exists. Hartman was inclined to think it did, whereas Ellis saw it as a useful but a definitional construct. Ellis asked: "Does my aliveness or humanity really give me value?" Ellis doubted it. "Being alive," Ellis said, "I can choose to see myself as valuable—or as worthless. If I choose the former definition, I will most probably get good results. But will I truly be or become valuable? Only because I say so."

Ellis argued about this with Hartman in a friendly manner, but they never resolved the argument. They also never agreed that Hartman's interesting test of human value, now carried on by Leon Pomeroy, was a valid assessment inventory. Hartman cordially invited Ellis to continue their discussion at his home in Mexico, but Ellis never had the time to go there to see him before Hartman died.

Around 1970 William Davis of the University of Tennessee at Knoxville invited Ellis to write a paper in Davis's edited volume, Value and Valuation: Aetiological Studies in Honor of Robert A. Hartman *(Davis, 1972), which the University of Tennessee Press was to publish. Ellis was delighted to do so and wrote an essay that is somewhat longer than the version included in this book. Davis was pleased with the paper, showed it to Hartman, and found that Hartman was enthusiastic about it, saying that this paper alone merited Ellis's receiving a doctorate in philosophy.*

Ellis considers that although this essay still stands in its original form, he wanted to add the following to its many points objecting to our making a global evaluation of ourselves, instead of merely evaluating our deeds and performances in the light of our specific goals and purposes:

1. As Leonard Rorer has pointed out, it is virtually impossible to find any valid criterion for rating one's self or one's being. Most people would probably use a criterion like "character." Thus, they would say, "I am a good person when I have a good character and act honestly, fairly, and nicely to others, and I am no good when I have a bad character." But this assumes that "character" itself is measurable (which is dubious because it includes several traits, such as "honesty" and "tact," that are quite different—and even somewhat contradictory). However, even if we all agree that John has a fine character and claim that therefore he is a "good person," we are first of all dealing with his extrinsic value or value to others. Second, someone could well hold that, whatever his character, "good" people are very bright, or quite personable, or great athletes, and that John is none of these.

2. What is the real goal of rating one's self or being? First, to get the egoistical pleasure of feeling good about oneself. But, as shown above, you will get that pleasure only if and when you consistently do well and win others' great approval. And even while you are succeeding at these "good" tasks, you will be telling yourself, "I must continue to do well at all times—and suppose I don't!" So you will be quite anxious.

Second, the real purpose of rating your self, your being, is almost always to be holier than thou, to be better than other humans, and presumably to get to heaven in a golden chariot. But no human can become superhuman.

3. When you negatively rate any of your traits, your usual purpose is to correct or improve that trait and thereby make your life more effective and enjoyable. But when you rate your self, your being, you are going to have one devil of a time changing your entire personal- *ity, your essence. Even if you change your basic philosophy—which RET tries to help you do—you hardly change it* completely—*and it might be quite dangerous if you did! You then might change your "good" wants (e.g., to remain alive and happy) as well as your "bad" demands (e.g., to be a safe driver while drinking too much).*

4. When you have the concept "I am a good person," you normally also believe, "and I can be a bad person," and therein lies trouble.

5. When you see yourself as a "bad person," you usually think that because you have done something so bad that it is awful *(and that you are consequently awful). But awful acts and awful people are really nonexistent because an* awful *deed means, really, that it is so bad that it must not exist—when, of course, it* does *exist. And an* awful *(or* horrible *or terrible) action is actually definitional and not truly measurable. Is it one that is 80% bad? Ninety percent? Ninety-nine percent? One hundred percent? Which* act or person *is truly* awful? *The terms* awful, horrible, and terrible, *moreover, have such a surplus meaning that they imply that an act or a person is* more *than "bad"—at least 101% bad. But how can this be?*

Thus, although it can be seen that Ellis's views on this issue are still evolving, the following paper is important in that it includes one of the most important aspects of RET, its view of human worth.

REFERENCES

Davis, J. W. (Ed.). (1972). *Value and valuation: Aetiological studies in honor of Robert A. Hartman.* Knoxville, TN: University of Tennessee Press.

Hartman, R. (1959). *The measurement of value.* Crotonville, NY: General Electric.

Tillich, P. (1953). *The courage to be.* New York: Oxford.

Almost all modern authorities in psychotherapy believe that the individual's estimation of his own value or worth is exceptionally important and that if he seriously denigrates himself or has a poor self-image, he will impair his normal functioning and make himself miserable in many significant ways. The proponents of rational–emotive psychotherapy are no different than most and, in fact, go even further in stressing that a disproportionately high percentage of disturbed people become so because they estimate themselves negatively. Consequently, one of the main functions of psychotherapy is to enhance the individual's self-respect (or "ego strength," "self-confidence," "self-esteem," "feelings of personal worth," or "sense of identity") so that he may thereby solve the problem of self-evaluation (see Adler, 1927, 1931; Ellis, 1962, 1966; Ellis & Harper, 1967; Kelly, 1955; Lecky, 1945; Rogers, 1961).

Moreover, when an individual does not value himself very highly, innumerable other problems result. He frequently will focus so intensely on what a rotten person he is that he will distract himself from problem-solving and will become increasingly inefficient. He may falsely conclude that a rotter such as he can do virtually nothing right, and he may stop trying to succeed at the things he wants to accomplish. He may look at his proven advantages with a jaundiced eye and tend to conclude that he is a "phony" and that people just haven't as yet seen through him. Or he may become so intent on "proving" his value that he will be inclined to grovel for others' favors and approval and will conformingly give up his own desires for what he thinks (rightly or wrongly) they want him to do (Ellis, 1967; Hoffer, 1955; Lecky, 1945; Nietzsche, 1961). He may tend to annihilate himself, either literally or figuratively, as he desperately tries to achieve or to please (Becker, 1964; Hess, 1966; Watzlawick, 1967). He may favor noncommitment and avoidance, and become essentially "nonalive," and he may sabotage many or most of his potentialities for creative living (May, 1969). He may become obsessed with comparing himself to others and their achievements and tend to be status-seeking rather than joy-exploring (Farson, 1966; Harris, 1963). He may frequently be anxious, panicked, terrified (Branden, 1964; Coopersmith, 1968; Ellis, 1962; Rosenberg, 1962). He may tend to be a short-range hedonist and to lack self-discipline (Hoffer, 1955). Often he may become defensive and thus act in a "superior," grandiose way (Adler, 1964; Anderson, 1962, 1966; Low, 1967). He may compensatingly assume an unusually rough or "masculine" man-

This is a shorter version of a chapter that first appeared in *Value and Valuation: Aetiological Studies in Honor of Robert A. Hartman* edited by William Davis (Knoxville: University of Tennessee Press, 1972).

ner (Adler, 1931; Maslow, 1966). He may become quite hostile toward others (Anderson, 1966; Low, 1967). He may become exceptionally depressed (Anderson, 1964). He may withdraw from reality and retreat into fantasy (Coopersmith, 1968; Rosenberg, 1962). He may become exceptionally guilty (Ellis, 1967; Geis, 1965). He may present a great false front to the world (Rosenberg, 1962). He may sabotage a number of special talents which he possesses (Coopersmith, 1968). He may easily become conscious of his lack of self-approval, may berate himself for having little or no confidence in himself, and may thereby reduce his self-image even more than he has done previously (Ellis, 1962; Ellis & Harper, 1967). He may become afflicted with numerous psychosomatic reactions, which then encourage him to defame himself still more (Coopersmith, 1968; Rosenberg, 1962).

An obvious question therefore presents itself: If the individual's perception of his own value or worth so importantly affects his thoughts, emotions, and actions, how and why does a person foolishly denigrate himself, and how is it possible to help him consistently to appraise himself so that, no matter what kind of performances he achieves and no matter how popular or unpopular he is in his relations with others, he almost invariably accepts or respects himself? Oddly enough, modern psychotherapy has not often posed this question—at least not in the form just stated. Instead, it has fairly consistently asked another, and actually almost antithetical, question: Since the individual's self-acceptance seems to depend on (1) his succeeding or achieving reasonably well in his society and on (2) his having good relations with others, how can he be helped to accomplish these two goals and thereby to achieve self-esteem?

The answer, I think, lies in the distinction between self-acceptance and self-esteem. At first blush they appear to be very similar; but actually, when they are clearly defined, they are quite different. Self-esteem—as it is fairly consistently used by Branden (1964), Rand (1961, 1964), and other devotees of Ayn Rand's objectivist philosophy—means that the individual values himself because he has behaved intelligently, correctly, or competently. When taken to its logical extremes, it "is the consequence, expression and reward of a mind *fully* committed to reason" (Branden, 1965; italics mine); and "an *unbreached rationality*—that is, an unbreached determination to use one's mind to the fullest extent of one's ability, and a refusal *ever* to evade one's knowledge or act against it—is the *only* valid criterion of virtue and the *only* possible basis of authentic self-esteem" (Branden, 1967; italics mine).

While this is a highly interesting position, there is a great deal of trouble with the inelegance of its philosophic premise. Granted that man's thinking of himself as bad or worthless is usually pernicious and that his thinking of himself as good or worthwhile is more beneficial, I see no reason why these two hypotheses exhaust the possibilities of useful choices. I believe, instead, that there is a third choice that is much more philosophically elegant, less definitional, and more likely to conform to empirical reality. And that is the seldom-posited assumption that value is a meaningless term when applied to man's being, that it is invalid to call him either "good" or "bad," and that if educators and psychotherapists can teach people to give up all "ego" concepts and to have no "self-images" whatever, they may considerably help the human dilemma and enable men and women to be much less emotionally disturbed than they now tend to be.

This is the essence of self-acceptance. Self-acceptance means that the individual fully and unconditionally accepts himself whether or not he behaves intelligently, correctly, or competently and whether or not other people approve, respect, or love him (Bone, 1968; Ellis, 1962, 1966; Rogers, 1961). Whereas, therefore, only well-behaving (not to mention perfectly behaving) individuals can merit and feel self-esteem, virtually all humans are capable of feeling self-acceptance. And since the number of consistently well behaving individuals in this world appears usually to be exceptionally small and the number of exceptionally fallible and often ill-behaving persons appears to be legion, the consistent achievement of self-esteem by most of us would seem to be remote, while the steady feeling of self-acceptance would seem to be quite attainable.

Must man actually be a self-evaluator? Yes and no. On the yes side, he clearly seems to be the kind of animal who is not merely reared but is also born with strong self-evaluating tendencies. For nowhere in the world, to my knowledge, does civilized man simply accept that he is alive, go about the business of discovering how he can enjoy himself more and discomfort himself less, and live his century or so of existence in a reasonably unself-conscious, non-damning, and nondeifying manner. Instead he invariably seems to identify and rate his *self* as well as his *performances*, to be highly ego-involved about accomplishing this and avoiding that deed, and to believe and feel strongly that he will end up in some kind of heaven or hell if he does the "right" and eschews the "wrong" thing.

But is it really worth it? Does man absolutely have to rate himself as a person and evaluate others as people? My tentative answer to both of these questions, after spending a quarter of a century busily engaged as a psychotherapist, writer, teacher, and lecturer, is: "No." By very hardheaded thinking, along with active work and practice, he can persistently fight against and minimize this tendency; if he does, he will, in all probability, be considerably healthier and happier than he usually is. Instead of strongly evaluating his and other people's selves, he can pretty rigorously stick to rating only performances; instead of damning or deifying anyone or anything, he can adhere to reality and be truly demonless and godless; and instead of inventing demands and needs, he can remain with desires and preferences. If he does so, I hypothesize, he will not achieve utopia (which itself is changeless, absolutistic, and unrealistic), but he most probably will achieve more spontaneity, creativity, and satisfaction than he has ever previously achieved or presently tends to attain.

Now I will detail some of the main reasons for my espousing man's taking a nonevaluative attitude toward himself (while still evaluating many of his traits and performances):

1. Both positive and negative self-evaluation are inefficient and often seriously interfere with problem-solving. If one elevates or defames himself because of his performances, he will tend to be self-centered rather than problem-centered, and these performances will, consequently, tend to suffer. Self-evaluation, moreover, is usually ruminative and absorbs enormous amounts of time and energy. By it one may possibly cultivate his "soul" but hardly his garden!

2. Self-rating only works well when one has many talents and few flaws; but, statistically speaking, few are in that class. It also tends to demand universal competence. But, again, few can measure up to such a demand.

3. Self-appraisal almost inevitably leads to one-upmanship and one-downmanship. If one rates himself as being "good," he will usually rate others as being "bad" or "less good." If he rates himself as being "bad," others will be seen as "less bad" or "good." Thereby he practically forces himself to compete with others in "goodness" or "badness" and constantly feels envious, jealous, or superior. Persistent individual, group, and international conflicts easily stem from this kind of thinking and feeling; love, cooperation, and other forms of fellow-feeling are minimized. To see oneself as having a better or worse *trait* than another person may be unimportant or even beneficial (since one may use his knowledge of another's superior trait to help achieve that trait himself). But to see oneself as being a better or worse *person* than another is likely to cause trouble for both.

4. Self-evaluation enhances self-consciousness and therefore tends to shut one up within himself, to narrow his range of interests and enjoyments. "It should be our endeavor," said Bertrand

Russell (1952), "to aim at avoiding self-centered passions and at acquiring those affections and those interests which will prevent our thoughts from dwelling perpetually upon ourselves. It is not the nature of most men to be happy in a prison, and the passions which shut us up in ourselves constitute one of the worst kinds of prisons. Among such passions some of the commonest are fear, envy, the sense of sin, self-pity, and self-admiration."

5. Blaming or praising the whole individual for a few of his acts is an unscientific overgeneralization. "I have called the process of converting a child mentally into something else, whether it be a monster or a mere nonentity, *pathogenic metamorphosis*," Jules Henry (1963) declared. "Mrs. Portman called [her son] Pete 'a human garbage pail'; she said to him, 'you smell, you stink'; she kept the garbage bag and refuse newspapers on his high chair when he was not in it; she called him Mr. Magoo, and never used his right name. Thus he was a stinking monster, a nonentity, a buffoon." But Henry failed to point out that had Mrs. Portman called her son Pete "an angel" and said to him, "You smell heavenly," she would have equally converted him, by the process of pathogenic metamorphosis, into something he was not; namely, a godlike being. Peter is a human person who sometimes smells bad (or heavenly); he is not a *bad-smelling* (or heavenly smelling) *person*.

6. When human selves are lauded or condemned, there is a strong implication that people should be rewarded or punished for being "good" or "bad." But, as noted above, if there were "bad" people, they would already be so handicapped by their "rottenness" that it would be thoroughly unfair to punish them further for being "rotten." And if there were "good" people, they would already be so favored by their "goodness" that it would be superfluous or unjust to reward them for it. Human justice, therefore, is very badly served by self-evaluations.

7. To rate a person high because of his good traits is often tantamount to deifying him; conversely, to rate him low because of his bad traits is tantamount to demonizing him. But since there seems to be no way of validating the existence of gods and devils and since man can well live without this redundant hypothesis, it merely clutters human thinking and acting and probably does much more harm than good. Concepts of god and the devil, moreover, obviously vary enormously from person to person and from group to group; they add nothing to human knowledge; and they usually serve as obstructions to precise intrapersonal and interpersonal communication. Although it is possible that people who behave stupidly and weakly may derive benefits from inventing supernatural beings, there is no evidence that those who act intelligently and strongly have any need of them.

8. Bigotry and lack of respect for individuals in their own right are consequences of self- and other-evaluation. For if you accept A because he is white, Episcopalian, and well-educated and reject B because he is black, Baptist, and a high school dropout, you are clearly not respecting B as a human—and, of course, are intolerantly disrespecting millions of people like him. Bigotry is arbitrary, unjust, and conflict-creating; it is ineffective for social living. As George Axtelle (1956) has noted, "Men are profoundly social creatures. They can realize their own ends more fully only as they respect one another as ends in themselves. Mutual respect is an essential condition of effectiveness both individually and socially. Its opposites, hatred, contempt, segregation, exploitation, frustrate the realization of values for all concerned and hence they are profoundly destructive of all effectiveness." Once you damn an individual, including yourself, for having or lacking any trait whatever, you become authoritarian or fascistic; for fascism is the very essence of people-evaluation (Ellis, 1965a, 1965b).

9. By evaluating an individual, even if only in a complimentary way, one is often trying to change him or trying to control or manipulate him; and the kind of change envisioned may or may not be good for him. "Often," Richard Farson (1966), notes, "the change which praise asks one to make is not necessarily beneficial to the person being praised but will redound to the convenience, pleasure or profit of the praiser." Evaluation may induce the individual to feel obligated to his evaluator; to the degree that he lets himself feel compelled or obligated to change himself, he may be much less of the self that he would really like to be. Positive or negative evaluation of a person, therefore, may well encourage him to be less of a self or of a self-directed individual than he would enjoy being.

10. Evaluation of the individual tends to bolster the Establishment and to block social change. For when one gives himself a report card, he not only becomes accustomed to telling himself, "My deeds are wrong, and I think I'd better work at improving them in the future," but also, "I am wrong, I am a 'no-goodnik' for performing these poor deeds." Since "wrong" acts are largely measured by societal standards, and since most societies are run by a limited number of "upper level" people who have a strong, vested interest in keeping them the way they are, self-evaluation usually encourages the individual to go along with social rules, no matter how arbitrary or foolish they are, and especially to woo the approval of the powers that be. Conformism, which is one of the worst products of self-rating, generally means conformity to the time-honored and justice-dishonoring rules of the "Establishment."

11. Self-appraisal and the measuring of others tends to sabotage

empathic listening. Close and authentic relationships between two people, as Richard Farson (1966) points out, are often achieved through intensive listening: "This does not merely mean to wait for a person to finish talking, but to try to see how the world looks to this person and to communicate this understanding to him. This empathic, non-evaluative listening responds to the person's feelings as well as to his words; that is, to the total meaning of what he is trying to say. It implies no evaluation, no judgment, no agreement (or disagreement). It simply conveys an understanding of what the person is feeling and attempting to communicate; and his feelings and ideas are accepted as being valid for him, if not for the listener." When, however, one evaluates a person (and oneself) as one listens to the other person, one is usually prejudicedly blocked from fully understanding him, seeing him as he is, and uncompetitively understanding and getting close to him.

12. Person-rating tends to denigrate human wants, desires, and preferences and to replace them with demands, compulsions, or needs. If you do not measure your selfness, you tend to spend your days asking yourself, "Now what would I really like to do, in my relatively brief span of existence, to gain maximum satisfaction and minimum pain?" If you do measure your selfhood, you tend to keep asking, "What do I have to do to prove that I am a worthwhile person?" As Richard Robertiello (1964) has observed, "People are constantly negating their right to take something just purely because they want it, to enjoy something simply because they enjoy it. They can hardly ever let themselves take anything for pure pleasure without justifying it on the basis of having earned it or suffered enough to be entitled to it or rationalizing that, though they enjoy it, it is really an altruistic act that they are doing for someone else's good. . . . It seems as if the greatest crime is to do something simply because we enjoy it and without any thought of doing good for anyone else or of serving an absolute need in us that is essential for our continued survival." Such is the folly born of self-deservingness!

13. Placing a value on a human being tends to sabotage his free will. One has little enough self-direction in the normal course of events! Even his most "voluntary" activities are significantly influenced by his heredity and environment; when he thinks that one of his thoughts, feelings, or actions is really "his," he is ignoring some of its most important biosocial causes. As soon as one labels himself as "good" or "bad," as a "genius" or as an "idiot," he so seriously stereotypes himself that he will almost certainly bias and influence much of his subsequent behavior. For how can a "bad person" or an "idiot" determine, even to a small degree, what his

future actions will be, and how can he work hard at achieving his goals? Moreover, how can a "good person" do non-good acts, or a "genius" turn out mediocre works along with his outstanding ones? What asinine, creativity-downing restrictions one almost automatically places on himself when he thinks in terms of these general designations of his selfness!

14. To give a human an accurate global rating is probably impossible for several reasons:

a. The traits by which he is to be rated are very likely to change from year to year, even from moment to moment. Man is not a thing or an object, but a process. How can an ever-changing process be precisely measured and rated?

b. The characteristics by which a person is to be evaluated have no absolute scale by which they can be judged. Traits which are highly honored in one social group are roundly condemned in another. A murderer may be seen as a horrible criminal by a judge but as a marvelous soldier by a general. A man's qualities (such as his ability to compose music) may be deemed fine in one century and mediocre in a later age.

c. To rate a human globally, special weights would have to be given to each kind of positive and negative action that he performed. Thus, if a man did a friend a small favor and also worked very hard to save a hundred people from drowning, his latter act would normally be given a much higher rating than his former act; if he told a lie to his wife and also battered a child, his second deed would be considered much more heinous than his first. But who is to give an exact weight to his various deeds, so that it could finally be determined how globally "good" or "bad" he is? It might be convenient if there existed on earth some kind of St. Peter, who would have a record of every single one of his deeds (and, for that matter, his thoughts) and who could quickly assess him as a potential angel or as hell-bound. But what is the likelihood of such a St. Peter's ever existing (even in the form of an infallible computer)?

d. What kind of mathematics could we employ to arrive at a single, total rating of a human being's worth? Suppose an individual does a thousand good acts, and then he fiendishly tortures someone to death. Shall we, to arrive at a general evaluation of his being, add up all his good acts arithmetically and compare this sum to the weighted sum of his bad act? Shall we, instead, use some geometric means of assessing his "goodness" and "badness"? What system shall we employ to "accurately" measure his "value"? Is there, really, any valid kind of mathematical evaluation by which he can be rated?

e. No matter how many traits of an individual are known and employed for his global rating, since it is quite impossible for him or anyone else to discover all of his characteristics and to use them in arriving at a single universal rating, in the final analysis the whole of him is being evaluated by some of his parts. But is it ever really legitimate to rate a whole individual by some (or even many) of his parts? Even one unknown, and hence unevaluated, part might significantly change and, hence invalidate the final rating. Suppose, for example, the individual is given (by himself or others) a 91% general rating (that is, is considered to have 91% of "goodness"). If he unconsciously hated his brother most of his life and actually brought about the early demise of this brother, but if he consciously only remembers loving his brother and presumably helping him to live happily, he will rate himself (and anyone but an all-knowing St. Peter will rate him) considerably higher than if he consciously admitted his hatred for his brother and causing this brother needless harm. His "real" rating, therefore, will be considerably lower than 91%; but how will this "real" rating ever be known?

f. If an individual is given a very low global rating by himself and others—say, he winds up with a 13% general report card on himself—it presumably means that: (1) he was born a worthless individual; (2) he never possibly could become worthwhile; and (3) he deserves to be punished (and ultimately roasted in some kind of hell) for being hopelessly worthless. All of these are empirically unverifiable hypotheses which can hardly be proved or disproved and which tend (as stated above) to bring about much more harm than good.

g. Measuring a human being is really a form of circular thinking. If a man is "good" because he has "good" traits, his "goodness," in both instances, is based on some kind of value system that is definitional; for who, again, except some kind of deity is to say what "good" traits truly are? Once his traits are defined as being "good," and his global "goodness" is deduced from his specific "goodnesses," the concept of his being globally "good" will almost inevitably prejudice one's view of his specific traits—which will then seem "more good" than they really may be. And once his traits are defined as being "bad," the concept of his being globally "bad" will almost inevitably prejudice one's view of his specific traits—which will then seem "more bad" than they really may be. If the "good" traits of a person who is rated as being globally "good" are prejudicedly seen as being "more good" than they really are, one will keep seeing him, by prejudice, as being "good," when he may not actually be. Globally rating him, in other words, includes making a prophecy about his specific "good" traits; rating his specific traits as "good" includes making a prophecy about his global "goodness." Both of these prophecies, in all probability, will turn out to be "true," whatever the facts of his specific and general "goodness" actually are; for "goodness" itself can never accurately be determined, since the entire edifice of "goodness" is based, as I have said, on concepts which are largely definitional.

h. Perhaps the only sensible way of making a global rating of an individual is on the basis of his aliveness: that is, assuming that he is intrinsically good just because he is human and alive (and that he will be nongood or nonexistent when he is dead). Similarly, we can hypothesize, if we want to accept redundant and unnecessary religious assumptions, that an individual is good because he is human and because Jehovah, Jesus, or some other deity in whom he believes, accepts, loves, or gives grace to all humans. This is a rather silly assumption, since we know (as well as we know anything) that the individual who believes in this assumed deity exists, while we have no way of proving the existence (or nonexistence) of the deity in which he believes. Nonetheless, such an assumption will work, in that it will refer back to the more basic assumption that a human is globally "good" just because he is human and alive. The trouble with this basic concept of general human "goodness" is that it obviously puts *all* humans in the same boat—makes them all equally "good" and leaves no room whatever for any of them to be "bad." Consequently, it is a global rating that is not really a rating, and it is entirely definitional and is rather meaningless.

i. The concept of giving any human a general or global evaluation may be an artifact of the inaccurate way in which almost all humans think and communicate with themselves and each other. Korzybski (1933, 1951) and some of his main followers, such as Hayakawa (1965) and Bourland (1969), have pointed out for a good many years that just as pencil$_1$ is not the same thing as pencil$_2$ so individual$_1$ is hardly the same as individual$_2$. Consequently, generalizing about pencils and about individuals is never entirely accurate. Bourland has especially campaigned, for the last decade, against our using any form of the verb *to be* when we speak about or categorize the behavior of a person. Thus, it is one thing for us to note that "Jones has (or possesses) some outstanding mathematical qualities" and another to say that "Jones is an outstanding mathematician." The former sentence is much more precise and probably "truer" than the latter. The latter sentence, moreover, implies a global rating of Jones that is hardly warranted by the facts, if these can be substantiated, of Jones's possessing some mathematical qualities. If Korzybski and his followers are correct, as they in all probability are (at least to some degree), than global terms and ratings of humans are easily made (indeed, it is most difficult for us not to make them) but would better be fought against and transformed into more specific evaluations of their performances, talents, and traits. Such generalized (or overgeneralized) grades exist (since we obviously keep employing them), but it would be much better if we minimized or eliminated them.

j. All of man's traits are different—as apples and pears are different. Just as one cannot legitimately add and divide apples and pears and thereby get a single, accurate, global rating of an entire basket of fruit, so one cannot truly add and divide different human traits and thereby obtain a single, meaningful, global rating of a hurnan individual.

What conclusions can be drawn from the foregoing observations and deductions about psychotherapy and human value? First, that self-reference and self-evaluation are a normal and natural part of man. It seems to be much easier for him to rate his self, his being, as well as his performances, than it is for him only to assess the latter and not the former.

When man does appraise himself *globally*, he almost invariably gets into trouble. When he terms himself "bad," "inferior," or "inadequate," he tends to feel anxious, guilty, and depressed, and to falsely confirm his low estimation of himself. When he terms himself "good," "superior," or "adequate," he tends to feel forever unsure of maintaining his "goodness," to spend considerable time and energy "proving" how worthwhile he is, but still to sabotage his relations with himself and others.

Ideally, it would seem wise for man to train himself, through rigorous thinking about and working against some of his strongest inborn and environmentally bolstered tendencies, to refuse to evaluate himself at all. He had better continue, as objectively as he can, to assess his traits, talents, and performances, so that he can thereby lead a longer, pain-avoiding, and satisfaction-filled life. But, for many reasons which are considered in detail in this chapter, he would better also accept rather than rate his so-called self and strive for the enjoyment rather than the justification of his existence. According to Freud (1963), the individual attains mental health when he follows the rule. "Where id was, there shall ego be." Freud, however, did not mean by *ego* man's self-evaluating but his self-directing tendencies. According to my own views (Ellis, 1962, 1966, 1968, 1971) and the principles of rationale–emotive therapy, man attains maximum understanding of himself and others and minimum anxiety and hostility when he follows the rule "Where ego was, there shall the person be." By *ego*, of course, I mean man's self-rating and self-justifying tendencies.

For man, as an individual living with other individuals in a world with which he interacts, is too complex to be measured or given a report card. He may be legitimately "valued," in the sense of accepting and abiding by the empirically determinable facts that (1) he exists, (2) he can suffer satisfaction and pain while he exists, (3) it is usually within his power to continue to exist and to experience more satisfaction than pain, and (4) it is therefore highly probable that he "deserves" to (that is, would better) go on existing and enjoying. Or, more succinctly stated, man has value because he decides to remain alive and to value his existence. Observations and conclusions other than those based on these minimal assumptions may well be foolishly egocentric and fictional, and in the final analysis human—all too human, but still essentially inhumane.

REFERENCES

Adler, A. (1927). *Understanding human nature*. New York: Greenberg.

Adler, A. (1931). *What life should mean to you*. New York: Greenberg.

Alder, A. (1964). *Social interest: A challenge to mankind*. New York: Capricorn.

Anderson, C. (1962). *Saints, sinners and psychiatry.* Portland, OR: Commonwealth Fund.

Anderson C. (1964). Depression and suicide reassessed. *Rational Living, 1*(2), 31–36.

Axtelle, G. E. (1956). Effectiveness as a value concept. *Journal of Educational Sociology, 29*, 240–246.

Becker, E., (1964) *The revolution in psychiatry*. New York: Free Press.

Bone, H. (1968). Two proposed alternatives to psychoanalytic interpreting. In E. F. Hammer (Ed.), *Use of interpretation in treatment* (pp. 160–196). New York and London: Grune & Stratton.

Bourland, D. D. (1969, May 23). Language. *Time*, p. 69.

Branden, N. (1964). Pseudo-self-esteem. *Objective Newsletter*, 3(6), 22–23.

Branden, N. (1965). *Who is Ayn Rand?* New York: New American Library.

Branden, N. (1967). Self-esteem. *Objectivist, 6* (March), 1–17; (April), 5–10; May, 8–10; (June), 5–8.

Coopersmith, S. (1968). Studies in self-esteem. *Scientific Monthly, 218*(2), 96–106.

Danielsson, B. (1956). *Love in the South Seas*. New York: Reynal.

Danielsson, B. (1967). Sex life in Polynesia. In A. Ellis & A. Abarbanel (Eds.), *The encyclopedia of sexual behavior* (pp. 832–840). New York: Hawthorn.

Ellis, A. (1962). *Reason and emotion in psychotherapy.* New York: Lyle Stuart.

Ellis, A. (1965a). *Sex without guilt.* New York: Lyle Stuart.

Ellis, A. (1965b). *Suppressed: Seven key essays publishers dared not print.* Chicago: New Classics House.

Ellis, A. (1967). Psychotherapy and moral laxity. *Psychiatric Opinion, 4*(5), 18–21.

Ellis, A. (1968). *Is objectivism a religion?* New York: Lyle Stuart.

Ellis, A. (1971). *Growth through reason.* Palo Alto, CA: Science & Behavior Books.

Ellis, A., & Gullo, J. M. (1970). *Murder and assassination.* New York: Lyle Stuart.

Ellis, A., & Harper, R. A. (1967). *A guide to rational living.* Englewood Cliffs, NJ: Prentice-Hall.

Ellis, A., with Wolfe, J. L. & Moseley, S. (1966). *How to prevent your child from becoming a neurotic adult.* New York: Crown.

Farson, R. A. (1966). A praise reappraised. *Encounter, 1,* 13–21.

Freud, S. (1963). *Collected papers.* New York: Doubleday-Anchor.

Geis, H. J. (1965) *Guilt feelings and inferiority feelings: An experimental comparison.* Unpublished doctoral dissertation, Columbia University, New York.

Harris, S. J. (1963, December 12). A man's worth is not relative. *Detroit Free Press.*

Hartman, R. S. (1959). *The measurement of value.* Crotonville, NY: General Electric.

Hartman, R. S. (1960). Sputnik's moral challenge. *Texas Quarterly, 3*(3), 9–22.

Hartman, R. S. (1962). *The individual in management.* Chicago: Nationwide Insurance.

Hartman, R. S. (1967). *The structure of value.* Carbondale, IL: Southern Illinois University Press.

Hayakawa, S. I. (1965). *Language in action.* New York: Harcourt, Brace.

Henry, J. (1963). *Culture against man.* New York: Random House.

Hess, J. L. (1966, October 14). Michelin's two stars lost, Paris chef shoots himself. *The New York Times.*

Hoffer, E. (1955). *The passionate state of mind.* New York: Harper.

Kelly, G. (1955). *The psychology of personal constructs.* New York: Norton.

Korzybksi, A. (1933). *Science and sanity.* Lancaster, PA: Lancaster Press.

Korzybski, A. (1951). The role of language in the perceptual process. In R. R. Blake & G. V. Ramsey (Eds.), *Perception* (pp. 170–202). New York: Ronald Press.

Lecky, P. (1945). *Self-consistency.* New York: Island Press.

Low, A. (1967). *Lectures to relatives of former patients.* Boston: Christopher.

Marston, A. R. (1965, Winter). Self reinforcement: The relevance of a concept in analogue research to psychotherapy. *Psychotherapy,* p. 2.

Maslow, A. H. (1966). *Psychology and the human dilemma.* Princetown, NJ: Van Nostrand.

May, R. (1969). *Love and will.* New York: Norton.

Nietzsche, F. W. (1961). In H. J. Blackman (Ed.), *Reality, man and exist-ence: Essential works of existentialism*. New York: Bantam.

Rand, A. (1961). *For the new intellectual*. New York: New American Li-brary.

Rand, A. (1964). *The virtue of selfishness*. New York: New American Li-brary.

Robertiello, R. (1964). *Sexual fulfillment and self-affirmation*. Larchmont, NY: Argonaut.

Rogers, C. C. (1961). *On becoming a person*. Boston: Houghton Mifflin.

Rosenberg, M. (1962). The association between self-esteem and anxiety. *Psychiatric Research, 1,* 135–152.

Russell, B. (1952). *The conquest of happiness*. New York: Bantam.

Watzlawick, P. et al. (1967). *Pragmatics of human communication*. New York: Norton.

Discomfort Anxiety: A New Cognitive–Behavioral Construct

5

INTRODUCTION

By 1978 Ellis was showing his clients and the therapists he supervised how important low frustration tolerance (LFT) was in creating and maintaining human disturbance. But till then he had not quite seen that LFT was often a form of anxiety than can be fairly clearly differentiated from ego anxiety.

The 28-year-old client whose case is presented in the following paper had, as a result of RET and previous therapy, overcome a great deal of self-downing but still often referred to his being "very anxious." Ellis concluded that the client had a classic case of "discomfort anxiety." He discovered that as soon as be brought "discomfort anxiety" to the attention of his supervisees and other therapists, they found this construct very useful in their attempts to help clients.

Ironically, Ellis was somewhat hasty in labeling LFT "ego anxiety," even though the two disturbances clearly overlap and are basically the same. Ellis now holds that LFT not only creates some forms of anxiety but also some forms of depression and self-pity, and these feelings, although they have something in common with anxiety (especially common irrational beliefs), are not exactly the same. LFT, therefore, may more appropriately be named discomfort disturbance because it is often involved in depression, self-pity, love slobbism, extreme jealousy, addiction, compulsion, and other disorders, as well as in anxiety.

Nonetheless, the strength of the following paper is that it clearly distinguishes between two exceptionally common elements in emotional disturbance: ego-oriented and discomfort-oriented processes. As Ellis shows, these elements are not entirely different. Discomfort disturbance goes with a thought like "I, special me, must get exactly what I want when I want it!" and therefore includes ego grandiosity.

94

Ego disturbance stems from thoughts like "I cannot stand *failing and being rejected because I'll then get less goodies in life (which* I *must not get. If I cannot acquire these goodies, there must be something radically wrong with* me!*").*

Similarly, ego disturbance often includes the thought "I am such a worthless slob that therefore I need to be taken care of and catered to, or else I will be unable to get what I really want." Discomfort disturbance often includes the idea "Since I must have exactly what I want and frequently cannot get it, I am an incompetent and inadequate individual!"

Ego and discomfort disturbance often overlap or coalesce. Ellis has found that many people, however, have severe ego disturbance and little discomfort disturbance; and many others have much of the latter and little of the former. The most disturbed people, he has usually found, have high degrees of both.

There are two major forms of discomfort disturbance, or LFT: (1) anger at other people (e.g., "I absolutely need *you to care for me and do my bidding, and you are a real turd if you don't!") and (2) anger at world conditions (e.g., "I absolutely* need *conditions to be arranged so that I am cared for and get everything I want, and the world is a horrible place if I am deprived!").*

Because these two forms of LFT are closely related, Ellis says that humans almost invariably disturb themselves in only two major ways: by thinking in absolutist terms that produce ego disturbance and discomfort disturbance. He encourages his supervisees to look for both of these processes in anxious, depressed, self-hating, enraged, and self-pitying people, and he argues that in doing so they will soon be able to zero in on the key source of their clients' emotional–behavioral disturbance.

DISCOMFORT ANXIETY VERSUS EGO ANXIETY

For the past several years, largely on the basis of clinical evidence derived from my practice of rational-emotive therapy (RET), I have been distinguishing between two major forms of anxiety: discomfort anxiety (DA) and ego anxiety (EA). *Discomfort anxiety* I define as emotional tension that results when people feel (1) that their comfort (or life) is threatened, (2) that they *should* or *must* get what they want (and *should not* or *must not* get what they don't want), and (3) that it is *awful* or *catastrophic* (rather than merely inconvenient or disadvantageous) when they don't get what they supposedly *must*. *Ego anxiety* I define as emotional tension that results when people feel (1) that their self or personal worth is threatened. (2) that they *should* or *must* perform well and/or be approved by others, and (3) that it is *awful* or *catastrophic* when they don't perform well and/or are not approved by others as they supposedly *should* or *must* be.

Ego anxiety is a dramatic, powerful feeling that usually seems overwhelming; is often accompanied by feelings of severe depression, shame, guilt, and inadequacy and frequently drives people to therapy (or to suicide!). Discomfort anxiety is often less dramatic but perhaps more common. It tends to be specific to certain "uncomfortable" or "dangerous" situations, and consequently shows up in such phobias as fear of heights, open spaces, elevators, and trains. But it can also easily generalize to uncomfortable *feelings* themselves, such as feelings of anxiety, depression, and shame. Thus, DA may be a primary symptom (e.g., anxiety about elevators) or a secondary symptom (e.g., anxiety about feeling anxious about elevators).

As a secondary symptom, DA may generalize to almost *any* kind of anxiety. Thus, people may first feel anxious about feeling anxious about elevators; but they may later worry about whether they are *also* going to feel anxious about trains or escalators; and they may therefore actually make themselves exceptionally uncomfortable (anxious) about *many* forms of anxiety (discomfort) and may thereby become pandemically anxious. Or they may at first feel anxious about a specific event (e.g., about entering an elevator) and later, realizing that they may well become anxious about that event, they may also make themselves anxious about any symbol of that event (e.g., a picture of an elevator) or about any thought of

This chapter amalgamates two papers first published in *Rational Living:* Discomfort anxiety: A new cognitive–behavioral construct (parts 1 and 2), *14* (1979) and *15* (1980), respectively.

that event (e.g., the thought "Suppose I have to take an elevator when I visit my friend. Wouldn't that possibility be awful?").

Because it is often less dramatic than ego anxiety (or self-downing) and because it may be a secondary rather than a primary symptom, discomfort anxiety may easily be unrecognized and may be somewhat wrongly labeled as general or free-floating anxiety. Thus, if people are anxious about going in elevators, they may clearly recognize their anxiety or phobia and label it "elevator phobia." But if they are anxious about being anxious (that is, fearful of the uncomfortable sensations they will probably feel if they enter an elevator or if they even think about entering an elevator), they may feel very anxious but may not see clearly *what* they are anxious about. Nor may their therapists!

The construct of discomfort anxiety helps to explain several phenomena relating to emotional disturbance in clearer and more therapeutic ways. Thus, if clients tell me they are so terrified of snakes that they feel extremely upset whenever they see even a picture of a snake, I can pretty well guess that they hardly think the *picture* will bite them. I can quickly surmise that they are not only afraid of snakes but also of their anxiety itself—of the uncomfortable *feelings* they will predictably have when they think about (or view a picture of) a snake.

My problem with these clients, therefore, is to get them first to stop awfulizing about their feelings of anxiety; to help them accept their discomfort (or potential discomfort) as a damned bother (and not as a holy honor!). Then, when they truly see that it's not awful to *feel* anxious, they can stop obsessing about this feeling and work on anti-awfulizing about the original feared object, the snakes. Their discomfort anxiety about their feelings helps keep them from confronting these feelings and working through them.

A research study that possibly shows the explanatory and therapeutic value of the construct of discomfort anxiety is that of Sutton-Simon (1979), who found some seemingly contradictory results that may be explained by the use of this construct. She noted that, in a study of subjects with fears of heights, subjects with social anxiety, and subjects with fears of heights plus social anxieties, those with fears of heights did not display significant irrationality on the Jones (1968) Irrational Beliefs Test (IBT); while those with social anxiety did show significant irrationality on the IBT.

This would be expected, according to the construct posited in this chapter, since fear of heights would presumably largely involve discomfort anxiety, while social anxiety would largely involve ego anxiety. Sutton-Simon (1979) observes that ego anxiety may be cross-situational, while discomfort anxiety may be specific to situations, although one person may experience discomfort anxiety in many situations. DA may be "hooked up" to the particular cues of the situation, while EA may be more of a quality of a person.

Although the construct of discomfort anxiety presented here seems to have some new and useful elements, it overlaps with several previous hypotheses about emotional disturbance and its treatment. Thus, Low (1952) pointed out that disturbed individuals often get upset about their symptoms of anxiety and panic, and that they may be helped by defining these symptoms as uncomfortable but not dangerous. Ellis (1962, 1979) emphasized secondary symptoms of disturbance, such as anxiety about anxiety, and stressed the role of low frustration tolerance and short-range hedonism in disturbed behavior and in clients' resistance to changing this behavior. Weekes (1969, 1972, 1977) highlighted the importance of anxiety about anxiety, especially in agoraphobia. Rehm (1977) offered a self-control model of depression that stresses hedonic as well as ego factors in this disturbance. The present formulations go somewhat beyond these other theories in developing a construct of discomfort anxiety and in distinguishing it more clearly from ego anxiety.

DISCOMFORT ANXIETY AND DEPRESSION

The concept of discomfort anxiety also tends to give a better explanation of the origins and treatment of depression than many of the other explanations. Abramson and Sackheim (1977) point out a seeming paradox in depression. On the one hand, depressed individuals—as Beck (1976) emphasizes—blame themselves and look upon themselves as unable to help themselves; they are distinct self-downers. But on the other hand, they insist, in a somewhat grandiose manner, that they must have certainty and must control the outcome of the events in their lives; and they depress themselves when they don't actually have that kind of full control. They are therefore both self-denigrating and self-deifying, which seems to be something of a paradox.

In RET terms, and in terms of ego anxiety and discomfort anxiety, this paradox seems quite resolvable. In RET, it is hypothesized that the individual tends to have three basic irrational beliefs (iB's) about himself or herself and the universe: (1) "I *must* succeed at the important things that I do in life amd win the approval of significant people in my life, and it is *awful* when I don't. I am therefore not as good as I *should* be, and I am therefore worthless."

(2) "You *must* treat me kindly, fairly, and considerately, and it is *horrible* when you don't. You are therefore a crumb or a louse." (3) "The conditions under which I live *must* be easy, or at least not too difficult, and *must* give me all the things I really want quickly and without too much of a hassle; and it is *terrible* when they aren't that way. The world is a really rotten place in which to live and *should* not be the way it indubitably is."

Very often, depressed people have two of these basic ideas—the first and the third—and sometimes they have the second as well. There is no reason, of course, why they should not have two or three; and I also do not see why the first and the third, when they are strongly held, necessarily conflict with each other. The first one, "I *must* succeed at the important things that I do in life and win the approval of significant people in my life; and it is *awful* when I don't!" seems to be essentially self-downing. But its perfectionism is essentially grandiose, since the implication is that "I *must* be outstanding, perfect, and godlike; and if I am not what I must be in these respects, *then* it is *awful* and I am a worthless or rotten person." This same kind of grandiosity is also implied in the third irrationality; namely, "Because I am (or *should* be) a great person for whom everything goes easily and well in life, *therefore* the conditions under which I live must not be too difficult, and therefore it is *terrible* and the world is a horrible place if they are that difficult."

Implicit grandiosity, therefore, underlies virtually all emotional disturbance; namely, the unspoken (or spoken!) demand and command that "*I* must succeed and be universally approved; *you* must treat me kindly and fairly; and the *world conditions* must be easy and immediately gratifying for me." When these demands and commands are not met—as, of course, in reality, they usually are not—then I "logically" make myself anxious, despairing, depressed, or angry. Without these omnipotent insistences, I would only tend to make myself sorry, regretful, annoyed, and irritated.

Discomfort anxiety is particularly important in anxiety and depression, as I think will be shown in the following case illustration. Several years ago I saw a man of 28, who was severely anxious or panicked, as well as angry and depressed, virtually every day of the year, and had been so for 10 years prior to that time. He had been in intensive psychotherapy since the age of 15; and had improved moderately during this time, so that he at least had been able to go through college and work steadily as a bookkeeper. But he had been institutionalized twice, for a period of a year at a time; had not been able to achieve any intimate relations with women; and had led a very restricted and highly routinized existence. He frequently became so depressed that he seriously considered suicide.

On the surface, this man's problem was ego anxiety, since he insisted that he had to do things well and win others' approval, and he put himself down severely whenever he failed to do so. He said that he hated himself, had no self-confidence, and had an enormous fear of failure; and he was afraid to make any major decisions, for fear that he might make a mistake and would then have to castigate himself for this mistake.

Actually, however, this client had benefited somewhat from previous therapy, particularly from reading Ellis and Harper's (1975) book, *A New Guide to Rational Living*, which he used virtually as his bible. In many respects, he felt relatively little shame or guilt as, for example, when he dressed sloppily and was criticized for not socializing, and when he acted quite selfishly, even with friends and relatives whom he most loved and respected. So I began to suspect that his main problem was discomfort anxiety, rather than ego anxiety, although he also had aspects of the latter (as perhaps almost every human does). In a typical fit of anxiety, depression, and anger, he would think and act in the following ways:

1. He would become exceptionally "anxious" or "panicked" when he had to wait in line at a store or wait to be served at a bar. Here, he seemed to be demanding that conditions be easier and that he be served immediately; he had fairly clear-cut low frustration tolerance or discomfort anxiety.

2. Once he became "panicked," he would tell himself, "I *must* not overreact in this manner; what a worm I am!" and would experience ego anxiety. But, often much more strongly, he would insist to himself, "I *must* not be panicked and feel such horrible discomfort at being panicked!" and would experience secondary symptoms of discomfort anxiety.

3. He would then notice that he was continually panicked over hassles and difficulties; and when he saw that this was so (largely as a result of the RET he was undergoing), he would then insist that life was *too* hard and that it *was* awful that he kept being set upon in these horrible ways. He would naively ask me, "Don't *you* feel terrible when people force you to do what you really don't want to do, such as wait on line for a long time at a store?" When I answered that I certainly did not like that kind of thing but that I accepted it and thereby was able to edit out almost entirely some of the inconvenience I was caused, he simply could not understand how I could accept it. He considered it intrinsically horrible to be

balked in any desire, even relatively little ones like wanting to be waited on quickly at a store, and thought that everyone in the universe thought it equally horrible.

4. As he kept upsetting himself in these ways, he realized that he was, at least in the degree of his upsetness, different from other people. So he again put himself down for that and went back, once more, to ego anxiety. Then he also felt horrified about the uncomfortableness of continually feeling panicked and reverted, once more, to discomfort anxiety about this continual discomfort; that is, he would not accept it and viewed it as being a virtually unlivable state. Again, he felt suicidal (though not actively so) because of these continued feelings; and again he wondered about his suicidalness and whether he was a rotten person, much different from and worse than others, for having such feelings. At times, however, he merely accepted such feelings and thought that he was quite justified in thinking about killing himself because of the "horrible" discomforts of living.

5. Because this client defined almost all of his strong wants or desires as absolute needs—which is the philosophical essence of discomfort anxiety—he reemphasized his irrational belief, "I *must* do well!" For he devoutly believed that only by doing well would he get more of the things that he absolutely "needed." When he did not perform beautifully, therefore, he not only downed himself for his inadequacy but also felt that his performance was below his "need" level, and he thereby experienced discomfort anxiety as well as ego anxiety.

All in all, this client's DA continually intermingled with and helped reinforce his EA, and vice versa. Like many severely disturbed people, he probably would have functioned poorly with only EA, for he often seriously downed himself for his errors and for experiencing others' disapproval. But it is unlikely that he would have been as critically disturbed as he was without his suffering from both ego anxiety and discomfort anxiety. From observing him and many other clients like him, I hypothesize that some individuals suffer emotionally because of their ego anxiety and some because of their discomfort anxiety, and that those who have a combination of severe EA and DA are even more disturbed than those who have one or the other and are also less likely to change themselves or to benefit from any form of psychotherapy.

Another often-noted phenomenon that can be explained nicely by the hypothesis of discomfort anxiety is the observation that people who suffer severe depression frequently have lost their parents or other significant persons early in their lives; that this kind of depression is also related to job loss, to serious economic reversal, or to retirement from a satisfactory position; and that, as Levitt and Lubin (1975) show, depression proneness is not related to such traditional demographic variables as age, sex, and race, but instead increases as educational background, annual income, and ability to improve one's financial situation decrease. If these observations are true, we can easily conclude that people who are deprived of parental or economic satisfactions early or later in their lives suffer loss of status and consequent ego anxiety, and that they therefore are more prone to having severe feelings of depression. But we can perhaps more logically conclude that people who are deprived in these affectional and economic ways often (though not, of course, always) have low frustration tolerance or discomfort anxiety, and that a combination of actual frustration plus their discomfort anxiety *about* this frustration often drives them over the brink into the arms of severe depressive reactions. Frustration, Dollard, Doob, Miller, Mowrer, and Sears (1939) once wrongly claimed, leads to aggression. In itself, it doesn't. Nor does it lead to depression. But frustration *of people with abysmal discomfort anxiety* (for which there may exist a biological proneness or vulnerability, as well as a reinforcement or escalation resulting from unusually frustrating events) may lead to almost any kind of disturbed reaction, including aggression and depression.

As Beck (1967, 1976) and Ellis (1962) point out, depression is usually linked with ego anxiety, with people deprecating themselves for their poor performances and believing that, therefore, because *they* are worthless or hopelessly incompetent, they cannot handle life situations and particularly difficult situations that are occurring or may occur. But even in this ego anxiety aspect of depression, discomfort anxiety is probably also a factor, for depressed individuals are not merely telling themselves that they are so incompetent that they cannot master normal life situations and prove how "worthwhile" or "great" they are. They are also probably telling themselves that they are so hopelessly inept that they cannot ward off present and future *inconveniences* and *discomforts*, and that therefore their lives are, and will continue to be, terrible and horrible.

Depression also involves another and perhaps more common element of discomfort anxiety. For depressed people frequently have such abysmally low frustration tolerance that they refuse to accept ordinary or mild hassles, let alone unusual ones, and they can easily whine and wail when they don't have *good enough* events in their lives, or when they once had it easy and comfortable, but now that they have lost their jobs or lost money they don't any longer have it *that* good.

Years ago, before I realized how important a factor discomfort anxiety usually is in the case of severe feelings of depression, I mainly showed my depressed clients that they did *not* have to rate themselves for doing poorly in life (or for doing less well than others were doing) and that they could accept themselves unconditionally, *whether or not* they performed well and *whether or not* significant others approved of them. This helped them immensely in many instances, but in others I found that it was hardly sufficient.

I now *also* look for their discomfort anxiety, and I practically always seem to find it. If I am able to help them, as I often am, to give up their demanding and commanding that conditions be easier and more immediately gratifying, and their insisting that they get what they want quickly and effortlessly, I find not only that they get over their profound depressions, sometimes in fairly short order, but that they also have much less of a tendency to return to a depressed state when something unfortunate occurs in their lives at a later date.

TREATING DISCOMFORT ANXIETY

I do not find it easy to help people raise their level of frustration tolerance and thereby reduce or eliminate their discomfort anxiety. I am fairly convinced that virtually all human beings have a strong biological tendency to defeat themselves by being short-range hedonists and going for immediate rather than long-range gain (Ellis, 1976). That is why so many of them refuse to give up addictions such as smoking, overeating, alcohol abuse, and procrastination, which they "know" are harmful and which they keep resolving to overcome. But when they are induced by various kinds of therapy, including RET, to stay with discomfort, to see that it is *only* inconvenient and *not* unbearable, they often increase their frustration tolerance, overcome their discomfort anxiety, and make significant changes in their dysfunctional feelings and behaviors.

One reason for this lack of change in clients who have significant elements of both ego anxiety and discomfort anxiety is that they often bring up these two elements as if they were *one* problem. Consequently, their therapists mistakenly shuttle back and forth trying to help them with this supposedly *single* problem and end up trying, in a sense, to solve a quadratic equation with two unknowns—which is impossible to do! Thus, in the case of the client mentioned earlier, he could be said to have had two somewhat distinct problems, both of which started from the same premise. The premise would be, "I must get a good result at the things I do, especially a good result at producing my own feelings." This premise would lead to two rather different conclusions: (1) "When I do the wrong things and produce the wrong kind of feelings, I can't stand the *discomfort* I create. Under these conditions, the world is too hard for me to live in happily and I might just as well be dead!" (2) "When I do the wrong things and produce the wrong kind of feelings, I can't stand *myself* for acting so foolishly. Under these conditions, I am hopelessly inept, will always fail to get what I want, and hardly deserve to go on living!"

If clients with discomfort anxiety present material that shows these two irrational ideas, the therapist may get "hooked" into their system by trying to show them how to accept gracefully the discomfort that the world brings them and that they themselves produce. If the therapist fails to zero in on the client's problems *one at a time*, then the two will get confused with each other and the disputing of the client's irrational ideas will be so confounded that a satisfactory solution is unlikely.

It is important, therefore, for the therapist to recognize these two *different* (though perhaps overlapping) points clearly, and to deal first with one and then with the other, so that clients finally see that they have two disparate irrational ideas and that both of them produce dysfunctional emotional and behavioral results. Thus, if the therapist initially focuses on clients' discomfort anxiety, the clients may give up the idea that they *must* not experience "wrong" feelings because the discomfort of experiencing them is *too* difficult and *should not* be that difficult. After doing this, the therapist then probably has a better chance of zeroing in on clients' ego anxiety and helping them give up the idea that they *must not* experience "wrong" feelings because they are *lousy people* for acting ineptly. Either one of the irrational beliefs may be clearly seen and uprooted if the therapist considers them *independently*. But if they are tackled together, or if the therapist and client keep shuttling back and forth from one to the other, then there is a good chance that neither will be seen clearly nor given up.

If I am correct about the existence of discomfort anxiety (DA) and ego anxiety (EA) and their tendency to reinforce each other when they coexist in an individual, then these concepts serve to explain some other aspects of human disturbance and psychotherapy that have long been noted in the literature. For one thing, many indulgent forms of psychotherapy have often produced good, albeit temporary, results. Thus, large numbers of malfunctioning individuals have felt better for awhile and achieved transient symptom removal as a result of hypnosis, suggestion, reassurance, approval, and catharsis. I believe that most of these clients actually start to *feel* better rather than to *get* better in any permanent sense, but they definitely often do improve (Ellis, 1968, 1970, 1974). I would speculate that they do so largely because these indulgent techniques of therapy temporarily allay their discomfort anxiety. Even though it returns fairly soon—because their basic notion that they *must not* suffer frustration and deprivation has not been surrendered and may even be augmented—they at least feel significantly better and relatively symptom-free for a short period of time.

Another interesting phenomenon that can be partially explained by the concept of discomfort anxiety is the case of individuals who are converted to some highly implausible and probably irrational idea, such as the idea that God or Jesus has a personal interest in them and will save them from harm. Such people consequently achieve a distinct personality change, such as becoming recovered alcoholics. I hypothesize that these people, through their devout belief in some kind of magical cure, become highly motivated to work at their discomfort anxiety and to go through present pain to reap the rewards of future gain. Perhaps, for reasons that might be called wrong, they do the right thing: discipline themselves to give up alcohol, drugs, overeating, smoking, or gambling. They then see that they *can* control their own destiny, whereas previously they incorrectly thought that they could not. They may even acquire some sensible ideas along with the irrational ones that initially led them to discipline themselves and ameliorate their low frustration tolerance.

Still another aspect of therapy that can be explained by the concept of discomfort anxiety is the phenomenon of therapists leading many clients to believe in false or scientifically groundless ideas and thereby inadvertently helping these clients to become less disturbed. Thus, orthodox Freudians show people that their parents treated them cruelly when they were children and that this past cruelty makes them neurotic today (Freud, 1965); primal therapists go even further than this and teach their clients that they all suffered from intense primal pain as a result of their parents' iniquity and that if they now scream, yell, and release this pain, they will significantly improve their ability to function (Janov, 1970). Both of these concepts are probably false, for they are largely stimulus–response rather than stimulus–organism– response theories, and they posit early childhood stimuli that were most likely nonexistent.

Interestingly enough, however, when a Freudian analyst or a primal therapist induces clients to mull over their past histories and experience feelings of intense distress in connection with these feelings, they are probably dealing with individuals who, because of their extreme discomfort anxiety, frequently refuse to face their anxious, angry feelings and instead suppress or repress them. Consequently, they do not give themselves a chance to deal with or change these feelings. In forcing such clients to get in touch with and face the discomfort of these feelings—albeit for the wrong reasons and often in a highly exaggerated way—Freudian and primal therapists may unwittingly help them see that feelings of anxiety and anger are *not* unbearable and horrible and may therby help them to overcome some of their discomfort anxiety.

Several behavioral techniques, especially in vivo desensitization and implosion therapy, also seem explicable in terms of the concept of discomfort anxiety. Thus, I have found (Ellis, 1962), as have Marks, Viswanathan, Lipsedge, & Gardner (1972), that flooding or in vivo desensitization works much better with severely disturbed phobic or obsessive–compulsive individuals than more gradual or imaginal methods of therapy. I think this is because these individuals avoid discomfort at all cost and consequently will not confront their phobias or compulsions in order to overcome them. If they can be forced to do this, they eventually discover that doing what they intensely fear, or not doing what they absolutely think they *must* do, helps them to surrender some of their discomfort anxiety, enables them to start working on eliminating their dysfunctional behavior, and eventually helps them not only to *feel* better but actually to *get* better.

One of the persistent puzzles about neurotic individuals is that they can easily upset themselves by not only encountering a "fearful" situation but by imagining it, hearing about it, or seeing it (as in a radio broadcast or television show). Wolpe (1978) cites this as an indication that cognitive therapy often does not work because (1) "most neurotic patients are afraid of situations that they clearly know are not objectively dangerous"; (2) "the stimulus to a neurotic anxiety response may be such that it is inconceivable that it could be regarded as a threat—for example, anxiety at the sight of a test tube full of blood"; and (3) "a patient who is continually anxious may be found to have a specific persistent fear (e.g., fear of going insane); strong reassurance may convince him or her to the contrary, yet the anxiety may not materially diminish."

Wolpe (1978) may well be wrong here, because he uses the word "know" loosely, as if irrationality is totally "known." Thus, a neurotic individual may partly "know" that a situation is not objectively dangerous but also "know" that it is. She or he may be "convinced" that a fear of going insane is false but also be "convinced" that it is true. Rarely, in fact, do we "know" anything with

100% absoluteness; instead, we simultaneously partly believe it and partly do not.

More to the point, all of Wolpe's (1978) examples can be explained by the concept of discomfort anxiety. Thus, neurotic individuals may "know" that riding the rollercoaster at an amusement park is not threatening or dangerous, but they also may know that they are likely to experience anxiety if they ride it and therefore be afraid of their anxiety (and its consequent discomfort) rather than of the cars themselves. They may "know" that the sight of a test tube full of blood will not threaten them with pain of bloodletting, but they also may know that it reminds them of their anxiety about bloodletting and be threatened by this anxiety (discomfort) rather than by bloodletting. They may "know" that they have little chance of going insane, but they may still have both discomfort anxiety ("Wouldn't it be horribly uncomfortable if I *did* go crazy?") and ego anxiety ("I would be a weak, rotten person if I *did* go crazy!"). As noted already, when people have discomfort anxiety they tend to be afraid of any reminder of a "feared object," not because the representation of the object is seen as "frightening" but because their anxious, uncomfortable reaction to the object is viewed as "horrible" or "unbearable."

Mineka & Kihlstrom (1978) have reviewed the literature on experimental neurosis, including the experiments of Gantt (1944), Liddell (1944), Masserman (1943), Pavlov (1927), and Wolpe (1958), and have developed the hypothesis that the common thread running through the entire literature in this area is that in each case important life events become unpredictable, uncontrollable, or both. They also point out that there are striking parallels between experimental neurosis and learned helplessness following exposure to uncontrollable shock, which in turn has been linked to depression (Seligman, 1975). If there is some validity to the hypothesis of Mineka and Kihlstrom (1978) about experimental neurosis and to those of Seligman (1975) about learned helplessness, as I think there probably is, their theories can easily be related to my hypothesis of discomfort anxiety. I would guess that when humans (and several species of other animals) are faced with life events that they consider important to control and to succeed at, and when these events turn out to be consistently unpredictable, uncontrollable, or both, they not only tend to feel uncomfortable but they also conclude that these situations are *too* uncomfortable and there is no *use* trying to make them more comfortable. Therefore, they give up completely or develop what G. V. Hamilton (1925) called a persistent nonadjustive reaction and become "depressed" or otherwise "neurotic."

I am hypothesizing that what I call discomfort anxiety (DA) is a biological tendency of humans and of certain other animals (e.g., rats or guinea pigs); that organisms of this sort innately strive to predict what is going on around them, to control their environments so that they get more of what they want and less of what they don't want, and thereby to survive satisfactorily or "happily." When they perceive that there is a high degree of probability that they will be able to do this, they persist in their adjustive reactions and therefore are "healthy" or "non-neurotic." When they perceive (rightly or wrongly) that they probably cannot control their life situations and get what they want, they either gracefully live with their continued frustrations (developing a philosophy of accepting the inevitable) or they refuse to accept this grim reality (whimpering and whining and developing a philosophy of desperate nonacceptance, a neurotic or nonadjustive outlook that frequently results in depression and withdrawal).

I am also hypothesizing that human phobias are particularly related to discomfort anxiety. When people have, for example, a phobia of airplanes, they usually have some element of ego anxiety; that is, they devoutly believe that *they*, now that they are alive, should live practically forever and *must* not die before their time; and they also frequently believe that it is shameful for them to display their fear of airplanes in front of others (e.g., flight personnel and plane passengers), and consequently they have to stay out of planes to avoid this "shameful" activity.

More important, however, they seem to have enormous discomfort anxiety about the supposed unpredictability of the plane's falling ("Yes, I know there is little chance of it's falling, but suppose it does!"), and they also have discomfort anxiety about their own initial anxiety reactions (which are often exceptionally uncomfortable). They therefore avoid plane flights, often to their own disadvantage.

In desensitizing these individuals to the thing they fear (e.g., plane flights), therapists have their choice of many methods, including systematic desensitization (SD) (Wolpe, 1958), imaginative implosion (Stampfl & Levis, 1967), and in vivo desensitization in the course of rational–emotive therapy (Ellis, 1962, 1971, 1973; Ellis & Whiteley, 1979; Ellis & Grieger, 1977). These seem to be radically different methods of desensitization, but as Teasdale (1977) points out, they have one thing in common: repeated presentation of a fear stimulus with no apparent disastrous consequence.

It seems that people with airplane (or other) phobias keep telling themselves, for one reason or another, "Going in a plane is too frightening, too painful; I can't stand it; I would practically fall apart at the seams if I had to experience this terrible event!" and they keep reindoctrinating themselves with this "fear" and reinforcing their belief in it by *not* going up in a plane. Every time they refuse to do so, they keep telling themselves (overtly or tacitly), "If I did fly, it *would* be horribly uncomfortable and now that I am avoiding flying, I can see how relatively comfortable I feel!" Moreover, by fearfully refusing to confront their phobia and *do* something to overcome it, it becomes almost impossible to get rid of it.

In virtually all kinds of desensitizing procedures, as Teasdale (1977) notes, they *do* something about their phobia: They actively confront it, either imaginatively or in vivo, and they *discover* that (1) the unpredictable event has more predictability than they originally thought it did; (2) nothing disastrous happens to them and they are *only* uncomfortable, and not, as they imagined, utterly *destroyed* by the confrontation; (3) they learn a technique such as SD, implosion therapy, or RET that gives them some possibility of *coping* with their anxiety in the future; (4) they learn that although they cannot control the feared event (the possibility of the plane's falling), they can definitely control some of their own *reactions* to it and therefore face a much "safer" kind of situation should they actually confront the feared object.

Let us make one other observation about the concept of discomfort anxiety (DA) in explaining and dealing with phobias. Emmelkamp, Kuipers, and Eggeraat (1978), in a study showing that in vivo desensitization works better with agoraphobics than do three different kinds of cognitive restructuring without in vivo retraining, point out that clinical agoraphobics probably differ from subjects in analog studies in that they have a higher degree of physiological arousal in anxiety-engendering situations (Lader, 1967) than do the former subjects. They note that "it is quite possible that cognitive restructuring constitutes an effective form of treatment for low physiological reactors (such as the subjects of analog studies), while such treatment will be effective for high physiological reactors (such as agoraphobics) only after the autonomic component has been reduced."

In a comment on the Emmelkamp et al. (1978) paper, I quite agree with their observation (Ellis, 1979). For if it is true that agoraphobics (and many other serious phobics) are high physiological reactors—and my own clinical findings for many years lead me to strongly support this hypothesis—then I would assume that they tend to feel more discomfort, and presumably more discomfort anxiety, than certain other disturbed individuals. Consequently, it seems likely they would tend to develop more phobias and hold on to them more strongly than would "lighter" or less physiologically involved phobics. The discomfort anxiety theory helps explain why agoraphobics are somewhat different from other phobics and why they are so difficult to treat.

In many important respects, then, the concept of discomfort anxiety seems to shed light on human disturbance and on psychotherapeutic processes. It especially leads the way toward creating and utilizing more effective, more elegant, and more long-lasting forms of psychological treatment. I suggest, for example, that many or most of the therapeutic methods used today are in themselves forms of indulgence, and that in the long run they reinforce people's discomfort anxiety and possibly do more harm than good. Take, for instance, muscular relaxation methods, which are so popular among behavior therapists. While there is no question that such techniques frequently work and result in considerable symptom removal, like all methods of therapy, they also have ideological implications, some of which seem to be iatrogenic:

1. Usually, as in Wolpe's (1958, 1973) systematic desensitization, relaxation is used in a gradual way to interrupt clients' feelings of anxiety. The very gradualness of this procedure, I suggest, may easily reaffirm these clients' beliefs that they *must* slowly, easily, and by comfortable degrees, tackle their anxieties, and that as soon as they experience any intense feelings of fear they *have* to relax their muscles and thereby distract themselves from these feelings. Such beliefs, of course, may well serve to increase, rather than to decrease, their discomfort anxiety.

2. Relaxation methods essentially consist of cognitive distraction rather than cognitive restructuring. If, for example, clients are afraid of elevators and they imagine themselves getting closer and closer to elevators and then, as they feel anxious about this imagined closeness, they focus on relaxing their muscles, they automatically distract themselves from the idea "I *must not* enter elevators; it would be *awful* if something happened to me when I rode in them!" They may well decrease their anxiety by this distraction procedure, but they usually have not *worked at* really *giving up* their irrational beliefs about riding in elevators. Relaxation and other forms of cognitive distraction are almost always much easier than actively combating and rethinking one's basic irrationalities. They consequently reinforce people's notions of the horror of work, for instance, and thus may increase their discomfort anxiety.

3. Cognitive distraction, though a viable method of psychotherapy, probably is not as effective in most instances as in vivo desen-

sitization. By employing it with clients, the therapist avoids getting them to face the actual elevators or other irrationally feared objects, and thereby gives them an inelegant method of solving their problems. Again, it tends to sustain or augment their discomfort anxiety.

It is tempting for me to overemphasize the significance of discomfort anxiety and to relate all forms of emotional disturbance to this concept. Thus, humans tend to believe that they *must* perform well and have approval, that others *must* treat them properly, and that the conditions under which they live *must* be easy and enjoyable. When these three *must*urbatory views are not affirmed by reality—which is often the case in this frustrating world—they usually conclude that they *can't stand* their own, others', or the world's imperfections and that it is *awful and terrible* that such unpleasantness is allowed to occur. In some respects, they seem to have low frustration tolerance (LFT) or discomfort anxiety as an aspect of virtually all their emotional disturbances—their self-downing, their hostility, and their self-pity. In a sense, then, we could say that virtually all "emotional" disturbances arise from LFT.

My clinical perception and judgment, however, tells me that this formulation omits some essential data about people and their disturbances. Although ego anxiety and discomfort anxiety are found in almost all individuals, and, as noted already, significantly interrelate and reinforce each other, I think it is best to view them as separate but interlocking behaviors. In that way, they have maximum explanatory and therapeutic usefulness.

REFERENCES

Abramson, L. Y., & Sackheim, H. A. (1977). A paradox in depression: Uncontrollability and self-blame. *Psychological Bulletin, 84*, 838–851.

Beck, A. T. (1967). *Depression*. New York: Hoeber-Harper.

Beck, A. T. (1976). *Cognitive therapy and the emotional disorders*. New York: International Universities Press.

Dollard, J., Doob, L., Miller, N. E., Mowrer, O.H., & Sears, R. R. (1939). *Frustration and aggression*. New Haven, CT: Yale University Press.

Ellis, A. (1962). *Reason and emotion in psychotherapy*. New York: Lyle Stuart.

Ellis, A. (1968). What really causes therapeutic change? *Voices, 4*(2), 90–97.

Ellis, A. (1970). The cognitive element in experiential and relationship psychotherapy. *Existential Psychiatry, 28*, 35–42.

Ellis, A. (1971). *Growth through reason.* Palo Alto, CA: Science and Behavior Books; Hollywood, CA: Wilshire Books.

Ellis, A. (1973). *Humanistic psychotherapy: The rational–emotive approach.* New York: Julian Press and McGraw-Hill Paperbacks.

Ellis, A. (1974). Cognitive aspects of abreactive therapy. *Voices, 10*(1), 48–56.

Ellis, A. (1976). The biological basis of human irrationality. *Journal of Individual Psychology, 32,* 145–168.

Ellis, A. (1979). A note on the treatment of agoraphobics with cognitive modification versus prolonged exposure *in vivo. Behavior Research and Therapy, 17*(2), 162–163.

Ellis, A., & Grieger, R. (1977). *Handbook of rational–emotive therapy.* New York: Springer Publishing Co.

Ellis, A., & Harper, R. A. (1975). *A new guide to rational living.* Englewood Cliffs, NJ: Prentice-Hall; Hollywood, CA: Wilshire Books.

Ellis, A., & Whiteley, J. M. (Eds.). (1979). *Theoretical and empirical foundations of rational–emotive therapy.* Monterey, CA: Brooks/Cole.

Emmelkamp, P. M. G., Kuipers, A. C., & Eggeraat, J. B. (1978). Cognitive modification versus prolonged exposure *in vivo:* A comparison with agoraphobics as subjects. *Behaviour Therapy and Research, 16,* 33–41.

Freud, S. *Standard edition of the complete psychological works of Sigmund Freud.* London: Hogarth, 1965.

Gantt, W. H. (1944). Experimental basis for neurotic behavior. *Psychosomatic Medicine Monographs,* Nos. 3 & 4.

Hamilton, G. V. (1925). *An introduction to objective psychopathology.* St. Louis: C. V. Mosby.

Janov, A. (1970). *The primal scream.* New York: Delta.

Jones, R. G. (1968). *A factored measure of Ellis' irrational belief system, with personality and maladjustment correlates.* Unpublished doctoral dissertation, Texas Technological University, Lubbock, TX.

Lader, M. H. (1967). Palmer skin conductance measures in anxiety and phobic states. *Journal of Psychosomatic Research, 11,* 271–281.

Levitt, E. E., & Lubin, B. (1975). *Depression,* New York: Springer Publishing Co.

Lidell, H. S. (1944). Conditioned reflex method and experimental neurosis. In J. McV. Hunt (Ed.), *Personality and the behavior disorders.* New York: Ronald.

Low, A. A. (1952). *Mental health through will training.* Boston: Christopher.

Marks, I. M., Viswanathan, R., Lipsedge, M. S., & Gardner, R. (1972). Enhanced relief by flooding during waning diazepam effect. *British Journal of Psychiatry, 121,* 493–505.

Masserman, J. H. (1943). *Behavior and neurosis.* Chicago: University of Chicago Press.

Mineka, S., & Kihlstrom, J. F. (1978). Unpredictable and uncontrollable events: A new perspective on experimental neurosis. *Journal of Abnormal Psychology, 87,* 256–271.

Pavlov, I. P. (1927). *Conditioned reflexes.* London: Oxford University Press.

Rehm, L. P. (1977). A self-control model of depression. *Behavior Therapy, 8,* 787–804.

Seligman, M. E. P. (1975). *Helplessness.* San Francisco: W. H. Freeman.

Stampfl, P. G., & Levis, D. J. (1967). Essentials of implosive therapy. *Journal of Abnormal Psychology, 72,* 496–503.

Sutton-Simon, K. (1979). A study of irrational ideas of individuals with fears of heights, with social anxiety, and with fear of heights plus social anxieties. *Cognitive Therapy and Research, 3*(2), 193–204.

Teasdale, J. D. (1977). Psychological treatment of phobias. In N. S. Sutherland (Ed.), *Tutorial essays in psychology* (Vol. 1). Hillsdale, NJ: Erlbaum.

Weekes, C. (1969). *Hope and help for your nerves.* New York: Hawthorn.

Weekes, C. (1972). *Peace from nervous suffering.* New York: Hawthorne.

Weekes, C. (1977). *Simple effective treatment of agoraphobia.* New York: Hawthorne.

Wolpe, J. (1958). *Psychotherapy by reciprocal inhibition.* Stanford, CA: Stanford Univeristy Press.

Wolpe, J. (1973). *The practice of behavior therapy.* New York: Pergamon.

Wolpe, J. (1978). Cognition and causation in human behavior and its therapy. *American Psychologist, 33,* 437–446.

Is Rational–Emotive Therapy (RET) "Rationalist" or "Constructivist"?

6

INTRODUCTION

Ellis considers that it may have been the greatest mistake he ever made in regard to RET to use the word rational *to partly describe it. As he might have recognized (but did not) at the time he coined its original title,* rational therapy (RT), *in 1955, innumerable people seemed to be allergic to the word* rational *and bristled whenever they heard it used. So he might have much better used the term* cognitive, cognitive–behavioral, *or* cognitive–emotive–behavioral *therapy instead.*

For people often wrongly believe that rational *means unemotional, but it practically never does when applied to personality change. As the dictionary notes,* rational *means "of, based on, or derived from reasoning; sensible; practical; judging soundly." But the dictionary does not make clear that rational or reasonable judgment implies people's deciding which of their* desires *and* preferences *to follow and is really based on our* emotions *and* feelings.

If, for example, I want to be rational about my decision to buy a car, I weigh my desires for *or* feelings about *cost, speed, convenience, appearance, and the like; I determine which of these aspects are more important to me personally; and then I presumably select a car that has more of what I* desire *and less of what I* don't *desire about it. The rationality of my decision involves judgment, to be sure; but my judgments are mainly about my feelings. In a very important sense, then, my decision is both rational (logical, sensible, practical) and emotional—not one or the other.*

Rational usually means choosing sensibly and reasonably among feelings. And that is what it especially means in RET. Similarly with the word stoical. *It does not mean unfeeling or unemotional, except in extreme cases. Thus, I stoically accept the* pain *of giving up alcohol, sugar, and cigarettes in order to enjoy the* pleasures *of sobriety, low blood sugar, and freedom from cancer. I stoically go to the* trouble *of exercising to achieve the* satisfaction *of good health. I do not stoically take on pain for the sake of pain, for that would be foolish masochism.*

When Ellis first used the term rational therapy *(RT) to describe rational–emotive therapy (RET), he did so because he thought it was sensible to maximize human pleasure and minimize pain—especially to abet mental and emotional enjoyment and to reduce emotive–behavioral self-defeatism. RET, therefore, has always been a hedonism-oriented theory and practice, particularly favoring long-range rather than short-range hedonism. But from the start many critics of RET have insisted (wrongly!) that RET is interested only in logical, objective, precise, linear thinking and hardly at all in emotion, enjoyment, and pleasure.*

To head off some of the early critics of RET, Ellis, together with Bob Harper (c. 1960), started to think of a more suitable name than RT, and they finally decided to use the name rational–emotive therapy (RET) to show people that it was not truly rationalist nor stoical, that it always used highly emotive as well as cognitive processes, and that it was not merely scientific (in the sense of being logical and empirical) but also stressed the philosophy *of science, which includes openness, flexibility, and lack of dogma (Ellis, 1962). Increasingly, over ensuing years, RET has emphasized that the somewhat narrow logico-empiricism of most other cognitive therapists, such as Aaron Beck, Marvin Goldfried, Maxie Maultsby, Donald Meichenbaum, and Victor Rainy, constitutes "good" but not elegant therapy and that the latter form of treatment—elegant, or preferential, RET—includes helping clients to make a* profound philosophic change *(Ellis & Dryden, 1987.)*

In spite of Ellis's frequent statements of this preferential or elegant rational–emotive approach to therapy, a number of writers, often of religious or mystical schools of thought, have continued to attack RET as being too rational, too logico-empirical, too consciousness-oriented, too left brained, too linear rather than circular in its concepts, and too neglectful of feelings (Evans, 1984–1985; Finley, 1987; Grieger, 1985; Parker, 1987; Sharkey & Maloney, 1986, Wilber, 1989). Ellis has replied to some of these accusations of RET's "rationalism" (Ellis, 1984–1985, 1987a, 1987b, 1988b, 1988c) but has sometimes not taken them too seriously because they have mostly come from theorists opposed to cognitive–behavioral therapy, which he naturally expects to oppose RET. Recently, however, important cognitive-

behaviorists have strongly held that there are two main camps of cognitive therapy, the "rationalist" and the "constructivist" camps and that RET is clearly in the former camp (Guidano, 1988; Mahoney, 1988). Ellis was really surprised when he first read about this supposed rationalist–constructivist dichotomy because he is skeptical that it really exists and wonders whether any modern cognitive therapies are really in the "rationalist" category, as Guidano and Mahoney claim (Ellis, 1988a, 1988d).

To make matters even more surprising, some of the main "constructivist" positions that Guidano, Mahoney, and Reda outline, have been posited by and used therapeutically in RET for about a quarter of a century and are included in Reason and Emotion in Psychotherapy (Ellis, 1962), and other "constructivist" RET positions were made explicit in RET in the late 1960s and in the 1970s (e.g., Ellis, 1968, 1973).

Ellis wrote the following paper because the recent cognitive–behavioral critics of RET wrongly understand the original "rationalist" terms of the 1950s, because they almost completely ignore its later aspects, because they claim originality for views that RET has long presented, and because they misrepresent theories and practices that RET truly holds. Ellis here shows how they have set up an RET straw person and then gleefully ripped it to smithereens. He considered that it was important to present the paper at the World Congress on Cognitive Therapy in Oxford, England, in June 1989 to show what modern RET is really like and how it fits far more closely into the "constructivist" rather than the "rationalist" camp of cognitive–behavioral therapies. In Ellis's view, the picture of RET that Guidano (1988), Mahoney (1988), and some other "constructivists" present is a travesty. He hopes that the following paper will help it to be more accurately perceived.

REFERENCES

Ellis, A. (1962). *Reason and emotion in psychotherapy*. Secaucus, NJ: Lyle Stuart.

Ellis, A. (1968). *Is objectivism a religion?* New York: Lyle Stuart.

Ellis, A. (1973). *Humanistic psychotherapy: The rational–emotive approach*. New York: McGraw-Hill.

Ellis, A. (1984–1985). Yes, how reasonable is rational–emotive therapy? *Review of Existential Psychology and Psychiatry, 9*, 135–139.

Ellis, A. (1987a). Religiosity and emotional disturbance: A reply to Sharkey and Maloney. *Psychotherapy, 24*, 826–827.

Ellis, A. (1987b). Reply to Parker on fanaticism and absolutism. *Journal of Counseling and Development, 66*, 156–157.

Ellis, A. (1988a). Are there "rationalist" and "constructivist" camps of the cognitive therapies? *Cognitive Behaviorist, 10*, 13–17.

Ellis, A. (1988b). Comments on Finley's "Critique of rational–emotive philosophy." *Psychotherapy, 25*, 147–148.

Ellis, A. (1988c). Comments on R. M. Grieger's "Contextual model of the ABCs of RET." *Journal of Rational–Emotive and Cognitive–Behavioral Therapy, 6*, 189–195.

Ellis, A. (1988d). Further comments on dichotomies and classifications in the cognitive therapies. *Cognitive Behaviorist, 10*, 22–23.

Ellis, A., & Dryden, W. (1987). *The practice of rational–emotive therapy*. New York: Springer Publishing Co.

Evans, J. (1984–1985). Albert Ellis' conception of rationality: How reasonable is RET? *Review of Existential Psychology & Psychiatry, 19*(2–3), 129–134.

Finley, R. D. (1987). Critique of rational–emotive philosophy. *Psychotherapy, 24*, 271–276.

Grieger, R. (1985). From a linear to a contextual model of the ABCs of RET. *Journal of Rational–Emotive Therapy, 3*(2), 75–99.

Guidano, V. F. (1988). A systems, process-oriented approach to cognitive therapy. In K. S. Dobson (Ed.), *Handbook of cognitive–behavioral therapies*, (pp. 307–356). New York: Guilford.

Mahoney, M. J. (1988). The cognitive sciences and psychotherapy: Patterns in a developing relationship. In K. S. Dobson (Ed.), *Handbook of the cognitive–behavioral therapies* (pp. 357–386) New York: Guilford.

Parker, D. (1987). Ellis on fanaticism and absolutism. *Journal of Counseling and Development, 66*, 573.

Sharkey, P. W., & Maloney, H. N. (1986). Religiosity and emotional disturbance: A test of Ellis's thesis in his own counseling center. *Psychotherapy, 23*, 640–641.

Wilber, K. (1989). Let's nuke the transpersonalists: A response to Albert Ellis. *Journal of Counseling and Development, 67*, 332–335.

Recent discussants of cognitive–behavioral therapies have emphasized new developments in the field, especially the emergence of "constructivist" or "systems-process-oriented" theories and practices and have contrasted these with what they term the "rationalist" approach to psychotherapy (Dobson, 1988; Guidano, 1988; Mahoney, 1988). Among the "rationalist" approaches, along with the cognitive therapies of Beck (1976; Beck, Rush, Shaw, & Emery, 1979), D'Zurilla and Goldfried (1971), and Meichenbaum (1977), they have especially singled out rational–emotive therapy (RET) as being highly stoical and "rationalist."

I have elsewhere (Ellis, 1988a, 1988b) briefly argued against this kind of dichotomizing and held that none of the cognitive–

behavioral therapies that Mahoney (1988) notably labels as "rationalist" is actually in that camp. In the present paper I shall more comprehensively show that RET is not only nonrationalist but that it is in several important respects more constructivist and more process-oriented than just about all of the other cognitive therapies, including those of Guidano (1988) and Mahoney (1988). Although RET originally favored logical positivism and fairly strict empiricism (Ellis, 1958, 1962) and therefore partly followed what Mahoney calls the "rationalist" approach, I was, ironically enough, led by Mahoney's book *The Scientist* (1976) to abandon logical positivism and to follow the more modern "constructivist" views of Bartley (1962) and Popper (1959) and thereby to change some of its philosophical underpinnings. Even before that, I radically changed my views on the place of emotion in psychotherapy (Ellis, 1969, 1973) and on the importance of heredity rather than early conditioning in the "causation" of emotional and behavioral disorders (Ellis, 1962, 1963). Present-day RET, therefore, has changed significantly from some of its early formulations; and if it ever was "rationalist," it hardly is so today!

CONSTRUCTIVIST ASPECTS OF RET

Let me review some of the main theories and practices that Guidano (1988) calls "process-oriented" and that Mahoney (1988) calls "constructivist" to see exactly how RET agrees and disagrees with them today.

Deep Cognitive Structures

Guidano's (1988) systems- and process-oriented approach to therapy "emphasizes the active-generative, and intentional dimensions of personal knowing processes. In this approach assessment procedures are aimed at identifying invariant deep structures that provide the entire individual knowledge organization with coherence and stability. The strategy of therapy is therefore based upon the elaboration of alternative models of the self and the world such that the deep structures can adopt a more flexible and adaptive articulation" (p. 307).

I don't like the terms "invariant" and "entire individual knowledge" in this statement, but otherwise I agree with it. RET assumes that people learn from their parents and culture many "deep" standards, preferences, values, and rules of living (because they are innately gullible and teachable especially when young) and that they also have a strong biological tendency to overgeneralize (Korzybski, 1933) and to transmute their rules into dogmatic, absolutist shoulds, oughts, and musts (Ellis, 1962, 1973, 1977, 1988c; Ellis & Becker, 1982; Ellis & Dryden, 1987; Ellis & Harper, 1975). They apply *both* their preferences and rules *and* their musturbatory dogmas to themselves and the world and thereby create coherence and stability in their lives. RET does its best to help them retain and achieve their personal values and preferences but to be much more flexible and adaptive about their dogmatic musts. Like Guidano's therapy, it explores the relationship between their desires and rigid commands so that they can develop the former and change the latter; but it doesn't rely on their "naturally" doing so, and encourages and teaches them how to do so when their healthy reconstructive tendencies (which, as humans, they usually have) are not being adequately used.

Motor Theories of the Mind

Guidano and Mahoney follow Weimer's (1977) motor theory of the mind instead of conventional sensory theories that depict the mind as a mere collector of sensations. From this perspective, information processing (input) and behavior (output) are no longer considered functionally different. "The classical empiricist argument, according to which abstractions are just the result of the association of sensations, is deeply challenged" (Guidano, 1988. p. 310).

RET goes along with this hypothesis, and I have said for many years that even if a human male were raised by wolves on a desert island, he would probably have the innate ability to abstract, to generalize—and to invent dogmatic shoulds and musts and thereby make himself depressed about his not being able to run as fast as the other wolves (Ellis, 1963, 1987a). Humans are *born* (not merely raised) as abstractors and would not be able to abstract *without* sensations but most probably do not do so *because* of their sensations.

Tacit and Explicit Levels of Knowing

Following Polanyi (1966), Hayek (1978), Weimer (1975), and other theorists, Guidano and Mahoney see tacit or unconscious cognitive structures as "deep" and "superconscious," while explicit or surface cognitive structures are much more conscious or superficial. "The tacit level is the higher, organizing one since it includes the whole set of basic ordering processes constituting the system, while the explicit structure is composed of processes that mediate one's actual relationship with the environment" (Guidano, 1988, p. 311).

I am not sure whether the tacit level is a "higher" one, but RET holds that people's dogmatic and absolutist musts, which for the most part are implicit, tacit, and unconscious, are usually deeper and more powerful instigators of their disturbed emotions and behaviors than are their largely conscious, explicit preferences and values. RET holds, moreover, that humans (unlike other animals) quite unconsciously *create* or *invent* their rigid musts and that they do *not* (as most therapists of other schools believe) get them from their parents and other early teachers (Ellis, 1963, 1976a, 1987a, 1988c, 1989a; Ellis & Dryden, 1987). So RET is unusually constructivist about self-defeating unconscious cognitions.

Attachment Process and Self-Identity

Relying heavily on the theories of Bowlby (1969, 1973, 1980), Guidano (1988) holds that "a unique relationship with an attachment figure, yielding a sort of template, provides the child with a framework within which otherwise fragmentary information about self and the world can be organized within a structured whole" (p. 312).

RET holds that this statement contains truth but is probably exaggerated. Children innately become attached, especially to mother and father figures; and their early attachments, if reciprocated, seem to help them gain a sense of self-identity and to organize their lives. But I don't think we have evidence that they would have *no* identity and *no* organized sense of the world if they had only light affectionate attachments or group attachments during their early childhood.

What seems quite important, from an RET constructivist view, is that most children *create* strong attachments to other humans (especially to their parents but also to others) and that they very often take their strong *preferences* for affection and love and *transmute* them into dire *necessities*. For survival, they really *have to* be fed, clothed, and otherwise cared for. But they usually *think* that they absolutely *must* be attended to and loved, when they could most probably not only survive but actually be happy if they were not adored. RET contends that they have a powerful inborn tendency, probably in the majority of cases, to *demand* and *command* that they be attended to and loved. Because they *like* this kind of affection, they *assume* that they need it; and they thereby *construct* many of their own early problems—and then continue this kind of construing for the rest of their lives.

The RET view of human attachment is somewhat similar to that of Bowlby, Guidano, and Mahoney, but it is more constructivist in that it hypothesizes that children are born with a strong tendency to become attached to their early caretakers and to therefore feel very pained and saddened when they are not attended to and loved. But it also sees them as highly prone to *create* a love *need* out of their love *desire* and thereby to *produce* feelings of depression when they are emotionally deprived. Children (and adults), RET says, largely *make themselves* lose their identity (feeling nonexistent and worthless) when their preferences ("needs") for love are not met. It is not a *loss* of affection alone that seriously bothers them but partly their *view* of that loss (Ellis, 1985a, 1985b, 1987b). The RET theory of childhood depression, therefore, is exceptionally constructivist.

Personal Identity and Self-Evaluation

Guidano (1988) states that personal identity "is fundamentally an inferred knowledge of oneself, biased by one's own tacit self-knowledge" and that it "provides a set of basic expectations that direct the individual's patterns of self-perception and self-evaluation in accordance with the selected self-image. The degree of congruence existing between beliefs about one's own value on the one hand, and estimates of one's own behaviors and emotions on the other, corresponds to the degree of self-acceptability and self-esteem" (p. 317).

RET accepts this formulation but is more specific in its theory of self-evaluation. It assumes that humans are born with tendencies to rate or evaluate, first, their performances and traits and, second, their personal identities or "selves," even though doing this second kind of rating is an overgeneralization and is inaccurate. Thus, I can legitimately say, "I often play tennis well," but I cannot correctly conclude, "I am marvelous at tennis" or "I am great at sports." And I cannot accurately conclude, "Because I often play tennis well, I am a fine, noble person." But people tacitly (as well as, sometimes, by explicit learning), inaccurately evaluate both their abilities and their selves. RET holds that they have strong innate (as well as acquired) tendencies to do this.

Because self-evaluation leads to both self-esteem and self-deprecation, RET tries to help people make their tacit or unconscious self-ratings conscious and to continue, for practical purposes, to measure their deeds and performances but to be very cautious about evaluating themselves. Ideally, it shows them how to rate *only* what they think, feel, and do and *not* to rate their self or being at all (Ellis, 1957, 1962, 1972b, 1973, 1976b, 1988c; Ellis

& Becker, 1982; Ellis & Harper, 1975). It clearly distinguishes between their achieving self-esteem, which has the Achilles heel of
implying self-disesteem, and unconditional self-acceptance, which
means accepting oneself *whether or not* one performs well. And it
particularly emphasizes that self-evaluations are *constructions* that
are tacitly invented (as well as *accepted* from others' evaluations)
and that they therefore can be consciously changed.

Models of Reality

Guidano (1988) states that "if the mind is considered as an active system imposing its order on the environment, it becomes
clear that some life events can assume a critical personal meaning
only through the particular individual knowledge organization and
are criticized for that organization alone. In other words, it is not
the 'real' social world but how it is construed that plays the crucial role, and the ongoing tacit ordering of life events into personal
meanings is primary" (pp. 320–321).

RET has posited a similar view of "reality" for many years. I
have often pointed out that in the ABCs of RET, Activating Events
in the "real" world (A's) *contribute* to disturbed emotional and
behavioral Consequences (C's), but one's Belief Systems (B's) *largely*
"create" or "cause" C (Ellis, 1965, 1973, 1977, 1985b, 1988c; Ellis
& Dryden, 1987; Ellis & Harper, 1975). I have also shown that C
influences and affects A and B; that the relationships among A, B,
and C are not linear but circular; and that just as cognitions
influence feelings and behaviors, so do the latter influence
thoughts and affect each other (Ellis, 1962, 1984, 1985a, 1985b,
1988c; Ellis & Dryden, 1987). So RET, though not aligned with
what is usually called systems family therapy, is in its own right a
pioneering form of systems therapy (Ellis, Sichel, Yeager, DiMattia,
& DiGiuseppe, 1989).

Deep-Change Processes

Guidano (1988) holds that "deep change processes . . . correspond to changes in patterns of attitude toward oneself as a result of
the reconstruction of sets of deeper rules emerging from tacit self-
knowledge. The changed attitude toward oneself will consequently
produce a modification of personal identity, which will in turn
entail a restructuring of the attitude to reality through which the
world can be seen and dealt with in a different manner" (p. 322).

RET has again foreshadowed this view by seeing most psychotherapy as leading to a beneficial but superficial change—in the

course of which clients *feel* better but do not really *get* better (Ellis, 1972a)—and therefore advocating that therapy help clients achieve what I call "a profound philosophic change," one that truly enables them to *get* better (Ellis, 1962, 1972a, 1985b). RET encourages clients to make this profound or deep change by revealing their tacit dogmatic musts (as well as their more superficial, and probably derivative, unrealistic inferences); and it particularly helps them to change their perfectionistic, grandiose demands on themselves that lead to self-deprecation and loss of personal identity. It also shows them how to give up their grandiosity and egocentricity about other people and about the world and thereby more completely modify their personal identity *and* their distorted views of reality.

Life-span Development

Guidano (1988) states that a life theme "is best defined as something that is progressively and dynamically constructed day by day, year by year, on the basis of events that have characterized an individual's existence, of how he or she has integrated these events and dealt with them, and of the consequences that derived from this process. The consequences of his or her choices and action become in turn further events that, unified in individual memory, allow him or her to build an even more uniform and comprehensive image of self and his or her life. Using Hayek's (1978) words once more, we might say that the products of conscious rationality are the result of human actions, but not of human design" (p. 324).

RET goes along with the first part of this statement but is skeptical of Hayek's allergy against human design. It assumes that humans are innately predisposed to build more uniform and comprehensive images of their lives, and that they do so on the basis of their prior choices, actions, and the consequences that derive from these choices and actions (or, better, from their *views* of these consequences). But RET assumes that creativity and design are also innate human tendencies. We are *born* (as well as raised) to design and redesign—to *observe* our poor life-styles and to (consciously and unconsciously) *try* (plan *and* act) to change them. Moreover, because we are language-centered and persuadable creatures, we can imbibe and adopt other people's designs, plans, and teachings. Though Hayek's and Guidano's views of life-span development, unlike some behavioristic views, are indeed constructivist, the RET assumption that humans can *deliberately* and *creatively* design their own changes, and can also deliberately *choose* (or *not* choose) to adopt others' plans and designs, would seem to be even more constructivist. In other words, RET seems to favor personal choice, or "free will" and conscious decision making, even more than do Hayek and Guidano.

Approaches to Truth and Reality

Guidano (1988) sets up a straw-person definition of truth that supposedly the empiricist–associationistic approaches to therapy, including RET, follow and states that according to RET "truth is considered singular, static, and external to all humans" (p. 326). Instead, he points out, "rationality, rather than being something static and absolute, like an entity, has a relationistic and interactive nature" (p. 326). He also notes that although clients' assumptions may not be logical nor empirically valid, they are nonetheless rational because they provide internal coherence and reliability to their knowledge organization and are therefore rational to *them*. He holds that clients' basic assumptions underlying their way of experiencing reality "are viewed as being in need of modification not because they are irrational but because they represent an outmoded solution" (p. 327).

Guidano makes some good points here but almost completely misunderstands RET's view of irrationality. As I think I clearly stated (Ellis, 1979), "RET posits no abolutistic or invariant criteria of rationality" and "RET therapists do *not* select clients' values, goals, and purposes or show them what their basic aims and purposes *should* be" (p. 40). RET defines "irrational" behavior as thoughts, feelings, and actions that people create or construct that frequently defeat or sabotage their *own personal* goals, values, and interests. RET hypothesizes that there is a high degree of correlation between people's behaving self-defeatingly and their holding unrealistic, antiempirical, illogical, rigid, and absolutist beliefs about themselves, about others, and about the world; and that if they become (that is, *make* themselves) flexible, skeptical, open-minded, scientific thinkers, they are likely to change their self-sabotaging behaviors. But it also acknowledges that people with unrealistic, illogical, musturbatory cognitions sometimes get through life productively and happily (Ellis, 1985b, 1988c; Ellis & Dryden, 1987).

Guidano (1988) states that some basic assumptions of clients "are viewed as being in need of modification not because they are irrational but because they represent an outmoded solution" (p. 327). RET would say that, using its definition of "rational" as "self-helping," these outmoded solutions were *once* "rational" but are *now* "self-defeating" and hence "irrational." It would also point out that many of the "good" solutions that children create (e.g., having temper tantrums when they are frustrated) never really were very "good" because they needlessly upset themselves, only sometimes induced others to treat them better, and often brought on *more* opposition and frustration. Often, children construct bad solutions to their early problems and the fact that they get poor results from doing so doesn't prevent them from continuing these poor solutions into adulthood. For one thing, they may falsely *see* their early solutions as "good"; or they may *view* them as "bad" but not *realize* what they are doing to create them or may *assume* that they cannot change their self-defeating reactions. So when therapists state that people's early constructions and ideas *had to be* "good" and "useful" just because they once existed and were perpetuated, they may be quite mistaken.

Guidano (1988) holds that because people's developmental processes produce an individual knowledge organization that belongs uniquely to each individual, it is "real" to them, has some kind of intrinsic validity, and therefore therapists must intervene, *not* "to persuade the client to accept more 'rational' points of view but [use] a strategy to modify the client's demarcation between real and not-real in order to allow him or her to assimilate (e.g., to consider now as real) neglected past memories and new available experiences" (p. 327).

Guidano seems to be alleging here that no matter how irrational (self-defeating) clients' ideas and behaviors are, they are *real* and *intrinsically valid* to these clients and therefore must not be disputed by the therapist. This is a strange outlook for a therapist to have! Suppose a woman believes that because her neglectful father did not love her sufficiently, as he *should* have done, she is a worm who now absolutely *needs* every neglectful man's love to make her worthwhile, and she therefore compulsively runs after unloving men. Her irrational beliefs are, of course, *real*, and her compulsive behavior is *intrinsically valid* to her. But what therapist worth his or her salt would not dispute them and help her give them up? Guidano assumes that this woman would have repressed her past memories of her father's neglect and that bringing them to light, as a psychoanalyst would do, would cure her. He forgets that most clients like her would vividly remember their past and would *therefore* irrationally conclude that they *must* be loved by neglectful men today. More important, he assumes that if she did repress the memory of her father's past neglect and now, through therapy, experienced it for *real*, she would automatically give up her irrational demand for neglectful men's love today and rationally conclude that she did *not* need it. Quite an assumption!

One main reason I abandoned psychoanalysis in 1953, after practicing it for six years, was that I discovered that when neglected past memories were brought to clients' consciousness, they *still* thought and behaved very irrationally—sometimes more than ever! The woman I have just used as an illustration was an actual client of mine who, when I helped her see how unloving her father actually was, insisted that this *proved* that men were not to be trusted as lovers and that therefore she *had* to win their affection. She became *more* compulsive about getting men to love her—until (as many psychoanalysts do) I abandoned digging into her past and rationally disputed her *present* dire need for neglectful men's love. Only *then* was she able to throw herself into new available experiences with more loving men. Why Guidano assumes that clients' assimilating neglected past experiences as *real* normally helps people to accept new healthy experiences is not at all clear to me. My experience when I practiced psychoanalysis usually showed me the opposite. The more I helped my clients focus on and understand the past, the *less* they usually thought rationally about and allowed themselves enjoyable experiences in the present and future.

Role of Developmental Analysis

Under the guise of making a thorough assessment of clients and their disturbances, Guidano (1988) again takes the highly psychoanalytic position that "any distortion of the patterns of family attachment will be reflected ... in the child's developing self-identity. Hence, from a developmental viewpoint, psychotherapy should be regarded in light of attachment processes and of their relevance in building up the maladaptive conceptions of self that prevent the progression toward more integrated levels of self-knowledge and instead foster the emergence of those regressive oscillations in life-span development that we call clinical disturbances" (p. 338).

Here Guidano is beating the drum for several psychoanalytic theories that are most probably invalid:

1. The child's developing self-identity almost entirely depends on "the patterns of family attachment." On the contrary, as almost any *non*psychoanalytic therapist can easily see, children with "good" and "bad" self-identities are reared in a wide variety of distorted and nondistorted patterns of family attachment; and we now have an enormous amount of data that tends to show that children (and adults) with defective self-identity—especially those

whom we call psychotic or borderline personalities—are influenced more by innate biological tendencies than by their early family environment (Adler, 1989; Bradley & Hirsch, 1986; Rosenthal & Kety, 1968), as I hypothesized a quarter of a century ago (Ellis, 1963).

2. Guidano assumes that clinical disturbances stem from "regressive oscillations in life-span development." But my own observations, as well as considerable research data, tend to show that the vast majority of seriously disturbed individuals did not achieve a "good" life-span development and then have "regressive oscillations." Most of them seem to have been cognitively, emotionally, and behaviorally deficient since their earliest years, never particularly progressed "toward more integrated levels of self-knowledge," and wound up just as disturbed or even more disturbed in their adolescence and adulthood as they were in their first few years of life (Chess, Thomas, & Birch, 1965; Green, Bax, & Tsitsikas, 1989; Werner, 1989).

Guidano's so-called developmental theory of disturbance really goes back to semiconstructivist psychoanalytic, stimulus–response theories of personality. It sees family stimuli as very strongly creating childhood disturbance and sees the child as constructively (and destructively) reacting to these stimuli. It is an interactional theory, to be sure, but is not nearly as constructivist as the RET theory. RET holds that young children, mainly for biological reasons, *bring themselves* to family processes and do so on quite an individualistic basis. They usually are, as Bowlby (1969, 1973) rightly shows, born quite attachable but vary widely in how attachable or relatable they are. The more attachable ones, even when they are reared by healthy, loving families, feel more deprived and sad than the less attachable ones when they are not greatly or continually loved. But in addition to being more or less attachable, children are also, largely (though not entirely) for biological reasons, more or less dogmatic, demanding, and disturbable. Hence, when they are deprived (or *see themselves* as deprived) of family support, they either musturbatorily *make* themselves panicked (instead of concerned) and depressed (instead of sad and frustrated) and consequently largely *construct* their clinical disturbances.

The RET theory of the role of developmental analysis, therefore, seems to be distinctly *more* constructivist than that of the stimulus →organism→response theories of Guidano and Mahoney, of the psychoanalysts that they tend to follow, and of radical behaviorists whom they barely mention.

Guidano (1988) states that "it seems quite evident from clinical experience that both obesity and anorexia have their start in a similar stressful event: a strong disappointment coming from a loved person, usually a parent. The difficult effects resulting from the same event have to be attributed to the different developmental stage in which that event occurred" (p. 328).

As first a psychoanalyst and then a practitioner of rational–emotive theory, I have treated more than 1,000 obese and more than 100 anorectic clients, and it is not evident to me that they all overate or underate because of strong disappointment coming from a loved person. A number of them were quite loved during childhood, and they fully acknowledged that they were. Moreover, they developed eating disorders at all ages and "developmental stages." Almost all of the obese individuals I have seen *constructed* several main irrational beliefs: (1) "I absolutely *must* not be deprived of immediate gratification, especially good-tasting food"; (2) "Whenever I feel emotionally upset—especially panicked and depressed—I *can't stand* that *feeling* and *have to* distract myself by and quiet myself down with *food, food, food*"; (3) "Because I foolishly stuff myself with extra food, as I absolutely *should* not, I am an incompetent, worthless person who *can't* control my appetite!" No matter how much or little they were loved or in what developmental stage they were in, my obese clients *brought* these kinds of self-defeating beliefs to their eating processes and thereby largely *constructed* their overeating behaviors.

Similarly, my anorectic clients almost always *brought* perfectionist ideas to family situations and dogmatically held that they *had* to be completely thin to be worthwhile. Even when they knew full well that their anorexia was alienating people whose love they craved, they rigidly held to their perfectionist demands. A great many other clinicians and researchers have shown that obese and anorectic individuals *bring* irrational ideas to family and other life situations and thereby largely *construct* their eating disorders (Fairburn, 1985; Garner & Bemis, 1985; Peveler & Fairburn, 1989).

Clients' Resistance to Change

Guidano (1988) says that clients resist therapy because the therapist's "reasonable" attitude "is perceived by the client as threatening because it is so encoded in his or her representational models of self and others" (p. 329). This is a *somewhat* constructivist theory of resistance, and RET would tend to agree. But RET is even more constructivist in that it hypothesizes that most clients are *born* resisters and would therefore tend to resist almost *any* therapist who would try to help them change (Ellis, 1985b). RET once again assumes that people bring *themselves* (their tendencies to selectively *see* and *interpret* their family members and other environmental influences *individually*) to life situations; that they largely *train themselves* to become disturbed; that they then *reinforce themselves* to feel relatively comfortable with and to hold onto rather than let go of their disturbances (e.g., feel good when they refuse to go on elevators that they have *made themselves* phobic about); that they *habituate themselves* to self-defeating thoughts, feelings, and behaviors; and that they finally (consciously and unconsciously) *hang onto* their disturbances even when they partly "see" how pernicious they are and when they engage in psychotherapy. The RET theory of resistance, then, appears to be distinctly more constructivist (and individualistic) than Guidano's—and Mahoney's (1988)—theories.

Superficial and Deep Changes

Guidano and Mahoney pride themselves on trying to help clients achieve deep rather than superficial change; and Guidano (1988) notes that "a superficial change coincides with the reorganization of the client's attitude toward reality without revising his or her personality" (p. 330).

RET not only agrees with this goal of helping clients achieve a deep personality change but has pioneered in this goal for many years (Ellis, 1962, 1971, 1973, 1977, 1985b, 1987a, 1987b, 1988c; Ellis & Harper, 1975). More concretely than Guidano, RET strives for what it calls a *profound philosophic change* or *basic attitudinal change*—and especially for helping clients minimize absolutist, dogmatic, musturbatory thinking and adopt a flexible, scientific, alternative-seeking, open attitude toward themselves, others, and the world.

Guidano seems to confuse RET with several other healing therapies, such as those of Bandura (1986), Beck (1976), Lazarus (1966; Lazarus & Folkman, 1984); Maultsby (1984); Meichenbaum (1977), Raimy (1975), and Seligman (1975). These cognitive–behavioral therapies, as Guidano implies, largely deal with clients' "unrealistic" or "false" inferences, attributions, and overgeneralizations— for example, "Because my parents scolded me, I must have done the wrong thing; they don't love me at all; I'll always act badly, and I'm a worthless person for being the way I am." All of these conclusions tend to be opposed to reality; and RET, like most other cognitively oriented therapies, shows clients how to dispute and change them (Ellis, 1962, 1973, 1988c, 1989b).

RET has emphasized since the early 1970s, however, that when therapists dispute *only* people's disturbed and unrealistic inferences and attributions they are doing superficial, not deep, therapy. According to RET theory, these nonempirical inferences almost always *stem from* and are *derivatives of* underlying *deeper* philosophic assumptions from which the inferences are *constructed*. Thus, in the illustrations in the preceding paragraph, clients *infer* that their parents' scolding them means that they have done the wrong thing, that their parents do not love them at all, that they'll always act badly, and that they are worthless individuals because they hold the basic *demands* that they *absolutely must* always perform well and *have to* be *completely* loved by their parents and by other significant people. Without stoutly holding such impossible and perfectionistic *commands* they would rarely derive these unrealistic and illogical inferences (Ellis, 1985b, 1987a, 1987b, 1988c, 1989b; Ellis & Yeager, 1989; Ellis, Young, & Lockwood, 1987).

However deeply Guidano and Mahoney go into their clients' developmental processes, they do not seem to recognize that the tacit, process-oriented cognitions that are, as they rightly say, extremely important to people's *personality organization* are not the specific deep ideologies that probably led to their *disturbances*. They therefore fail to consider seriously and to help clients change their tacit (and explicit) Jehovian commands and musts. In this respect, they are again less constructivist (and more stimulus-oriented) than are modern RET practitioners.

Strategy for Therapeutic Change

Guidano (1988) says that he fully subscribes to Bowlby's personal letter to him (July 1982), which states that the principal tasks of the therapist are "(a) encouraging and enabling the patient to explore his cognitive models; (b) helping the patient to recognize the cognitive models he is actually using; (c) helping him trace how he has come to have them, which I believe to have been in large measure due to his having accepted what his parents have constantly *told* him—both about themselves and about himself; (d) encouraging him to review the models in the light both of their history and also of the degree to which they correspond to his own *first-hand* experience of himself and his parents; (e) helping him to recognize the sanctions his parents have used to insist that he adopts their model and not his own. Only after this process has been gone through many times are the revised models likely to be stable" (pp. 331–332).

Although points (a) and (b) of this Bowlby–Guidano technique are derived from RET and cognitive–behavioral therapy (CBT), the psychoanalytic orientation of the other points seems to be inefficient and nonconstructivist. Let me be specific:

(c) People do *not* become disturbed by what their parents *tell* them but by their *deciding to accept* parental rules and to *make* them into rigid, musturbatory demands.

(d) Helping clients to review their cognitive models in the light of their history implies that their early experiences created these models—instead of *their* creating and constructing them *about* these experiences. Helping clients to see the degree that their cognitive models correspond to their own *firsthand* experiences of themselves and their parents ignores the important point that they *also* partly created these "experiences" *themselves*, by *viewing* their parental relations in a prejudiced, distorted light and then, during psychoanalytically-oriented therapy, by *inventing* many of their memories of what "actually" happened years ago.

(e) Helping clients to understand the sanctions their parents have used to insist that they adopt parental cognitive models and not their own again leads them up the (psychoanalytically oriented) garden path. For it was not these sanctions that *made* them adopt parental cognitive models but the clients' individualized *decisions* to abide (or not to abide) by these sanctions. Many parents, of course, did not impose strict sanctions; and even when they did, many youngsters *refused* to be intimidated by them. Early imbibed cognitions, especially those imposed by sanctions, do not *have* to be carried into later life. Carrying them on is a *choice* and stems from the cognitions of the child, not merely those imposed by the parents. More important, Bowlby and Guidano seem to forget that many parents are lenient, liberal, and nondemanding, and some children are *not*. Thus, parents are often liberal religionists, non-religionists, or antireligionists, whereas their children choose—that is, *make themselves*—devout religionists. The psychoanalytic (Freud, 1965) and transactional analysis (Berne, 1972) theory that parents impose cognitive tapes on their children and thereby, especially in their interpersonal relations, maim them forever has considerable contradictory evidence to assail it.

If the Bowlby–Guidano strategy for therapeutic change were accurately followed, all effective cognitive–behavioral therapy would presumably take at least a year, and often (as psychoanalysis does) 2 to 10 years. Oddly enough, however, many RET clients, including hundreds of my own, seem to have made a profound philosophic, emotive, and behavioral change, and have maintained their greatly revised cognitive models in a stable manner, after from 5 to 15 sessions. And I have spoken to and corresponded with scores of people who have radically changed their disturbed attitudes and actions without any psychotherapy, merely from reading RET books and listening to RET cassettes. Others have done so by conversion to religious, sociopolitical, or other philosophies. So I am most skeptical of the desirability or the "necessity" of the kind of long-term cognitive reconstruction mandated by Bowlby and Guidano. Once again, I see Guidano as largely a strong environmentalist who hardly consistently follows the constructivist position that is much more native to RET.

Guidano (1988) states that "the knowledge content capable to revising the client's cognitive models is already available in some way. What is not available is the client's selective attention in recognizing it. Then the therapist should pay great respect to the client's self-knowledge. In general, it is useless and even dangerous to put new knowledge into a client's head in every possible way, since the information useful for the client comes from his or her deep structures and cannot be replaced by the therapist's conceptions about life" (p. 332).

This sounds like some psychoanalytically oriented propaganda to me and is not greatly constructivist. It amounts to saying that clients, in their deep unconscious minds, have very healthy self-knowledge that has only to be released by the therapists making their unconscious conscious and that it is dangerous for the therapist to do anything *but* this and is especially dangerous to give clients new knowledge. RET would much more constructivistically put it this way: (1) Clients imbibe (decide to accept) and invent healthy (self-helping) *and* unhealthy cognitions, many of which are tacit or unconscious; (2) they create self-defeating dogmas *and* self-actualizing cognitive changes and solutions to their life events that are creatively scientific *and* unscientific; (3) a good therapist will pay respect to clients' self-helping *and* self-defeating cognitions but especially point out the differences between the two and respect clients' great creative capacities to enhance the former and minimize the latter; (4) an effective cognitive–behavioral therapist will often find it very useful to teach clients new knowledge (including new *ways* of thinking, new problem-solving methods, and new skills) that other people have often found helpful.

The therapist will present this new knowledge tentatively and experimentally, never as dogma, and will give clients the *choice* of using it, modifying it, or ignoring it. He or she will *not* practice consumerism disguised as "transference" or as a "strong therapeutic alliance" and thereby encourage clients to adapt the therapist's ideas out of their dire need to win his or her approval (Ellis, 1989a). Following this kind of position, RET assumes that one of the most constructivist and creative of humans' tendencies is the ability to attend to *new* knowledge imparted by therapists, teachers, and educational materials; to *consider* its plausibility; to *select* and *modify* parts of it for growth purposes; and to *utilize* it for present and future change. If people were not able to *use* therapeutic (and other) teaching creatively, psychotherapy would hardly exist. What we call *experience*—including therapeutic experience—largely consists of taking the direct and indirect instruction of others and selectively *making* parts of it our "own" percepts and precepts. Even Milton Erickson, whose followers often apotheosize him for "indirectly" hypnotizing and changing clients, usually was directive. Jay Haley (1973), one of his main proponents, noted that "since most of Erickson's therapy is directive, an important part of the art is to persuade people to follow his directives" (p. 205).

Guidano (1988) states that "in order to make the tacit explicit ... one has to respect the client's tacit level since it represents the essential directionality to be followed. For example, it is useless and dangerous to try to convince individuals with depressive organizations that their inner view of themselves is absurd or to criticize their basic feelings about loneliness, ephemerality, and the futility of life. In some ways, these are the only possibilities they have of establishing a relationship with reality" (p. 333).

What an anticonstructivist view! Guidano seems to be saying that since depressives tacitly and solidly construct a very futile attitude, this "essential directionality" *has to be* followed by the therapist, who *must not* actively–directively oppose it. He seems to forget that the clients creatively *chose* this futility of life attitude and are now *choosing* to maintain it. Being human constructivists, they now *can* construct new attitudes and feelings about loneliness, ephemerality, the futility of life, and their own worthlessness—especially *if* therapists actively–directively help them to do so. For example, since first using RET in 1955, I have very forcefully and directly shown about 500 suicidal clients that their lives were not futile and that they could unconditionally accept themselves in spite of their love and work failures; and to my knowledge none of them killed themselves while I was still seeing them. Moreover, I almost always actively talked them out of their feelings of hopelessness within 1 to 10 sessions, and then often spent the next 9 months or so helping them overcome their long-standing feelings of severe depression.

Guidano (1988) states that my and other therapists' use of "classic behavioral and cognitive techniques" or RET with this kind of suicidal and depressive client amounts only to "disproving client's superficial beliefs and expectations . . . so allowing deeper structures to emerge. In this sense a process-oriented therapist does not consider the achievement of a therapeutic goal as a matter of choosing the 'right' technique, but rather, he or she always uses techniques (or even 'invents' new techniques) that fit into the strategy of guiding the client's process to make the tacit explicit" (p. 334).

Well, shades of Freudianism again! Almost 100 years of psychotherapy have now shown that the main Freudian goal of making the unconscious conscious is one of the most *in*efficient techniques ever invented. Of the many schools of psychoanalysis that now exist—including those that follow Adler, Jung, Ferenczi, Rank, Reich, Horney, Sullivan, Alexander, Fromm, Klein, Winnicott, Lacan, and Schafer—none really emphasizes making the unconscious conscious, and most of them are much more active–directive than Guidano's claims to be. It is indeed an irony that I created RET and became grandfather of cognitive–behavioral therapy in 1955 mainly as a revolt against the abysmal therapeutic inefficiency of psychoanalysis and that now Guidano and Mahoney, as far as I can see, have brought back some of its worst inefficiencies with a vengeance!

Guidano also assumes that making clients' unconscious conscious will somehow automatically—and I would add magically— help them to *change* their self-defeating and self-damning tacit philosophies. I fail to see why this is true. If I believe that I am a worthless person because I unconsciously imbibed my parents' experiencing me as such and (subtly and overtly) denigrating me, and if I now consciously see, with Guidano's help, what my tacit cognitions about me and my parents have been, why can't I *still* insist that they are right and that I really *am* valueless? More important, if I *don't* ever know the history of my parents' denigrating me and even repress that "shameful" history, why can't I now, using RET, give up my *still existing* demand that my parents (and significant others) must love me, and why can't I *thus* unconditionally accept myself?

RET says I definitely can, and, using RET, I have helped literally thousands of severe self-deprecators to profoundly change their philosophies and radically—and revolutionarily—accept themselves. In so doing, I have rarely worked at making their "deep" unconscious conscious but mainly at showing them that just beneath their level of conscious awareness they now hold tacit musturbatory beliefs. Once they begin to see this, they and I work very hard to help them to dispute, to emotively and behaviorally *change* their now conscious dogmas and insistences.

My use of the word *revolutionarily* in the preceding paragraph reminds me that, as almost everyone now recognizes, the cognitive revolution began in psychology in the early 1950s (Neisser, 1967), and shortly thereafter the cognitive–behavioral therapy revolution started in 1955 (Ellis, 1957, 1958; Kelly, 1955). Now Guidano (1988) and Mahoney (1988) are attempting to revolutionize cognitive therapy by making it more constructivist and less rationalist. But these constructivists forget that scientific revolutions, as Kuhn (1970) has shown, largely take place not by mere discovery but by teaching, writing, and propaganda. I contend that profound therapeutic change also constitutes a "revolution" in clients' ways of thinking, feeling, and behaving and that when clients effect this "revolution," they creatively use both the direct and indirect teachings of the therapists. I also hypothesize that the most revolutionary changes in the clients—what we call the elegant solution in RET—are significantly correlated with therapists' (and other people's) direct teaching or persuasion (Frank, 1973).

Integration of Deep Cognition, Emotion, and Behavior

Mahoney (1988) states that cognitive constructivists hold that "acting, feeling, and knowing are inseparable expressions of adaptation and development" (p. 370). He is correct about this but significantly forgets that the same point has been clearly made in RET since 1956, before he and Guidano entered the field of psychotherapy (Ellis, 1958, 1962). Ellis (1962) stated: "The theoretical foundations of RET are based on the assumption that human thinking and emotion are *not* two disparate or different processes, but that they significantly overlap and are in some respects, for all practical purposes, essentially the same thing. Like the other two basic life processes, sensing and moving, they are integrally interrelated and never can be seen wholly apart from each other" (p. 38).

RET not only is highly cognitive but also unusually emotive and behavioral. Unlike many other cognitive–behavioral therapies, it emphasizes the close relationship between "hot" cognitions and emotions and therefore consistently uses a variety of dramatic, evocative, forceful verbal and action-oriented techniques.

Mahoney (1988) holds that "rationalist" therapies denigrate emotions and claims that "all intense emotions (regardless of valence) have a disorganized effect on behavior" (p. 374). It is not clear what "rationalist" therapies he is referring to in this criticism, but

RET has never been opposed to intense emotions (e.g., strong feelings of sadness, disappointment, and grief) but only to disruptive, self-defeating emotions (e.g., panic, depression, and self-hatred). Unlike most other therapies, RET clearly distinguishes between *appropriate* and *in*appropriate feelings (Crawford & Ellis, 1989; Ellis, 1957, 1962, 1971, 1973, 1977, 1987b, 1988c; Ellis & Becker, 1982; Ellis & Dryden, 1987; Ellis & Harper, 1975). RET often helps people to feel *more* strongly than they did when they first came to therapy—but not to feel just for the sake of feeling. And it emphasizes the enhancement of self-actualizing, happy feelings, not merely the elimination of destructive ones (Ellis, 1988c; Ellis & Becker, 1982).

Therapeutic Relationship

Guidano (1988) and Mahoney (1988), along with Freud (1965) and Rogers (1961), stress the importance of the therapeutic relationship for personality change, and they wrongly assumed that RET and other cognitive therapies ignore this aspect. On the contrary, RET particularly stresses that therapists had better always give individual and family clients unconditional acceptance, or what Rogers calls unconditional positive regard, and that they not merely *tell* but *show* their clients that they are accepted by their therapists *whether or not* they perform adequately and *whether or not* they are nice and lovable. But in addition to *showing* and *modeling* unconditional acceptance, RET couples practitioners *teach* clients how to accept themselves philosophically, not because of but also independently of their therapist's acceptance (Ellis, 1973, 1977, 1988c; Ellis & Harper, 1975). This double-barreled RET approach uniquely emphasizes people's ability to *choose* and *construct* their own self-acceptance and is therefore more constructivist than the psychoanalytically oriented approaches of Mahoney and Guidano.

Mahoney (1988) claims that classical "rationalists" see relapse and recidivism in therapy resulting from insufficient use of knowledge and information imparted during therapy, whereas cognitive constructivists see setbacks and regression as "naturally and virtually inevitable aspects of psychological development" (p. 378). Mahoney seems to forget that this position was clearly formulated in RET back in the 1960s (Ellis, 1962) and has been part and parcel of RET practice since that time (Ellis, 1973, 1987a, 1988c; Ellis & Dryden, 1987). Unlike strategic and systems family therapy, RET assumes that family members not only largely *disturb themselves* about what happens to them in the family system but that they also consistently *re*disturb themselves even when a beneficial change in the system is arranged. As I observed in 1965, people are born with a *talent* for defeating their own and their family's interests, *easily* do so and *naturally* fall back to doing so again during the entire period of their lives.

If clients profoundly change their basic, deep-seated, disturbance-creating philosophies, RET holds, and if they keep working to keep them flexible, they often can achieve the "elegant" solution of rarely (not *never*) upsetting themselves in the present and future and of quickly un-upsetting themselves when they do fall back. So they have the ability, if they work hard at effective therapy, of making themselves *less* but not *non*-upsettable (Ellis, 1987a). In this way, RET seems to be more constructivist than the cognitive therapies of Mahoney, Guidano, Reda, Liotti, and other cognitive constructivists.

CONCLUSION

Mahoney, Guidano, and other modern constructivists and process-oriented therapists are partly on the right track and are making some interesting additions to traditional cognitive therapy. But they sometimes also revert to inefficient and sidetracking psychoanalytically oriented methods of therapy. RET, in both its individual and family therapy approaches, attempts to use the most effective and hardheaded of the so-called rationalist methods, including active–directive changing of unrealistic and irrational beliefs, skill training, problem solving, bibliotherapy, in vivo desensitization, and reinforcement procedures. It also employs many of the methods of the cognitive constructivists, including the disclosing of tacit philosophies; the achievement of a profound philosophical change in clients' attitudes toward themselves, toward others, and toward life situations; the use of the therapist's relationship with clients to show them how to accept themselves unconditionally; and the employment of many dramatic, emotive, and experiential exercises to change clients' feelings as well as their thoughts and behaviors. RET is particularly interested in effecting both individual and familial change as quickly and as efficiently as feasible. It is therefore rational (efficaciously hedonic) *and* emotive (energetically experiential). Or at least it tries to be!

REFERENCES

Adler, T. (1989). Study finds genetic defect linked with schizophrenia. *American Psychological Association Monitor, 20*(1), 15.

Bandura, A. (1986). *Social foundations of thought and action: A social cognitive theory*. Englewood Cliffs, NJ: Prentice-Hall.

Bartley, W. W. (1962). *The retreat to commitment*. New York: Knopf.

Beck, A. T. (1976). *Cognitive therapy and the emotional disorders*. New York: International Universities Press.

Beck, A. T., Rush, A. J., Shaw, B. F., & Emery, G. (1979). *Cognitive therapy of depression*. New York: Guilford.

Berne, E. (1972). *What do you say after you say hello?* New York: Grove.

Bowlby, J. (1969). *Attachment and loss: 1. Attachment*. New York: Basic Books.

Bowlby, J. (1973). *Attachment and loss: 2. Separation*. New York: Basic Books.

Bowlby, J. (1980). *Attachment and loss: 3. Loss: Sadness and depression*. New York: Basic Books.

Bradley, P. B., & Hirsch, S. R. (Eds.). (1986). *The psychopharmacology and treatment of schizophrenia*. Oxford: Oxford University Press.

Chess, S., Thomas, T., & Birch, H. G. (1965). *Your child is a person*. New York: Viking.

Crawford, T., & Ellis, A. (1989). A dictionary of rational–emotive feelings and behaviors. *Journal of Rational–Emotive and Cognitive–Behavioral Therapy, 7*(1), 3–27.

Dobson, K. S. (1988). The present and future of the cognitive–behavioral therapies. In K. S. Dobson (Ed.), *Handbook of cognitive–behavioral therapies* (pp. 387–414). New York: Guilford.

D'Zurilla, T. J., & Goldfried, M. R. (1971) Problem-solving and behavior modification. *Journal of Abnormal Psychology, 78*, 107–126.

Ellis, A. (1957). *How to live with a neurotic: At home and at work*, New York: Crown.

Ellis, A. (1958). Rational psychotherapy. *Journal of General Psychology, 59*, 35–49.

Ellis, A. (1962). *Reason and emotion in psychotherapy*, Secaucus, NJ: Lyle Stuart.

Ellis, A. (1963). *The treatment of borderline and psychotic individuals*. New York: Institute for Rational–Emotive Therapy.

Ellis, A. (1965). Workshop in rational–emotive therapy. New York: Institute for Rational–Emotive Therapy.

Ellis, A. (1969). A weekend of rational encounter. *Rational Living, 4*(2), 1–8.

Ellis, A. (1971). *Growth through reason*. North Hollywood, CA: Wilshire Books.

Ellis, A. (1972a). Helping people get better rather than merely feel better. *Rational Living, 7*(2), 2–9.

Ellis, A. (1972b). *Psychotherapy and the value of a human being*. New York: Institute for Rational–Emotive Therapy.

Ellis, A. (1973). *Humanistic psychotherapy: The rational–emotive approach.* New York: McGraw-Hill.

Ellis, A. (1976a). The biological basis of human irrationality. *Journal of Individual Psychology, 32,* 145–168.

Ellis, A. (1976b). RET abolishes most of the human ego. *Psychotherapy, 13,* 343–348.

Ellis, A. (1977). *Anger—how to live with and without it.* Secaucus, NJ: Citadel Press.

Ellis, A. (1979). The theory of rational–emotive therapy. In A. Ellis & J. M. Whiteley (Eds.), *Theoretical and empirical foundations of rational–emotive therapy* (pp. 33–60). Monterey, CA: Brooks/Cole.

Ellis, A. (1984). Is the unified-interaction approach to cognitive-behavior modification a reinvention of the wheel? *Clinical Psychology Review, 4,* 215–218.

Ellis, A. (1985a). Expanding the ABC's of rational–emotive therapy. In M. Mahoney & A. Freeman (Eds.), *Cognition and psychotherapy* (pp. 313–323). New York: Plenum.

Ellis, A. (1985b). *Overcoming resistance: Rational–emotive therapy with difficult clients.* New York: Springer Publishing Co.

Ellis, A. (1987a). The impossibility of achieving consistently good mental health. *American Psychologist, 42,* 364–375.

Ellis, A. (1987b). A sadly neglected cognitive element in depression. *Cognitive Therapy and Research, 11,* 121–146.

Ellis, A. (1988c). *How to stubbornly refuse to make yourself miserable about anything–yes, anything!* New York: Lyle Stuart.

Ellis, A. (1989a). Ineffective consumerism in the cognitive–behavioral therapies and in general psychotherapy. In W. Dryden & P. Trower (Eds.), *Cognitive psychotherapy: Stasis and change.* London: Cassell.

Ellis, A. (1989b). Rational–emotive therapy. In R. J. Corsini & D. Wedding (Eds.), *Current psychotherapies* (4th ed.). Itasca, IL: Peacock.

Ellis, A., & Becker, I. (1982). *A guide to personal happiness.* North Hollywood, CA: Wilshire Books.

Ellis, A., & Dryden, W. (1987). *The practice of rational–emotive therapy.* New York: Springer Publishing Co.

Ellis, A., & Harper, R. A. (1975). *A new guide to rational living.* North Hollywood, CA: Wilshire Books.

Ellis, A., Sichel, J., Yeager, R., DiMattia, D., & DiGiuseppe, R. (1989). *Rational–emotive couples therapy.* New York: Pergammon.

Ellis, A., & Yeager, R. (1989). *Why some therapies don't work: The dangers of transpersonal psychology.* Buffalo, NY: Prometheus.

Ellis, A., Young, J., & Lockwood, G. (1987). Cognitive therapy and rational–emotive therapy: A dialogue. *Journal of Cognitive Psychotherapy, 1*(4), 137–187.

Fairburn, C. G. (1985). Cognitive–behavioral treatment for bulimia. In D. M. Gardner & P. E. Garfinkel (Eds.), *Handbook of psychotherapy for anorexia nervosa and bulimia.* New York: Guilford.

Frank, J. D. (1973). *Persuasion and healing.* Baltimore: Johns Hopkins University Press.

Freud, S. (1965). *Standard edition of the complete psychological works of Sigmund Freud*. London: Hogarth.

Garner, D. M., & Bemis, K. M. (1985). Cognitive therapy for anorexia nervosa. In D. M. Garner & P. E. Garfinkel (Eds.), *Handbook of psychotherapy for anorexia nervosa and bulimia*, New York: Guilford.

Green, J., Bax, D. M., & Tsitsikas, H. (1989). Neonatal behavior and early temperament. *American Journal of Orthopsychiatry, 59*, 72–81.

Guidano, V. F. (1988). A systems, process-oriented approach to cognitive therapy. In K. S. Dobson (Ed.), *Handbook of cognitive–behavioral therapies* (pp. 307–356). New York: Guilford.

Haley, J. (1973). *Uncommon therapy: The psychiatric techniques of Milton H. Erickson*. New York: Norton.

Hayek, F. A. (1978). *New studies in philosophy, politics, economics, and the history of ideas*. Chicago: University of Chicago Press.

Kelly, G. (1955). *The psychology of personal constructs*, vols. 1 & 2. New York: Norton.

Korzybski, A. (1933). *Science and sanity*. San Francisco: International Society of General Semantics.

Kuhn, T. S. (1970). *The structure of scientific revolution*. Chicago: University of Chicago Press.

Lazarus, R. S. (1966). *Psychological stress and the coping process*. New York: McGraw-Hill.

Lazarus, R. S., & Folkman, S. (1984). *Stress, appraisal, and coping*. New York: Springer Publishing Co.

Mahoney, M. J. (1976). *The scientist*. Cambridge, MA: Ballinger.

Mahoney, M. J. (1988). The cognitive sciences and psychotherapy: Patterns in a developing relationship. In K. S. Dobson (Ed.), *Handbook of the cognitive–behavioral therapies* (pp. 357–386). New York: Guilford.

Maultsby, M. C., Jr. (1984). *Rational behavior therapy*. Englewood Cliffs, NJ: Prentice-Hall.

Meichenbaum, D. (1977). *Cognitive-behavior modification*. New York: Plenum.

Neisser, U. (1967). *Cognitive psychology*. New York: Appleton-Century-Crofts.

Peveler, R. C., & Fairburn, C. G. (1989). Anorexia nervosa in association with diabetus mellitus: A cognitive–behavioral approach to treatment. *Behaviour Research and Therapy, 27*, 95–99.

Polanyi, M. (1966). *The tacit dimension*. New York: Doubleday.

Popper, K. R. (1959). *The logic of scientific discovery*. New York: Harper & Bros.

Raimy, V. (1975). *Misunderstandings of the self*. San Francisco: Jossey-Bass.

Rogers, C. R. (1961). *On becoming a person*. Boston: Houghton-Mifflin.

Rosenthal, D., & Kety, S. S. (Eds.). (1968). *The transmission of schizophrenia*. Elmsford, NY: Pergamon.

Seligman, M. E. P. (1975). *Helplessness*. San Francisco: Freeman.

Weimer, W. B. (1975). The psychology of inference and expectation. In G. Maxwell & R. M. Anderson (Eds.), *Induction, probability and confirmation*. Minneapolis: University of Minnesota Press.

Weimer, W. B. (1977). A conceptual framework for cognitive psychology. In R. Shaw & J. D. Bransford (Eds.), *Acting, perceiving and knowing.* Hillsdale, NJ: Erlbaum.

Werner, E. E. (1989). High-risk children in young adulthood. *American Journal of Orthopsychiatry, 59,* 72–81.

Practice

II

The Basic Practice of RET

7

INTRODUCTION

This chapter was written by Ellis and Windy Dryden for their book The Practice of Rational–Emotive Therapy *(Ellis & Dryden, 1987) to summarize some of the most important aspects of RET practice. As such, it presents a succinct and up-to-date outline of some of the most important RET techniques.*

Because Ellis's original presentations of RET were designed to stress its main aspects that were quite different from those of popular therapies in the 1950s, Ellis often failed to mention or discuss in detail some of the ways in which RET overlaps with general psychotherapy—such as the ways in which it handles the therapeutic relationship, inducts clients into RET, and assesses clients' thoughts, feelings, and behaviors. Ellis and other RETers later dealt with these aspects of rational–emotive practice.

Ellis believes that this chapter neatly summarizes these early neglected aspects of RET and thereby brings the descriptions of some of its basic practice up to date.

Parts of this chapter were adapted from Dryden and Ellis (1986) and W. Dryden and A. Ellis, "Rational–Emotive Therapy," in K. S. Dobson (Ed.), *Handbook of Cognitive–Behavioral Therapies.* New York: Guilford, 1987 (Used by permission), and have been previously published in *The Nurse Practitioner: The American Journal of Primary Health Care, 12*(7), July 1987.

In this chapter we outline the basic practice of RET. First, we consider aspects of the therapeutic relationship between clients and therapists in RET. Second, we deal with issues pertaining to inducting clients into RET and assessing their problems in RET terms. Third, we specify basic treatment strategies in RET. Fourth, we specify the major treatment techniques that are employed during RET. Fifth, we note a number of obstacles that emerge in the process of RET and how they might be overcome. Finally, we distinguish between preferential and general RET (or cognitive–behavior therapy—CBT) and specify their differences.

THE THERAPEUTIC RELATIONSHIP

RET is an active–directive form of psychotherapy in that therapists are active in directing their clients to identify the philosophical source of their psychological problems and in showing them they can challenge and change their irrational, musterbatory evaluations. As such, RET is an educational form of therapy. I (AE) have sometimes conceptualized the role of the effective RET therapist as that of an authoritative (but not authoritarian!) and encouraging teacher who strives to teach his or her clients how to be their own therapists once formal therapy sessions have ended (Ellis 1979b, 1984).

Therapeutic Conditions

Given the above role, RET therapists strive to *unconditionally accept* their clients as fallible human beings who often act self-defeatingly but are never essentially bad (or good). No matter how badly clients behave in therapy, the RET therapist attempts to accept them as people but will frequently, if appropriate, let them know his or her reactions to the client's negative behavior (Ellis, 1973).

In our role as therapists we strive to be as open as therapeutically feasible and will not hesitate to give highly personal information about ourselves should our clients ask for it, except when we judge that clients would use such information against themselves. RET therapists often disclose examples from their own lives concerning how they experienced similar problems and, more importantly, how they have gone about solving these problems. Thus, they strive to be *therapeutically genuine* in conducting sessions.

RET therapists tend to be *appropriately humorous* with most of their clients since they think that much emotional disturbance

stems from the fact that clients take themselves and their problems, other people, and the world too seriously. RET therapists
thus strive to model for their clients the therapeutic advantages of
taking a serious but humorously ironic attitude toward life. They
endeavor, however, not to poke fun at the clients themselves but at
their self-defeating thoughts, feelings, and actions (Ellis, 1977a,
1977b, 1981). In the same vein, and for similar purposes, RET
therapists tend to be informal and easygoing with most of their
clients. However, RET opposes therapists unethically indulging
themselves in order to enjoy therapy sessions at their clients' expense (Ellis, 1983b).

RET therapists show their clients a special kind of empathy.
They not only offer them "affective" empathy (i.e., communicating
that they understand how their clients feel) but also offer them
philosophic empathy (i.e., showing them that they understand the
philosophies that underlie these feelings).

Thus, with certain modifications, they agree with Rogers's (1957)
views concerning therapist empathy, genuineness, and unconditional positive regard. However, rational–emotive therapists are
very wary of showing the vast majority of their clients undue
warmth. RET holds that if RET therapists get really close to their
clients and give them considerable warmth, attention, caring, and
support, as well as unconditional acceptance, then these therapists
run two major risks (Ellis, 1977c, 1982a).

The first major risk is that therapists may unwittingly reinforce
their clients' dire needs for love and approval—two irrational
ideas that are at the core of much human disturbance. When this
happens, clients appear to improve because their therapists are
indeed giving them what they believe they must have. They begin
to "feel better" but do not necessarily "get better" (Ellis, 1972a).
Their "improvement" is illusory because their irrational philosophies are being reinforced. Since they seem to improve, their therapists have restricted opportunities to identify these ideas, show
them how they relate to their problems, and help them challenge
and change them. Consequently, while such clients are helped by
their therapists, they are not shown how they can help themselves
and are thus vulnerable to future upset.

The second major risk is that therapists may unwittingly reinforce their clients' philosophy of low frustration tolerance (LFT), a
major form of discomfort disturbance. Clients with LFT problems
"almost always try to seek interminable help from others instead
of coping with life's difficulties themselves. Any kind of therapy
that does not specifically persuade them to stop their puerile
whining and to accept responsibility for their own happiness tends

to confirm their belief that others *must* help them. Close relation-ship therapy is frequently the worst offender in this respect and thereby does considerable harm" (Ellis, 1977c, p. 15). [See Chapter 8.]

However, since RET is relative in nature and is against the for-mulation of absolute, dogmatic therapeutic rules, it does recognize that under certain conditions (e.g., where a client is extremely depressed, accompanied by powerful suicidal ideation, etc.), dis-tinct therapist warmth may be positively indicated for a restricted period of time (Ellis, 1985a).

Therapeutic Style

I (AE) recommend that RET therapists adopt an active–directive style with most clients and a particularly forceful version of that style with some very disturbed and resistant clients (Ellis, 1979a). However, not all RET therapists concur with this view. Some rec-ommend a more passive, gentle approach under specific or most conditions with clients (e.g., Garcia, 1977; Young, 1974a, 1977). Eschenroeder (1979) notes that it is important to ask in RET, "Which therapeutic style is most effective with which kind of cli-ent?" (p. 5). In the same vein, recent proponents of eclectic forms of therapy argue that style of therapeutic interaction had better be varied to meet the special situations of individual clients (Beutler, 1983; Lazarus, 1981). While this is a scantily researched area in RET, it may be best for RET therapists to avoid (1) an overly friendly, emotionally charged style of interaction with "hysterical" clients, (2) an overly intellectual style with "obsessive–compulsive" clients, (3) an overly directive style with clients whose sense of autonomy is easily threatened (Beutler, 1983), and (4) an overly active style with clients who easily retreat into pas-sivity. This line of reasoning fits well with the notion of flexibility that rational–emotive therapists advocate as a desirable therapeu-tic quality. Varying one's therapeutic style in RET does not mean departing from the theoretical principles on which the content of therapy is based. As Eschenroeder (1979) points out, in RET "there is no one-to-one relationship between theory and practice" (p. 3).

Personal Qualities of Effective
Rational–Emotive Therapists

Unfortunately, no research studies have been carried out to de-termine the personal qualities of effective rational–emotive thera-pists. Rational–emotive theory, however, does put forward a number of hypotheses concerning this topic (Ellis, 1978), but it is important to regard these as both tentative and awaiting empirical study.

1. Since RET is a fairly structured form of therapy, its effective practitioners are usually comfortable with structure but flexible enough to work in a less structured manner when the need arises.

2. RET practitioners tend to be intellectually, cognitively, or philosophically inclined and become attracted to RET because the approach provides them with opportunities to fully express this tendency.

3. Since RET is often to be conducted in a strong active–directive manner, effective RET practitioners are usually comfortable operating in this mode. Nevertheless, they have the flexibility to modify their interpersonal style with clients so that they provide the optimum conditions to facilitate client change.

4. RET emphasizes that it is important for clients to put their therapy-derived insights into practice in their everyday lives. As a result, effective practitioners of RET are usually comfortable with behavioral instruction and teaching and with providing the active prompting that clients often require if they are to follow through on homework assignments.

5. Effective rational–emotive therapists tend to have little fear of failure themselves. Their personal worth is not invested in their clients' improvement. They do not need their clients' love and/or approval and are thus not afraid of taking calculated risks if therapeutic impasses occur. They tend to accept both themselves and their clients as fallible human beings and are therefore tolerant of their own mistakes and the irresponsible acts of their clients. They tend to have, or persistently work toward acquiring, a philosophy of high frustration tolerance, and they do not get discouraged when clients improve at a slower rate than they desire. Thus, effective practitioners tend to score highly on most of the criteria of positive mental health, and they serve as healthy role models for their clients.

6. RET strives to be scientific, empirical, antiabsolutistic, and undevout in its approach to people's selecting and achieving their own goals (Ellis, 1978). Thus, effective practitioners of RET tend to show similar traits and are definitely not mystical, anti-intellectual, or magical in their beliefs.

7. RET advocates the use of techniques in a number of different modalities (cognitive, imagery, emotive, behavioral, and interpersonal). Its effective practitioners are thus comfortable with a multimodal approach to treatment and tend not to be people who like to stick rigidly to any one modality.

Finally, I (AE) note that some rational–emotive therapists often modify the preferred practice of RET according to their own natural personality characteristics (Ellis, 1978). Thus, for example, some therapists practice RET in a slow-moving, passive manner, do little disputing, and focus therapy on the relationship between them and their clients. Whether such modification of the preferred practice of RET is effective is a question awaiting empirical inquiry.

INDUCTING CLIENTS INTO RET

When clients seek help from rational–emotive therapists, they vary concerning how much they already know about the type of therapeutic process they are likely to encounter. Some may approach the therapist because they know he or she is a practitioner of RET, while others may know nothing about this therapeutic method. In any event it is often beneficial to explore clients' expectations for therapy at the outset of the process. Duckro, Beal, and George (1979) have argued that it is important to distinguish between preferences and anticipations when expectations are assessed. Clients' preferences for therapy concern what kind of experience they want, while anticipations concern what service they think they will receive. Clients who have realistic anticipations for the RET therapeutic process and have a preference for this process, require, in general, far less induction into rational–emotive therapy than clients who have unrealistic anticipations of the process and/or preferences for a different type of therapeutic experience.

Induction procedures, in general, involve showing clients that RET is an active–directive structured therapy oriented to discussion about clients' present and future problems and one that requires clients to play an active role in the change process. Induction can take a number of different forms. First, therapists may develop and use a number of pretherapy role induction procedures where a typical course of RET is outlined and productive client behaviors demonstrated (Macaskill & Macaskill, 1983). Second, therapists may give a short lecture at the outset of therapy concerning the nature and process of rational-emotive therapy. Third, therapists may employ induction-related explanations in the initial therapy sessions using client problem material to illustrate how these problems may be tackled in RET and to outline the respective roles of client and therapist.

ASSESSMENT OF CLIENTS' PROBLEMS

The next stage of therapy concerns assessment. Assessment of the kind and degree of emotional disturbance of clients is held to be important in RET for several reasons:

- To determine how seriously disturbed clients are, so that therapists can see how likely they are to benefit from any form of therapy, including RET, and so that they can also decide which RET techniques (of the many possible ones that are available) may be most suitably employed (and which techniques avoided) with each particular client under the conditions in which he or she may be expected to live.
- To determine—or at least guess with a fair degree of accuracy—how difficult clients are likely to be, how they will probably take to the main RET procedures, and how long psychotherapy with each of them is likely to be required.
- To discover which type of therapist involvement, e.g., a more or less active or a more or less passive and supportive kind, is likely to help the individual client.
- To discover what types of skill deficiencies clients have and what kinds of training (either in the course of RET or outside of therapy) they might best undertake to remedy some of their skill deficiencies. Thus, on the basis of this assessment, certain kinds of skill training, such as assertiveness, social skills, communication, or vocational training, may be recommended for specific clients.

RET practitioners are at liberty to use all kinds of assessment procedures but generally favor the types of cognitive–behavioral interventions described in Kendall and Hollon (1980). They tend to take a dimmer view of diagnostic procedures such as the Rorschach and other projective techniques than they do of more objective personality questionnaires and behavioral tests, largely because the former often have dubious validity, incorporate questionable psychoanalytic and psychodynamic interpretations, and usually are not particularly relatable to effective treatment processes.

Together with many other RET practitioners, we take the view that although assessment interviews and some standard diagnostic tests may at times be useful in exploring clients' disturbances, perhaps the best form of assessment consists of having several RET sessions with the client. Some of the advantages of this kind of therapy-oriented assessment are:

1. In the course of such an assessment procedure, clients can get to work almost immediately on their problems, can gain therapeutically while being assessed, and can be helped to suffer less pain, hardship, and expense while undergoing treatment.

2. The preferable techniques to be used with different clients are often best determined mainly through experimenting with some of these techniques in the course of the therapeutic process. While the use of standard personality tests, such as the MMPI, may help the therapist start off with some RET methods rather than other methods with a given client, only by actually experimenting with certain specific methods is the therapist likely to see how the client reacts to them and consequently how they had better be continued or discontinued.

3. Assessment procedures divorced from ongoing psychotherapy (such as giving a whole battery of tests prior to beginning therapy) may be iatrogenic for a number of clients. During this testing process, especially if the assessment procedures are long-winded and take some time to complete, clients may imagine "horrors" about themselves that led them astray and make it more difficult for them to benefit from therapy.

4. Certain conventional assessment procedures—for example, the Rorschach and TAT—may wrongly predict problems, symptoms, and dynamics that many clients do not really have and may help lead their therapists up the garden path and away from more scientifically based evaluations.

5. Clients sometimes take diagnoses obtained from complicated assessment procedures as the gospel truth, feel that they have thereby received a valid "explanation" of what ails them, and wrongly conclude that they have been helped by this "explanation." RET assessment procedures, including using therapy itself as an integral part of the assessment process, primarily focus on what clients had better do to change rather than emphasize clever diagnostic "explanations" of what ails them.

Because RET is strongly cognitive, emotive, and behavioral, it not only assesses clients' irrational Beliefs but also their inappropriate feelings and their self-defeating behaviors. The usual RET assessment process almost always includes the following:

Clients are helped to acknowledge and describe their inappropriate feelings (e.g., anxiety, depression, anger, and self-hatred), and these are clearly differentiated from their negative appropriate feelings (e.g., disappointment, sadness, frustration, and displeasure).

They are led to acknowledge and delineate their self-defeating behaviors (e.g., compulsions, addictions, phobias, and procrastination) rather than to overemphasize idiosyncratic but non-deleterious behaviors (e.g., unusual devotion to socializing, sex, study, or work).

They are asked to point out specific Activating events in their lives that tend to occur just prior to their experienced disturbed feelings and behaviors.

Their rational Beliefs that accompany their Activating events and that lead to undisturbed Consequences are assessed and discussed.

Their irrational Beliefs that accompany their Activating events and that lead to disturbed Consequences are assessed and discussed.

Their irrational Beliefs that involve absolutistic "musts" and grandiose demands on themselves, others, and the universe are particularly determined.

Their second-level irrational Beliefs that tend to be derived from their absolutistic "shoulds" and "musts"—that is, their "awfulizing," their "I-can't-stand-it-itis," their "damning" of themselves and others, and their unrealistic overgeneralizations—are also revealed.

Their irrational Beliefs that lead to their disturbance about their disturbances—that is, their anxiety about their anxiety and their depression about being depressed—are particularly revealed and discussed.

As these specialized RET assessment and diagnostic procedures are instituted, specific treatment plans are made, normally in close collaboration with the clients, to work first on the most important and self-sabotaging emotional and behavioral symptoms that they present and later on related and possibly less important symptoms. RET practitioners, however, always try to maintain an exceptionally open-minded, skeptical, and experimental attitude toward the clients and their problems, so that what at first seem to be their crucial and most debilitating ideas, feelings, and actions may later be seen in a different light, and emphasis may be changed to working on other equally or more pernicious irrationalities that might not be evident during the clients' early sessions.

RET therapists, in general, spend little time gathering background information on their clients, although they may ask them to fill out forms designed to assess which irrational ideas they spontaneously endorse at the outset of therapy (see Figure 7.1).

Consultation Center

Institute for Advanced Study in Rational Psychotherapy

45 East 65th Street • New York, N. Y. 10021

Personality Data Form — Part 2

Instructions: Read each of the following items and circle after each one the word STRONGLY, MODERATELY, or WEAKLY to indicate how much you believe in the statement described in the item. Thus, if you strongly believe that it is awful to make a mistake when other people are watching, circle the word STRONGLY in item 1; and if you weakly believe that it is intolerable to be disapproved by others, circle the word WEAKLY in item 2. DO NOT SKIP ANY ITEMS. Be as honest as you can possibly be.

Acceptance

1. I believe that it is awful to make a mistake when other people are watching — STRONGLY MODERATELY WEAKLY.

2. I believe that it is intolerable to be disapproved of by others — STRONGLY MODERATELY WEAKLY.

3. I believe that it is awful for people to know certain undesirable things about one's family or one's background — STRONGLY MODERATELY WEAKLY.

4. I believe that it is shameful to be looked down upon by people for having less than they have — STRONGLY MODERATELY WEAKLY.

5. I believe that it is horrible to be the center of attention of others who may be highly critical — STRONGLY MODERATELY WEAKLY.

6. I believe it is terribly painful when one is criticized by a person one respects — STRONGLY MODERATELY WEAKLY.

7. I believe that it is awful to have people disapprove of the way one looks or dresses — STRONGLY MODERATELY WEAKLY.

8. I believe that it is very embarrassing if people discover what one really is like — STRONGLY MODERATELY WEAKLY.

9. I believe that it is awful to be alone — STRONGLY MODERATELY WEAKLY.

154

10. I believe that it is horrible if one does not have the love or approval of certain special people who are important to one — STRONGLY / MODERATELY / WEAKLY.

11. I believe that one must have others on whom one can always depend for help — STRONGLY / MODERATELY / WEAKLY.

Frustration

12. I believe that it is intolerable to have things go along slowly and not be settled quickly — STRONGLY / MODERATELY / WEAKLY.

13. I believe that it's too hard to get down to work at things it often would be better for one to do — STRONGLY / MODERATELY / WEAKLY.

14. I believe that it is terrible that life is so full of inconveniences and frustrations — STRONGLY / MODERATELY / WEAKLY.

15. I believe that people who keep one waiting frequently are pretty worthless and deserve to be boycotted — STRONGLY / MODERATELY / WEAKLY.

16. I believe that it is terrible if one lacks desirable traits that other people possess — STRONGLY / MODERATELY / WEAKLY.

17. I believe that it is intolerable when other people do not do one's bidding or give one what one wants — STRONGLY / MODERATELY / WEAKLY.

18. I believe that some people are unbearably stupid or nasty and that one must get them to change — STRONGLY / MODERATELY / WEAKLY.

19. I believe that it is too hard for one to accept serious responsibility — STRONGLY / MODERATELY / WEAKLY.

20. I believe that it is dreadful that one cannot get what one wants without making a real effort to get it — STRONGLY / MODERATELY / WEAKLY.

21. I believe that things are too rough in this world and that therefore it is legitimate for one to feel sorry for oneself — STRONGLY / MODERATELY / WEAKLY.

22. I believe that it is too hard to persist at many of the things one starts, especially when the going gets rough — STRONGLY / MODERATELY / WEAKLY.

23. I believe it is terrible that life is so unexciting and boring — STRONGLY / MODERATELY / WEAKLY.

24. I believe it is awful for one to have to discipline oneself — STRONGLY / MODERATELY / WEAKLY.

Figure 7.1

155

Injustice

25. I believe that people who do wrong things should suffer strong revenge for their acts STRONGLY MODERATELY WEAKLY.

26. I believe that wrong doers and immoral people should be severely condemned STRONGLY MODERATELY WEAKLY.

27. I believe that people who commit unjust acts are bastards and that they should be severely punished STRONGLY MODERATELY WEAKLY.

Achievement

28. I believe that it is horrible for one to perform poorly STRONGLY MODERATELY WEAKLY.

29. I believe that it is awful if one fails at important things STRONGLY MODERATELY WEAKLY.

30. I believe that it is terrible for one to make a mistake when one has to make important decisions STRONGLY MODERATELY WEAKLY.

31. I believe that it is terrifying for one to take risks or to try new things STRONGLY MODERATELY WEAKLY.

Worth

32. I believe that some of one's thoughts or actions are unforgivable STRONGLY MODERATELY WEAKLY.

33. I believe that if one keeps failing at things one is a pretty worthless person STRONGLY MODERATELY WEAKLY.

34. I believe that killing oneself is preferable to a miserable life of failure STRONGLY MODERATELY WEAKLY.

35. I believe that things are so ghastly that one cannot help feel like crying much of the time STRONGLY MODERATELY WEAKLY.

36. I believe that it is frightfully hard for one to stand up for oneself and not give in too easily to others STRONGLY MODERATELY WEAKLY.

37. I believe that when one has shown poor personality traits for a long time, it is hopeless for one to change STRONGLY MODERATELY WEAKLY.

38. I believe that if one does not usually see things clearly and act well on them, one is hopelessly stupid STRONGLY MODERATELY WEAKLY.

39. I believe that it is awful to have no good meaning or purpose in life STRONGLY MODERATELY WEAKLY.

156

Control

40. I believe that one cannot enjoy himself today because of his poor early life — STRONGLY MODERATELY WEAKLY.

41. I believe that if one kept failing at important things in the past, one must inevitably keep failing in the future — STRONGLY MODERATELY WEAKLY.

42. I believe that once one's parents train one to act and feel in certain ways, there is little one can do to act or feel better — STRONGLY MODERATELY WEAKLY.

43. I believe that strong emotions like anxiety and rage are caused by external conditions and events and that one has little or no control over them — STRONGLY MODERATELY WEAKLY.

Certainty

44. I believe it would be terrible if there were no higher being or purpose on which to rely — STRONGLY MODERATELY WEAKLY.

45. I believe that if one does not keep doing certain things over and over again something bad will happen if one stops — STRONGLY MODERATELY WEAKLY.

46. I believe that things must be in good order for one to be comfortable — STRONGLY MODERATELY WEAKLY.

Catastrophizing

47. I believe that it is awful if one's future is not guaranteed — STRONGLY MODERATELY WEAKLY.

48. I believe that it is frightening that there are no guarantees that accidents and serious illnesses will not occur — STRONGLY MODERATELY WEAKLY.

49. I believe that it is terrifying for one to go to new places or meet a new group of people — STRONGLY MODERATELY WEAKLY.

50. I believe that it is ghastly for one to be faced with the possibility of dying — STRONGLY MODERATELY WEAKLY.

Figure 7.1 (continued)

Rather, they are likely to ask clients for a description of their major problem(s). As clients describe their problems, RET therapists intervene fairly early to break these down into their ABC components. If clients begin by describing A (the Activating event), then the therapists ask for C (their emotional and or behavioral reactions). However, if clients begin by outlining C, therapists ask for a brief description of A.

In RET, A and C are normally assessed before B and are usually assessed in the order that clients report them. C refers to both emotional and behavioral consequences of the preferential or musturbatory evaluations made at B. Careful assessment of emotional C's is advocated in RET, since they serve as a major indicator of what type of evaluations are to be found at B. In this regard, it is important to reiterate that "appropriate" negative emotions are different from "inappropriate" negative emotions. Emotions such as sadness, regret, annoyance, and concern are termed "appropriate" in RET in that they are deemed to stem from rational, preferential evaluations at B and encourage people to attempt to change, for the better, obnoxious situations at A. The "inappropriate" versions of the above emotional states are depression, guilt, anger, and anxiety. These are deemed to stem from irrational, musturbatory evaluations at B and tend to interfere with people's constructive attempts to change undesirable situations.

When emotional C's are being assessed, it is important to realize three important points. First, clients do not necessarily use effective terminology in the same way RET therapists do. It is often helpful to inform them about the nature of the unique discriminations made between "appropriate" and "inappropriate" negative emotional states so that therapist and client can come to use shared emotional "language." Second, emotional C's are often "chained" together. For example, anger is frequently chained to anxiety in that one can experience anger to "cover up" feelings of inadequacy. And one can feel depressed after a threat to one's self-esteem emerges (Wessler, 1981). Finally, rational–emotive therapists had better realize that clients do not always want to change every "inappropriate" negative emotion as defined by RET theory; that is, they may not see a particular "inappropriate" emotion (e.g., anger) as being truly "inappropriate" self-defeating. Thus, a good deal of flexibility and clinical acumen is called for in the assessment of emotional C's to be targeted for change.

While C is assessed mainly by the client's verbal report, occasionally clients experience difficulty in accurately reporting their emotional and behavioral problems. When this occurs, RET therapists may use a number of methods to facilitate this part of the assessment process. Thus a variety of emotive (e.g., Gestalt two-chair dialogue, psychodrama), imagery, and other techniques (e.g., keeping an emotion/behavior diary) can be used in this respect (Dryden, 1984).

While we have chosen to highlight the assessment of emotional C's, similar points can be made about the assessment of behavioral C's. As noted earlier, withdrawal, procrastination, alcoholism, and substance abuse are generally regarded as dysfunctional behaviors and related to irrational, musturbatory evaluations at B (Ellis, 1982b).

When B is assessed, some rational–emotive therapists prefer to fully assess the client's inferences in search of the most relevant inference that is linked to the client's musturbatory evaluations, given that C is self-defeating. This is known as *inference chaining* (Moore, 1983). An example of this procedure is described below:

THERAPIST:	So what was your major feeling here?
CLIENT:	I guess I was angry.
THERAPIST:	Angry about what? (Here the therapist has obtained C and is probing for A)
CLIENT:	I was angry that he did not send me a birthday card. (Client provides inference about A)
THERAPIST:	And what was anger-provoking about that? (Probing to see whether this is the most relevant inference in the chain)
CLIENT:	Well . . . He promised me he would remember. (Inference 2)
THERAPIST:	And because he broke his promise? (Probing for relevance of inference 2)
CLIENT:	I felt that he didn't care enough about me. (Inference 3)
THERAPIST:	But let's assume that for a moment. What would be distressing about that? (Probing for relevance of inference 3)
CLIENT:	Well, he might leave me. (Inference 4)
THERAPIST:	And if he did? (Probing for relevance of inference 4)
CLIENT:	I'd be left alone. (Inference 5)
THERAPIST:	And if you were alone? (Probing for relevance of inference 5)
CLIENT:	I couldn't stand that. (Irrational Belief)
THERAPIST:	OK, so let's back up a minute. What would be most distressing for you, the birthday card incident, the broken promise, the fact that he doesn't care, being left by your husband, or being alone? (Therapist checks to see which inference is most relevant in the chain)
CLIENT:	Definitely being alone.

This example shows that not only are inferences chained together but, as mentioned earlier, emotions are too. Here anger was chained with anxiety about being alone. While this rational–emotive therapist chose then to Dispute the client's irrational Belief underlying her anxiety, he still has to deal with her anger-creating Belief. Other rational–emotive therapists may have chosen to take the first element in the chain (anger about the missing birthday card) and Disputed the irrational Belief related to anger. Skillful RET therapists do succeed in discovering the hidden issues underlying the "presenting problem" during the Disputing process. It is important for RET therapists to assess correctly *all* relevant issues related to a presenting problem. How they do this depends upon personal style and how particular clients react to different assessment procedures.

When irrational musturbatory Beliefs are assessed clients are helped to see the link between these irrational Beliefs and their "inappropriate" affective and behavioral Consequences at C. Some rational–emotive therapists like to give a short lecture at this point on the role of the "musts" in emotional disturbance and how they can be distinguished from "preferences." I (AE), for example, often use the following teaching dialogue:

ELLIS: Imagine that you prefer to have a minimum of $11 in your pocket at all times and you discover you only have $10. How will you feel?

CLIENT: Frustrated.

ELLIS: Right. Or you'd feel concerned or sad but you wouldn't kill yourself. Right?

CLIENT: Right.

ELLIS: OK. Now this time imagine that you absolutely *have to* have a minimum of $11 in your pocket at all times. You *must* have it; it is a *necessity*. You *must*, you *must*, you *must*, have a minimum of $11, and again you look and you find you only have $10. How will you feel?

CLIENT: Very anxious.

ELLIS: Right, or depressed. Right. Now remember it's the same $11 but a different Belief. OK, now this time you still have that same belief. You *have to* have a minimum of $11 at all times; you *must*. It's absolutely *essential*. But this time you look in your pocket and find that you've got $12. How will you feel?

CLIENT: Relieved, content.

ELLIS: Right. But with that same Belief—you *have to* have a minimum of $11 at all times—something will soon occur to you to scare you shitless. What do you think that would be?

CLIENT: What if I lose $2?

ELLIS: Right. What if I lose $2, what if I spend $2, what if I get
          robbed? That's right. Now the moral of this model—which
          applies to all humans, rich or poor, black or white, male or
          female, young or old, in the past or in the future, assuming
          that humans are still human—is: People make themselves
          miserable if they don't get what they think they *must* but they
          are also panicked when they do—because of the *must*. For
          even if they have what they think they *must*, they could al-
          ways lose it.

CLIENT: So I have no chance to be happy when I don't have what I
          think I *must*—and little chance of remaining unanxious when
          I do have it?

ELLIS: Right! Your *must*urbation will get you nowhere—except de-
          pressed or panicked!

An important goal of the assessment stage of RET is to help
clients distinguish between their primary problems (e.g., depression, anxiety, withdrawal, addiction) and their secondary problems, that is, their problems about their primary problems (e.g.,
depression about depression, anxiety about anxiety, shame about
withdrawal, and guilt about addiction). Rational–emotive therapists often assess secondary problems before primary problems
because these often require prior therapeutic attention—since, for
example, clients frequently find it difficult to focus on their original problem of anxiety when, for example, they are severely blaming themselves for being anxious. Secondary problems are assessed
in the same manner as primary problems.

When particular problems have been adequately assessed according to the ABC model and clients clearly see the link between
their irrational Beliefs and their dysfunctional emotional and behavioral Consequences, then therapists can proceed to the Disputing stage. The initial purpose of Disputing is to help clients gain
intellectual insight into the fact that there is no evidence in support
of the existence of their absolutistic demands, or the irrational
derivatives of these demands ("awfulizing," "I-can't-stand-it-itis,"
and "damnation"). There exists only evidence that if they stay with
their nonabsolutistic preferences and if these are not fulfilled they
will get unfortunate or "bad" results, while if they are fulfilled
they will get desirable or "good" results. Intellectual insight in
RET is defined as an acknowledgment that an irrational Belief
frequently leads to emotional disturbance and dysfunctional behavior and that a rational Belief almost always abets emotional
health. But when people see and hold rational Beliefs only weakly
and occasionally, they have intellectual insight that may not help

them change (Ellis, 1963, 1985b). So RET does not stop with intellectual insight but uses it as a springboard for the working-through phase of RET. In this phase clients are encouraged to use a large variety of cognitive, emotive, and behavioral techniques designed to help them achieve emotional insight. Emotional insight in RET is defined as a very strong and frequently held Belief that an irrational idea is dysfunctional and that a rational idea is helpful (Ellis, 1963). When a person has achieved emotional insight, he or she thinks-feels-behaves according to the rational Belief.

Two other points relevant to the assessment stage of RET bear mention. First, therapists had better be alert to problems in *both* areas, ego and discomfort disturbance (see Chapters 4 and 5). In particular, ego and discomfort disturbance often interact, and careful assessment is often required to disentangle one from the other. Second, RET practitioners pay particular attention to other ways that humans perpetuate their psychological problems and attempt to assess these carefully in therapy. Thus, humans often seek to defend themselves from threats to their "ego" and sense of comfort. Therapists are often aware that much dysfunctional behavior is defensive and help their clients to identify the irrational Beliefs that underlie such defensive dysfunctional behavior. In addition, psychological problems are sometimes perpetuated because the person defines their consequences as payoffs. These payoffs also require careful assessment if productive therapeutic strategies are to be implemented.

TREATMENT STRATEGIES IN RET

There are two forms of RET—preferential and general (Ellis, 1980). General RET is synonymous with cognitive behavior therapy (CBT), while preferential RET is unique in a number of important respects. The emphasis here will be on preferential RET (although it should be noted that RET therapist routinely use strategies derived from both forms of RET). The major goal of preferential RET is an ambitious one: to encourage clients to make a profound philosophic change in the two main areas of ego disturbance and discomfort disturbance. This involves helping clients, as far as is humanly possible, to give up their irrational musturbatory thinking processes and to replace them with rational nonabsolute thinking as discussed in Chapter 1.

In preferential RET, the major goals are to help clients pursue their long-range basic goals and purposes and to help them do so as effectively as possible by fully accepting themselves and tolerating unchangeable uncomfortable life conditions. Practitioners of preferential RET further strive to help clients obtain the skills that they can use to prevent the development of future disturbance. In encouraging clients to achieve and maintain this profound philosophic change, rational–emotive therapists implement the following strategies. They help their clients see that

1. Emotional and behavioral disturbances have cognitive antecedents, and these conditions normally take the form of absolutistic devout evaluations. RET practitioners train their clients to observe their own psychological disturbances and to trace these back to their ideological roots.
2. People have a distinct measure of self-determination and can thus *choose* to work at undisturbing themselves. Thus, clients are shown that they are not slaves to their biologically based irrational thinking processes.
3. People can implement their choices and maximize their freedom by actively working at changing their irrational musturbatory Beliefs. This is best achieved by employing cognitive, emotive, and behavioral methods—often in quite a forceful and vigorous manner (Ellis, 1979a).

With the majority of clients, from the first session onward RET therapists are likely to use strategies designed to effect profound philosophic change. The therapist begins therapy with the hypothesis that this particular client may be able to achieve such change and thus begins preferential RET, which he or she will abandon after collecting sufficient data to reject the initial hypothesis. We regularly implement this viewpoint, which is based on the notion that the client's response to therapy is the best indicator of his or her prognosis. It is not known what proportion of RET therapists share and regularly implement this position.

When it is clear that the client is not able to achieve philosophic change, whether on a particular issue or in general, the therapist often switches to general RET and uses methods to effect inferential and behaviorally based change. A good example of this change in strategy is one reported by a therapist of our acquaintance. He was working with a middle-aged married woman who reported feeling furious every time her aging father telephoned her and enquired "Noo, what's doing?" She inferred that this was a gross invasion of her privacy and absolutistically insisted that he had no right to do so. The therapist initially intervened with a preferential RET strategy by attempting to Dispute the client's dogmatic Belief and tried to help her see that there was no law in the universe that stated that he *must* not do such a thing. Meeting initial resistance, the therapist persisted with different variations of this theme, all to no avail. Changing tack, he began to implement a general RET strategy designed to help the client question her inference that her father was actually invading her privacy. Given her father's age, the therapist inquired, was it not more likely that his question represented his usual manner of beginning telephone conversations rather than an intense desire to pry into her affairs? This inquiry proved successful in that the client's rage subsided because she began to reinterpret her father's motives. Interestingly enough, although he returned to the specialized strategy later, the therapist never succeeded in helping his client to give up her irrational musturbatory Belief! However, some clients are more amenable to reevaluating their irrational musturbatory Beliefs *after* they have been helped to correct distorted inferences. We had better do research on this topic if we are to answer the question, "Which strategy is most appropriate for which clients at which stage in therapy?" Meanwhile, it is important to note that RET therapists, if they follow our lead, are unique in that they are more likely to challenge musturbatory cognitions and to dispute these self-defeating Beliefs on their clients much earlier in the therapeutic process than do other cognitive–behavioral therapists. Further differences between preferential RET and general RET (or cognitive–behavior therapy) will be discussed at the end of this chapter.

MAJOR TREATMENT TECHNIQUES IN RET

RET represents a major form of electicism known as "theoretically consistent eclecticism" (Dryden, 1987) in that techniques are liberally borrowed from other therapeutic systems but employed for purposes usually consistent with RET's underlying theory. In particular, RET therapists are mindful of the short-term and long-term effects of particular therapeutic techniques and will rarely employ a technique that has beneficial immediate but harmful long-range consequences. While rational–emotive therapists employ a large number of cognitive, emotive, and behavioral techniques, only the major ones will be discussed here. It should be noted at the outset that probably all the following techniques have cognitive, emotive, and behavioral elements to them and that "pure" techniques (e.g., purely cognitive) probably do not exist.

Techniques are grouped below to show which psychological process predominates.

Cognitive Techniques

Probably the most common technique employed by RET therapists with the majority of their clients is the *Disputing of irrational Beliefs*. There are three subcategories of Disputing (Phadke, 1982). *Detecting* consists of looking for irrational Beliefs—particularly "musts," "shoulds," "oughts," and "have to's"—that lead to self-defeating emotions and behaviors. *Debating* consists of the therapist asking a number of questions that are designed to help the client give up irrational Beliefs. Questions such as "Where is the evidence . . .?" "In what way does this Belief have truth or falseness?" and "What makes it so?" are frequently employed. The therapist proceeds with such questioning until the client acknowledges the falseness of his or her irrational Belief and, in addition, acknowledges the truth of its rational alternative. *Discriminating* involves the therapist helping the client to clearly distinguish between his or her nonabsolute values (his wants, preferences, likes, and desires) and his or her absolutistic values (his needs, demands, and imperatives). Rational–emotive therapists are often very creative in their use of Disputing sequences (e.g., Young, 1984a, 1984b, 1984c) and sometimes employ such methods in a highly dramatic fashion (Dryden, 1984). A formal version of Disputing that includes some of its main components is known as DIBS (Disputing irrational Beliefs). I (AE) have outlined its form thus:

QUESTION 1: What irrational Belief do I want to dispute and surrender?

ANSWER: I must be as effective and sexually fulfilled as most other women.

QUESTION 2: Can I rationally support this Belief?

ANSWER: _____

QUESTION 3: What evidence exists of the truth of this Belief?

ANSWER: _____

QUESTION 4: What evidence exists of the falseness of my Belief that I must be as orgasmic as other women are?

ANSWER: _____

QUESTION 5: What are the worst possible things that could actually happen to me if I never achieved the orgasm that I think I must achieve?

ANSWER: _____

QUESTION 6: What good things could happen or could I make happen if I never achieved the heights of orgasm that I think I must achieve?

ANSWER: _____

(Ellis, 1979b,pp.79–80)

DIBS is one example of *cognitive homework* that is frequently given to clients to do between sessions after the client has been trained to use them. Another example appears in Figure 7.2. The purpose of this form is to provide a clear framework for clients to do Disputing for themselves.

Clients can also use audiocassettes as an aid to the Disputing process. They can listen to audiotapes of therapy sessions and also Dispute their own irrational Beliefs on tape (*Disputing on tape*). Here they initiate and sustain a dialogue between the rational and irrational parts of themselves.

Clients who do not have the intellectual skills necessary to perform cognitive Disputing are usually helped to develop *rational self-statements* that they can memorize or write out on 3" × 5" cards and repeat at various times between sessions. An example developed by one of us (WD) with a client was "Just because my being overweight is bad doesn't mean that I am bad. My overeating makes me too heavy and is therefore wrong, but I can correct it and get better results."

Three cognitive methods that therapists often suggest to their clients to help them reinforce that new rational philosophy are (1) *bibliotherapy*, where clients are given self-help books and materials to read (e.g., Ellis & Becker, 1982; Ellis & Harper, 1975; Young, 1974b); (2) listening to *audiocassettes of RET lectures* on various themes (e.g., Ellis, 1971, 1972b, 1976); and (3) *using RET with others*, where clients use RET to help their friends and relatives with their problems. In doing so they gain practice at using rational arguments (Ellis & Abrahms, 1978).

A number of semantic methods are also employed in RET. *Defining* techniques are sometimes employed, the purpose of which is to help clients use language in a less self-defeating manner. Thus, instead of "I can't ..." clients are urged to use "I haven't yet. ...." *Referenting* techniques are also employed (Danysh, 1974). Here, clients are encouraged to list both the negative and positive referents of a particular concept such as "smoking." This method is employed to counteract clients' tendencies to focus on the positive aspects of a harmful habit and to neglect its negative aspects.

RET therapists also employ a number of imagery techniques. Thus, *rational–emotive imagery* (Ellis, 1979b; Maultsby & Ellis,

1974) is often employed. Clients thereby gain practice at changing their "inappropriate" negative emotions to "appropriate" ones (C) while maintaining a vivid image of the negative event at A. Here they are in fact learning to change their self-defeating emotions by changing their underlying Beliefs at B. *Time projection* imagery methods are also employed in RET (Lazarus, 1984). Thus, a client may say that a particular event would be "awful" if it occurred. Rather than directly challenging this irrational Belief at this stage, the therapist may temporarily go along with this but help the client to picture what life might be like at regular intervals after the "awful" event has occurred. In this way clients are indirectly helped to change their irrational Belief because they come to "see" that life goes on after the "awful" event, that they will usually recover from it, and that they can continue to pursue their original goals or develop new ones. Such realizations encourage the person to reevaluate his or her irrational Belief. Finally, a number of therapists have successfully employed RET in a *hypnosis* paradigm (e.g., Boutin & Tosi, 1983; Golden, 1983).

Emotive Techniques

Rational–emotive therapy has often been falsely criticized for neglecting emotive aspects of psychotherapy. However, this is far from the truth, and RET therapists frequently employ a number of emotive techniques. As has already been shown, RET therapists offer their clients the emotional attitude of *unconditional acceptance*. No matter how badly clients behave, their therapists strive to accept them as fallible humans but do not go along with their bad behavior. RET therapists use a variety of emotive techniques that are designed to help clients challenge their irrational Beliefs. First, a number of *humorous* methods are employed to encourage clients to think rationally by not taking themselves too seriously (Ellis, 1977a, 1977b). Second, RET therapists do not hesitate to model a rational philosophy through *self-disclosure*. They honestly admit that they have had similar problems and show that they overcame them by using RET. Thus I (WD) frequently tell clients that I used to feel ashamed of my stammer. I then relate how I accepted myself with my speech impediment and how I forced myself to tolerate the discomfort of speaking in public whenever the opportunity arose. Third, RET therapists frequently use a number of *stories, mottoes, parables, witticisms, poems,* and *aphorisms* as adjuncts to cognitive Disputing techniques (Wessler & Wessler, 1980). Fourth, we have written a number of rational hu-

RET SELF-HELP FORM

Institute for Rational-Emotive Therapy
45 East 65th Street, New York, N.Y. 10021
(212) 535-0822

(A) ACTIVATING EVENTS, thoughts, or feelings that happened just before I felt emotionally disturbed or acted self-defeatingly: _____

(C) CONSEQUENCE or CONDITION—disturbed feeling or self-defeating behavior—that I produced and would like to change: _____

(B) BELIEFS—Irrational BELIEFS (IBs) leading to my CONSEQUENCE (emotional disturbance or self-defeating behavior). Circle all that apply to these ACTIVATING EVENTS (A).	(D) DISPUTES for each circled IRRATIONAL BELIEF. Examples: *"Why MUST I do very well?"* *"Where is it written that I am a BAD PERSON?"* *"Where is the evidence that I MUST be approved or accepted?"*	(E) EFFECTIVE RATIONAL BELIEFS (RBs) to replace my IRRATIONAL BELIEFS (IBs). *Examples: "I'd PREFER to do very well but I don't HAVE TO." "I am a PERSON WHO acted badly, not a BAD PERSON." "There is no evidence that I HAVE TO be approved, though I would LIKE to be."*
1. I MUST do well or very well!	....	....

2. I am a BAD OR WORTHLESS PERSON
when I act weakly or stupidly.

3. I MUST be approved or accepted by people I
find important!

4. I NEED to be loved by someone who matters
to me a lot!

5. I am a BAD, UNLOVABLE PERSON if I get
rejected.

6. People MUST treat me fairly and give me
what I NEED!

Figure 7.2

169

7. People MUST live up to my expectations or it is TERRIBLE!

....

....

....

8. People who act immorally are undeserving, ROTTEN PEOPLE!

....

....

....

9. I CAN'T STAND really bad things or very difficult people!

....

....

....

10. My life MUST have few major hassles or troubles.

....

....

....

11. It's AWFUL or HORRIBLE when major things don't go my way!

12. I CAN'T STAND IT when life is really unfair!

13. I NEED a good deal of immediate gratification and HAVE to feel miserable when I don't get it!

Additional Irrational Beliefs:

(F) FEELINGS and BEHAVIORS I experienced after arriving at my EFFECTIVE RATIONAL BELIEFS: _____

I WILL WORK HARD TO REPEAT MY EFFECTIVE RATIONAL BELIEFS FORCEFULLY TO MYSELF ON MANY OCCASIONS SO THAT I CAN MAKE MYSELF LESS DISTURBED NOW AND ACT LESS SELF-DEFEATINGLY IN THE FUTURE.

Joyce Sichel, Ph.D. and Albert Ellis, Ph.D. Copyright © 1984 by the Institute for Rational–Emotive Therapy.

Figure 7.2 (continued)

morous songs that are designed to present rational philosophies in
an amusing and memorable format (Ellis, 1977a, 1977b, 1981). The
following is a rational humorous song written by one of us (WD) to
the tune of "God Save the Queen":

God save my precious spleen
Send me a life serene
God save my spleen!
Protect me from things odious
Give me a life melodious
And if things get too onerous
I'll whine, bawl, and scream!

In an important paper, I (AE) first advocated the use of force
and energy in the practice of psychotherapy (Ellis, 1979a). [See
Chapter 10.] RET is unique among the cognitive–behavioral therapies in emphasizing the employment of such interventions that
fully involve clients' emotions. Thus, RET therapists suggest that
clients can help themselves go from intellectual to emotional insight by *vigorously Disputing* their irrational Beliefs. Vigor is often
employed by clients in *rational role reversal*, where they forcefully
and dramatically adopt the role of their rational "self," whose goal
is to successfully Dispute self-defeating Beliefs as articulated by
their irrational "self." Force and energy also play a significant part
in RET's now famous *shame-attacking exercises* (Ellis, 1969; Ellis &
Becker, 1982). Here clients deliberately seek to act "shamefully" in
public in order to accept themselves and to tolerate the ensuing
discomfort. Since clients had better neither harm themselves nor
other people, minor infractions of social rules often serve as appropriate shame-attacking exercises (e.g., calling out the time in a
crowded department store, wearing bizarre clothes designed to
attract public attention, and going into a hardware store and asking if they sell tobacco). *Risk-taking exercises* come into the same
category. Here clients deliberately force themselves to take calculated risks in areas where they wish to make changes. While disputing relevant irrational Beliefs, I (AE) overcame my anxiety
about approaching women by deliberately forcing myself to speak
to 100 women in the Bronx Botanical Gardens. I (WD) pushed
myself to speak on national and local radio as part of a campaign
to overcome my public-speaking anxiety. Both of us took these
risks while showing ourselves that nothing "awful" would result
from such experiences. *Repeating rational self-statements in a passionate and forceful manner* is also often used in conjunction with
such exercises (Ellis, 1985b).

Behavioral Techniques

RET has advocated the use of behavioral techniques (particularly *homework assignments)* from its inception in 1955 because it is realized that cognitive change is very often facilitated by behavioral change (Emmelkamp, Kuipers, & Eggeraat, 1978). Since RET therapists are concerned to help clients raise their level of frustration tolerance, they encourage them to carry out homework assignments based on *in vivo desensitization* and *flooding* paradigms rather than those that are based on the gradual desensitization paradigm (Ellis, 1979b; Ellis & Abrahms, 1978; Ellis & Becker, 1982; Ellis & Grieger, 1977). However, pragmatic considerations do have to be considered, and some clients refuse to carry out such assignments. When this occurs, RET therapists would negotiate a compromise encouraging such clients to undertake tasks that are sufficiently challenging for them but that are not overwhelming, given their present status (Dryden, 1985).

Other behavioral methods frequently employed in RET include (1) *"stay in there" activities* (Grieger & Boyd, 1980), which present clients with opportunities to tolerate chronic discomfort while remaining in *"uncomfortable"* situations for a long period of time; (2) *antiprocrastination exercises*, where clients are encouraged to push themselves to start tasks sooner rather than later, while again tolerating the discomfort of breaking the "mañana" habit; (3) the use of *rewards and penalties,"* which are employed to encourage clients to undertake uncomfortable assignments in the pursuit of their long-range goals (Ellis, 1979b) [stiff penalties are found to be particularly helpful with chronically resistant clients (Ellis, 1985b); and (4) Kelly's *fixed role therapy,* sometimes employed in RET, where clients are encouraged to act "as if" they already think rationally, to enable them to get the experience that change is possible.

A number of other behavioral methods are employed in both preferential and general RET (e.g., various forms of *skills training methods).* When these are used in preferential RET, they are done to encourage philosophic change; whereas in general RET they are employed to teach clients skills that are absent from their repertory. When skill training is the goal in preferential RET, it is employed *along with* Disputing of irrational Beliefs and while some measure of philosophic change is being sought.

Techniques That Are Avoided in RET

By now it will be clear that RET is a multimodal form of therapy that advocates the employment of techniques in the cognitive, emotive, and behavioral modalities. However, because the choice of therapeutic techniques is inspired by RET theory, the following available therapeutic techniques are avoided or used sparingly in the practice of RET (Ellis, 1979b, 1983a, 1984).

- Techniques that help people become more dependent (e.g., undue therapist warmth as a strong reinforcement and the creation and analysis of a transference neurosis).
- Techniques that encourage people to become more gullible and suggestible (e.g., pollyannaish positive thinking).
- Techniques that are long-winded and inefficient (e.g., psychoanalytic methods in general and free association in particular; encouraging clients to give lengthy descriptions of Activating experiences at A).
- Methods that help people feel better in the short term rather than get better in the long term (Ellis, 1972a) (e.g., some experiential techniques like fully expressing one's feelings in a dramatic, cathartic, and abreactive manner, i.e., some Gestalt methods and primal techniques; the danger here is that such methods may encourage people to practice irrational philosophies underlying such emotions as anger).
- Techniques that distract clients from working on their irrational philosophies (e.g., relaxation methods, Yoga, and other cognitive distraction methods). These methods may be employed, however, *along with* cognitive Disputing designed to yield some philosophic change.
- Methods that may unwittingly reinforce clients' philosophy of low frustration tolerance (e.g., gradual desensitization).
- Techniques that include an antiscientific philosophy (e.g., faith healing and mysticism).
- Techniques that attempt to change Activating events (A) before or without showing clients how to change their irrational Beliefs (B) (e.g., some strategic family systems techniques).
- Techniques that have dubious validity (e.g., neurolinguistic programming).

Finally, to reiterate, RET therapists do not absolutistically avoid using the above methods. They may on certain occasions with certain clients utilize such techniques, particularly for pragmatic purposes. For example, if faith healing is the only method that will prevent some clients from harming themselves, then RET therapists might either employ it themselves or, more probably, refer such clients to a faith healer (Ellis, 1985b).

OVERCOMING OBSTACLES TO CLIENT PROGRESS

When RET is practiced efficiently and effectively and when clients understand and are prepared to continually implement its basic concepts, then it can achieve remarkable results. However, frequently (and perhaps more frequently than most therapists are prepared to admit!) various obstacles to client progress are encountered in the practice of RET (and indeed all other forms of therapy). Three major forms of obstacles are deemed to occur in RET: (1) "relationship" obstacles, (2) therapist obstacles, and (3) client obstacles (Ellis, 1985b). [See also Chapter 13.]

"Relationship" Obstacles to Client Progress

These can be first attributed to poor therapist–client matching. Such mismatching may occur for many reasons. Thus, clients "may have a therapist who, according to their idiosyncratic tastes or preferences, is too young or too old, too liberal or too conservative, too active or too passive" (Ellis, 1983e, p. 29). If these "relationship match" obstacles persist, then it is preferable for that client to be transferred to a therapist with more suitable traits. Other relationship obstacles may occur because the therapist and client may get on "too well" and get distracted from the more mundane tasks of therapy. In such cases, the paradox is that if the client improves, the "life" of the satisfactory relationship is threatened. As a result, collusion may occur between therapist and client to avoid making therapy as effective an endeavor as it might otherwise be. This problem can be largely overcome if the therapist helps first himself or herself and then the client to overcome the philosophy of low frustration tolerance implicit in this collusive short-range hedonism.

Therapist Obstacles to Client Progress

There are two major types of therapist obstacles: skill-oriented obstacles and disturbance-oriented obstacles. When obstacles to client progress can be mainly attributed to therapist skill deficits, these may appear in a variety of forms, but most commonly therapists may impede client progress by

1. Improperly inducting clients into therapy and failing to correct unrealistic expectations such as "my therapist will solve my problems for me."

2. Incorrectly assessing clients' problems and thus working on "problems" that clients do not have.
3. Failing to show clients that their problems have ideological roots and that C is largely (but not exclusively) determined by B and not by A. Inexpert therapists often fail to persist with this strategy or persist with an ineffective strategy.
4. Failing to show clients that the ideological roots of their problems are most frequently expressed in the form of devout, absolutistic "musts" or one of the three main derivatives of "musturbation." Instead, inexpert RET therapists frequently dwell too long on their clients' antiempirical or inferentially distorted thinking.
5. Assuming that clients will automatically change their absolute thinking once they have identified it. Inexpert RET therapists either fail to Dispute such thinking at all or use Disputing methods sparingly and/or with insufficient vigor. In addition, inexpert therapists routinely fail to (1) give their clients homework assignments, which provide them with opportunities to practice Disputing their irrational Beliefs, (2) check on their client's progress on these assignments, and (3) help their clients to identify and change their philosophic obstacles to continually working at self-change.
6. Failing to realize that clients often have problems about their problems and thus working only on a primary problem when the client is preoccupied with a secondary problem.
7. Frequently switching from ego to discomfort disturbance issues within a given session so that clients get confused and thus distracted from working on either issue.
8. Working at a pace and a level inappropriate to the learning abilities of clients so that these clients are insufficiently involved in the therapeutic process due to confusion or boredom.

For these reasons it is highly desirable for RET therapists to strive to continually improve their skills by involving themselves in ongoing supervision and training activities (Dryden, 1983; Wessler & Ellis, 1980, 1983).

Client progress can also be hindered because therapists may bring their own disturbance to the therapeutic process [see Chapter 14].

Client Obstacles to Client Progress

In order to really benefit from RET, clients had better achieve three forms of insight, namely: (1) Psychological disturbance is mainly determined by the absolutistic Beliefs that they hold about themselves, others, and the world; (2) even when people acquired and created their irrational Beliefs in their early lives, they perpetuate their disturbance by reindoctrinating themselves in the present with these Beliefs; (3) only if they constantly work and practice in the present and future to think, feel, and act against these irrational Beliefs are clients likely to surrender their irrationalities and make themselves significantly less disturbed.

As shown in a study by one of us (Ellis, 1983a) on treatment failures in RET (see Chapter 12), clients' own extreme level of disturbance is a significant obstacle to their own progress. A full discussion of what "special" therapeutic methods and techniques to employ with such clients is presented in chapter 13).

Termination preferably takes place in RET when clients have made some significant progress and when they have become proficient in RET's self-change technique. Thus, terminating clients should preferably be able to (1) acknowledge that they experience "inappropriate" negative emotions and act dysfunctionally when they do, (2) detect the irrational Beliefs that underpin these experiences, (3) discriminate their irrational Beliefs from their rational alternatives, (4) challenge these irrational Beliefs, and (5) counteract them by using cognitive, emotive, and behavioral self-change methods. In addition, it is often helpful for therapists to arrange for their clients to attend a series of follow-up sessions after termination to monitor their progress and deal with any remaining obstacles to sustained improvement.

PREFERENTIAL RET VERSUS GENERAL RET (CBT)

We have already alluded to the differences between preferential RET and general RET (which, I [AE] have argued, is synonymous with broad-based cognitive–behavior therapy [CBT] [Ellis, 1980]). Let us close this chapter by noting these differences in greater detail. Preferential RET

1. Has a distinct philosophic emphasis that is one of its central features and that other forms of CBT appear to omit. Thus, it stresses that humans appraise themselves, others, and the world in terms of (1) rational, preferential, flexible, and tolerant philosophies and in terms of (2) irrational, musturbatory, rigid, intolerant, and absolutistic philosophies.

2. Has an existential–humanistic outlook that is intrinsic to it and that is omitted by most other CBT approaches. Thus, it sees

people "as holistic, goal-directed individuals who have importance in the world just because they are human and alive; it unconditionally accepts them with their limitations, and it particularly focuses upon their experiences and values, including their self-actualizing potentialities" (Ellis, 1980, p. 327). It also shares the views of ethical humanism by encouraging people to emphasize human interest (self and social) over the interests of deities, material objects, and lower animals.

3. Favors striving for pervasive and long-lasting (philosophically based) rather than symptomatic change.

4. Attempts to help humans eliminate all self-ratings and views self-esteem as a self-defeating concept that encourages them to make conditional evaluations of self. Instead, it teaches people *un*conditional self-acceptance (Ellis, 1972a).

5. Considers psychological disturbance to reflect an attitude to taking life "too" seriously and thus advocates the appropriate use of various humorous therapeutic methods (Ellis, 1977a, 1977b, 1981).

6. Stresses the use of antimusturbatory rather than antiempirical Disputing methods. Since it considers that inferential distortions often stem from dogmatic "musts," "shoulds," etc., preferential RET favors going to the philosophic core of emotional disturbance and Disputing the irrational Beliefs at this core rather than merely Disputing antiempirical inferences, which are more peripheral. Also, preferential RET favors the use of forceful logico-empirical Disputing of irrational Beliefs whenever possible rather than the employment of rationally oriented, coping self-statements. When feasible, preferential RET teaches clients how to become their own scientists instead of parroting therapist-inculcated rational Beliefs.

7. Employs but only mildly encourages the use of palliative cognitive methods that serve to distract people from their disturbed philosophies (e.g., relaxation methods). Preferential RET holds that such techqniques may help clients better in the short term but do not encourage them to identify challenge and change in the long term the devout philosophies that underpin their psychological problems. Indeed, these palliative methods may make it harder for people to engage in philosophic Disputing since they may be less likely to do this when they are calm and relaxed than when they are motivated by their emotional distress. For these reasons, preferential RET also employs problem-solving and skill training methods, along with, but not instead of, teaching people to work at understanding and changing their irrational Beliefs.

8. Gives a more central explanatory role to the concept of dis-

comfort anxiety in psychological distiurbance than do other cognitive–behavioral therapies. Discomfort anxiety is defined as "emotional hypertension that arises when people feel (1) that their life or comfort is threatened, (2) that they *must* not feel uncomfortable and *have to* feel at ease, and (3) that it is awful or catastrophic (rather than merely inconvenient or disadvantageous) when they don't get what they supposedly must" (Ellis, 1980, p. 331). While other cognitive–behvioral therapies recognize specific instances of discomfort anxieties (e.g., "fear of fear"), they tend not to regard discomfort disturbance to be as centrally implicated in psychological problems as does preferential RET.

9. Emphasizes, more than other approaches to CBT, that humans frequently make themselves disturbed about their original disturbances. Thus, in preferential RET therapists actively look for secondary and tertiary symptoms of disturbances and encourage clients to work on overcoming these before addressing themselves to the primary disturbance.

10. Has clear-cut theories of disturbance and its treatment but is eclectic or multimodal in its techniques. However, it favors some techniques (e.g., active Disputing) over others (e.g., cognitive distraction) and strives for profound or elegant philosophic change where feasible.

11. Discriminates between "appropriate" and "inappropriate" negative emotions. Preferential RET considers such negative emotions as sadness, annoyance, concern, regret, and disappointment as "appropriate" affective responses to thwarted desires based on a nondevout philosophy of desire and views them as healthy when they do not needlessly interfere with people's goals and purposes. However, it sees depression, anger, anxiety, guilt, shame/ embarrassment, self-pity, and feelings of inadequacy usually as "inappropriate" emotions based on absolutistic demands about thwarted desires. Preferential RET considers these latter feelings as symptoms of disturbance because they very frequently (but not always) sabotage people from constructively pursuing their goals and purposes. Other CBT approaches do not make such fine discriminations between "appropriate" and "inappropriate" negative emotions.

12. Advocates therapists giving unconditional acceptance rather than giving warmth or approval to clients. Other cognitive– behavioral therapies tend not to make this distinction. Preferential RET holds that therapist warmth and approval have their distinct dangers in that they may unwittingly encourage clients to strengthen their dire needs for love and approval. When RET therapists unconditionally accept their clients, they also serve as good

role models, in that they also help clients to unconditionally accept themselves.

13. Stresses the importance of the use of vigor and force in
counteracting irrational philosophies and behaviors (Dryden, 1984;
Ellis, 1979a). Preferential RET is alone among the cognitive–
behavioral therapies in stressing that humans are, for the most
part, biologically predisposed to originate and perpetuate their
disturbances and often, thus, experience great difficulty in changing the ideological roots of these problems. Since it holds this
view, it urges both therapists and clients to use considerable force
and vigor in interrupting clients' irrationalities.

14. Is more selective than most other cognitive–behavioral therapies in choosing behavioral change methods. Thus, it favors the
use of penalization in encouraging resistant clients to change. Often these clients will not change to obtain positive reinforcements
but may be encouraged to change to avoid stiff penalties. Furthermore, preferential RET has reservations concerning the use of social reinforcement in therapy. It considers that humans are too
reinforceable and that they often do the right thing for the wrong
reason. Thus, they may change to please their socially reinforcing
therapist, but in doing so they have not been encouraged to think
and act for their own sake. Preferential RET therapists aim to help
clients become maximally noncomformist, nondependent, and individualistic and would thus use social reinforcement techniques
sparingly. Finally, preferential RET favors the use of in vivo desensitization and flooding methods rather than the use of gradual
desensitization techniques since it argues that the former procedures best help clients to raise their level of frustration tolerance
(Ellis, 1983c).

While RET therapist *prefer* to use preferential RET wherever
feasible, they do not dogmatically insist that it be employed.
When, on pragmatic grounds, they employ general RET, their therapeutic practice is frequently indistinguishable from that of other
cognitive–behavioral therapists.

REFERENCES

Beutler, L. E. (1983). *Eclectic psychotherapy: A systematic approach.* New
    York: Pergamon.
Boutin, G. E., & Tosi, D. J. (1983). Modification of irrational ideas and
    test anxiety through rational stage direct hypnotherapy (RSDH). *Jour-
    nal of Clinical Psychology, 39,* 382–391.

Danysh, J. (1974). *Stop without quitting*. San Francisco: International Society for General Semantics.

Dryden, W. (1983). Audiotape supervision by mail: A rational–emotive approach. *British Journal of Cognitive Psychotherapy, 1*(1), 57–64.

Dryden, W. (1984). Rational–emotive therapy. In W. Dryden (Ed.), *Individual therapy in Britain* (pp. 235–263). London: Harper & Row.

Dryden, W. (1985). Challenging but not overwhelming: A compromise in negotiating homework assignments. *British Journal of Cognitive Psychotherapy, 3*(1), 77–80.

Dryden, W. (1987). Theoretically consistent eclecticism: Humanizing a computer "addict". In J.C. Norcross (Ed.), *Casebook of eclectic psychotherapy*. New York: Brunner/Mazel.

Duckro, P., Beal, D., & George, C. (1979). Research on the effects of disconfirmed client role expectations in psychotherapy: A critical review. *Psychological Bulletin, 86*, 260–275.

Ellis, A. (1963). Toward a more precise definition of "emotional" and "intellectual" insight. *Psychological Reports, 13*, 125–126.

Ellis, A. (1969). A weekend of rational encounter. *Rational Living, 4*(2), 1–8.

Ellis, A. (1972a). Helping people get better: Rather than merely feel better. *Rational Living, 7*(2), 2–9.

Ellis, A. (1972b). *Psychotherapy and the value of a human being*. New York: Institute for Rational–Emotive Therapy.

Ellis, A. (1973). *Humanistic psychotherapy: The rational–emotive approach*. New York: McGraw-Hill.

Ellis, A. (Speaker). (1976). *Conquering low frustration tolerance* [Cassette recording]. New York: Institute for Rational–Emotive Therapy.

Ellis, A. (1977a). Fun as psychotherapy. *Rational Living, 12*(1), 2–6.

Ellis, A. (Speaker). (1977b). *A garland of rational humorous songs*. [Cassette recording]. New York: Institute for Rational–Emotive Therapy.

Ellis, A. (1977c). Intimacy in psychotherapy. *Rational Living, 12*(2), 13–19.

Ellis, A. (1978). Personality characteristics of rational–emotive therapists and other kinds of therapists. *Psychotherapy: Theory, Research and Practice, 14*, 329–332.

Ellis, A. (1979a). The issue of force and energy in behavioral change. *Journal of Contemporary Psychotherapy, 10*(2), 83–97.

Ellis, A. (1979b). The practice of rational–emotive therapy. In A. Ellis & J. M. Whiteley (Eds.), *Theoretical and empirical foundations of rational–emotive therapy* (pp. 61–100). Monterey, CA: Brooks/Cole.

Ellis, A. (1980). Rational–emotive therapy and cognitive behavior therapy: Similarities and differences. *Cognitive Therapy and Research, 4*, 325–340.

Ellis, A. (1981). The use of rational humorous songs in psychotherapy. *Voices, 16*(4), 29–36.

Ellis, A. (1982a). Intimacy in rational–emotive therapy. In M. Fisher & G. Stricker (Eds.), *Intimacy* (pp. 203–217). New York: Plenum.

Ellis, A. (1982b). The treatment of alcohol and drug abuse: A rational–emotive approach. *Rational Living, 17*(20), 15–24.

Ellis, A. (1983a). Failures in rational–emotive therapy. In E. B. Foa & P. M.

G. Emelkamp (Eds.), *Failures in behavior therapy* (pp. 159–171). New York: Wiley.

Ellis, A. (1983b). How to deal with your most difficult client: You. *Journal of Rational–Emotive Therapy, 1*(1), 3–8.

Ellis, A. (1983c). The philosophic implications and dangers of some popular behavior therapy techniques. In M. Rosenbaum, C. M. Franks, & Y. Jaffe (Eds.), *Perspectives in behavior therapy in the eighties* (pp. 138–151). New York: Springer Publishing Co.

Ellis, A. (1983e). Rational-emotive therapy (RET) approaches to overcoming resistance, I: Common forms of resistance. *British Journal of Cognitive Psychotherapy, 1*(1), 28–38.

Ellis, A. (1984). Rational–emotive therapy. In R. J. Corsini (Ed.), *Current psychotherapies* (3rd ed.) (pp. 196–238). Itasca, IL: Peacock.

Ellis, A. (1985a). Dilemmas in giving warmth or love to clients: An interview with Windy Dryden. In W. Dryden (Ed.), *Therapist's dilemmas* (pp. 5–16). London: Harper & Row.

Ellis, A. (1985b). Expanding the ABCs of rational–emotive therapy. In M. Mahoney & A. Freeman (Eds.), *Cognition and psychotherapy* (pp. 313–323). New York: Plenum.

Ellis, A., & Abrahms, E. (1978). *Brief psychotherapy in medical and health practice.* New York: Springer Publishing Co.

Ellis, A., & Becker, I. (1982). *A guide to personal happiness.* North Hollywood, CA: Wilshire.

Ellis, A., & Grieger, R. (Eds.). (1977). *Handbook of rational–emotive therapy* vol. 1). New York: Springer Publishing Co.

Ellis, A., & Harper, R. A. (1975). *A new guide to rational living.* North Hollywood, CA: Wilshire.

Emmelkamp, P. M. G., Kuipers, A. C. M., & Eggeraat, J. B. (1978). Cognitive modification versus prolonged exposure in vivo: A comparison with agoraphobics as subjects. *Behaviour Research and Therapy, 16,* 33–41.

Eschenroeder, C. (1979). Different therapeutic styles in rational–emotive therapy. *Rational Living, 14*(1), 3–7.

Garcia, E. J. (1977). Working on the E in RET. In J. L. Wolfe & E. Brand (Eds.), *Twenty years of rational therapy* (pp. 72–87). New York: Institute for Rational–Emotive Therapy.

Golden, W. L. (1983). Rational–emotive hypnotherapy. *British Journal of Cognitive Psychotherapy, 1*(2), 47–56.

Grieger, R., & Boyd, J. (1980). *Rational–emotive therapy: A skills-based approach.* New York: Van Nostrand Reinhold.

Kendall, P., & Hollon, S. (Eds.). (1980). *Assessment strategies for cognitive–behavioral interventions.* New York: Academic Press.

Lazarus, A. A. (1981). *The practice of multimodal therapy.* New York: McGraw-Hill.

Lazarus, A. A. (1984). *In the mind's eye.* New York: Guilford.

Macaskill, N. D., & Macaskill, A. (1983). Preparing patients for psychotherapy. *British Journal of Clinical and Social Psychiatry, 2,* 80–84.

Maultsby, M. C., Jr., & Ellis, A. (1974). *Techniques for using rational–emotive imagery.* New York: Institute for Rational–Emotive Therapy.

Moore, R. H. (1983). Inference as "A" in RET. *British Journal of Cognitive Psychotherapy, 1*(2), 17–23.

Phadke, K. M. (1982). Some innovations in RET theory and practice. *Rational Living, 17*(2), 25–30.

Rogers, C. R. (1957). The necessary and sufficient conditions of therapeutic personality change. *Journal of Consulting Psychology, 21*, 95–103.

Wessler, R. A. (1981). So you are angry: Now what's your problem? *Rational Living, 16*(1), 29–31.

Wessler, R. A., & Wessler, R. L. (1980). *The principles and practice of rational–emotive therapy.* San Francisco: Jossey-Bass.

Wessler, R. L., & Ellis, A. (1980). Supervision in rational–emotive therapy. In A. K. Hess (Ed.), *Psychotherapy supervision* (pp. 181–191). New York: Wiley.

Wessler, R. L., & Ellis, A. (1983). Supervision in counseling: Rational–emotive therapy. *Counseling Psychologist, 11*, 43–49.

Young, H. S. (1974a). A framework for working with adolescents. *Rational Living, 9*(1), 3–7.

Young, H. S. (1974b). *A rational counseling primer.* New York: Institute for Rational–Emotive Therapy.

Young, H. S. (1977). Counseling strategies with working class adolescents. In J. L. Wolfe & E. Brand (Eds.), *Twenty years of rational therapy* (pp. 187–202). New York: Institute for Rational–Emotive Therapy.

Young, H. S. (1984a). Practising RET with Bible-Belt Christians. *British Journal of Cognitive Psychotherapy, 2*(2), 60–76.

Young, H. S. (1984b). Practising RET with lower-class clients. *British Journal of Cognitive Psychotherapy, 2*(2), 33–59.

Young, H. S. (1984c). Teaching rational self-value concepts to tough customers. *British Journal of Cognitive Psychotherapy, 2*(2), 77–97.

Intimacy in Rational–Emotive Therapy 8

INTRODUCTION

People keep asking Ellis about his views on intimacy in psychotherapy for two main reasons. First, Ellis has been known since the 1940s for his liberal sex views, and therefore some people wrongly assume that he favors sex between therapists and their clients, even though he has often written and spoken against this kind of intimacy.

Second, because RET is a highly direct and didactic mode of therapy and does not usually coddle clients, and because it is so different from Freudian, Sullivanian, Rogerian, and other relationship-obsessed forms of treatment, people are curious about its specific "transference" aspects. Ellis was frequently asked about RET's views on intimacy and had not often outlined them in detail; therefore, he welcomed the chance to do so when Martin Fisher and George Stricker asked him to write a chapter for their book, Intimacy. *The chapter, reprinted here, includes more material on the RET view of intimacy than any other paper that Ellis has written.*

Reprinted from M. Fisher and G. Stricker (Eds.) *Intimacy*, 1982, New York: Plenum.

Intimacy has a special place in the theory and practice of rational–emotive therapy (RET), and I shall try to outline in this chapter how it fits—and does not fit—into the therapeutic process, and how RET tries to be of maximum help to those clients who wish to achieve a greater degree of intimacy in their own lives.

DEFINITION OF INTIMACY

According to the dictionary, intimacy consists of several things: (1) a relationship between two (or more) individuals that is most private or personal; (2) a very friendly, familiar, or close relationship; and (3) a sexual or erotic relationship. These definitions are good enough in general, but rational–emotive therapy more specifically distinguishes between healthy and unhealthy intimacy; and, as will be shown below in more detail, it particularly looks upon love, friendship, and sexuality as healthy or self-helping when they are based on strong desires, preferences, or wishes, and as (usually) unhealthy or self-defeating when they are based on absolutistic needs, demands, or commands.

RET, moreover, does not sacredize anything—including intimacy and love. Some psychotherapists—such as deForest (1954), Ferenczi (1952–1955), List (1961), and Suttie (1948)—virtually deify intimacy and hold that people are warped and disturbed unless they receive a great deal of warmth and approval during their early childhood and continue to achieve an intense degree of intimacy with significant others during their adult years. These "authorities" fail to note that although human attachment is usually one of the most enjoyable and absorbing pursuits, it is hardly the be-all and end-all of existence; and they ignore the fairly obvious fact that literally millions of people live most of their lives in a distinctly nonintimate and nonloving manner, and yet some of them are extremely happy and productive.

RET, therefore, looks upon intimacy as a choice rather than as a necessity, sees its disadvantages as well as advantages, does not try to cram it down the gullets of all individuals, sees its limitations as a part of the therapeutic process, clearly distinguishes between its healthy and its unhealthy aspects, and tries to develop effective techniques of helping those who want to achieve it to do so in a relatively brief period of time and in a manner that is likely to produce lasting results.

INTIMACY BETWEEN THERAPISTS AND CLIENTS

Assuming that human intimacy can be healthy and good and that it can add considerably to an enjoyable existence, is it appropriate or beneficial when it occurs, in a fairly strong manner, between therapists and their clients? Although I have always been a rather strong proponent of sexual liberalism, and although I have written some of the most influential books that have helped bring about the revolution in sex attitudes that has taken place during the past three decades, I have always opposed sexual intimacy in the course of psychotherapy. Thus, I presented a paper on erotic feelings in the therapy relationship at the American Psychological Association annual convention in Philadelphia in 1963, in which I showed that sex relations between therapists and clients practically never work out well and are irrational and iatrogenic (Ellis, 1963). Some of the main points that I made at that time, and still hold to, include the following. (1) Clients tend to get sidetracked from their therapeutic goals when they overfocus on having sex with their therapist. (2) Therapists lose objectivity and effectiveness when they concentrate on their clients' sexual attractiveness rather than on helping them think, emote, and act more healthfully. (3) Clients who have sex with therapists almost always crave for an involved love relationship instead of a more limited sex affair and tend to become exceptionally disappointed, and often disturbed, when sex with their therapist does not lead to the emotional involvement they really crave. (4) Therapists are both in legal and professional jeopardy when they become sexually intimate with their clients, and this jeopardy will tend to detract them from full-fledged therapeutic interests. (5) From a rational-emotive standpoint, therapists who have sex–love relationships with their clients, instead of helping these clients to combat their irrational ideas (that they absolutely need love and that it is awful and horrible when the world doesn't immediately give them exactly what they want), actually help these clients confirm rather than surrender these self-sabotaging beliefs. (6) By giving in to their own short-range hedonism and low frustration tolerance, therapists act as poor models for their clients and do not help these clients to give up their own demands for easy and immediate gratification.

For these and other reasons, RET opposes sexual intimacy between therapists and clients, though it recognizes that occasionally more good than harm may come of such contacts (Shepard, 1972). Since sexual affairs seem to be relatively rare in the course of therapy but other kinds of intimacy between therapists and clients are much more common, the question arises: What is the RET attitude toward nonsexual closeness? Does this kind of intimacy provide the excellent results that many of its proponents claim? Or does it, somewhat like sexual intimacy, generally lead to more harm than good?

This is not an easy question to answer, and perhaps has no general answer that would apply to all therapeutic situations. Certainly there is considerable evidence, at least of an anecdotal nature, that closeness between some therapists and some of their clients has seemingly led to favorable therapeutic outcomes. Some of the advantages claimed for this kind of closeness include the following. (1) If therapists maintain close, caring, superempathic relationships with their clients, they may help motivate them to continue in therapy and to work at helping themselves. (2) They may, by their example of accepting their clients, and even liking them despite their poor and self-defeating behavior, help them to unconditionally accept themselves. (3) Since clients' main problems often consist of relating poorly to people, therapists may train them, in the course of intimate relationships, to relate adequately to the therapists—and, presumably, to others as well. (4) Therapists can use their relationships with clients as reinforcers; and by first doing things for their therapist's approval, clients may later learn to enjoy doing these things in their own right and to condition themselves to do them without the need for approbation. (5) By being warmly on their clients' side, therapists may help them solve some of the practical problems of their existence, and thereby give them problem-solving techniques that they can subsequently take over on their own. (6) By letting clients hook into their own healthy energies, determination, stability, and independence, therapists may serve as good models and encourage their clients to take on such traits themselves. (7) Because their intimacy with their therapists gives them real pleasure, clients may look for similar satisfactions elsewhere and lead a happier life.

All these advantages of relating closely or warmly to clients are not to be put down; and the literature is replete with hundreds of examples of clients using therapeutic closeness to their own advantage and thereby ultimately being able to dispense with it and lead independent and more self-sufficient existences (Rogers, 1961; Whitaker & Malone, 1953). But there is, alas, another side to this coin; and this other side seems to show that, at least with many clients, distinct disadvantages may follow from their intimacy with their therapists. Some of these are as follows.

1. Therapists may reinforce clients' dire needs for love and approval, which frequently are the central core of their disturbance (Bard, 1980; Ellis, 1957a, 1962, 1971, 1973a, Grieger & Boyd, 1980; Hauck, 1973; Walen, DiGiuseppe, & Wessler, 1980; Wessler & Wessler, 1980). Almost all seriously disturbed individuals tend to be perennial babies, who are theoretically able to be self-sufficient but who stubbornly insist—nay, absolutely command—that their worth to themselves or their happy existence on this earth utterly depends on some significant person's approving or loving them. By getting really intimate with clients, and even by giving them what may be considered full acceptance without particular warmth (but what they often *interpret* as the therapist's truly caring for them), therapists frequently help reinforce clients' conviction that they *must* have approval and that they *absolutely cannot* live happily without it. Many therapists who variously call themselves psychoanalytic, existential, Rogerian, or humanistic, have made this error and have helped vast numbers of clients to become more dependent and more disturbed. Even in the course of highly rational and didactic therapy, such as RET, or during classical behavior therapy, therapists run the risk of their clients' concluding that they are in therapy to *be* helped rather than to *help themselves;* and they consequently allow too much dependency to develop. In less didactic and more relationship-oriented therapies, this risk becomes immensely greater.

2. As I noted a quarter of a century ago (Ellis, 1957a, 1957b), a second major irrational idea that humans are exceptionally prone to believe, and that lies at the very core of their disturbance, is that the conditions of their lives absolutely *should not, must not* be as difficult as they are, and that things *must* be made easier and more enjoyable, or else life is awful, terrible, and horrible, and existence hardly worth continuing. They have, in other words, abysmally low frustration tolerance (LFT) or discomfort anxiety (Ellis, 1979), the essence of which is their strong tendency, probably innate as well as acquired, to whine and scream for immediately available, easier satisfactions. What we call emotional disturbance is largely self-indulgence, lack of discipline, and childish demandingness: that is, exaggerating the significance of the hassles that virtually all of us experience and whiningly insisting that they must not continue. People with LFT almost always try to seek indulgent help from others instead of coping with life's difficulties themselves. Any mode of therapy that does not specifically persuade them to stop their puerile whining and to accept responsibility for their own unhappiness tends to confirm their belief that others *must* help them. Close-relationship therapy is fre-

quently the worst offender in this respect and thereby contributes to doing considerable harm.

3. The Freudians have emphasized the dangers of countertransference for many years (Freud, 1965; Wolman, 1959); and even though they frequently overstate these hazards, they sometimes make sense. For practically all humans are born and reared with a strong tendency to see things from their own biased frames of reference and to project onto others some of their own bigotries and disturbances; and therapists are hardly the exception to this rule! In virtually all relationships, moreover, we tend to like or to dislike others intensely and to see them as acting "well" or "badly" in the light of our prejudiced likes and dislikes—as literally hundreds of experiments in the field of social psychology and personal attraction show (Baron & Byrne, 1977; Freedman, Carlsmith, & Sears, 1978). The closer our relationship with others, moreover, the more prejudiced our view of their behavior tends to be. Since effective therapy is somewhat dependent on reality testing and on therapists' ability to see their clients objectively and to help them achieve what *they* really want (and not what their associates or the therapist thinks they *should* want), intimacy in therapy tends to breed exaggerated countertransference and consequent bias, and often seriously interferes with healthy therapeutic goals.

4. What I have just said would appear an especial danger for highly existential, encounter types of therapy. For if you, as a therapist, really have ideal existential encounters with your clients and use these encounters to have the kind of intimacy *you* desire and to help yourself with *your* problems as much as you try to help them with *theirs*, as therapists such as Mullan and Sanguiliano (1960) seem to advise, it seems to me unethical if you charge any fees for your service and inaccurate if you call what you are having a truly therapeutic relationship. In therapy, the interests of the client clearly had better come first and those of the therapist a fairly poor second. And in a truly warm, utterly authentic and open existential encounter, this would not be true; and poor or low-level therapy, at least for the clients, would probably develop in many instances.

5. The establishment of very close and warm relationships between therapists and their clients often seems to include an essentially false and hypocritical element. For paid friendship, as Schofield (1964) has aptly termed psychotherapy, is almost necessarily limited and temporary; and real friendship is not. Thus, if I know you as a friend or lover and decide to help you with some of your emotional problems, I not only will not charge you for my

services but will devote a good deal of time to helping you: I will speak to you whenever you are sorely troubled; I will lend you money or do other practical favors for you; and I will continue to see you indefinitely as a friend after you have conquered your trouble and you no longer desire my special therapeutic help. As a therapist, however, I will hardly treat you in this unrestricted or unlimited manner; and if I pretend that you really are my friend and then refuse to do some of these friendly things for you, you will ultimately see that my "intimate" relation with you is largely a pretense and may well become disillusioned and bitter about it.

6. In the long run, an intimate relationship between client and therapist may well frustrate clients more than the lack of such a relationship. If therapists become too intimate with their clients, and mainly stick to helping them to become more intimate with others as well and to learn to gracefully lump frustration when such intimacy does not exist, the clients tend to do both these things: to work for intimacy outside of therapy and thereby to frustrate themselves less and to increase their frustration tolerance when such intimacy is (as it often is) nonexistent. But if therapists give them "intimacy," and them eventually limit this closeness (which they almost always have to do, sooner or later) or withdraw it completely (at the end of therapy), their clients will ultimately be provided with more rather than less frustration. Moreover, as indicated above, they may well fail to cope with their LFT and may tend to raise it. How, then, are they *really* helped by the "intimacy" with their therapists?

7. Since most clients are prone to making themselves feel very hostile, and since you are offering them limited or pseudointimacy, many of them may easily wind up becoming more hostile than ever; and this certainly won't help them—unless, of course, you then employ RET or other antihostility techniques to help them work through their hostile feelings!

As can be seen from these points, developing a considerable degree of intimacy with clients has distinct disadvantages. It probably won't kill them, and at times it may even to some degree benefit them. But it certainly may harm as well as aid. It you use it, beware! Fully realize its great liabilities and do your best to compensate for them. Don't forget that, whether you like it or not, many clients will do their damnedest to achieve intimacy with you, for that is not only their desire but, in oh so many cases, their crazy "need." So no matter what you do, some kind of real or pseudointimacy will often develop. But at least see that you *know* it is being established, *know* its disadvantages, and *know* how to limit them.

Another word of warning: psychotherapy, like every other form of fee-oriented relationship, is distinctly a business as well as an art and a science. Professional therapists therefore want to make a decent living; and, today, they not only have to compete with other therapists but with many business-oriented organizations—such as Silva Mind Control and erhard seminars training (est)—that keep using every possible Madison Avenue selling technique to get people involved in their "educational" or "training" procedures (which are really a slightly disguised form of psychotherapy). With all this competition, many legitimate therapists may be tempted to forego modes of therapy that in the long run will prove most beneficial to their clients and, instead, try to bind these clients with the legerdermain of love. Watch this temptation! Care for your clients by all means, but try to care for them so that you largely, if not completely, help them more than your own pocket-book!

IDEAL GOALS OF THERAPEUTIC INTIMACY

Considering that, as just noted, intimacy has its advantages and disadvantages in the therapeutic process, is there any ideal goal that therapists had better seek in trying the "intimacy-schmintamacy" game with their clients? RET has its own preju-dices here, and mainly opts for therapy that is quite humanistic but also unusually efficient (Ellis, 1977a, 1980). This means that therapy preferably should (1) zero in on clients' core problems rather than mainly on their presenting complaints, (2) help them to see how they are basically causing their own disturbances and are not truly disturbed by what happened to them many years ago or by contemporary environmental conditions, (3) show them how to make profound philosophic rather than slight symptomatic changes in their lives; (4) prepare them to not only get over their present difficulties but to cope with any possible future hassles that are likely to arise, and (5) get them to a point where they can ultimately be their own therapists and not need outside help to keep them from making themselves miserable and from actualiz-ing their own potentials for enjoyment.

Are these goals of RET compatible with a heavy emphasis on intimacy in therapy? Yes and no. On the one hand, as Meichen-baum (1977) has pointed out, even the most direct and persuasive form of RET can be done with a Rogerian-oriented manner and does not have to be done as I personally would do it. Several RET therapists have recently stressed doing rational–emotive therapy in a warm, caring framework (Bard, 1980; Ellis & Grieger, 1977; Garcia, 1977; Lange & Jakubowski, 1976; Silverstein, 1977; Walen et al., 1980; Wessler & Wessler, 1980).

Some of the aspects of intimacy that can be legitimately emphasized in rational–emotive therapy include the following.

1. Therapists can be unusually open with their clients, including openness about their own personal lives and views. RET therapists, having presumably worked on their own dire needs for approval, can afford to take risks in expressing themselves during therapeutic sessions; and if they lose the approval or respect of some of their clients thereby, that too is bad but hardly catastrophic!

2. RET particularly emphasizes what Standal (1959) and Rogers (1961) call unconditional positive regard but what is called full acceptance in rational–emotive therapy. RET practitioners try to teach almost all their clients that they can unconditionally accept themselves, *whether or not* they perform competently and *whether or not* others like or respect them (Ellis, 1972a, 1976). They therefore do their very best to show their clients that they both accept themselves and these clients unconditionally, no matter how they behave or what wrongs they do themselves or others. This kind of acknowledgment and affirmation of the clients as humans is an aspect of intimacy that is particularly indigenous to RET.

3. If RET clients are especially interested in how their therapists feel about them, these therapists can usually feel free to give honest and open answers; since they do not feel obliged to like all their clients, they are not ashamed of their own positive or negative feelings, and they are able to show clients who feel hurt or downed by their responses that they (and not the therapists) are hurting themselves and that they are able to feel appropriately sorry and displeased by this kind of "rejection," but never have to put themselves down or defame themselves because of it

4. When they feel warm or affectionate toward their clients, as they may sometimes spontaneously feel, RET therapists are able to express these feelings but at the same time point out the dangers of the clients' taking that warmth too seriously and aggrandizing themselves because of it. Similarly, RET therapists are able, at appropriate times, to use social reinforcement (e.g., approving of the fact that clients are doing their homework assignments) and simultaneously show the clients that *it* is good that they have done well in therapy, but that this does not make them *good people*.

5. While RET therapists are usually quite authoritative, in that they teach clients how they are upsetting themselves and how they

can start refusing to do so, they are minimally authoritarian and are opposed to saddling their clients with their own goals, values, and ideals. At the same time, RET invariably attempts to help clients think clearly for themselves and not to unthinkingly accept anyone's view, including the therapist's, unless they test it experimentally and objectively. Clients are therefore encouraged to give up their low frustration tolerance and to stop depending strongly on anyone or any set of environmental conditions. The likelihood of their becoming too dependent on the therapist is thereby minimized.

6. When deep transference between therapist and client exists (in the psychoanalytic sense of this term) and the client falls in love with or becomes overly attached to the therapist, this kind of transference relationship is viewed as part of the client's disturbance: First, the client is overidentifying the therapist with some prior loved figure, such as a mother or father; and second, the client is making himself/herself overly needy and dependent, rather than merely affectionate, toward the therapist. The irrational beliefs behind this kind of overintense feeling on the part of the client are quickly brought to the surface, forthrightly disputed, and soon surrendered. Instead of a transference neurosis being encouraged during RET, it is distinctly combatted if it happens to arise.

7. The rule is generally followed in RET that intimate social and other relationships between the therapist and clients are banned for the duration of the therapy and for some period of time after it ends (since clients may at times require renewed sessions with the therapist). When a sufficient amount of time has passed after therapy has ended, and when the clients seem to be maintaining their gains and no longer seem in need of help, close attachments between them and their therapist may develop and be maintained.

HEALTHY AND UNHEALTHY KINDS OF LOVE AND INTIMACY

As noted above, RET tries to help all clients (and other people) who want to achieve more intimacy to do so. But it clearly distinguishes between healthy and unhealthy kinds of love and intimacy. Healthy love is based on the desire, sometimes quite powerful and consuming but still a desire, that people become quite involved with, attached to, related to, or loved by other selected individuals whom they find interesting, fascinating, or lovable. When, however, people love unhealthfully or self-destructively, they do not

194   Practice

merely want or prefer to be involved intimately with others; they demand, dictate, insist, or command, in a highly absolutistic manner, that they find unusually attractive individuals, usually of the opposite sex; that they act exceptionally well and impressively with these people; that these individuals love them completely, devotedly, and lastingly; and that they love their beloveds in a thoroughly intimate, deep, abiding, and everlasting manner (Ellis, 1973b).

If an individual's goals, aims, and purposes about loving and being loved remained wishes, that would be fine and healthy. But if they are, as they ever so often are, absolutistic dire needs or mandates, if they are incorporated in the utter necessity that they should, ought, or must be achieved, then these individuals hardly have healthy or fulfilling love. Rather, they usually have the essence of emotional disturbance. Compulsive, all-consuming love quite frequently has several corollary irrationalities about it.

1. It is frequently based on misperception. The beloved is actually a person with fairly ordinary traits but is perceived as having remarkable and entirely unique characteristics.
2. It often involves fixation. The obsessed lover may be treated very well by a member of the other sex (such as a father, an uncle, or a brother) during the lover's early years and "therefore" keeps falling in love, for the rest of his/her days, with other members of this sex who have traits somewhat similar to those of this original beloved.
3. It may involve magical identification. Lovers desperately "need" to be strong or good-looking (often because of their own feelings of inadequacy) and keep falling in love with others who presumably have these traits, magically believing that they will come to possess them if the beloved can be induced to love them.
4. It is often narcissistic. The lover really likes some of his/her own qualities (such as good posture) and only becomes highly enamored and involved with individuals who have these same qualities, no matter what their other characteristics are.
5. It is sometimes motivated by hostility. Lovers may hate their parents or other authority figures and (consciously or unconsciously) become infatuated with individuals who would tend to be most offensive to these hated people.
6. It desperately seeks for security. The lover cannot stand any form of rejection and thinks he/she needs to be loved totally and forever; consequently, the lover only becomes enchanted with partners who seem to be utterly safe in this respect and will presumably return his/her love indefinitely.

7. It frequently involves caretaking needs. Lovers believe that they cannot stand on their own feet and that the world is too hard for them, so they become enormously attached to those who will presumably take care of them and make things easy for the rest of their lives.

While healthy love tends to add significantly to life, and sometimes tends to be the most valuable and important aspect of the lover's existence, unhealthy love usually leads to intense feelings of anxiety, jealousy, depression, inertia, hostility, and feelings of worthlessness. Scratch seriously disturbed individuals and they tend to love or seek love in a desperate, demanding manner. Or else they are so severely needy of approval and/or competence that they autistically are into themselves most of the time, and have virtually no ability to love, and sometimes no desire to do so. Adler (1968) and Sullivan (1961), among many other therapists, have pointed out that emotional disturbance largely shows itself in dysfunctions of interpersonal relations and social interest; and there is considerable evidence to back their hypotheses.

Assuming that a client loves unhealthfully or that he/she desires to achieve a greater and more satisfactory degree of intimacy in life, what are some of the main ways that rational–emotive therapy can help this individual? Here are some of the techniques that RET frequently uses in his regard.

Cognitive Methods

RET can usually show intimacy-seeking people how they are seriously blocking themselves with their absolutistic philosophies or self-statements, especially: (1) "I *must* perform competently and be approved by significant others or else it is *awful* and I am a *rotten person!*" (2) "You must approve and become intimate with me, and give me all I need in this respect, or else it is *terrible*, and you are a *nasty individual!*" (3) "Conditions *must* be arranged so that I easily and quickly get all the important things I want, including love and approval; and if they are not, it is *horrible*, I *can't stand* it, and my life is abominable and hardly worth living!" RET shows nonrelating individuals that they almost always do have these *must*-urbatory beliefs, and it teaches them how to use the logico-empirical method of science to question, challenge, and dispute them. Thus, it shows those who desperately seek intimacy that they don't *have to* be approved by others, though that would be lovely; that it is hardly *awful* but only highly *inconvenient* if they are not loved; and that they are never *rotten people* but, at worst, people with poor behavior, if they fail to achieve the intimacy that they demand.

RET therapists also use the methods of general semantics (Korzybski, 1933) to teach love-needy individuals to speak to themselves and others more precisely, without using overgeneralizations and "allness." If they say, "I *always* fail," RET points out that they have failed up to now, but that hardly means always. If they exclaim, "I *need* so-and-so to love me!" it shows them that they would prefer this love, but that hardly makes it a necessity. If they insist, "I *can't stand* being alone!" it demonstrates that they *can* stand it, although they may be highly inconvenienced by loneliness.

RET teaches love-starved individuals a philosophy of tolerance—of how to fully accept themselves and others, of long-range instead of short-range hedonism, of inevitable human fallibility and lack of perfectionality, of flexibility and avoidance of dogma, and of scientific thinking. It employs many psychoeducational techniques, including pamphlets and books, tape recordings, lectures, films, and workshops. It uses modeling to show people how they can pattern themselves after those who display effective love and self-accepting behavior rather than after those who do poorly in these respects.

RET also uses cognitive distraction—such as relaxation techniques—to help people temporarily stop making themselves anxious, angry, and depressed and give themselves leeway to work at more appropriate feelings. It employs humor, including paradoxical intention, to help rip up people's exaggerated notions of loving and being loved and to get them to adopt more realistic ideas of mating and relating. It gives people a considerable amount of relevant information about love, sex, marriage, friendship, and other aspects of intimacy, so that they will better know what these relationships are all about and be able to cope with them successfully.

Emotive Methods

Although it is largely concerned with helping people who have intimacy difficulties to make a profound philosophic change in their disturbance-creating views, and thereby to stop upsetting themselves, RET is a comprehensive, multimodal method of psychotherapy that frequently uses dramatic, evocative, emotive methods to help clients face, challenge, and surrender their irrational beliefs. Thus, it uses rational—emotive imagery (Maultsby, 1975; Maultsby & Ellis, 1974) in the course of which clients are led

to implosively imagine some of the worst things that might happen to them in their intimate relations, to let them feel extremely
anxious or depressed as they do so, to change their feelings to
appropriate ones of sorrow, disappointment, and frustration, and
to keep practicing the new cognitions and the new feelings that
they then experience.

RET has invented and frequently uses shame-attacking exercises
(Ellis, 1972b; Ellis & Abrahms, 1978), in which clients are given
the assignments of deliberately doing "shameful" or "foolish"
things in public—such as telling a member of the other sex some
negative things about themselves—and making themselves, in the
process, not feel ashamed or humiliated. They are given role-
playing tasks, in the course of which they reenact difficult encounters (such as talking to a person with whom they are madly in
love), let themselves feel upset while doing so, and learn to handle
their feelings, work through them, and behave effectively in these
encounters. They are shown how to write out on three-by-five
cards various rational or coping statements—for example, "I do
not have to have so-and-so become intimate with me, though I
would like this!" and "I *can* stand being rejected, and this does *not*
prove that I am a *rotten person!*"—and how to say these very
forcefully and vigorously to themselves (or out loud) several times
a day, until they really begin to believe them. They are given, as
noted above, unconditional acceptance by RET therapists, even
when they are acting poorly and foolishly defeating themselves.

Behavioral Methods

RET, from its very beginnings, has always favored the use of
behavioral as well as cognitive and emotive methods of therapy,
and it particularly uses these with clients who have a dire need for
love and who think that they will die if they are not intimate with
certain significant others. Thus, it makes use of many homework
assignments, particularly the in vivo performance of acts that people find "scary" or "horrible"—such as encountering new members
of the other sex or telling a loved person about one's feelings for
him or her. It shows people that they are rarely going to change
their "love slobbism" or their procrastinating in trying to gain
intimacy until they painfully—yes, painfully—do the things they
consider "too hard" and stay in difficult situations until they become familiar and possibly enjoyable.

RET uses a good deal of operant conditioning and arranges to
have clients reinforce themselves when they do valuable but difficult behaviors—such as doing their cognitive homework or doing

shame-attacking exercises. It also favors stiff penalties, such as burning a $100 bill, when clients continually promise themselves that they will change their ways but fail to carry out these promises. In getting people to bite the bullet and to do the things they are afraid of doing, it frequently encourages them to do these things floodingly and implosively rather than gradually and comfortably, since it holds that self-assignments that are done in this manner tend to lead to more profound cognitive and emotive changes than assignments that are done more cautiously (Ellis, 1979–1980; Emmelkamp, Kuipers, & Egeraat, 1978). RET also does a great deal of skill training, such as assertive training and communication training, and does so in an active–directive manner, by showing clients how to do their own problem solving and to do it in action and not merely in their heads. But it does the skill training and problem solving along with helping people to profoundly change their basic disturbance-creating philosophies (Ellis, 1977c).

SUMMARY AND CONCLUSION

Rational–emotive therapy (RET) is largely concerned with love and intimacy as a choice or a preference and views it as one of the major disturbances when clients and other people irrationally believe that they absolutely must have intimate relations with others (including their therapists), that it is awful when they don't, that they can't stand loneliness and differentiation from other humans, and that they are rotten people when they do not successfully carry on loving relationships with significant others. In line with this view, RET sees a good deal of psychotherapy as useless or iatrogenic when it encourages clients to exacerbate rather than to minimize their dire needs for love. RET therapists consequently avoid getting into relationships with their clients where the latter become slavishly attached to the therapist and where they become more, rather than less, emotionally dependent on their intimate relationship with him or her.

When clients want to achieve a healthy (that is, unneedy and undemanding) intimacy with people in their real lives, RET specializes in helping them do so by showing them that they create their own absolutistic needs for love (and for success, competence, and other forms of satisfaction) and that they have the power to change these into strong preferences and wishes and to accept sexual, amative, and other forms of frustration when these are inevitable. It uses a large variety of cognitive, emotive, and behavioral techniques of therapy, but instead of employing them for symptom removal or for palliative improvement, attempts to help most clients achieve a profound degree of cognitive restructuring or philosophic change so that they are able to meet future as well as present disappointments and defeats without needlessly upsetting themselves or defensively withdrawing from intimate relationships.

REFERENCES

Adler, A. (1968). *Understanding human nature*. Greenwich, CT: Fawcett.
Bard, J. (1980). *Rational–emotive therapy in practice*. Champaign, IL: Research Press.
Baron, R. A., & Byrne, D. (1977). *Social psychology*. Boston: Allyn and Bacon.
deForest, I. (1954). *The leaven of love*. New York: Harper.
Ellis, A. (1957a). *How to live with a "neurotic."* New York: Crown.
Ellis, A. (1957b). Outcome of employing three techniques of psychotherapy. *Journal of Clinical Psychology, 13*, 334–350.
Ellis, A. (1962). *Reason and emotion in psychotherapy*. Secaucus, NJ: Lyle Stuart and Citadel Press.
Ellis, A. (1963, August). *To thine own therapeutic lust be true???* Paper presented at the American Psychological Association Convention, Philadelphia.
Ellis, A. (1971). *Growth through reason*. Palo Alto, CA: Science and Behavior Books; Hollywood, CA: Wilshire Books.
Ellis, A. (1972a). Psychotherapy and the value of a human being. In J. W. Davis (Ed.), *Value and valuation*. Knoxville: University of Tennessee Press.
Ellis, A. (1972b). *How to stubbornly refuse to be ashamed of anything* [Cassette recording]. New York: Institute for Rational Living.
Ellis, A. (1973a). *Humanistic psychotherapy: The rational–emotive approach*. New York: Crown and McGraw-Hill Paperbacks.
Ellis, A. (1973b). Unhealthy love: Its causes and treatment. In M. E. Curtin (Ed.), *Symposium on love*. New York: Behavioral Publications.
Ellis, A. (1976). *RET abolishes most of the human ego*. New York: Institute for Rational Living.
Ellis, A. (1977a). How to be efficient though humanistic. *Dawnpoint, 1*(1), 38–47.
Ellis, A. (1977b). *How to live with—and without—anger*. New York: Reader's Digest Press.
Ellis, A. (1977c). Skill training in counseling and psychotherapy. *Canadian Counsellor, 12*(1), 30–35.
Ellis, A. (1979–1980). Discomfort anxiety: A new cognitive–behavioral construct. *Rational Living, 14*(2), 2–8; 15(1), 25–30.

Ellis, A. (1980). The value of efficiency in psychotherapy. *Psychotherapy*, 17, 414–419.

Ellis, A., & Abrahms, E. (1978). *Brief psychotherapy in medical and health practice*. New York: Springer Publishing Co.

Ellis, A., & Grieger, R. (1977). *Handbook of rational–emotive therapy*. New York: Springer Publishing Co.

Emmelkamp, P. M. G., Kuipers, A. C. M., & Eggeraat, J. B. (1978). Cognitive modification versus prolonged exposure *in vivo*. *Behaviour Research and Therapy*, 16, 33–41.

Ferenczi, S. (1952–1955). *Selected papers on psychoanalysis*. New York: Basic Books.

Freedman, J. L., Carlsmith, J. M., & Sears, D. O. (1978). *Social psychology*. Englewood Cliffs, NJ: Prentice-Hall.

Garcia, E. (1977). Working on the E in RET. In J. L. Wolfe & E. Brand (Eds.), *Twenty years of rational therapy*. New York: Institute for Rational Living.

Freud, S. (1965). *Standard edition of the complete psychological works of Sigmund Freud*. New York: Basic Books.

Grieger, R., & Boyd, J. (1980). *Rational–emotive therapy: A skills based approach*. New York: Van Nostrant Reinhold.

Hauck, P. A. (1973). *Overcoming depression*. Philadelphia: Westminster.

Korzybski, A. (1933). *Science and sanity*. Lakewood, CT: Institute for General Semantics.

Lange, A., & Jakubowski, P. (1976). *Responsible assertive behavior*. Champaign, IL: Research Press.

List, J. S. (1961). *Education for living*. New York: Philosophical Library.

Maultsby, M. C., Jr. (1975). *Help yourself to happiness*. New York: Institute for Rational Living.

Maultsby, M. C., Jr., & Ellis, A. (1974). *Technique for using rational–emotive imagery*. New York: Institute for Rational Living.

Meichenbaum, D. (1977). *Cognitive behavior modification*. New York: Plenum.

Mullan, H., & Sanguiliano, I. (1960). The discovery of existential components inherent in contemporary psychotherapy. *Journal of Existential Psychiatry*, 11, 330–345.

Rogers, C. R. (1961). *On becoming a person*. Boston: Houghton Mifflin.

Schofield, W. (1964). *Psychotherapy: The purchase of friendship*. Englewood Cliffs, NJ: Prentice-Hall.

Shepard, M. (1972). *The love treatment*. New York: Wyden.

Silverstein, L. (1977). *Consider the alternative*. Minneapolis: CompCare Publications.

Standal, S. (1959). *Unconditional positive regard*. Unpublished doctoral dissertation, University of Chicago.

Sullivan, H. S. (1961). *Conceptions of modern psychiatry*. New York: Norton.

Suttie, I. (1948). *The origins of love and hate*. London: Kegan Paul.

Walen, S., DiGiuseppe, R., & Wessler, R. (1980). *A practitioner's guide to rational–emotive therapy*. New York: Oxford.

Wessler, R. A., & Wessler, R. L. (1980). *The principles and practice of rational–emotive therapy.* San Francisco: Jossey-Bass.

Whitaker, C., & Malone, T. (1953). *Roots of psychotherapy.* New York: McGraw-Hill.

Wolman, B. (1959). *Countertransference.* New York: Grune & Stratton.

The Use of Rational Humorous Songs in Psychotherapy

9

INTRODUCTION

Ellis has used humor in RET ever since its inception in 1955 because his view is that the irrational beliefs that people create to needlessly upset themselves are, when looked at from a sane vantage point, ironic and truly comic. Ellis notes that the results of these irrational beliefs are frequently hilarious. Therefore, counterattacking them by reducing them to absurdity and by other humorous sallies is, as Ellis might say, poetic justice!

At his notorious Friday Night Workshops, Ellis especially uses humor to show volunteers that sacredly held dogmas with which they foolishly upset themselves are truly inane. He does this not only to help those who bring up specific problems but also to help members of the audience who have their own unpresented disturbances and can therefore well understand, and laugh at, the volunteers' self-defeating ideas.

As noted in the following paper, Ellis first realized the virtues of rational humorous songs when he used them in a symposium on humor and therapy at the American Psychological Association convention in Washington on September 3, 1976. Since then he (and many other therapists and group leaders) have used them hundreds of times with individual and group clients and with tens of thousands of members of the public.

Rational humorous songs are now an integral part of RET and no book presenting the essential Albert Ellis would be complete without a chapter on this rational-emotive element.

THEORETICAL PERSPECTIVE

Although humor can be appropriately and effectively employed in almost any kind of therapy—even those, like psychoanalysis, that take the therapist and the client much too seriously!—it is particularly appropriate to rational–emotive therapy (RET). In fact, if I didn't have such a fine sense of humor myself, and were I not able to laugh uproariously at myself while I foolishly (and unfunnily) practiced psychoanalysis for several years, I surely would have never originated RET. And had I not been able to take the not so humorous barbs of RET opponents with a huge bucket of salt for many years, RET would never have survived, and certainly not have become as popular as it now is.

Rational–emotive therapy, at its very core, deals with the asinine overseriousness of humans that tends to drive them, as Alfred Korzybski (1933) once beautifully said, *un*sane. Its basic theory says that, when people have what we call "emotional" problems, they largely create them with their own crooked, irrational thinking. They tend to give profound significance to the events of their lives, which, to be healthy and happy, they had better well do! Yet they also give themselves, others, and the conditions under which they live *exaggerated*—or almost totally unhumorous—significance, thereby foolishly upsetting themselves. Foolishly? Yes, and quite *needlessly.*

When, in the dim, dead days of my youth, I foolishly practiced classical psychoanalysis and psychoanalytically oriented psychotherapy, I rarely used humor in my explanations or interpretations. Freud forbid! But when I started to do RET in 1955, I soon found that almost all the irrational Beliefs that my clients fervently held, and with which they were royally befuddling or befogging themselves, had a clear-cut humorous, ironic, and undelightfully perverse quality. I discovered, for example, that almost all my nutty clients ironically held a highly mistaken idea: that they could control and change others. They simultaneously held onto another lulu of an idea: that they had virtually no control over and could not ever importantly change themselves.

Even more humorously, the vast majority of my clients devoutly believed that other people, by the mere use of words, gestures, and attitudes, could magically get into their guts and make them feel hysterical or enraged. My clients ended up believing that they

Reprinted from W. F. Fry, Jr., and W. A. Salameh (Eds.), *Handbook of Humor in Psychotherapy: Advances in the Clinical Use of Humor* (pp. 265–285), 1987, Sarasota, FL: Professional Resource Exchange, Inc.

could do nothing, absolutely nothing, to minimize or stop these self-sabotaging feelings!

Well, the list went on and on. I began to see that virtually all strongly held irrational beliefs that accompany and largely create human disturbance are silly, and I also came to recognize the even more hilarious and cockeyed fact that billions of humans all over the world imbibe, create, and maintain similar idiocies. Practically all these people are desperately striving, under conditions that are often hellishly rough, to make themselves happy and effective. Yet, lo and behold! With a rare degree of innate and acquired talent they are creatively unscrewing themselves!

TECHNIQUE

As I clearly noticed the almost incredible ironies and inconsistencies of human disturbance, I soon began to point these out to my clients (and friends!). I showed them that when they were furious at other people they ludicrously became obsessed with people whose behavior they despised. Moreover, when they made themselves panicked about succeeding, they almost invariably consumed so much time and energy with their worrying that they seriously interfered with their succeeding. I found that these forms of Disputing people's irrational Beliefs often (not always!) worked well, and I kept using them more and more in RET.

At the same time I began to use other forms of humor quite consistently in my individual and group psychotherapy sessions (Ellis, 1977a). Thus, when my clients insisted that they automatically or unconsciously kept overeating or smoking against their own wills, and when they denied that they used any Beliefs (at point B) to make themselves act self-defeatingly, I would say something like, "What do you keep telling yourself immediately before you cram that stuff down your gullet and into your craw? 'I hate food? I just eat to keep up my strength? I'll fix my dead mother by showing her that I can eat all I want without getting fat?' Or do you mean to tell me that the food automatically jumps out of the refrigerator, onto your plate, into your mouth and forces you to swallow it?" Using humor in this manner—and taking care to only attack my clients' *behaviors* and never their *personhood*— I began to get excellent results. Not that I made humor the core of my RET techniques, but I normally included it as one of the vivid and forceful techniques, along with some very serious discussion, teaching, and active Disputing of clients' irrational *mus*turbation (Ellis, 1977a, 1977b).

As I was increasing my use of humor in RET, I also used serious and comic song lyrics to help clients overcome their irrationalities. My hobby for many years—indeed, since I was 16—had been the composing of songs, and especially the setting of new lyrics to famous tunes, such as melodies of Tchaikowsky, Grieg, Johann Strauss, Jr., Victor Herbert, and Rudolf Friml. So when I became a rational–emotive therapist I wrote a number of songs that (I imagined) cleverly ripped up people's self-sabotaging ideas and helped them acquire self-actualizing philosophies. For example, one of my fairly serious songs was this one:

ACHIEVING RATIONALITY
(Tune: "Oh, Susanna" by Stephen Foster)

When I give up reality and start to go berserk,
At greater rationality, I work, work, work, work, work!
Emotional totality most properly includes
A lot of rationality, as well as loony moods.
I go crazy if I just sit and shirk,
Achieving rationality means work, work, work, work, work!

I used these humorous and serious songs, giving them to my individual and group therapy clients and having them sing them many times to themselves until the songs' messages sank in and reinforced the other rational–emotive self-messages. As far as I could tell, I often obtained excellent therapeutic results with these songs.

Then a landmark in my life as a therapist accidentally occurred. I was invited by my associate, Dr. Robert A. Harper, to appear on a symposium, "Humor, Play and Absurdity in Psychotherapy," at the American Psychological Association's annual meeting in Washington on September 3, 1976. Along with papers presented by Harold Greenwald and Will Schutz, I presented a paper on "Fun as Psychotherapy," showing how humor is used in RET. I included in my paper several of the rational humorous songs I had been composing since 1973. Somewhat to my surprise, 1 was the hit of the convention—not for my Bronx-accented baritone but for the fact that I had the guts to sing in public at an otherwise highly conventional convention.

I saw that the humorous songs went over much better than my previously used serious song lyrics. Consequently, I began to use them more and more with my clients and my public audiences and also made them available in the form of a songbook and a cassette recording published by the Institute for Rational–Emotive Therapy. The rest is history. I now rarely give a talk or workshop without requests for and inclusion of some of these rational humorous songs!

There are many ways of using rational humorous songs in RET and in other forms of psychotherapy. My associates and I at the Institute for Rational–Emotive Therapy in New York use the songs in the following ways:

1. When they first come for psychotherapy, all the clients at our clinic are given a packet of RET articles, such as *How to Maintain and Enhance Your Rational–Emotive Therapy Gains* (Ellis, 1984), and "Showing Clients That They Are Not Worthless Individuals" (Ellis, 1965). Included in this packet is a double-faced sheet containing 16 song lyrics set to well-known tunes such as Strauss's "Beautiful Blue Danube," Friml's "Rose Marie", and Lady Scott's "Annie Laurie."

2. From time to time, clients who are anxious are given homework assignments of singing to themselves, a number of times per week, an anxiety-attacking song. Clients who are depressed agree to take the assignment of singing to themselves a depression-attacking song. Perfectionistic clients may take this rational humorous song to sing to themselves:

PERFECT RATIONALITY
(Tune: "Funiculi, Funicula" by Denza)

Some think the world must have a right direction,
And so do I; And so do I!
Some think that, with the slightest imperfection
They can't get by—and so do I!
For I, I have to prove I'm superhuman,
And better far than people are!
To show I have miraculous acumen—
And always rate among the Great!

Perfect, Perfect rationality
Is, of course, the only thing for me!
How can I ever think of being
If I must live fallibly?
Rationality must be a perfect thing for me!

Depressed clients may take the homework assignment of singing to themselves, several times during the week, either or both of these antidepression songs:

WHEN I AM SO BLUE
(Tune: "Beautiful Blue Danube" by Johann Strauss, Jr.)

When I am so blue, so blue, so blue,
I sit and I stew, I stew, I stew!
I deem it so awfully horrible
That my life is rough and scarable!
Whenever my blues are verified
I make myself doubly terrified,
For I never choose to refuse
To be so blue about my blues!

I'M DEPRESSED, DEPRESSED!
(Tune: "The Band Played On" by Ward)

When anything slightly goes wrong with my life,
I'm depressed, depressed!
Whenever I'm stricken with chickenshit strife,
I feel most distressed!
When Life isn't fated to be consecrated
I can't tolerate it at all!
When anything slightly goes wrong with my life,
I just bawl, bawl, bawl!

3. In the course of RET group therapy and marathons, the group members are often encouraged to sing some rational humorous songs together—to liven the proceedings, to give them a lift, and to serve as a shame-attacking exercise for some group members (Ellis, 1971b). In RET shame-attacking exercises, people are encouraged to do foolish or "shameful" acts, such as singing aloud when they have a god-awful voice. By doing so, they can work on giving up their self-downing thoughts and feelings, so that they no longer perfectionistically feel ashamed.

4. I also use rational humorous songs in the RET workshops I conduct for the public, such as the infamous Friday Night Workshops I conduct every week at the Institute for Rational–Emotive Therapy. In the course of this workshop, I demonstrate actual sessions of RET with members of the audience who volunteer to have a public session and agree to talk to me and the other members of the audience about their personal problems. I often have the entire group sing out some of the rational humorous songs in unison, thus introducing them to the principles of rational–emotive therapy. Workshop members are also given a sheet of these songs to take home with them and to use for therapeutic purposes on their own.

5. RET clients (and readers of RET-oriented articles and books) are encouraged to compose their own rational humorous songs. They are further encouraged to use such songs for themselves and with their friends to help spread some of the sensible and sane philosophies of living promoted by RET.

PERTINENT USES

As noted above, RET is used with many different clients, particularly neurotics who have severe problems of anxiety, depression, hostility, self-pity, and self-downing. It is also commonly employed with people experiencing behavior problems such as addiction, procrastination, avoidance, shyness, and various kinds of low frustration tolerance or short-range hedonism (Ellis, 1962, 1985: Ellis & Knaus, 1977). It does not pretend to cure psychotics but is often helpful in getting schizophrenics and manic-depressives to accept themselves and their serious limitations more fully so that they can function more effectively in their social and work lives.

Rational humorous songs are used in RET with a wide variety of clients, including some highly disturbed individuals. But they have their limitations when employed with psychotics, who may lack almost any kind of a sense of humor and who may interpret them iatrogenically, such as paranoid schizophrenics.

Some of the common neurotic syndromes with which the songs have proved most helpful (with examples of suitable songs used in these cases) are these:

1. For clients with abysmally low frustration tolerance or discomfort anxiety:

WHINE, WHINE, WHINE
(Tune: Yale "Whiffenpoof Song"
composed by a Harvard man in 1896!)

I cannot have all my wishes filled—
  Whine, whine, whine!
I cannot have every frustration stilled—
  Whine, whine whine!
Life really owes me the things I miss,
Fate has to grant me eternal bliss!
Since I must settle for less than this—
  Whine, whine, whine!

MAYBE I'LL MOVE MY ASS
(Tune: "After the Ball" by Harris)

After you make things easy and you provide the gas;
After you squeeze and please me, maybe I'll move my ass!
Make my life nice and breezy, fill it with sassafras!
And possibly, if things are easy, I'll move my ass!

2. For clients with hang-ups about the past:

LET'S LEAVE THE OLD FOLKS AT HOME
(Tune: "Old Folks at Home" by Stephen Foster)

Let us suppose my goddamned mother filled me with pap.
I listened and I let her smother—and carry on her crap!
Let us suppose my crazy father called me a shit.
I heard it and I let it bother—and I still do my bit!
Sure my childhood was confining, full of lousy strokes.
Now I am still depressed and whining, far from my goddamned folks!
Though my past was rather stinking, I am free to roam.
So let me change my nutty thinking—and leave the old folks at home!

3. For clients who are love-slobs and who feel that they must—
yes, absolutely must!—be approved by others:

I AM JUST A FUCKING BABY!
(Tune: "Meet Me in St. Louis, Louis" by Kerry Mills)

I am just a fucking baby, drooling everywhere!
How can my poor life Okay be if you do not care!?
If you tell me No or Maybe, you will quarter me and slay me!
For I am just a fucking baby!—please take care, take care!

I AM JUST A LOVE SLOB!
(Tune: "Annie Laurie" by Lady Scott)

Oh, I am just a love slob, who needs to have you say
That you'll be truly for me forever and a day!
If you won't guarantee forever mine to be,
I shall whine and scream and make life stormy,
And then la-ay me doon and dee!

4. For clients who are irrationally hostile:

LOVE ME, LOVE ME, ONLY ME!
(Tune: "Yankee Doodle"—Unknown folk song)

Love me, love me, only me or I'll die without you!
Make your love a guarantee, so I can never doubt you!
Love me, love totally; really, really try dear;
But if you demand love, too, I'll hate you till I die, dear!

Love me, love me all the time, thoroughly and wholly;
Life turns into slushy slime' less you love me solely!
Love me with great tenderness, with no ifs or buts, dear.
If you love me somewhat less, I'll hate your goddamned guts, dear!

5. For clients who refuse to accept reality:

GLORY, GLORY HALLELUJAH,
PEOPLE LOVE YA TILL THEY SCREW YA!
(Tune: "Battle Hymn of the Republic"—Unknown folk song)

Mine eyes have seen the glory of relationships that glow
And then falter by the wayside as love passions come—and go!
I've heard of great romances where there is no slightest lull—
But I am skeptical!
Glory, glory hallelujah! People love ya till they screw ya!
If you'd cushion how they do ya, then don't expect they won't!
Glory, glory hallelujah! People cheer ya till they boo ya!
To recover when they screw ya, then don't expect they won't!

6. For clients who have secondary symptoms of disturbance and who upset themselves about their upsetness:

BEAUTIFUL HANG-UP
(Tune: "Beautiful Dreamer" by Stephen Foster)

Beautiful hang-up, why should we part
When we have shared our whole lives from the start?
We are so used to taking one course,
Oh, what a crime it would be to divorce!
Beautiful hang-up, don't go away!
Who will befriend me if you do not stay?
Though you still make me look like a jerk,
Living without you would be too much work!

I WISH I WERE NOT CRAZY!
(Tune:"Dixie" by Dan Emmett)

Oh, I wish I were really put together—
Smooth and fine as patent leather!

Oh, how great to be rated innately sedate!
But I'm afraid that I was fated
To be rather aberrated—
Oh, how sad to be mad as my Mom and my Dad!

Oh, I wish I were not crazy! Hooray! Hooray!
I wish my mind were less inclined
To be the kind that's hazy!
I could agree to really be less crazy—
But I, alas, am just too goddamned lazy!

CLINICAL PRESENTATION

In the following case the use of rational humorous songs was particularly effective. Dinah (fictional name) came to see me for rational–emotive therapy after 7 years of psychoanalytic and Gestalt therapy, neither of which had helped alleviate her chronic severe depression. At the age of 33 she was almost continually depressed because her work as a teacher of emotionally disturbed children was full of frustrations and because she never had been able to maintain a meaningful relationship with a man. She had already been left by two husbands who found her to be unusually angry and depressed. Antidepressant medication helped her briefly; yet whenever anything went wrong in her vocational or love life, she reverted to severe feelings of depression and to thoughts about suicide.

I used several RET cognitive methods with Dinah—especially the Disputing of irrational Beliefs, the repetition of rational coping statements, cognitive distraction, and the reframing of her "horrors" as "inconveniences." I also used a number of emotive–evocative methods with Dinah, including shame-attacking exercises, the use of very forceful self-statements, and recorded self-dialogues. Another emotive–evocative method I used was rational–emotive imagery (Maultsby & Ellis, 1974), in the course of which she would imagine some of the worst things that might happen to her and make herself feel *only* appropriately sad and disappointed and not inappropriately angry and depressed.

Included in the behavioral RET homework assignments I used with Dinah were antiprocrastination assignments and the employment of reinforcements when she did her promised lesson plans, as well as self-imposed penalties when she avoided doing them.

This comprehensive cognitive–emotive–behavioral RET approach soon began to help Dinah, but her progress in overcoming her feelings of depression was slow. Finally, when she almost desperately asked for something *extra* to do that we had not already tried, I suggested that she vigorously sing to herself one or more of my rational humorous songs, at least 10 times a day. I also suggested that she sing some of these songs aloud (as shame-attacking exercises) and that she teach them to others.

At first, she thought that the use of rational humorous songs was a crazy idea and balked at implementing it. But I persuaded her to try this assignment experimentally for 3 weeks. She reluctantly agreed and started singing the songs to herself unenthusiastically for the first few days. To her surprise, they really reached her gut, and she often burst out into hilarious laughter when singing them. This so reinforced her that she soon found herself singing them with great gusto—sometimes silently, sometimes aloud to herself, and sometimes to her friends and relatives.

After 10 days, Dinah reported:

I truly began to see the real irony of my depression and my over-rebelliousness. I saw how utterly childish I was to anger myself at my depressed mother—to demand that a nut like her act un-nuttily! And I fully realized that, just like she frequently upset herself, I whined and yapped about things I couldn't change—like those pathetically disturbed kids I teach. How ridiculous! I even began to understand—though this was very hard for me—that being loved by a man would be nice and soothing but that it wouldn't change *me* as a person, nor give *me* the extreme pleasure of actively and creatively loving. And what especially got through to me was the point you have made several times—that who *needs* a needy person? And that the more I depressed myself about not being adored, the less lovable I made myself! For who enjoys a *whiner*?

Thereafter, Dinah still had her problems, and from time to time again she made herself depressed and angry. But she did this much less frequently, intensely, and prolongedly. By regaling her students and friends with my rational humorous songs, she also found that she significantly helped some of them—which gave her a new and antidepressing vital absorbing interest.

Some of the songs that helped Dinah were included above, especially "When I Am So Blue," "I'm Depressed, Depressed," "Whine, Whine, Whine," and "I Am Just a Fucking Baby!" One more song that particularly helped her overcome her lifelong habit of procrastinating was this one:

OH, HOW I HATE TO GET UP AND GET GOING!
(Tune: "Oh, How I Hate to Get Up in The Morning"
by Irving Berlin)

Oh, how I hate to get up and get going!
Oh, how I love to procrastinate!
For the hardest thing I know
Is to hear the whistle blow,
"You gotta get on, you gotta get on,
You gotta get on and stop slowing!"

Someday, I promise that I will get going—
Someday, but never, of course, today!
I think I'll still procrastinate
And always get my ass in late,
And piss the rest of my life away!

SYNTHESIS

RET is, of course, hardly the only school of psychotherapy that almost routinely uses humor. As I previously noted (Ellis, 1977a), "my therapeutic brand of humor consists of practically every kind of drollery ever invented—such as taking things to extreme, reducing ideas to absurdity, paradoxical intention, puns, witticisms, irony, whimsy, evocative language, slang, deliberate use of sprightly obscenity, and various other kinds of jocularity" (p. 3).

I can safely say that RET uses humor on principle, not merely for practical reasons. It teaches that emotional disturbance does not stem from giving value or significance to things but from giving them *exaggerated* or *sacredized* importance. What we usually call neurosis largely follows from people demanding and commanding that (a) "I absolutely MUST do well and be approved by significant others!" (b) "You HAVE TO treat me kindly and fairly!" and (c) "The conditions under which I live unconditionally SHOULD be nice and easy!" Lots of luck on any or all of these Jehovian commands!

RET hypothesizes that if people consistently look at things skeptically, scientifically, flexibly, and humorously they will usually not make themselves seriously anxious, depressed, or enraged. Lots of luck on that one, too!

Humans *will* be human—that is, screwed-up and fallible. To help them be less disturbedly and more enjoyably human, RET advocates heavy doses of logic and humor. Why? Because, once again, neurosis largely consists of taking things *too* seriously. Thus, according to RET, when people make themselves feel anxious and angry, they do the following:

- Highly exaggerate the significance of things.
- Fail to see their light or funny side.
- Criticize not only their own and others' *acts* and *deeds* but thoroughly damn *themselves* and other *people.*
- Overgeneralize and see things in black and white, all-or-nothing terms.
- Awfulize and catastrophize about problems and inconveniences.
- Frame things in absolutistic, dogmatic, necessitous, *must*urbatory ways.

What are the most effective antidotes to awfulizing, catastrophizing, I-can't-stand-it-itis, and shithood? Rationality and empiricism, says RET, and, of course, humor. What are some of the main cognitive, emotive, and behavioral advantages of using humor in rational–emotive therapy? First, here are a number of cognitive advantages:

1. Humor helps clients laugh at their failings and train themselves to refuse to take anything *too* seriously.
2. It relieves the monotony and overseriousness of some of the grave and heavy aspects of therapy.
3. It tends to help clients gain objective distance with respect to their self-defeating behaviors and makes it easier for them to acknowledge and attack their self-sabotaging.
4. It distracts disturbed people from some of their intensely anxious and depressed thoughts and feelings, makes them temporarily feel better, and allows them to be able to concentrate on the processes of change.
5. It punctures clients' grandiosity, which may be a basic cause of their emotional problems.
6. By nicely revealing human foibles, it shows clients how incredibly fallible they and others can be.
7. Humor exaggerates and counterattacks the overly serious exaggerations that lead to disturbances.
8. It gives alternative ideas and plans that help puncture overgeneralizing and black-and-white thinking.
9. It pithily presents realistic and rational philosophies, such as Mark Twain's observation, "My life has been filled with terrible misfortunes—most of which never happened!" and

Oscar Wilde's homily, "Anything that's worth doing is worth doing badly!"
10. It is largely incompatible with the categorical imperatives and absolutistic musts that lie behind most neurotic disturbances.
11. It interrupts and tends to break up old ingrained and rigid habits of thinking.
12. Humor activates a philosophy of joy and happiness that constitutes the basis for sane living, including a philosophy of striving for long-range as well as short-range pleasure.
13. It helps people see that they *can* control and change their disruptive feelings, deal with their practical problems, and have good options in the present and future.
14. It paradoxically indicates that bad things can have good aspects and that good things can have bad aspects.
15. It can be used as an effective teaching device by therapists to help get RET concepts across to clients.
16. If people take a humorous attitude toward their disturbances, they can accept the *challenge* of seeing things unawfulizingly, of reframing "horrible" events differently, and of seeing the "good" aspects of "bad" things.

Humor, when used in RET, also has many emotive, evocative, and dramatic advantages, such as these:

1. It shows how life, despite its hassles, can be quite hilarious and enjoyable.
2. It distracts clients from their painful feelings and gives them immediate constructive pleasure. It is often incompatible with emotional pain and distress.
3. As Fry (1978) has shown, humor enhances creativity and spontaneity, which themselves constitute rational goals of therapy.
4. RET-oriented shame-attacking exercises can be done humorously—as when clients yell out the stops in subway trains or buses or tell a stranger, "I just got out of the loony bin. What month is this?" Humor like this shows people that nothing is truly "shameful" and that they can fully accept themselves even when others think they are acting very foolishly.
5. Humor particularly interrupts and destroys the feelings of rage and hostility that create much internal and external havoc in our world (Dworkin & Efran, 1967; Frenkel, 1971; Whitaker, 1975).

6. Humor can add a sense of play to life as well as to psychotherapy.

7. It can often provide more interesting and more dramatic ways of making rational points than are provided by grave discussion and debating. With humor, RET practitioners can often display more dramatic ways of teaching rational arguments.

8. By using humor, therapists can let their clients see them as people rather than as mere "professionals." In this respect, humorous interactions can often help therapists' relationships with clients.

9. Through humorous sallies, therapists can often manage to be more hard-headed and confronting than they would otherwise effectively be.

10. Humor has an emotive–persuasive quality that nonhumorous rational persuasion may lack.

11. Evocative humorous language (such as that frequently used in RET) can get over to people more incisively and tellingly than dry-as-dust language. When a little old lady client says to me, "I feel worthless," and I reply, "Oh, you really feel like a total shit!" she tends to hear me much better—for I am using the strong kind of language that she may use, not socially, but to herself.

Finally, RET-oriented humor can be effectively used as part of RET's behavioral methods. When so used, it has these action-oriented advantages:

1. It dramatically and incisively interrupts clients' old dysfunctional behavior patterns.

2. It can often be repeated, especially in the form of RET's rational humorous songs, so that it finally affects or "conditions" clients favorably.

3. When people keep using RET humor, especially its humorous songs, humorous messages tend to become unconsciously assimilated into their thoughts, feelings, and actions. These people then tend to "buy" the rational ideas embedded in this humor and explicitly or implicitly tend to act on these ideas. This form of assimilation is similar to the process that occurs when the ideas incorporated in popular songs, which are often irrational, tend to "catch" people and to motivate their behavior.

4. Humorous statements and songs can strongly interrupt and interfere with clients' self-defeating obsessions or compul-

sions, thus helping to get them started on new tracks. As Fay (1977) notes, humor gives people a greater sense of freedom.

5. If clients take a humorous attitude toward some of their self-defeating behaviors, they can often get themselves to perform "terrible" and "horrifying" acts—such as riding on trains or elevators—that they phobically think they "cannot" face doing.

6. By showing people how foolish they appear to others, humor can motivate them to change their self-sabotaging habits and behaviors.

7. As Fry (1978) has shown, humor often stimulates people to cope with and overcome negative stress.

In conclusion, let me say that rational–emotive therapy makes the use of humor an integral part of its therapeutic armamentarium. In the process of doing so, it holds these truths to be self-evident:

- That masturbation is good and delicious but *mus*turbation is evil and pernicious.
- That shouldhood almost inevitably leads to shithood.
- That lack of humor tends to create emotional tumor.
- That absolute "truths" are almost absolutely false—and most probably disturbing.
- That overgeneralizations are generally overdone.
- That self-esteem (rather than self-acceptance) is one of the greatest of human disturbances.
- That there are no human subhumans.
- That just about all people seem to be FFHs—fallible fucked-up humans.
- That life, for virtually all of us, is spelled H-A-S-S-L-E but that, with clear and flexible scientific thinking, we can stop making HASSLES into HORRORS.
- That nothing is awful or awe-ful—only, at worst, a pain in the ass.
- That if you want to start winning you'd better stop whining.

REFERENCES

DiGiuseppe, R. A., Miller, N. J., & Trexler, L. D. (1979). A review of rational–emotive psychotherapy outcome studies. In A. Ellis & J. M. Whiteley (Eds.), *Theoretical and empirical foundations of rational–emotive therapy* (pp. 218–235). Monterey CA: Brooks/Cole.

Dworkin, E. S., & Efran, J. S. (1967). The angered: Their susceptibility to varieties of humor. *Journal of Personality and Social Psychology, 6*, 233–236.

Ellis, A. (1962). *Reason and emotion in psychotherapy.* New York: Lyle Stuart.

Ellis, A. (1965). Showing clients they are not worthless individuals. *Voices, 1*, 74–77.

Ellis, A. (1971b). *How to stubbornly refuse to be ashamed of anything* [Cassette recording]. New York: Institute for Rational–Emotive Therapy.

Ellis, A. (1977a). Fun as psychotherapy. *Rational Living, 12*, 2–6. (Also available as cassette recording from the Institute for Rational–Emotive Therapy, New York).

Ellis, A. (Singer). (1977b). *A garland of rational songs* [Cassette recording]. New York: Institute for Rational–Emotive Therapy.

Ellis, A. (1984). *How to maintain and enhance your rational–emotive therapy gains.* New York: Institute for Rational–Emotive Therapy.

Ellis, A. (1985). *Overcoming resistance: Rational–emotive therapy with difficult clients.* New York: Springer Publishing Co.

Ellis, A., & Knaus, W. (1977). *Overcoming procrastination.* New York: New American Library.

Fay, A. (1977). *Making things better by making them worse.* New York: Hawthorne.

Frenkel, R. E. (1971). Clinical management and treatment of rage. *New York State Journal of Medicine, 71*, 1740–1743.

Fry, Jr., W. F. (1978, March). Humor, health, and hanging in, or out, or on—as the case may be. *Humor Events and Possibilities*, pp. 1, 3.

Korzybski, A. (1933). *Science and sanity.* San Francisco: International Society of General Semantics.

Maultsby, Jr., M. C., & Ellis, A. (1974). *Technique for using rational emotive imagery.* New York: Institute for Rational–Emotive Therapy.

Whitaker, C. (1975). Psychotherapy of the absurd: With special emphasis on the psychotherapy of aggression. *Family Process, 14*, 1–16.

The Issue
of Force and Energy
in Behavioral Change 10

INTRODUCTION

Ellis wrote the following article because, as time went by, and as he encountered more resistant and difficult clients, he thought about better ways to help them change their self-defeating behaviors and to make RET more efficient than the cognitive–behavioral therapies of Albert Bandura, Aaron Beck, William Glasser, Michael Mahoney, Maxie Maultsby, Jr., and Donald Meichenbaum. Ellis realized that a great cognitivist, George Kelly, had not advocated rational disputing in getting people to change but had largely used the emotive–behavioral technique of fixed role playing. Also, learning from Will Schutz and the encounter movement, Ellis had adapted several experiential techniques to RET in the late 1960s (Ellis, 1969) and had been much more forceful, confrontative, and provocative in his therapy methods than were many other nonrational therapists (Ellis, 1963) when RET was still very young.

Ellis became even more emotive–dramatic in his therapy sessions and workshops in the 1970s, and in thinking about why this procedure worked, he came up with the idea that people, particularly disturbed people, simultaneously held both weak and strong cognitions and that their emotions and behaviors almost always followed the latter. Thus, they often would weakly tell themselves, "I guess it really isn't terrible *but only* unfortunate *if I fail and get rejected," and they then would feel a little better. However, they would (largely unconsciously) also strongly tell themselves, "But it really is* terrible!" *and they would immediately feel anxious and depressed again.*

So, more and more, Ellis used emotive methods of helping his clients, especially rational–emotive imagery (Maultsby & Ellis, 1974) and forceful coping self-statements, such as "I definitely do not *have to win this match–though that would be very nice!" or "I can write this paper immediately, no matter* how *hard it is for me to finish it!"*

As Ellis's *dramatic, vehement methods of using RET began to produce good results, especially with difficult and recalcitrant clients, he
wanted to instill those methods into RET theory and to strongly
advocate their use by RET and would-be RET practitioners. So he
wrote the paper reprinted here and kept incorporating its message into
his writings, talks, and workshops.*

*At the time he wrote it, Ellis was not aware of Abelson's (1963)
distinction between "cool" and "hot" cognitions. But when he discovered this, he saw that Abelson had anticipated some of his own
thinking about emotions and cognitions. Ellis now classifies three
major kinds of thoughts:*

1. *Cold or cool cognitions that usually are not accompanied by any
   emotion—for example, "That is a man."*
2. *Warm or preferential cognitions that usually are accompanied by
   appropriate (self-helping) emotions—for example, "I like that
   man, and I wish he'd like me, too. But if he doesn't, too bad!"*
3. *Hot or absolutist cognitions that usually are accompanied by
   inappropriate (self-defeating) emotions—for example, "I like that
   man so much that he* has *to like me, too. If he doesn't, that's
   awful! I* can't *stand it, and I am a* rotten person!"

*Ellis considers that his article presents one of the most important
theories of RET—that not only do thoughts significantly affect emotions and importantly contribute to or "cause" disturbed feelings or
behavior but that strong or "hot" thoughts are often held simultaneously with weak or "warm" thoughts and tend to cause dysfunctional
pain as long as they are consciously or unconsciously promulgated
and maintained. If one has "intellectual" insight, one sees but only
lightly accepts rational beliefs; whereas if one has "emotional" insight, one sees and strongly accepts and acts upon rational beliefs.
As Ellis notes, there is quite a difference between these two types of
insights.*

REFERENCES

Abelson, R. P. (1963). Computer simulation of "hot" cognition.
In S. S. Tompkins & S. Messick (Eds.), *Computer simulation of personality.* New
   York: Wiley.
Ellis, A. (1963). Toward a more precise definition of "emotional" and "intellectual"
   insight. *Psychological Reports, 13,* 125–126.
Ellis, A. (1969). A weekend of rational encounter. *Rational Living, 4*(2), 1–8.
Maultsby, M. C., Jr., & Ellis, A. (1974). *Technique for using rational–emotive imagery.*
   New York: Institute for Rational–Emotive Therapy.

What I call the issue of force and energy in behavioral change is one that has been sadly neglected over the years. Although hundreds of psychotherapists utilize a great many forceful and energetic methods (Burton, 1969), they frequently do not acknowledge the concept of forcefulness in what they do, and sometimes they even deny it. The Freudians, for example, vigorously force their patients to fit themselves into the procrustean bed of their oedipal complexes, and they manipulate the "transference" relationship with these patients so that they become very dependent on the analysts. Yet they often speak and write as if psychoanalysis mainly appeals to the scientific and reasoning aspects of humans and as if it finally wins out through the pure voice of reason (Freud, 1965). Other therapists, such as the Rogerians (Rogers, 1961) and the Gestalt therapists (Perls, 1969), consciously employ highly emotive methods with their clients, but they rarely talk about the *force* or *vigor* of their unsubtle techniques.

When the concepts of force or energy are employed in behavioral change, they are more commonly (and usually quite unscientifically) related to hypotheses about the central forces or energies of the universe; people are told that (1) such forces indubitably exist; (2) you can get in touch with them by various transpersonal and mystical approaches; (3) you can thereby tap these universal forces and use them to your own personal ends; and (4) you can consequently overcome virtually all your emotional problems and enormously increase your potential for actualizing yourself. This kind of devout belief in universal forces and of the human ability to tap these forces and acquire immense personal power from zeroing in on the "energies" of the universe has been with us for literally thousands of years, but it is unfortunately becoming much more widespread in recent times. Innumerable books and articles state or imply that cosmic forces are there for the asking and that we can easily commune with them and thereby increase our own power of coping with ourselves and life (Albin & Montagna, 1977; Campbell, 1975; Harrell, 1976; Ingalls, 1976; Krippner, Davidson, & Peterson, 1973; Ostrander & Schroeder, 1974; Pulvino, 1975; Schutz, 1971; Smith, 1976; Targ & Puthoff, 1977; Weil, 1973). Protesting against this mystical trend in psychology and psychotherapy have been relatively few recent writers, including Alperson (1976), Duffy (1975), Ellis (1972, 1977b, 1977c), Flew (1976), and Kurtz (1976).

Reprinted from *Journal of Contemporary Psychotherapy*, Vol. 10, No. 2, Fall/Winter 1979, pp. 83–97. © 1979 Human Sciences Press.

THE BASIC ISSUE OF FORCE AND ENERGY IN BEHAVIORAL CHANGE

The real or basic issue of force and energy in behavioral change seems to have little or nothing to do with the mystical or transpersonal hogwash that presently abounds in the literature. It concerns the following question. Assuming that certain ideas or cognitions help individuals to change their basic personality structure (and rid themselves more temporarily and palliatively of certain psychological symptoms or disturbances), is it important that these ideas be conveyed by the therapists, or by the clients to themselves, in a pronouncedly vigorous, forceful, and dramatic manner? And if it is important that certain health-promoting ideas be forcefully invoked in therapy, what are some of the most effective ways of doing so?

As noted, little consideration has been given in the past to this particular problem of behavioral change. Many therapeutic writers have talked about intellectual insight and emotional insight and have held that the latter will lead to significant personality change, while the former will not (Alexander & French, 1946; Hobbs, 1962; Wolberg, 1967). Unfortunately, they have not been very precise in their definitions; I will discuss this problem shortly. I (and a certain number of other writers who have followed my lead) have defined emotion as "nothing more or less than a certain kind—a biased, prejudiced, or strongly evaluative kind—of thought" (Ellis, 1962, p. 41), and I have consequently discussed the problem of changing behavior by utilizing powerful, vigorous thinking processes (Ellis, 1957, 1962, 1971, 1973, 1977a; Ellis & Grieger, 1977; Ellis & Harper, 1975). A few psychotherapists, such as Finney (1972), have not particularly discriminated between vigorous and blander thinking but have used what could be called vigorous counterpropagandizing methods in their therapy.

All told, however, surprisingly little has been done in this respect, in spite of the fact that methods of propaganda and counterpropaganda have been studied, mostly by social psychologists, for many years and that, in the course of these studies, considerable attention has been paid to the powerful or less powerful ways in which persuasion has been promulgated (Hovland & Janis, 1959). So I think that we might safely conclude that although therapists frequently *use* vigorous persuasion or "brainwashing" methods in their encounters with clients, they have not been particularly keen on thinking about the concept of forcefulness or energeticness in their procedures; in fact, to some extent they may have even delib-

erately and defensively avoided this area of discussion and research.

THE PROBLEM OF INTELLECTUAL
AND EMOTIONAL INSIGHT

Clinical observers, as noted, have for many years noted the difference between intellectual and emotional insight and have
pointed out that when clients are intellectually aware of their
problems and understand the sources of these problems, they frequently make minor or minimal personality changes; when they
have emotional insight into these same problems, they frequently
make much more major changes. Unfortunately, the literature in
this respect is quite vague as to what the real difference between
emotional and intellectual insight is and as to why the former is
presumably more effective than the latter.

I gave some fairly careful thought to this problem some years
ago and came up with what I think is at least a partial solution to
these questions (Ellis, 1963). First, I tried to define emotional and
intellectual insight more precisely. In so doing, I noted that what
we usually call emotional insight has several important characteristics.

1. The client has some degree of intellectual insight—that is,
admits that she/he is disturbed and that his/her behavior is irrational or self-defeating. Without this "intellectual" acknowledgment
or admission, emotional or "fuller" insight will probably not occur.

2. The client usually realizes that his/her present behavior has
some antecedent causes and does not magically spring from nowhere. It does not "just" occur but has tended to occur for quite a
long period of time, and it occurs in conjunction with certain
activating experiences or stimuli.

3. The client assumes some kind of responsibility for the dysfunctional or self-defeating behavior, realizes that she/he has something to do with originating it and carrying it on. In the
rational–emotive therapy A-B-C model of personality, the client
realizes that A (an Activating Experience or Activating Event) does
not directly or mainly cause C (an emotional or behavioral Consequence, such as anxiety or depression). Instead, B (the client's
own Belief System) directly causes the feeling and the behavioral
Consequence, and the client is responsible for having and carrying
on this Belief System.

4. The client realizes that even if she/he was significantly

helped, usually during early childhood, to have certain irrational Beliefs (iBs) and to create self-defeating emotions with these Beliefs, she/he has now *chosen* to keep these Beliefs right now, in the present, and to keep affecting himself/herself by them.

5. The client clearly and strongly "sees" or "acknowledges" that she/he can now do something *to change* his/her irrational Beliefs and thereby to change the habitual disturbed feelings and disordered behaviors that spring directly from these Beliefs. This Belief on the part of the client is firm or strong and is solidly held much or most of the time.

6. The client feels determined to work at (yes, *work* at) changing his/her irrational Beliefs—to accept their falsity, acknowledge that they do not conform to empirical reality, to see their illogical or contradictory aspects, and to keep striving, because of the poor results they bring, to give them up and not return to believing them again. Working at changing Beliefs includes the client's (a) forcefully and repetitively disputing and challenging them, (b) forcing himself/herself to go through the pain and trouble of steadily contradicting them, (c) practicing feeling differently about them or their results (e.g., practicing feeling happy about giving up smoking instead of clinging to the idea that it is awful to go through the pain of giving it up), (d) directly and vigorously acting against the irrational Beliefs or against the actions to which they self-defeatingly lead (e.g., forcing oneself to put the lit end of a cigarette in one's mouth every time one takes a puff at the other end of it).

7. The client not only feels determined to work at challenging his/her irrational Beliefs but actually does this kind of work and does it often and vigorously. Thus, if the client has a swimming phobia, she/he had better keep convincing himself/herself, over and over again, that swimming is not terribly dangerous, and also repeatedly plunge into a swimming pool until she/he gets rid of this self-defeating idea.

8. This client fully realizes that his/her emotional disturbances are always under his/her own control and that she/he can continue to think and act his/her way out of them whenever they recur. This means continual determination and action, whenever a new emotional upset occurs, to conquer it as quickly as possible and to become convinced of some general Beliefs that will tend to prevent many kinds of future disturbances, Beliefs such as "Nothing is awful or terrible," "I can always accept myself, no matter what faults I have," "Many things are hassles but not horrors," and "All humans, including myself, are incredibly fallible and will keep making fairly serious mistakes forever, and that is unpleasant and inconvenient but hardly the end of the world!"

9. The client keeps admitting that there seems to be no other way to become and to remain undisturbed except by his/her continually working and practicing, in theory and action, against whatever disturbances may arise.

The preceding rules may be partially summarized by saying that people who have intellectual insight see how they create their own disturbances and what they can do about uncreating them, but tend to see these things lightly, occasionally, and weakly; those who have emotional insight see the same things intensely, often, and strongly. Sometimes, more to the point, people with emotional insight normally work very hard, very often, and very powerfully at giving up their self-defeating Beliefs and acting against them, while people with intellectual insight do this kind of work mildly, seldom, and weakly.

FALSE ISSUES IN UTILIZING FORCE AND ENERGY

If what I have just said about intellectual and emotional insight tends to be true, the main issue in utilizing force and energy to bring about behavioral change seems to be work and practice much more than it is an issue of mere insight or resolve to change. New Year's Resolutions are easy to make—but proverbially hard to keep. "Willpower" is easy to invoke—but difficult to put into practice. Concepts such as motivation, determination, will, intention, and resolve are all important in behavioral change, and it is possible that very little effective change takes place without people having a good degree of these "feelings." But just as bread is not enough for most people to live on and enjoy life, so willpower is not enough to incite and induce basic personality change unless we include, under willpower, not merely the resolve and determination to modify one's traits and behaviors but also the action, the work, the labor that one almost invariably must apply in order to back up this resolve.

That is why the transpersonal or mystical solutions just noted are usually false solutions. They assume the existence of general forces and energies as a central part of the universe; which probably has at least some partial validity, since human life seems unviable apart from a basic source of energy, such as that which we derive primarily from the sun. But they also assume some inert mass of such energy or force in some special or central place that can be easily tapped by humans and they can put to their own use—including their own psychological use. This hypothesis seems

very questionable, especially when it assumes that we can *directly*
zero in on universal forces and use them, at will, for our own
pleasures and our own straighter thinking.

But perhaps the most foolish part of this kind of hypothesis is
that *anyone* can *easily*, with a few simple mystical or religious
instructions, focus on the universal reservoir of Mighty Energy and
can use it for immediate personal satisfaction. This utopian view
fairly obviously stems from the feelings of low frustration tolerance that many or most people have, and that constitutes one of
their major disturbances! The idea that "I must have things easy,
and the universe must provide me quickly and effortlessly with
immediate and immense gratification" is one of the most asinine
*must*urbatory ideas with which humans victimize themselves and,
as one would well imagine, it leads them far astray from the work
and practice that they almost always use to bring about profound
behavioral changes in themselves (Ellis, 1971, 1973, 1977a).

Ironically, some religious and mystical sects, such as the Zen
Buddhists, refuse to take this easy way out to the heaven of vast
resources of Universal Energy; instead they teach their members
that they must discipline themselves, often in exceptionally rigorous and overzealous ways, if they are to get "in touch with the
infinite," attain "higher consciousness," or otherwise acquire those
Great Forces. Even though, as noted, such Energies and Forces
probably do not exist, or have a nonexistent connection with human psychic abilities, the disciplined procedures that these sects
advocate *do* often have a salutary effect on mental health. It is
extremely difficult to maintain one's low frustration tolerance
(LFT) when one is deliberately following rituals such as rising
early in the morning, meditating in uncomfortable positions for
hours on end, fasting a great deal of the time, wearing reasonable
facsimiles of hair shirts, and so forth.

Although, therefore, the utopian, spiritualistic philosophies of
these mystical sects are unverifiable and probably filled with er-
rant claptrap, the disciplined procedures that lead to "nirvana,"
"universal fulfillment," "higher consciousness," or what you will
may themselves provide the kind of work and practice that help
the devotees of these systems of thought (and they really are, for
all the denials of the gurus of these religions, systems of *thought*)
to achieve that aspect of emotional insight that includes work and
practice. In other words, if you foolishly believe that when you
rigorously diet, exercise, and give up smoking, some kind of St.
Peter will reward you by permitting you to enter the pearly gates
of Heaven after you have died, and you actually do consistently
diet, exercise, and refrain from smoking in accordance with this

silly hypothesis, there is a good chance that you will, first, achieve much better physical health than you otherwise would achieve, and, second, learn how to discipline yourself and acquire confidence in your own self-controlling talents. These two beneficial results will occur in spite of the nonsense that you believe, but this nonsense will (partially by accident) motivate you to follow some sensible procedures that may well help you emotionally.

The following questions still remain, of course: How could you engage in the same kinds of useful self-discipline *without* believing devoutly in the mystical (and disturbance-creating) nonsense that goes with it? How can you validate the results of your high frustration tolerance in its own right, to discover what aspects of it are advantageous and what aspects are disadvantageous, so that you (and others) become more disciplined in more sensible ways and do not become disciplined for the sake of discipline (or for the sake of some imagined deity) itself?

AN OPERATIONAL DEFINITION OF FORCE AND ENERGY IN BEHAVIORAL CHANGE

The hypothesis of rational–emotive therapy (RET) and of several other schools of psychotherapy is that emotional insight or intellectual insight, backed up by the individual's determination (will) to change and his/her consistent and hard work and practice at the process of actual change, will frequently result in pronounced and "elegant" modification of some important personality traits and behaviors (Beck, 1976; Goldfried & Davison, 1976; Lembo, 1976; Mahoney, 1974; Meichenbaum, 1977). Another rational–emotive therapy hypothesis is that when elegant cognitive or philosophic restructuring occurs, the individual not only tends to minimize or lose his/her disturbed symptoms but also maintains increased emotional health in the future and automatically feels much less disturbed about "traumatic" events when they occur in his/her later life (Ellis, 1977b, 1977c, 1978).

Assuming that these hypotheses have some validity, or that they are at least worth checking out, the following question arises. How may people specifically and concretely, forcefully and energetically change their disturbance-creating or irrational Beliefs so that they achieve a high degree of "emotional" insight? To answer this, let me first try to define operationally the concepts of force and energy in psychotherapy or behavioral change, so that I thereby accurately lay out what individuals had better *do* to employ it.

To be more precise in this respect, I will start with the example of a very typical irrational Belief that many people seem to have and that leads them to feel anxious, depressed, needlessly inhibited, and inadequate; this is the Belief that "I *must* perform adequately or well in this task and *have to* win the approval of others by doing so; if I significantly fail in these respects, it is *awful*, I *cannot stand* it, and I am a *rotten person (RP)* for behaving badly and for gaining the disapproval of others." Let us assume that you (or one of your clients or associates) has this kind of irrational Belief and that it is leading to anxious and depressed feelings and to various kinds of dysfunctional behaviors. How, using an operational approach to defining force and energy, can you vigorously and effectively surrender this set of irrational Beliefs and change these self-defeating emotions and behaviors?

Let me list the specific things you may do in this connection to achieve emotional insight or elegant philosophic reconstruction. Some of the following tasks overlap with each other, but each may be important in its own right.

1. You had better actively and strongly Dispute (at point D in rational–emotive therapy) your irrational Beliefs *quite often*. To do this, you would *frequently* challenge and question these Beliefs, using the logico-empirical methods of science, and ask yourself nonrhetorical queries such as: "Where is the evidence that I *must* perform adequately or well in this task? Why do I *have to* win the approval of others by doing so? What proof exists that it is *awful* (and not merely highly inconvenient) if I fail in these respects? Where is it written that I *cannot stand* failing and getting rejected? What data exist to show that I am truly a *rotten person* (instead of a person who may have *acted rottenly* on this occasion) if I fail and get rejected?"

The main essence here of gaining emotional and not intellectual insight (or, more accurately, of gaining *more complete* instead of *partial* insight) into the irrationality of your self-defeating Beliefs consists of your winding up with the new rational Effect (E in RET) or new empirically based philosophy more *commonly*, more *frequently*, and more *consistently* than you have done before. Even when you strongly or emotionally believe that you *must* perform well and win others' approval (or refrain from gaining their disapproval), you do not believe this 100% of the time. You *mostly* or *often* believe it. And if you get emotional or *forceful* insight into your Beliefs and their self-destructive qualities, you will come to believe this drivel only *occasionally* or much *less often* than you now do. Therefore you had better actively Dispute and surrender these crazy beliefs *quite often*.

2. You had better acquire a *more total* or *more prevailing* belief that you don't have to perform well and win others' approval (or avoid their disapproval), and that you can fully accept yourself (i.e., your aliveness and potential for happiness) if you perform badly. Again, as a human you rarely believe anything *totally* or *completely* but have conflicting views about innumerable things. Thus you probably believe that overeating is bad for you, but you also believe that it is somewhat good for you; you also believe that it is horribly unfair when people treat you unjustly, but you also believe that that is the way the world is and that you can bear their unjust treatment.

Disturbance-creating beliefs, such as the idea that you *have to* perform well and be approved by others, tend to be totalistic or complete; you devoutly and fully believe them, at least at the moment when you feel depressed and destroyed about performing badly and gaining others' disapproval. In general, you do not believe them in a complete or 100% manner, but you tend to believe them in a basic, underlying, and 80% or 90% way. To *really* or *basically* disbelieve them, therefore, you had better keep working at believing them in a much less totalistic and less prevailing manner. Thus, if you have a 95% belief that the world is round and a 5% belief that it is flat, you will probably not get into any serious trouble and can take a long trip with minimum qualms; however, if you have a 95% belief that it is flat and a 5% belief that it is round, your travel will tend to be highly restricted or you will travel in an exceptionally anxious state! In the latter case, your problem is to work on your 95% belief that the world is flat until you make it into a 5% or less belief.

3. You had better believe your rational Belief (rB) more strongly, intensely, or powerfully than your irrational Belief. Thus you can, if you wish, lightly or weakly believe that "I must perform well and win others' approval," but you had better more strongly and intensely believe that "I really don't *have to* perform well and win others' aprproval, although it would be highly preferable if I did." Exactly *how* you can measure the intensity of your beliefs is not entirely clear, since it overlaps with believing them often and totally, especially with the latter. But there does seem to be a power or intensity to beliefs, as Osgood (1971) has shown, and it is somewhat different from believing something often or totally.

Thus you can lightly or weakly believe that "I had better not eat a lot of palatable food" and believe in a stronger manner that "It would be better if I did eat a lot of palatable food." If so, you would tend to *act* on the latter instead of the former belief. But there are probably also other indications of strength of a belief, such as your having, when you hold a strong or powerful belief, an

intense feeling about its truth or (in more cognitive terms) an
intense conviction that it is true and that you had better act as if
it were true.

A strong belief, in other words, is one that you tend to hold
(a) with firm conviction, (b) in a relatively fixed and unchanging
manner, (c) with a high degree of probability or certainty, (d)
without cavil or qualification, (e) dogmatically, (f) wholly or totally, (f) almost all of the time, (g) absolutistically, even when
empirical evidence does not support it, and (h) perhaps in other
ways that I have not quite specified here. Rationally, you may
hold a strong belief because virtually all the evidence that you
have seems to support it; irrationally, you may hold it because
you "feel" that it is true, even though there is little evidence to
support it and much to refute it. In either instance, you tend to
feel that the belief is quite true or valid, and you tend to act on
it.

To make a strong irrational Belief weak and a weak rational
Belief stronger, you can do several things. If, for example, you take
the irrational Belief that "I must perform well and be approved by
so-and-so," you could try to weaken it in these ways: (a) Ask yourself, "Where is the empirical evidence that I *must* act in this manner and get these results?" Answer: "There is no such evidence,
since I obviously *can* (or have the ability to) perform badly and
win disapproval." (b) Ask yourself, "Does it seem likely that a
universal law exists that commands my performing well and winning the approval of others?" Answer: "Obviously not, since if that
law existed I would always and only have to perform well and win
others' approval, and clearly I am able to perform badly and gain
disapproval." (c) Ask yourself: "What horror or disaster will probably or possibly occur if I don't perform well and win the approval
of others?" Answer: "No horror or disaster! I will probably be
quite inconvenienced if I act badly and others don't like me, but I
will still be able to live and enjoy my life in various ways." (d) Ask
yourself: "Will I be a truly or totally rotten person if I do not
perform well and get others' acceptance?" Answer: "No, of course
not. I will then be a person with, at worst, a rotten trait, poor
performance, and a poor result, others' nonacceptance. But I will
not be thoroughly rotten and can perform quite well in many
respects in many other ways." (e) Ask yourself: "Will some force in
the universe define me as undeserving and damn me, during my
lifetime or some hypothetical afterlife, if I do not act well and get
others' approval?" Answer: "Not that I can see or prove! It is most
unlikely that some force in the universe is personally interested in
me, will spy on my poor performances and my unacceptability to
others, and will utterly damn me and make me undeserving of any

joy in the here and now or in some hypothetical afterlife if I behave poorly." (f) You can vigorously and powerfully try to interrupt your irrational Beliefs and replace them by rational Beliefs. Thus you can ask yourself, in a vehement manner: "Why the hell *must* I perform well and where is the goddamned evidence that I *have to* win others' approval?" And you can answer, with equal vigor: "There's *no* damned reason, no reason whatsoever why I must perform well! And if I do not win other's approval, hell, I do not! It will not kill me!" (g) You can dogmatically (and somewhat *irrationally!*) keep reindoctrinating yourself with a counterbelief that effectively gets you to give up your irrational, self-defeating Belief, for example, "I am a perfectly lovely, special *person*, who deserves everything good in life just because I am I! Therefore I do not have to perform well, but am still noble and special! And if others disapprove of me, that is their problem, and they hardly deserve my acquaintance or friendship anyway. To hell with them!"

You can use still other methods of strongly uprooting your irrational Beliefs and coming to more rational Beliefs: (a) deliberately work at changing your beliefs from time to time so that virtually none of them remains fixed and invariant; (b) get yourself to believe, for instance, that "I must perform well (or had better perform well) only in certain unusual situations, as when my life depends on it or I will truly cause some disaster to happen to me by performing poorly. I need others' approval only in special cases, as when I depend on them for life and limb"; (c) constantly interrupt your irrational Beliefs and replace them with rational Beliefs; and (d) work against your general absolutistic tendencies to believe devoutly in anything whatever and see that you only accept things skeptically, tentatively, and with a willingness to believe in the opposite. Practice keeping yourself open to new or contradictory beliefs.

4. Realize that having a belief system will not necessarily make you act on it (although it will distinctly help you to do so) and that determination to think, feel, and act against it will tend to get you to carry it out. See that you can be firmly determined, mildly determined, or not determined to think or do something and work at being firmly or strongly determined to give up your irrational Beliefs and to act against them. Along these lines, talk to yourself as follows: "I am utterly determined to accept myself even if I perform badly and people do not approve of me. If it is the last thing I do, I will work hard at unconditional self-acceptance. Knowing that I can live and enjoy myself no matter what others think of me is probably the most important view that I can ever have, and I *will* have it, I will, I *will*, I *will!*"

5. Strongly and determinedly push yourself into actions that will contradict your tendency to hold irrational Beliefs and will reinforce your tendency to have rational ones. Thus you could (a) risk failing at certain important tasks, instead of avoiding them; (b) deliberately fail at certain tasks to show yourself that you will not die of failure; (c) tell people whom you find significant bad things about yourself in order to risk their disapproval; (d) use rational–emotive imagery (Maultsby, 1975; Maultsby & Ellis, 1974; Ellis, 1977a; Ellis & Harper, 1975) to imagine yourself failing and to make yourself feel only disappointed and sorry instead of panicked and depressed when you imagine this.

6. Keep practicing and practicing at working against your irrational Beliefs, feeling appropriate rather than inappropriate emotions (e.g., disappointment and sorrow instead of depression and feelings of worthlessness) when you fail and acting in a risk-taking manner. Realize that it normally requires constant practice to make yourself *really* and *strongly* believe sane ideas and to act on them and that it requires still more practice, to some extent for the rest of your life, to get yourself to the point where you retain rational thinking and appropriate behaviors once you have initially attained them.

7. Accept the near inevitability of falling back on some or many occasions to your irrational Beliefs. As I have noted on several occasions (Ellis, 1962, 1973, 1976a, 1976b, 1977a; Ellis & Grieger, 1977; Ellis & Harper, 1975), humans not only have a strong tendency to think crookedly but to fall back to their crooked thinking once they temporarily overcome it. So, in all probability, do you! Accept the fact, therefore, that you most probably will return at times to silly ideas and self-defeating behaviors and that this is too bad, but not horrible; you are not a lesser person for falling back. At these times, merely focus on your behavior and how to change that instead of on your youness and how to condemn that. You can learn by most of your retrogressions, and you can have fewer and fewer of them as the years go by. But you most probably will not reduce them to zero, not as long as you are still human!

8. Accept the fact that no matter how many times you fall back to dysfunctional ways of thinking, emoting, and behaving, you can just about invariably give them up again and return to more satisfying ways; you can work at strongly determining that you *will force yourself* to uproot your self-defeating behaviors and go back to less defeating pathways. Determine to keep rehabituating yourself to more efficient and more satisfying ways of living; work at this determination and at the actions required to actualize it.

9. Do not be afraid, at times, to use temporary or palliative

techniques of changing yourself. You can, for example, learn relaxation methods (Benson, 1975; Jacobsen, 1942; Lazarus, 1976), various kinds of pleasurable diversions (Ellis, 1976b; Masters & Johnson, 1970), Yoga and meditation techniques (Shapiro & Zifferblatt, 1976), physical and body exercises (Lowen, 1970); emotive methods (Casriel, 1974; Janov, 1970; Lazarus, 1976, 1978), and other diversionary methods. You can also take tranquilizers, alcohol, marijuana, and various other types of drugs to help yourself be temporarily distracted and relaxed. But recognize that these methods usually do not lead to profound philosophic change, and sometimes interfere with it. They help you feel better but not get better. We might say, therefore, that they are often among the most dramatic forms of unforceful, unenergetic therapy; and that is why they tend to be so palliative and to leave you with an underlying shame-creating and hostility-instigating philosophy that will later rise to smite you. If you use distraction methods with the full knowledge that they usually bring temporary results and that they sometimes put you in a mood where you can *then* vigorously and determinedly work to change your underlying disturbance-creating assumptions, fine. If you employ them "curatively," they may well give poor results and ultimately lead you to more harm than good.

DISCUSSION

Scientists are becoming more and more aware of the enormous importance of human perception, cognition, and intention in world affairs. Psychotherapists have essentially said this for years (Adler, 1927/1968; Ellis, 1957, 1962, 1971, 1973, 1977a; Ellis & Harper, 1975; Maslow, 1962; Rogers, 1961). Now biological and physical scientists are also beginning to say it (Sperry, 1977).

When you want to have a significant effect, however, on your own life as well as the universe around you, it seems clear that your thinking clearly and rationally is often not enough—unless, under the heading of rational we also include an emotive element and acknowledge that efficient thinking involves a forceful, energetic, and determined element. Mild-mannered thinking (the kind that you do when you merely observe that smoking or overeating has disadvantageous elements and that it would probably be better if you did not engage in such behavior) may be a necessary but not sufficient condition for basic personality change. It had better be accompanied or followed by a more vigorous, dramatic kind of thinking that goes one step further to include the determination to act and the actual action that backs up this kind of change-oriented cognition.

Overgeneralized or mystical-minded concepts of a universal force or energy and of how humans are to get in touch with and utilize such forces are again not enough; in fact, they can be pernicious and reactionary as far as instigating basic personality change is concerned. It therefore behooves social scientists to specify more operationally and practically the kinds of force or vigor that we can inculcate in our attempts at rationality and with which we can effectively implement these attempts. Peculiarly, little attention has yet been given to this problem in psychology or psychotherapy; this article is an attempt at specifying some of the more important elements in forceful, energetic thought and action and at harnessing some of these elements in the process of personality change. It is also an attempt to set up some hypotheses that can be experimentally investigated and either validated or rejected. Important therapeutic progress may well come out of such (*forceful* and *energetic*) thinking and acting!

REFERENCES

Adler, A. (1968/1927). *Understanding human nature.* Greenwich, CT: Fawcett World, 1968 (Original work published 1927).

Albin, R., & Montagna, D. D. (1977). Mystical aspects of science. *Humanist, 37*(2), 44–46.

Alexander, F., & French, T. M. (1946). *Psychoanalytic therapy.* New York: Ronald.

Alperson, B. L. (1976). On shibboleths, incantations, and the confusion of the I-thou and the oh-wow. *Humanist, 36*(1), 12–14.

Beck, A. T. (1976). *Cognitive therapy and the emotional disorders.* New York: International Universities Press.

Benson, H. (1975). *The relaxation response.* New York: Avon.

Burton, A. (1969). *Encounter.* San Francisco: Jossey Bass.

Campbell, J. (1975). Seven levels of consciousness. *Psychology Today, 9*(4), 77–78.

Casriel, D. (1974). *A scream away from happiness.* New York: Grosset & Dunlap.

Duffy, A. (1975, June 2). Esalen: Slow death. *Village Voice,* pp. 8–9.

Ellis, A., (1957). *How to live with a"neurotic".* New York: Crown Publishers.

Ellis, A. (1962). *Reason and emotion in psychotherapy.* New York: Lyle Stuart.

Ellis, A. (1963). Toward a more precise definition of "emotional" and "intellectual" insight. *Psychological Reports, 13,* 125–126.

Ellis, A. (1971). *Growth through reason.* Palo Alto, CA: Science and Behavior Books, Hollywood, CA: Wilshire Books.

Ellis, A. (1972). What does transpersonal psychology have to offer to the art and science of psychotherapy. *Voices, 8*(3), 10–20.

Ellis, A. (1973). *Humanistic psychotherapy: The rational–emotive approach.* New York: Julian Press and McGraw-Hill Paperbacks.

Ellis, A. (1976a). The biological basis of human irrationality. *Journal of Individual Psychology, 32,* 145–168.

Ellis, A. (1976b). *Sex and the liberated man.* New York: Lyle Stuart.

Ellis, A. (1977a). *How to live with—and without—anger.* New York: Reader's Digest Press.

Ellis, A. (1977b). Religious belief in the United States today. *Humanist, 37*(2), 38–41.

Ellis, A. (1977c). Why scientific professionals believe mystical nonsense. *Psychiatric Opinion, 14*(2), 27–30.

Ellis, A. (1978). Rational–emotive therapy. In R. J. Corsini (Ed.), *Current psychotherapies* (rev. ed.). Itasca, IL: Peacock.

Ellis, A., & Grieger, R. (1977). *Handbook of rational–emotive therapy.* Vol. 1. New York: Springer Publishing Co.

Ellis, A., & Harper, R.A. (1975). *A new guide to rational living.* Englewood Cliffs, NJ: Prentice-Hall; Hollywood, CA: Wilshire Books.

Finney, B. C. (1972). Say it again: An active therapy technique. *Psychotherapy, 9,* 128–131.

Flew, A. (1976). Parapsychology revisited: Laws, miracles, and repeatability. *Humanist, 36*(3), 28–30.

Freud, S. (1965). *Standard edition of the complete psychological works of Sigmund Freud.* London: Hogarth.

Goldfried, M. R., & Davison, G. C. (1976). *Clinical behavior therapy.* New York: Holt, Rinehart and Winston.

Harrel, D. E., Jr. (1976). *All things are possible.* Bloomington, IN: Indiana University Press.

Hobbs, N., (1962). Sources of gain in psychotherapy. *American Psychologist, 17,* 741–747.

Hovland, C. I., & Janis, I. L. (1959). *Personality and persuasibility.* New Haven, CT: Yale University Press.

Ingalls, J. D. (1976). *Human energy: The critical factor for individuals and organizations.* Reading, MA: Addison-Wesley.

Jacobsen, E. (1942). *You must relax.* New York: McGraw-Hill.

Janov, A. (1970). *The primal scream.* New York: Dell.

Krippner, S., Davidson, R., & Peterson, N. (1973). Psi phenomena in Moscow. *Journal of Contemporary Psychotherapy, 6,* 79–88.

Kurtz, P. (1976, Spring). Gullibility and nincompoopery. *Religous Humanism,* pp. 1–7.

Lazarus, A. A. (1976). *Learning to relax* [Tape recording]. New York: Institute for Rational Living.

Lazarus, A. A. (1978). *In the mind's eye.* New York: Rawson.

Lembo, J. (1976). *The counseling process: A rational behavioral approach.* New York: Libra.

Lowen, A. (1970). *Pleasure.* New York: Lancer.

Mahoney, M. (1974). *Cognition and behavior modification.* Cambridge, MA: Ballinger.

Maslow, A. (1962.). *Toward a psychology of being.* Princeton, NJ: Van Nostrand.

Masters, W., & Johnson, V. A. (1970). *Human sexual inadequacy.* Boston: Little, Brown.

Maultsby, M. C., Jr., (1975). *Help yourself to happiness.* New York: Institute for Rational Living.

Maultsby, M. C., Jr., & Ellis, A. (1974). *Technique for using rational–emotive imagery.* New York: Institute for Rational Living.

Meichenbaum, D. (1977). *Cognitive behavior modification.* New York: Plenum.

Osgood, C. E. (1971). Exploration in semantic space. *Journal of Social Issues, 24,* 5–6.

Ostrander, S., & Schroeder, L. (1974). *Psychic discoveries behind the Iron Curtain.* New York: Bantam.

Perls, F. (1969). *Gestalt therapy verbatim.* Lafayette, CA: Real People Press.

Pulvino, C. J. (1975). Psychic energy: The counselor's undervalued resource. *Personnel and Guidance Journal, 54,*(1), 28–32.

Rogers, C. R., (1961). *On becoming a person.* Boston: Houghton Mifflin.

Schutz, W. C. (1971). *Here comes everybody.* New York: Harper & Row.

Shapiro, D. H., & Zifferblatt, S. M. (1976). Zen meditation and behavioral self-control: Similarities, differences, and clinical applications. *American Psychologist, 31,* 519–532.

Smith, R. F. (1976). *Prelude to science.* New York: Scribner's.

Sperry, R. W. (1977). Bridging science and values: A unifying view of mind and brain. *American Psychologist, 32,* 237–245.

Targ, R., & Puthoff, R. (1977). *Mind-reach.* New York: Delacorte Press.

Weil, A. (1973). *The natural mind.* Boston: Houghton Mifflin.

Wolberg, L. R. (1967). *The technique of psychotherapy.* New York: Grune and Stratton.

The Value of Efficiency in Psychotherapy

11

INTRODUCTION

Albert Ellis has always been interested in efficiency, both in life and in psychotherapy. In the following paper, published in 1980, Ellis specifies several criteria of psychotherapeutic efficiency. These are brevity, depth-centeredness, pervasiveness, extensiveness, thoroughgoingness, maintaining therapeutic progress, minimization of therapeutic harm, and promotion of prevention in psychotherapy. These ingredients of therapeutic efficiency help place the concept of therapeutic effectiveness in a wider perspective, and as such, this paper is seminal.

The issue of value in psychotherapy is exceptionally important, and the existential therapists in particular may be credited with highlighting this importance (Frankl, 1966; May, 1969). Some psychotherapeutic values, however, have often been neglected, and I shall stress in this paper one of these: namely, that of efficiency, which I think is somewhat different from the value of effectiveness. Usually, we test the "effectiveness" of a given form of therapy by showing that, in both controlled experiments and in clinical practice, it results in significant gains for clients when therapized groups are compared to placebo or nontherapized groups. But we

Reprinted from *Psychotherapy: Theory, Research and Practice*, 17(4), 1980, 414–419.

237

rarely test the "efficiency" of treatment methods to determine, on a cost-benefit basis, how much time and effort is normally spent by therapists and clients to achieve "effective" results and how pervasive, thoroughgoing, and long-lasting these "results" are. Yet, in view of pending efforts to establish suitable criteria for the setting of governmental and insurance company standards for reimbursing "competent" therapists under existing and suggested mental health plans, a cost-benefit approach to psychotherapy looms as increasingly important (Hogan, 1980; Pottinger, 1980; Strupp, 1980).

What are some of the main goals to strive for in therapy that is "efficient" as well as "effective"? After giving this mater serious thought for more than a quarter of a century, and after experimenting in my own practice with several different methods of psychological treatment ranging from classical psychoanalysis to rational–emotive therapy, I have come up with the following hypotheses about "efficient" psychotherapy.

BREVITY IN PSYCHOTHERAPY

Although Freud (1965) himself usually practiced what today would be called brief psychotherapy and saw most of his analysands for only a matter of months (Jones, 1956), psychoanalysis turned to a longer period of treatment, usually taking a minimum of two years in its classic form and often much longer than that. In recent years, however, many analytically oriented therapists have espoused brief treatment (Small, 1979), and much of today's nonanalytic therapy is relatively short (Ellis & Abrahms, 1978). This obviously has its advantages: since most clients are in pain when they come for therapy, they function on a low level of competency; they enjoy themselves little; and the longer they take to overcome their disturbances, the more they and their associates are likely to suffer. Psychotherapy, moreover, is usually expensive and time-consuming; and if it is possible to achieve effective treatment in a short period of time, more clients will tend to come, stay in it, and benefit from it in various ways. Governmental and other agencies, moreover, will be more enthusiastic about reimbursing therapists for brief rather than for prolonged therapy.

DEPTH-CENTEREDNESS IN PSYCHOTHERAPY

Many modes of therapy, especially psychoanalysis, advocate that psychotherapy be depth-centered (Freud, 1965; Jones, 1956; Kaplan, 1979). They assume that many symptoms, such as phobias, not only have an environmental and experiential core but that they also have some kind of deep-seated, underlying "cause" and that this has to be thoroughly understood and worked through over a period of therapeutic time before it can really be resolved. In existential and philosophic therapies it is also assumed that a symptom has depth-centered roots. Thus, rational–emotive therapy (RET) holds that people's phobias largely stem from a basic absolutistic or *must*urbatory philosophy—e.g., "I *must* not suffer any form of severe discomfort or failure when I ride in elevators!"—and that it probably will not be resolved unless clients understand their self-invented "needs" for certainty and unless they consistently think and act against these "necessities."

There are many advantages to therapists trying to help clients arrive at their fundamental disturbance-creating ideas and then to surrender these for less disturbing philosophies: (1) They can not only help reveal the sources of clients' current symptoms but also of prior and later ones, so that they obtain a more comprehensive and clearer knowledge of what they do to disturb themselves. (2) Clients may, in addition to eliminating their negative symptoms, show themselves how to lead a more joyous, creative, and fulfilled existence. (3) Depth-centered psychotherapy may promote a general understanding of human "nature" that may be relevant to many aspects of living, including social and political relations, international understanding, and artistic pursuits.

PERVASIVENESS IN PSYCHOTHERAPY

Pervasiveness in psychotherapy may be defined as the therapist's helping clients to deal with many of their problems, and in a sense their whole lives, rather than with a few presenting symptoms. Thus, a psychoanalyst who sees a woman who has poor sex with her husband will try to zero in not merely on that particular issue but also on her general relations with her mate and with other significant people in her life. And a rational–emotive therapist may first show this woman that she has great fear of failing sexually with her husband (because of her absolutistic philosophy, "I *have to* do well sexually and *must* win his approval!") but *also* show her how her dire "need" for success and love are interfering with her other marital and nonmarital functions.

Like depth-centeredness, the value of pervasiveness in psychotherapy has distinct benefits: (1) It shows clients how they can easily create several symptoms from the same underlying attitudes and feelings and how, by changing these attitudes, they can deal with or eliminate more than one or two presenting symptoms. (2)

It helps them to understand and relate better to other people. (3) It may enable them, especially if they learn to apply a form of treatment like RET, to deal therapeutically with their close associates (Ellis, 1957).

EXTENSIVENESS IN PSYCHOTHERAPY

Extensiveness in psychotherapy means that clients can be helped not only to minimize their negative feelings (e.g., anxiety, depression, rage, and self-pity) but also to maximize their potential for happy living (e.g., to be more productive, creative, and enjoying). Where "intensive" therapy usually deals with pain, inhibition, panic, and horror, "extensive" therapy also deals with exploring and augmenting pleasure, sensuality, and laughter. "Efficient" psychotherapy, therefore, includes "intensive" as well as "extensive" treatment, provides self-actualizing as well as de-inhibiting procedures, and thereby tries to provide additional gains in the cost-benefit issues that are inevitably involved in therapy.

THOROUGHGOINGNESS IN PSYCHOTHERAPY

Since what we call "thought," "emotion," and "behavior" are processes that hardly exist in any pure state but significantly overlap and interact, and since "emotional disturbance" has cognitive and behavioral as well as emotive aspects, "efficient" psychotherapy had better consider and often include multimodal techniques (Ellis & Grieger, 1977; Ellis & Whiteley, 1979; Lazarus, 1971, 1976; Wachtel, 1978). This does not mean that it will unselectively use any and all available methods, but it will tend to be a comprehensive system that will explore several pathways and will test these to see which usually work best and which had better be used minimally with different clients. The more comprehensive a therapist's armamentarium of techniques is, the more likely he or she is to find suitable procedures for especially unique or difficult clients.

MAINTAINING THERAPEUTIC PROGRESS

Symptom removal, as Wolpe (1973) has stated, may be quite valuable and may even lead to a real "cure." But it also has distinct limitations: (1) When a given symptom is removed or ameliorated, another may easily spring up later—not necessarily because of symptom substitution but as a derivative of the same basic self-defeating philosophy with which clients create their original symptoms. (2) Many clients feel so relieved by the temporary or partial removal of a painful symptom (e.g., depression) that they leave the core of it (or its close relatives) still standing. (3) Most clients have some degree of low frustration tolerance and therefore will welcome palliative procedures (e.g., tranquilizers or relaxation methods) to quickly alleviate their worst symptoms rather than working at more elegant philosophic changes that will result in more permanent changes.

For reasons such as these, "efficient" therapy does not merely strive for symptom removal but for more lasting therapeutic gain; and, no matter how pleased clients may feel about their "cures," it does not accept these unless there is some evidence that they will be maintained for a period of time and, preferably, keep improving after formal therapy has ended. In rational–emotive therapy in particular, one of the hallmarks of "elegant" or highly "efficient" psychotherapy is for treated individuals to feel significantly better at the close of therapy than they did at the beginning—but also to keep improving for a considerable period of time after therapy has officially ended (Ellis & Whiteley, 1979).

PREVENTIVE PSYCHOTHERAPY

Most modern systems of therapy strive to have their clients free of presenting symptoms at the close of treatment and still free of these same symptoms months or years after therapy has ended. Another fairly obvious efficiency goal is that of teaching clients to understand themselves so well, to see so clearly how they usually create their own emotional problems, and to understand so solidly what they can do to restore their own emotional equilibrium that they are able to approach the future with a basically un-upsetting philosophy. This is not easy, but it is presumably sometimes achievable. Just as medical patients can presumably learn from their physicians how to get over their current ailments and to prevent these from recurring, so can psychotherapy clients often learn from their therapists how to ward off future emotional ills and to keep themselves from returning to their old disturbed pathways. From a cost-benefit standpoint it seems obvious that any kind of treatment that provides this kind of preventive therapy will provide more gains than symptom-removal treatments (because the results are lasting and cumulative) and also entail less expense (because the nonrecurrence of the symptoms precludes future hours of therapy).

ILLUSTRATIVE CASE PRESENTATION

It is interesting to discuss "efficiency" in psychotherapy abstractly, as I have just done, and to hypothesize about its advantages. Let me be more concrete by presenting a clinical case that illustrates how some of these principles may be practiced. Calvin R., a forty-year-old physician, was exceptionally depressed when he came for rational–emotive therapy. He damned himself for his medical errors and for his failings as a husband and father. He was extremely hostile toward his wife whenever she disagreed with him about some important matter. And he fumed and frothed about even the smallest un-niceties of his life, such as a leaky roof or a run in his socks.

In terms of brevity, Calvin was seen for four months on a once-a-week basis: first for one hour and during the last two months for half-hour sessions. His therapy made little inroads into his very busy medical schedule.

In regard to depth-centeredness, he was helped to zero in on three basic *musts*, or absolutistic philosophies, which permeated almost his entire life and largely created his depressed feelings: (1) "I *must* do outstandingly well in my work and be approved by all my patients!" (2) "My wife *must* never disagree with me about important things and *has to* do these things my way!" (3) "Conditions under which I live *must* be easy and unhassled, and never frustrate me too badly!" Although Calvin was at first convinced that his depression was purely biological and endogenous (even though several self-prescribed antidepressants had not lifted it a bit), I was able to show him that every time he felt depressed he was invariably demanding (not wishing) that he do well and castigating himself when he did not perform outstandingly, and that he was frequently commanding that things be better than they were. He soon acknowledged that his *must*urbatory philosophy underlay his depressed and hostile feelings and that, with this Jehovian attitude, *he* was making himself disturbed.

In the area of pervasiveness, although Calvin at first only wanted to discuss his horror of failing at work, and occasionally his anger at his wife, he was shown that his self-downing and his low frustration tolerance invaded other areas of his life as well, including his sex activities and his social relations. In fact, he responded better at first in these two areas than he did in giving up his work perfectionism, and he was partly able to give up the latter by first surrendering the former.

Regarding extensiveness, Calvin was not only taught how to work against his presenting symptoms but to add interests and pleasures to his days—such as music and running—that enhanced his existence, distracted him somewhat from his incessant worrying, and gave him two more vital absorbing interests that made life more enjoyable.

In terms of thoroughgoingness, Calvin was not only treated with the highly cognitive methods of RET (Ellis, 1962) but given a number of emotive exercises and in vivo activity homework assignments as well. Thus, he especially seemed to benefit from shame-attacking exercises (Ellis, 1973), rational–emotive imagery (Maultsby, 1975), and deliberately staying in some painful situations (such as visiting with his boring in-laws) and showing himself that he could stand, if not like, the pain (Ellis & Abrahms, 1978).

Best of all, Calvin seemed remarkably able to maintain his therapeutic progress and to do preventive psychotherapy on his own and increase his gains. For he first, after four months of therapy, lost his depression, went back to a full schedule of work, and started getting along remarkably well with his wife and family in spite of some difficulties which they themselves presented. This seemed surprising, considering the brevity of his therapy. But even more surprising was what he reported when he returned to see me two years later to talk about his wife, who was severely panicked about driving a car (after she had previously driven one without trouble for twelve years) and who was going through a period of severe depersonalization. For Calvin was handling this situation remarkably well, in spite of the immense transportation and other difficulties it was causing his entire family.

To make matters worse, Calvin himself had become afflicted, for the past six months, with a rheumatic condition that handicapped him seriously in his practice; one of his sons turned out to be dyslexic and was behaving in a highly delinquent manner; both his parents were dying of cancer; and his economic situation, for a variety of reasons including some poor investments on his part, had deteriorated. In spite of all these adversities, this ex-client's spirits were unusually high. He had virtually no hostility or self-pity in the face of his family frustrations. He was not downing himself for his own economic blunders. And he was doing a reasonably good job in using some of the RET principles he had learned to help his wife, his children, and his parents cope with some of the serious emotional troubles that they all were undergoing.

This is the kind of "elegant" therapeutic result that I particularly strive for and like to see effected. Calvin not only overcame his presenting symptoms and maintained this change. Moreover, he improved significantly after therapy had ended and was at a stage, two years later, where virtually no normal kind of setback would he allow to disturb him too seriously—meaning, to make him depressed, panicked, hostile, or self-pitying.

OTHER KINDS OF EFFICIENCY IN PSYCHOTHERAPY

In addition to the ways just hypothesized, some other kinds of efficiency in psychotherapy may be obtained in the following ways:

1. Efficient therapy tends to be stated in clear and simple terms, so that it is relatively easily understood both by practitioners and their clients. Abstruse or esoteric modes of therapy may have desirable qualities, but they tend to have a limited appeal to therapists and, especially, to the people with whom they are used. Highly mystical and transpersonal forms of therapy, for example, are understood only by a minority of the populace, often aim at contradictory goals, and may easily lead their devotees up the garden path into questionably "healthy" results (Ellis, 1972).

2. Efficient psychotherapy is fairly easily teachable to therapists and does not require them to undergo years of training and apprenticeship, not to mention years of personal therapy themselves.

3. Efficient therapy is often intrinsically interesting to therapists and clients, and motivates the latter to stay with it and to use it in their outside lives. This aspect of therapy may indeed have boomerang effects: for some of the most questionable and potentially harmful forms of psychological treatment—such as fanatical cult therapies like that promulgated by Jim Jones—are intrinsically fascinating to their followers and strongly motivate them to make changes in their lives. But assuming that a form of psychotherapy has healthy and lasting effects, it seems more efficient for it to be intrinsically interesting rather than dull and to be motivating rather than unmotivating.

4. Efficient psychotherapy helps clients achieve maximum good with minimum harm to themselves (and others). Many therapies, including some of the most esoteric and bizarre ones, help bring about healthy or beneficial results for clients (Frank, 1975). But it has also been shown that some of these forms of treatment have

harmful results as well (Chapman, 1964; Garfield & Bergin, 1978; Gross, 1979; Hadley & Strupp, 1976; Lieberman, Yalom, & Miles, 1973; Maliver, 1972; Rosen, 1977). It may also be questioned whether some modes of cultist or mystical therapies (such as sha-manism or exorcism) do not create, as well as alleviate, distur-bance (Ellis, 1972, 1975). Behavioral or emotional change, when effected through psychotherapy, had better be conducive of human survival and happiness, including social as well as individual hap-piness; and if it leads to pernicious as well as beneficial social results, its efficiency had better be examined (Adler, 1964).

5. Efficient psychotherapy favors flexibility, lack of dogma, and provision and encouragement for its own change. It not only tends to help its clients be less absolutistic, rigid, unscientific, and de-vout but it also endorses scientific falsifiability; that is, it sets up its theories so that they are ultimately falsifiable; it views them skeptically and tentatively; and it constantly strives to check on their errors and invalidities (Popper, 1972; Russell, 1965). In this manner, it not only tries to achieve but does its best to maintain both effectiveness and efficiency.

DISCUSSION

This paper hypothesizes that therapy, even when it has been shown to have experimentally proven effectiveness, may still be inefficient, and it outlines several criteria of efficiency in psycho-therapy and their presumed advantages. Psychotherapies, being humanistically oriented and somewhat allergic to hardheaded real-ities, often neglect the value of efficiency in their work. This is hardly in the best interests of their clients! Efficiency is a dis-tinctly valuable concept for therapists, for their clients, and for the science of psychotherapy itself. Effectiveness is indeed an impor-tant aspect of psychological treatment, and we had better strive for therapy that works. But efficiency includes, in addition to ef-fectiveness, several other ingredients, such as depth-centeredness, pervasiveness, extensiveness, thoroughgoingness, maintaining ther-apeutic progress, and preventive psychotherapy. It also encourages minimization of therapeutic harm and scientific flexibility and falsifiability. All these aspects of presumably efficient therapy can probably be concretized and measured. If this is done, it will prob-ably be found that what we now call "effectiveness" as measured in most contemporary outcome studies of therapy, is significantly correlated with "efficiency" but that the latter involves important aspects of treatment that are commonly neglected in considering the former. Research along these lines would seem to be highly desirable.

REFERENCES

Adler, A. (1964). *Social interest: A challenge to mankind.* New York: Capricorn.

Chapman, A. H. (1964, September). *Psychiatry Digest,* pp. 23–29.

Ellis, A. (1957). *How to live with a "neurotic."* New York: Crown.

Ellis, A. (1962). *Reason and emotion in psychotherapy.* New York: Lyle Stuart.

Ellis, A. (1972). What does transpersonal psychology have to offer to the art and science of psychotherapy? *Voices, 8*(3), 10–20.

Ellis, A. (1973). *How to stubbornly refuse to be ashamed of anything* [Cassette recording]. New York: Institute for Rational Living.

Ellis, A. (1975). Critique of Frank's "The limits of humanism." *Humanist, 35*(6), 33–34.

Ellis, A., & Abrahms, E. (1978). *Brief psychotherapy in medical and health practice.* New York: Springer Publishing Co.

Ellis, A., & Grieger, R. (1977). *Handbook of rational–emotive therapy.* New York: Springer Publishing Co.

Ellis, A., & Whiteley, J. (Eds.). (1979). *Theoretical and empirical foundations of rational–emotive therapy.* Monterey, CA: Brooks/Cole.

Frank, J. D. (1975). The limits of humanism. *Humanist, 35*(5), 40–52.

Frankl, V. (1966). *Man's search for meaning.* New York: Washington Square Press.

Freud, S. (1965). *Standard edition of the complete psychological works of Sigmund Freud.* London: Hogarth.

Garfield, S. L., & Bergin, A. E. (1978). *Handbook of psychotherapy and behavior change,* 2nd ed. New York: Wiley.

Gross, M. L. (1979). *The psychological society.* New York: Simon & Schuster.

Hadley, S. W., & Strupp, H. W. (1976). Contemporary view of negative effects in psychotherapy. *Archives of General Psychiatry, 33,* 1291–1302.

Hogan, D. B. (1980, September). *Defining what a competent psychotherapist does: Problems and prospects.* Paper presented at the Annual Convention of the American Psychological Association, Montreal.

Jones, E. (1956). *The life and works of Sigmund Freud.* New York: Basic Books.

Kaplan, H. S. (1979). *Disorders of sexual desire.* New York: Brunner/Mazel.

Lazarus, A. A. (1971). *Behavior therapy and beyond.* New York: McGraw-Hill.

Lazarus, A. A. (1976). *Multimodal behavior therapy.* New York: Springer Publishing Co.

Lieberman, M. A., Yalom, I. D., & Miles, M. B. (1973). *Encounter groups: First facts.* New York: Basic Books.

Maliver, B. L. (1972). *The encounter game.* New York: Stein & Day.

Maultsby, M. C., Jr. (1975). *Help yourself to happiness.* New York: Institute for Rational Living.

May, R. (1969). *Love and will.* New York: Norton.

Popper, K. (1972). *Objective knowledge.* London: Oxford.

Pottinger, P. S. (1980, September). *Certifying competence not credentials.* Paper presented at the Annual Convention of the American Psychological Association, Montreal.

Rosen, R. D. (1977). *Psychobabble.* New York: Atheneum.

Russell, B. (1965). *The basic writings of Bertrand Russell.* New York: Simon & Schuster.

Small, L. (1979). *The brief psychotherapies.* New York: Brunner/Mazel.

Strupp, H. H. (1980, September). *Toward the measurement of therapists' contributions to negative outcomes.* Paper presented at the Annual Convention of the American Psychological Association, Montreal.

Wachtel, P. (1978). *Psychoanalysis and behavior therapy.* New York: Basic Books.

Wolpe, J. (1973). *The practice of behavior therapy.* New York: Pergamon.

Failures in Rational– Emotive Therapy   12

INTRODUCTION

RET—especially its cognitive restructuring method—has been proved to be effective in scores of controlled experiments and, together with cognitive–behavior therapy (CBT) (which Ellis often calls non-preferential or general RET), has a remarkably good record in this respect (DiGiuseppe, Miller, & Trexler, 1979; Haaga & Davison, 1989; McGovern & Silverman, 1984). But as Ellis observes here RET certainly has its failures!

For a number of years Ellis's main hypothesis, based on considerable clinical observation, has been that when RET is efficiently employed with intelligent and educated clients who stay in therapy for a year or more and it still fails to bring good results, frequently the failing clients either are exceptionally disturbed (psychotic or borderline) or have unusually low frustration tolerance and keep coming to therapy without doing much to work at the RET procedures they presumably come to learn.

When Edna Foa asked Ellis to do a chapter for her book with P. M. G. Emmelkamp, Failures in Behavior Therapy, *he decided to test this hypothesis and did the study described in the following paper. As noted, the study has distinct flaws and limitations, and its findings are not to be taken as gospel. However, research in progress at the Institute for Rational–Emotive Therapy in New York by Raymond DiGiuseppe, Russell Leaf, and other members of the research staff also tends to substantiate Ellis's clinical and experimental findings. So he still tentatively upholds the main conclusions of this paper and hopes to have them more solidly substantiated by further research.*

REFERENCES

DiGiuseppe, R. A., Miller, N. J., & Trexler, L. D. (1979). A review of rational–emotive psychotherapy outcome studies. In A. Ellis & J. M. Whiteley (Eds.),

Theoretical and empirical foundations of rational–emotive therapy (pp. 218–235). Monterey, CA: Brooks/Cole.

Haaga, D. A., & Davison, G. C. (1989). Outcome studies of rational–emotive therapy. In M. E. Bernard & R. DiGiuseppe (Eds.), *Inside rational–emotive therapy*. San Diego, CA: Academic Press.

McGovern, T. E., & Silverman, M. S. (1984). A review of outcome studies of rational–emotive therapy from 1977 to 1982. *Journal of Rational–Emotive Therapy*, *2*(1), 7–18.

Failures in psychotherapy are, of course, common. Failures in behavior therapy (BT) and cognitive–behavior therapy (CBT) may not be as common as they are in most other modes of therapy, but they certainly exist! This chapter will discuss failures in treatment in rational–emotive therapy (RET), a pioneering and popular form of CBT.

RET is a highly cognitive and philosophic school of psychological treatment, but it was also specifically designed, at its inception early in 1955, as a set of emotive–evocative and dehabituating behavioral procedures. Its theory and its practice are comprehensive and multimodal (Bard, 1980; Ellis, 1962, 1973; Ellis & Abrahms, 1978; Ellis & Grieger, 1977; Grieger & Boyd, 1980; Walen, DiGiuseppe, & Wessler, 1980; Wessler & Wessler, 1980). Its record of effective results, as tested by controlled experiments, is highly imperfect but still good (Ellis & Whiteley, 1979). Why, then, should this unusually cognitive-emotive-behavioral therapy have its distinct share of failures? An intriguing question.

CHARACTERISTICS OF CLIENTS WHO FAILED IN RET

I could try to answer this question by citing a clinical case or two in which, in spite of my presumed competent use of RET, I dismally failed to effect any client improvement. Such cases might

Reprinted from *Failures in Behavior Therapy* (pp. 159–171) by E. B. Foa and P. M. G. Emmelkamp, 1983, New York: Wiley.

be very instructive. All clinical presentations, however, tend to be subjectively anecdotal rather than more objectively empirical, and they almost always include no real control group. On the other hand, well-controlled studies of therapy too often are analogue rather than down-to-earth clinical studies and, therefore, have their own serious limitations (Kazdin & Wilson, 1978). Seeking a compromise (though still imperfect) solution to this kind of research problem, I shall try a somewhat unusual procedure by employing a fairly large number (no less than 50) of my own clinical cases where RET failed and by comparing them to an equal number of other clinical cases (again my own) where it definitely appeared to succeed. These cases all saw me for individual and/or group therapy; when they were in group they also had as my associate therapist one of our Fellows at the Institute for Rational–Emotive Therapy, who assist me in group. They were rated by me (and sometimes also by my associate group therapist) as to (1) whether they succeeded or failed during the period of their being treated with RET, and (2) whether they possessed the 21 characteristics investigated in this study (listed in Table 12.1). The kind of research design used in this study clearly has its serious limitations, inasmuch as I am the only individual therapist and the main group therapist, and I am the main (though not the only) evaluator of these cases. Nonetheless, this piece of research may have some real value.

To make this research even more definitive and useful, the cases of failure I shall discuss have been selected so that they only include individuals (1) who are of above average or of superior intelligence (in my judgment and that of their other group therapist); (2) who seemed really to understand RET and who were often effective (especially in group therapy) in helping others to learn and use it; (3) who in some ways made therapeutic progress and felt that they benefited by having RET but who still retained one or more serious presenting symptoms, such as severe depression, acute anxiety, overwhelming hostility, or extreme lack of self-discipline; and (4) who had at least one year of individual and/or group RET sessions and sometimes considerably more. In important respects, then, this group of failures consisted of fairly ideal RET clients; as did, too, the clients in the control group, who were also selected on the basis of the same four criteria but who, in addition, seemed to greatly improve, to be free of serious symptoms at the end of their RET experience, and for at least a year more remain improved.

How did the failures in this study fail? In one or more of the following ways:

Table 12.1. Characteristics of Clients in Rational–Emotive Therapy (RET)

Characteristic	Number Who Failed to Respond	Number Who Responded Quite Well	Significance of χ^2 Difference
Extremely anxious	42	45	Nonsignificant
Severely neurotic or borderline	33	32	Nonsignificant
Dire need for approval or love	38	39	Nonsignificant
Overinvolved with others	10	10	Nonsignificant
Self-downing	39	49	.01
Autistic	28	8	.01
Disorganized	18	9	.02
Grandiose	11	2	.02
Often not listening to others	10	1	.01
Organicity signs	15	8	.05
Psychotic	10	1	.01
Psychopathic	11	6	Nonsignificant
Serious addictions	25	16	.01
Severely and/or often angry	36	20	.01
Severely depressed	38	26	.01
Dislikable to others	23	3	.01
Severe low frustration tolerance	33	16	.01
Stubborn, resistant, rebellious	38	12	.01
Refusal to do cognitive disputing	36	0	.01
Refusal to do activity homework assignments	34	6	.01
Refusal to generally work at therapy	34	2	.01

1. They made initial good progress emotionally and/or behaviorally but then stopped and could not or would not advance to the level of symptom removal or achievement of greater potential that they wished to achieve through therapy.
2. They made (initial or later) good therapeutic progress but then retrogressed to a level near which, or even below which, they began therapy.
3. They made good "emotional" progress (e.g., lost much of their original feelings of anxiety, depression, hostility, or self-pity)

but remained stymied behaviorally (e.g., remained self-defeatingly addicted to overeating, alcohol, or procrastination).

4. They made good behavioral progress (e.g., dieted steadily or stopped procrastinating) but relatively little cognitive and/or emotional improvement (e.g., still had severe feelings of anxiety, depression, hostility, or self-pity).

A number of characteristics of all the clients in this study was rated by me and by their other group therapists at the Institute for Rational–Emotive Therapy in New York City (at whose clinic all the clients were seen), to determine whether the clients possessed these characteristics (listed in Table 12.1). All raters had some extensive experience with the clients. When my ratings of whether a client possessed one of the 21 traits included in the study were compared to the ratings of the other therapists who also knew the clients well, an agreement of 87% was found. The ratings of the clients (i.e., whether they possessed the listed characteristics) were done either at the end of therapy or after they had been in therapy for a year or more and were still continuing. The characteristics rated were not carefully defined, and the therapists doing the ratings were merely asked to state whether, in their opinion, the subjects had the stated characteristic. When the ratings were done, the therapists were not told what the purpose of the ratings was, nor were they told anything about the study I was doing on failures in RET.

The characteristics listed in Table 12.1 were chosen on the basis of my hunches that they might possibly be related to failure in RET. The terms "neurosis" and "psychosis," as well as similar characteristics listed in the table were given their usual (vague) meanings in this study. Those who were rated as "often not listening to others" were not deemed to be psychotic (although of those who were noted as not listening to others significantly more were probably in the psychotic than in the neurotic group). "Organicity signs" were defined as having discernible organic manifestations, such as tics, severe stuttering, peculiar eye movements, epilepsy, and the like.

When the clients were rated regarding salient characteristics included in this study, 2 × 2 tables were constructed showing the number of clients in each of these classifications who failed to respond and who responded quite well to RET; chi-squares were calculated for each set of 2 × 2 tables, to see whether significant differences were obtained for each table. Thus it was found that in the failure group, 36 (out of 50) clients were rated as often being quite angry, and 14 were rated as not often being quite angry; in the "responded well to RET" group, 20 (out of 50) clients were rated as often being quite angry, and 30 were rated as not often being this angry. For this 2 × 2 matrix, chi-square was calculated as being 11.1, which indicates a probability of less than .01 that a significant difference between these two distributions did not exist. The conclusion in this instance would be, therefore, that in all probability the failure clients were significantly more often rated as experiencing extreme anger than were the group of clients who responded well to RET.

Examination of Table 12.1 reveals the following:

1. In regard to the usual diagnoses of neurotic traits, the "failure" group did not tend to differ significantly from the "responded well" group. Both groups had a remarkably equal number of individuals who were rated as being very anxious, severely neurotic or borderline, having a dire need for others' approval, and overinvolved with others. In one respect, self-downing, the "responded well" group actually included a significantly larger number of individuals (49 to 39) than the "failure" group. One reason for the similarity of both groups in these neurotic respects probably stemmed from the manner in which they were selected in the study, inasmuch as the "responded well" group (unlike many other clients who benefit from RET) was deliberately chosen to include individuals who took a year or more to complete therapy and who, therefore, were, at least at the start of therapy, highly neurotic. The reason why the "responded well" group included even more self-downing clients than the "failure" group was probably because the latter group (as will be seen below) included significantly larger numbers of autistic, grandiose, and psychotic individuals, as well as significantly larger numbers of angry individuals, many of whom tend to down others rather than to denigrate themselves and hence to not focus as much on self-downing thoughts and behaviors.

2. Although the "failures" appeared in this study not to be rated significantly more often as neurotic than the clients who responded well to RET, they did appear more often to be rated psychotic or near-psychotic. Thus the "failures" included a significantly greater proportion of individuals who were checked off as being autistic, disorganized, grandiose, organic, and psychotic; they also included a greater proportion of individuals who were rated as being psychopathic, although this proportion did not reach statistical significance. In addition, they included a significantly greater proportion of individuals who were rated as chroni-

cally not listening to others (or to their therapist), a trait which may possibly be indicative of near-psychosis.

3. On almost all the characteristics studied of the "failure" and the "responded well to RET" clients that included strong elements of low frustration tolerance, the former group consistently had a significantly greater proportion of individuals than the latter group. These characteristics included addiction to some self-defeating behavior, anger at other people, depression, possession of dislikable social traits, severe low frustration tolerance, and stubbornness and rebelliousness.

4. As might well be expected, on all the characteristics in the study that related to unwillingness to work at therapy (and which also are presumably related to low frustration tolerance), the "failure" group showed a significantly higher proportion of individuals than the "responded well to RET" group. These characteristics included refraining from disputing irrational beliefs, avoidance of carrying out activity homework assignments, and general refusal to work at therapy.

What do these findings mainly indicate? First of all, they at least partly seem to provide evidence favoring several major hypotheses or hunches with which I started when I thought about what questions to investigate about the characteristics of clients who fail to benefit appreciably from RET even though they are bright, seem to understand the principles of this kind of therapy, and spend a year or more in regular individual or group RET sessions.

Hypothesis 1. Clients who fail in RET are more severely disturbed, and particularly more psychotic or organically ill, than those who repond well to RET.

As noted above, the failures did not seem to be significantly more often neurotic than those who reponded well. But this may have been an artifact of the method in which both groups were selected, inasmuch as those who responded well only included individuals who stayed in therapy for a year or more (as did also the failures); and RET is a method of therapy that less neurotic individuals often respond to quite quickly—in 20 sessions or less of either group or individual therapy. My impression, from long-term clinical experience with RET, is that when clients who respond well to it are picked at random, and include those who respond rather quickly as well as those who do so after a year or more of therapy, the latter group is significantly less disturbed than the former group and that, therefore, Hypothesis 1 tends to have some evidence to back it. This impression, however, could well instigate some more careful empirical study before it is considered to be substantiated.

In regard to the part of the hypothesis concerning psychotic and organically ill clients, the present study shows some clear-cut evidence that such individuals indeed wind up more frequently in the "failure" than in the "respond well to RET" group and that, therefore, there may be some validity to the notion that intensive and prolonged RET (like various other kinds of psychotherapy) works better with neurotic than with psychotic clients. This would hardly be a surprising conclusion.

Hypothesis 2. Clients with severe low frustration tolerance tend to fail in RET more frequently than those with higher frustration tolerance.

This hunch was distinctly borne out by the data of the study, in that clients in the "failure" category significantly more often displayed such characteristics as some kind of serious addiction, frequent eruptions of anger and hostility, severe depression, personal dislikability to others, stubbornness and rebelliousness, and severe general low frustration tolerance. It may be guessed that low frustration tolerance would interfere with using RET in a therapeutic situation in several ways:

1. It would tend to focus clients on the necessity for changing others and the external world conditions rather than on changing themselves.
2. It would create feelings, such as those of anger, that would notably distract them from using RET philosophies and procedures to change themselves.
3. Although RET (unlike classical behavior therapy) helps clients gain a good deal of insight to help themselves change their basic beliefs, like classical behavior therapy it does not hold that this kind of insight enables clients "automatically" to modify their beliefs and behaviors; instead, it shows them that they had better rely, mainly, on their own persistent *activity* (including cognitive and behavioral) to modify their self-defeating responses.

Clients with low frustration tolerance, therefore, who believe that conditions of life are too hard and that they must not be that hard, are less likely to work at changing themselves (or, for that matter, at changing external conditions) than those with higher frustration tolerance.

Hypothesis 3. Clients who not only have low frustration tolerance in general but who have it specifically in regard to working at therapy will tend to fail in RET more frequently than those who have a hardworking attitude toward therapy.

The data of this study consistently supported this hypothesis, inasmuch as the three characteristics that were investigated that related to clients' attitudes toward and work at therapy all turned up data favoring it. Thus failures in RET were significantly more often found to avoid disputing their irrational beliefs, to fail to do their activity homework assignments, and to refuse to work at other aspects of rational–emotive therapy. It would have been surprising if this had not been found; the fact that it was so consistently found may be exaggerated because the raters of how well or poorly all the clients in the study did at working at therapy may well have been contaminated by their knowledge that those in the "failure" group did fail, whereas those in the "responded to RET" group did not. This particular finding, therefore, had better be viewed more skeptically than some of the other findings of the study.

DISCUSSION OF THE RESULTS

RET is a form of psychotherapy that specifically includes the use of a number of cognitive, emotive, and behavioral procedures. Cognitively, it stresses the acceptance by clients of responsibility for largely creating their own crooked thinking and their inappropriate feelings, and the consequent understanding by these clients of their own irrational beliefs (especially their use of absolutistic shoulds, oughts, and musts) and their employment of the disputing of these irrationalities and the use of other cognitive methods to allay or distract themselves from irrationality. In its cognitive aspects, RET also emphasizes the persistent use of reason, logic, and the scientific method to uproot clients' irrational beliefs. Consequently, it ideally requires intelligence, concentration, and high-level, consistent cognitive self-disputation and self-persuasion. These therapeutic behaviors would tend to be disrupted or blocked by extreme disturbance, by lack of organization, by grandiosity, by organic disruption, and by refusal to do RET-type disputing of irrational ideas. All these characteristics proved to be present in significantly more failures than in those clients who responded favorably to RET.

RET also, to be quite successful, involves clients' forcefully and emotively changing their beliefs and actions, and their being stubbornly determined to accept responsibility for their own inappropriate feelings and to vigorously work at changing these feelings (Ellis & Abrahms, 1978; Ellis & Whiteley, 1979). But the failure clients in this study were significantly more angry than those who responded well to RET; more of them were severely depressed and inactive, they were more often grandiose, and they were more frequently stubbornly resistant and rebellious. All these characteristics would presumably tend to interfere with the kind of emotive processes and changes that RET espouses.

RET strongly advocates that clients, in order to improve, do in vivo activity homework assignments, deliberately force themselves to engage in many painful activities until they become familiar and unpainful, and notably work and practice its multimodal techniques. But the group of clients who signally failed in this study showed abysmally low frustration tolerance, had serious behavioral addictions, led disorganized lives, refrained from doing their activity homework assignments, were more frequently psychotic, and generally refused to work at therapy. All these characteristics, which were found significantly more frequently than were found in the clients who responded quite well to RET, would tend to interfere with the behavioral methods of RET.

This brings us to a fascinating question: Inasmuch as the failures more often tended to be individuals who could be said to have inbuilt resistances to RET (and, very likely, to many or most other forms of psychotherapy), and inasmuch as their low frustration tolerance and their refusal to work at changing themselves both in their regular existences and in the course of therapy seem to often accompany their extreme states of disturbance (particularly their tendencies to be exceptionally angry, autistic, depressed, disorganized, grandiose, organically ill, and psychotic), does this reveal a kind of "Catch-22" regarding which clients require and which actually make the best use of psychotherapy? Namely, is there a strong tendency for the clients who are most disturbed and who could most use therapy to be precisely those kinds of individuals whose severe disturbances will interfere most with their actually benefiting from psychological treatment? A good deal of prior research and clinical findings tend to support this hypothesis (Garfield & Bergin, 1978), and the findings of the present study appear to confirm it once again.

If this proposition is indeed in part true, it need not engender a feeling of hopelessness in clients and therapists. As I have noted elsewhere, the strong predispositions of humans to think irrationally and to be emotionally disturbed is probably largely biological as well as environmental; but this does not mean that biological tendencies to think, emote, and act in dysfunctional ways cannot be overcome (Ellis, 1976). Similarly, if severe emotional disturbance and resistance to therapeutic change are significantly correlated, this again does not mean that seriously disturbed individuals have to continue to resist improvement, nor that they cannot change. It merely means that the problem of helping people to modify themselves is more complicated and difficult than many of us have previously thought it to be and, therefore, we require therapy procedures that are not only "effective" (i.e., bring about improved results with groups of disturbed clients) but also "efficient" (i.e., help more clients more extensively, pervasively, and preventively (Ellis, 1980a).

As far as RET and CBT are concerned, this study would tend to show that there are clients with certain characteristics who are significantly more likely to resist improvement than other types of clients. In general, neurotic clients can and do make good progress as compared to those who are autistic, depressed, disorganized, grandiose, organically ill, or psychotic. In addition, clients with abysmally low frustration tolerance or what I have elsewhere called discomfort anxiety (Ellis, 1979, 1980c), resist treatment more often than those who have higher frustration tolerance. Finally, as would be expected, clients who refuse to work hard and persistently at the therapeutic process more often signally fail at therapy than those who do the work and practice that RET particularly calls for. If these findings prove to be supported by other data than that found in this highly challengeable study, the task of RET theorists and practitioners (and perhaps of all therapists) is to keep working to discover more efficient procedures and better ways of motivating "D.C.'s" (difficult customers) to use these procedures.

COMMENTS ON FAILURES IN RET

The previous discussion has dealt mainly with failure in RET as revealed by the specific study discussed in this chapter. Several other important questions of a more general nature may be raised, and I shall now attempt to answer some of these.

First, in what way is failure to benefit from RET similar and different from failure to respond to other systems of psychotherapy: for example, psychoanalysis, behavior therapy, and client-centered therapy? Regarding similarities, I would hypothesize that a large minority of all psychotherapy clients—I would guess from

20% to 30%—are so severely, so organically, or so psychotically disturbed that they will benefit minimally, and often hardly at all, from any of today's modes of psychotherapy, including RET. This does not necessarily mean that these kinds of clients cannot, under any conditions, appreciably change through psychotherapeutic contact, but mainly that their changing themselves is so difficult and requires such a considerable amount of persistent effort on their (and their therapists') part that they, therefore, will not make this effort to modify their thoughts, feelings, and behaviors.

I would guess that RET and classical behavior therapy are most similar in this respect, inasmuch as both these forms of psychological treatment strive to help clients make a profound philosophical–behavioral change, to surrender their disturbed symptoms, and (presumably) to maintain this relatively symptom-free condition. The exceptionally disturbed, and especially the psychotic and near-psychotic, clients referred to in the preceding paragraph may tend to be unable or unwilling to make this kind of change and, therefore, will "resist" RET and behavior therapy treatment. It is interesting to note that Wolpe (1973) has consistently held that behavior therapy in general, and systematic desensitization in particular, are not likely to be effective with psychotics.

Certain other kinds of therapies, however, whether or not their adherents design them this way, are easily construed by clients (and by therapists) to help clients "feel better" rather than "get better." Client-centered therapy, encounter groups, and cathartic therapies, for example, seem notable in this respect. Clients in these types of therapy, therefore, may really have different goals than clients in RET and classical behavior therapy, and may succeed at attaining these goals even when they are exceptionally disturbed and in the category of individuals who frequently do not benefit from RET and classical behavior therapy. It may also be hypothesized that some highly resistant clients may be more benefited by certain non-RET and non-BT forms of treatment in that, by these therapies, they at least feel better *with* their unchanging symptoms whereas they would not feel as well with these same remaining symptoms if they experienced RET or BT.

It may also be hypothesized that individuals who benefit most from RET tend to be reasonably educated and intelligent, and that those with less advantages in this respect may benefit more from certain other therapies, such as BT or cathartic treatment. This, however, would mainly be true of the elegant form of RET, which includes teaching clients how to use the scientific method and to do high-level cognitive disputing of their irrational beliefs. Lower-level RET, which teaches them how to use coping statements, would probably be as effective (or even more so) with less educated and less intelligent clients than would various kinds of non-RET treatments, including classical BT.

What are the most common "mistakes" in practicing RET that probably lead to failures? These have been discussed in detail in several books and articles (Ellis & Whiteley, 1979; Walen, DiGiuseppe, & Wessler, 1980; Wessler & Ellis, 1980; Wessler & Wessler, 1980), so I shall briefly summarize some of them as follows.

1. RET therapists sometimes teach the principles of RET to clients too rapidly and too abruptly, thereby interfering with their understanding and using these principles.
2. Therapists are too namby-pamby or unforceful in encouraging RET clients to surrender their irrational thinking and behavioral dysfunctions.
3. Therapists shuttle back and forth from one symptom (e.g., self-downing) to another (e.g., anger), and fail to help clients zero in effectively on one at a time before they confuse and confound it with the second symptom.
4. Therapists deal only or mainly with primary symptoms (e.g., fear of elevators) rather than with secondary symptoms as well (e.g., fear of having the painful fear of elevators).
5. Therapists not only fail to relate warmly or intimately to clients (which is quite allowable in RET) but also are negative, impatient, and hostile to clients; they sometimes try to teach unconditional self-acceptance to clients but fail to unconditionally accept these clients themselves.
6. Therapists have significant degrees of low frustration tolerance, and do not strongly persist in using RET with clients but instead discourage themselves with difficult clients, give up too easily, and act impatiently.
7. RET therapists are not too bright or not too good at disputing irrational beliefs themselves and, therefore, are not too helpful to clients in showing them how to do RET disputation.
8. Therapists concentrate almost exclusively on clients' self-downing characteristics and the irrational beliefs that lie behind these characteristics, and consequently ignore their low frustration tolerance or discomfort anxiety, which may be equally or almost as important in their disturbances.
9. Therapists concentrate heavily on their own hypotheses about clients and their irrational beliefs, and consequently

do not listen adequately to these clients and sometimes foist on them problems and solutions that they could well live without.

10. Therapists are too simplistic and focus mainly on highly obvious symptoms and the irrationalities that lie behind them, rather than going on to deal with more subtle symptoms and the basic and often more complicated irrationalities that are subsumed under them (Ellis, 1980b).

11. Therapists attempt to help clients feel calm, serene, or indifferent when they are plagued by problems and losses, instead of helping them feel appropriately, and often deeply, sorrowful, regretful, frustrated, or annoyed about these difficulties.

12. Therapists only acknowledge clients' irrational cognitions that supposedly cause their emotional and behavioral disturbances, and fail to look at the activating events and experiences that partially lead to these thoughts, and the important interactions between the thoughts and the experiences or events.

13. RET therapists too heavily focus on the important cognitive aspects of rational–emotive therapy and partially or mainly neglect the highly important emotive and behavioral methods that are an integral part of RET.

Are there any therapist variables that can impede or enhance success by RET? Some of the main therapist variables that tend to impede its success have just been listed. Some of the important variables that tend to enhance RET success probably include the following.

A high degree of intelligence by the therapist.

A vital interest by the therapist not only in helping clients change but in doing so through a multiplicity of methods, especially including those that deal with the disputing of irrational beliefs and with problem solving.

The sincere and vigorous use by the therapist of RET philosophy and methods in his or her own life and the conquering of some of his or her own disturbances by this use.

A high energy level on the part of the therapist and the determination to use this energy to vigorously and forcefully attack clients' irrational ideas and self-defeating behaviors and to teach these clients how to internalize and use this kind of attacking themselves.

Conviction by the therapist that the scientific method is not only good for understanding human processes and for research into psychotherapy but that it also has immense usefulness when specifically applied to the personal problems of disturbed individuals.

What are some of the reasons for premature termination (dropouts) in RET and for serious relapses on the part of clients who have previously made significant gains? A number of such reasons seem to exist, including these.

1. Because it is simple and offers clients something of a revolutionary approach to understanding and minimizing their disturbances, RET often helps bring about unusually fast results in the elimination of certain symptoms such as fear of social disapproval, sexual inadequacy, and feelings of intense hostility. When it works "too well" in these respects, clients falsely think they are completely "cured" in some instances and break off therapy after relatively few sessions, before they have worked through their problems in a thoroughgoing manner.

2. RET requires a considerable amount of work and effort by clients who want to make a profound philosophic and behavioral change. Some clients, especially those with abysmally low frustration tolerance (and who want magical help), either drop out fairly quickly or remain in therapy but refuse to do the required work and, therefore, do not make too significant gains or else temporarily change and then fall back to previous disturbed levels of behavior.

3. Therapists make various errors that encourage clients to drop out of therapy or to relapse after making initial gains (such as the errors in the thirteen points listed above).

4. As noted previously in this paper, strong biological predispositions toward severe disturbance and toward refusing to work at giving up such disturbance may encourage some individuals to quit RET quickly or prematurely and to first make progress and then retrogress.

5. Various situational factors occur (as they do in other forms of therapy) to encourage premature dropouts. Thus a woman who comes to therapy because she cannot relate adequately to men may accidentally, soon after therapy has begun, meet an almost ideal man to whom she can easily relate. Or she may use the RET techniques she has learned in the first few sessions to do better than she usually does with men, and may thereby get into an intimate relationship; and, her main therapeutic goal being quickly achieved, drop therapy before she has benefited very much from it.

6. While participating in RET therapy, clients may for various reasons start to devoutly believe in a different system of psychotherapy or of philosophy—such as psychoanalysis, Erhard Seminar Training (EST), or some orthodox religion—which is antithetical to some of the principles of RET and that leads them to drop RET or to surrender some of the gains that they have previously made with it.

In conclusion, it seems fairly obvious, from the results of the study of RET failures included in this chapter and from extensive clinical observation, that RET often fails for reasons similar to those why all other forms of psychotherapy and that it sometimes succeeds for reasons, including situational reasons, similar to those that lead to successes in other forms of psychological treatment. In many respects, however, RET differs significantly from most other kinds of therapy and also from general cognitive–behavior therapy with which it is closely identified (Ellis, 1980b; Ellis & Whiteley, 1979). Some important aspects of its failures and successes, therefore, seem to be indigenous to its specific theory and practice, as has been pointed out in the above discussion. Considerably more research in regard to its failures, however, had better be done so that its efficacy and its efficiency can be appreciably improved.

REFERENCES

Bard, J. A. (1980). *Rational emotive therapy in practice.* Champaign, IL: Research Press.

Ellis, A. (1962). *Reason and emotion in psychotherapy.* New York: Lyle Stuart.

Ellis, A. (1973). *Humanistic psychotherapy: The rational–emotive approach.* New York: Crown and McGraw-Hill Paperbacks.

Ellis, A. (1976). The biological basis of human irrationality. *Journal of Individual Psychology, 32,* 145–168.

Ellis, A. (1979). Discomfort anxiety: A new cognitive–behavioral construct: Part I. *Rational Living, 14*(2), 2–8.

Ellis, A. (1980a). Discomfort anxiety: A new cognitive–behavioral construct: Part 2. *Rational Living, 15*(1), 25–30.

Ellis, A. (1980b). Rational–emotive therapy and cognitive behavior therapy: Similarities and differences. *Cognitive Therapy and Research, 4,* 325–340.

Ellis, A. (1980c). The value of efficiency in psychotherapy. *Psychotherapy, 17,* 414–419.

Ellis, A., & Abrahms, E. (1978). *Brief psychotherapy in medical and health practice.* New York: Springer Publishing Co.

Ellis, A., & Grieger, R. (Eds.). (1977). *Handbook of rational–emotive therapy.* New York: Springer Publishing Co.

Ellis, A., & Whiteley, J. M. (Eds.). (1979). *Theoretical and empirical foundations of rational–emotive therapy.* Monterey, CA: Brooks/Cole.

Garfield, S. L., & Bergin, A. E. (Eds.). (1978). *Handbook of psychotherapy and behavior change* (2nd ed.). New York: Wiley.

Grieger, R., & Boyd, J. (1980). *Rational–emotive therapy: A skills based approach.* New York: Van Nostrand Reinhold.

Kazdin, A. E., & Wilson, G. T. (1978). *Evaluation of behavior therapy: Issues, evidence and research strategies.* Cambridge, MA: Ballinger.

Walen, S. R., DiGiuseppe, R., & Wessler, R. L. (1980). *A practitioner's guide to rational–emotive therapy.* New York: Oxford.

Wessler, R. A., & Wessler, R. L. (1980). *The principles and practice of rational–emotive therapy.* San Francisco: Jossey-Bass.

Wessler, R. L., & Ellis, A. (1980). Supervision in rational–emotive therapy. In A. K. Hess (Ed.), *Psychotherapy supervision.* New York: Wiley.

Wolpe, J. (1973). *The practice of behavior therapy.* New York: Pergamon.

Rational–Emotive Therapy Approaches to Overcoming Resistance

13

INTRODUCTION

Before 1983 Ellis had dealt with resistance to RET and to psychotherapy in general with literally tens of thousands of clients and with the hundreds of therapists he has helped to train in RET. Ellis had not written extensively on this subject, however, until Windy Dryden, who founded the British Journal of Cognitive Psychotherapy, *asked him to do a paper on it. Ellis agreed to write an article or two on resistance and ended up by writing four, of which the present essay is a combination of the first two. Later, Ellis expanded on them and published a book,* Overcoming Resistance: Rational–Emotive Therapy with Difficult Clients *(Ellis, 1985).*

Rational–emotive therapy takes a very active–directive, vigorous, evocative approach to resistance, quite unlike the approaches taken by most of the other psychotherapies, including the cognitive–behavior therapies of Aaron Beck, Maxie Maultsby, and Donald Meichenbaum. RET sees resistance as largely stemming from clients' discomfort disturbance or low frustration tolerance and holds that unusual efforts had better be made by both therapists and clients to help overcome it.

From A. Ellis and R. Grieger, *Handbook of Rational–Emotive Therapy*, Vol. 2, 1986, New York: Springer Publishing Co. This article combines two earlier articles: (1) Ellis, A., Rational–emotive therapy (RET) approaches to overcoming resistance, part 1, *British Journal of Cognitive Psychotherapy*, 1983, *1*(1), 28–38, and (2) Ellis, A., Rational–emotive (RET) approaches to overcoming resistance, part 2, *British Journal of Cognitive Psychotherapy*, 1983, *1*(2), 1–16. Reprinted by permission of *British Journal of Cognitive Psychotherapy*.

*RET therefore stresses force, vigor, drama, action, work, and practice
to combat resistance and sees antiresistance effort as a lifelong proposition for most clients.*

*Along these lines, Ellis believes that the future of effective psycho-
therapy will largely consist of devising and experimentally testing
methods of working with people who resist acknowledging their disturbances, who refuse to go for therapy, who deliberately choose easy
and relatively inefficient methods of psychological treatment, and
who resist collaborating with efficient therapists to hasten and intensify treatment. Ellis notes that resistance to basic personality change
is part of the human biosocial makeup and believes that clinical
scientists and scientific clinicians had better make concerted efforts
to minimize this kind of resistance.*

REFERENCES

Ellis, A. (1985). *Overcoming resistance: Rational–emotive therapy with difficult clients.* New York: Springer Publishing Co.

Resistance to psychotherapy, even by those who strongly aver
that they want to help themselves change and who spend considerable time, money, and effort in pursuing therapy, has been observed for many years. Ancient philosophers—such as Confucius,
Gautama Buddha, Epictetus, Seneca, and Marcus Aurelius—
recognized that people voluntarily pursuing personality change often resist their own and their teachers' best efforts. When modern
psychotherapy began to develop in the nineteenth century, some of
its main practitioners—such as James Braid, Hippolyte Bernheim,
Jean-Martin Charcot, Auguste Ambroise Liebault, and Pierre
Janet—made the theory of resistance and the practice of overcoming it key elements in their psychotherapies (Ellenberger, 1970).

Early in the twentieth century, psychotherapeutic resistance particularly came into its own with the elucidation of the Freudian
concept of transference (Freud, 1912/1965a) and with Freud expanding his earlier concept to include five main varieties of resist-

ance: resistances of repression, of transference, and of secondary gain (all stemming from the ego), resistance of the repetition compulsion (arising from the id), and resistance of guilt and self-punishment (originating in the superego) (Freud, 1926/1965b). Since this time, psychoanalysis (and many related forms of therapy) have, we might say, almost been obsessed with problems of resistance.

As several recent writers have aptly noted (Wachtel, 1982), views on what resistance is and how it can best be resolved in therapy largely depend on one's definition of this fascinating phenomenon. Personally, I like Turkat and Meyer's (1982) definition: "Resistance is client behavior that the therapist labels antitherapeutic" (p. 158) since it is both simple and comprehensive; and, as its authors suggest, it can also be operationalized to each client's individual experience and be seen as that specific form of behavior that is observed when this particular client acts nontherapeutically according to his or her therapist in these particular situations.

However accurate such a definition of resistance may be, it is too general to be of much clinical use, and it hardly explains the main "causes" of resistance, nor what can be done to overcome it. Rational–emotive therapy (RET), together with cognitive–behavioral therapy (CBT), assumes that when clients self-defeatingly and irrationally resist following therapeutic procedures and homework assignments, they largely do so because of their explicit and implicit cognitions or beliefs. RET, which tends to be more philosophical and more persuasive than some other forms of CBT—such as those of Bandura (1977), Mahoney (1980) and Meichenbaum (1977)—assumes that resisting clients have an underlying set of powerful and persistent irrational Beliefs (iB's), as well as an innate biosocial tendency to create new irrationalities, that frequently block them from carrying out the therapeutic goals and contracts that they overtly agree to work at achieving. Although RET does not agree with psychoanalytic and psychodynamic theory, which holds that client resistance is based on deeply unconscious, repressed thoughts and feelings, it does hypothesize that many—perhaps most—of the iB's that underlie client resistance are (1) at least partially implicit, unconscious, or automatic; (2) tenaciously held; (3) held concomitantly with strong feelings and fixed habit patterns of behavior; (4) to some extent held by virtually all clients; (5) difficult to change; and (6) likely to recur once they have been temporarily surrendered (Bard, 1980; Ellis, 1962, 1971a, 1973 1976, 1979, 1983b; Ellis & Grieger, 1977; Ellis & Whiteley, 1979; Walen, DiGiuseppe, & Wessler, 1980; Wessler & Wessler, 1980).

More specifically, RET assumes that clients who self-defeatingly resist therapy implicitly or explicitly tend to hold three main irrational Beliefs (iB's) or philosophies: (1) "I *must* do well at changing myself, and I'm an incompetent, hopeless client if I don't"; (2) "You (the therapist and others) *must* help me change, and you're rotten people if you don't"; and (3) "Changing myself *must* occur quickly and easily, and it's horrible if it doesn't!" Concomitantly with these irrational beliefs, resisters feel anxious, depressed, angry, and self-pitying about changing, and these disturbed feelings block their forcing themselves to change. Behaviorally, resisters withdraw, procrastinate, remain inert, and sabotage their self-promises to change. RET practitioners are largely concerned with helping resisters (and other clients) make a profound philosophic change so that they adopt a cooperative, confident, determined attitude toward self-change, rather than the self-blocking views that they hold. To effect this kind of cognitive restructuring, RET uses a wide variety of thinking, feeling, and activity methods.

Having said all of this, I shall spend the first part of this chapter trying to show, from an RET standpoint, what are the principal kinds of resistance, in what ways they usually arise, and what RET (and, hopefully, other) practitioners can do to understand and help themselves and their clients overcome therapy-sabotaging resistance. I shall first deal with common, "normal," or "usual" resistance, and in the later sections with unusual or highly stubborn resistances.

COMMON FORMS OF RESISTANCE

Some of the statistically common kinds of resistance that therapists encounter include the following:

"Healthy" Resistance

Clients sometimes resist change because therapists have their own fish to fry and mistakenly see these clients as having symptoms (e.g., hostility to their parents) or as having origins of their symptoms (e.g., oedipal feelings "causing" their sexual inadequacy) that the clients view as figments of the therapists' imagination. Rather than allow these therapeutic "authorities" to lead them up the garden path, such clients refuse to accept these interpretations and healthfully resist or flee from "treatment" (Basch, 1982; Ellis, 1962; Ellis & Harper, 1975; Lazarus & Fay, 1982).

From a rational–emotive view, clients who resist for healthy reasons are explicitly or implicitly telling themselves rational beliefs (rB's), such as "My therapist is probably wrong about my having this symptom or about the origins of my having it. Too bad! I'd better ignore his or her interpretations and perhaps get another therapist!" In the ABC theory of RET, at A (activating event) the clients experience their therapist's interpretations and directives (e.g., "You think you love your mother very much but unconsciously you really appear to loathe her"). At B (belief system), the clients tell themselves the rational beliefs just noted, and at C (emotional and behavioral consequences) they feel appropriately sorry about their therapist's misperceptions about their disturbances and they actively resist these misperceptions. They are therefore acting rationally and sanely and, according to RET, their resistance is self-helping and healthy. The one who has the real problem in these cases—and is "resisting" doing effective treatment—is their therapist!

Resistance Motivated by Client–Therapist Mismatching

Clients sometimes are "naturally" mismatched with their therapists, that is, manage to pick or be assigned to a therapist whom they just do not like, for whatever reasons. Thus, they may have a therapist who, to their idiosyncratic tastes or preferences, is too young or too old, too liberal or too conservative, too male or too female, too active or too passive. Because of this mismatching, they don't have too much rapport with their therapist and therefore resist him or her more than they would resist a more preferable therapist. If this becomes obvious during the therapy (which it never may), the therapists may try to compensate for what these clients see as their "flaws," and may succeed in doing so by being extra-nice to or hardworking with such clients. Or the clients may naturally overcome their antitherapist prejudices as the course of therapy intimately proceeds (just as husbands and wives may become more attached to their physically unattractive mates as time goes by and more emotional intimacy is achieved). Or the clients and/or their therapists may (often wisely) bring the relationship to a close.

Resistance Stemming from Clients'
Transference Disturbances

Following Freud (1912/1965a; 1900/1965c), psychoanalytic therapists assume that clients will unconsciously reenact with or transfer to their therapists the same kind of highly prejudiced relationships that they experienced with their parents during their early childhood. Thus, if a young woman has a middle-aged male analyst, she will strongly tend to fall in love with him (as she presumably once loved her father), will be jealous of his wife, will hate him when he refuses to go to bed with her, will try to control him as she tried to control her father, and so forth.

In RET, we take the view that these disturbed transference relations *sometimes* but not *necessarily* occur and that, when they do, they are usually sparked by some irrational beliefs (iB's). Thus, if this young woman strongly transfers her relationship from her father to her analyst, she is probably telling herself (and strongly believing) iB's like these: "Because my analyst is helpful and fatherly to me in some ways, he *must* be a complete father to me, and he *must* love me dearly!" "Because being loved by my father is enjoyable, I absolutely *must* be loved by my own father and by all fatherly people, including my therapist!" "If my father and my therapist do not totally love me—as I utterly *need* them to do—I am a worthless person!"

If and when, then, disturbed transference relations occur in therapy, rational–emotive practitioners look for the irrational beliefs (iB's) *behind* these disturbances, show clients how to see and change these ideas, and thereby teach them how to surmount these kinds of relationship resistances.

Resistances Caused by Therapists' Relationship Problems

Therapists, like clients, also sometimes have their relationship difficulties. These may be of three major kinds. (1) Therapists may naturally not like some of their clients, particularly those who are nasty, stupid, ugly, or otherwise unprepossessing. (2) Therapists may have what the psychoanalysts call severe countertransference difficulties and may therefore be bigoted against their clients. Thus, if a therapist hates her mother and one of her clients looks and acts like this mother, she may unconsciously want to harm rather than help this client. (3) Therapists may not have personal negative feelings toward their clients but may be insensitive to these clients' feelings and may not know how to maintain good therapeutic relations with them (Goldfried, 1982; Lazarus & Fay, 1982; Meichenbaum & Gilmore, 1982).

If the first or third of these therapist problems exists, it can be met by therapists' becoming aware of their own limitations and by compensating for them. Thus, therapists who personally do not like their clients can still focus on suitable helpful procedures and thereby surmount this handicap. I particularly notice that in using

RET I can focus so well on my clients' problems, and especially on showing them how to correct their thinking errors, that it hardly matters that I personally do not like some of them and would never select them as my friends (Ellis, 1971b, 1973).

RET therapists can also, especially with certain supersensitive clients, go out of their way to give these clients positive verbal reinforcement, to listen carefully and reflectively to their difficulties, to be open and honest with them, to give them active encouragement, to deliberately point out their good (as well as some of their self-defeating) characteristics, and otherwise to empathize with them in an almost Rogerian manner (Dryden, 1982; Ellis, 1977b; Johnson, 1980; Walen et al., 1980; Wessler & Wessler, 1980; Wessler, 1982). Although this kind of positive reinforcement has its distinct dangers (Ellis, 1983a; Turkat & Meyer, 1982), it can also at times be constructively used to overcome resistance.

If therapists are victims of countertransference and are negative to clients because of their own problems and bigotries, these can be resolved by looking for and disputing the irrational beliefs (iB's) creating their prejudices. Therapists who, for example, hate their clients who resemble the therapists' obnoxious mothers are irrationally telling themselves ideas like these: "Because my mother treated me badly, I can't stand *any* person who has some of her traits!" "This client *must not* behave the obnoxious way in which my mother acted! She's a horrible *person* for behaving in this crummy way!" Such irrational beliefs are fairly easily revealed if therapists use RET to probe their negative reactions to their clients. The kinds of overgeneralizations that lead to these beliefs are particularly uprooted through rational–emotive therapy (RET) and cognitive–behavioral therapy (CBT) (Ellis, 1962; Beck, 1976).

Resistance Related to Moralistic Attitudes of Therapists

In addition to the therapist-related resistances just mentioned, a common trait that many therapists possess and that blocks them in helping clients is their moralism: the profound tendency to condemn themselves and others for evil or stupid acts. Even though they are in the helping profession, they frequently believe that their seriously disturbed clients *should* not, *must* not be the way they are, especially when these clients abuse their therapists, come late, refuse to pay their bills, and otherwise behave obnoxiously or antisocially. Many therapists therefore overtly or covertly damn their clients for their wrongdoings and consequently help these clients damn themselves and become more, instead of less, disturbed. Naturally, many such clients often resist therapy.

RET practitioners particularly can combat this kind of resistance, since one of the key tenets of RET is that all humans, including all clients, merit what Rogers (1961) calls unconditional positive regard and what RET calls unconditional acceptance (Ellis, 1962, 1972a, 1973, 1976). This means that rational–emotive therapists look at their own (and others') moralism and the irrational beliefs (iB's) that underlie them, such as: "My client *should* work at therapy! She *must* not sabotage my efforts! How *awful* if she does! I *can't stand* it!" And RET practitioners work hard at extirpating these ideas and giving all their clients, no matter how difficult they are, unconditional self-acceptance. In this manner they help minimize therapist-encouraged resistance.

Resistance Linked to Clients' and Therapists' Other Love–Hate Problems

Although the Freudians assume that love–hate problems between clients and their therapists are invariably sparked by and intimately involved with transference difficulties—that is, stem from clients' and therapists' early family relationships—this is questionable. Client–therapist difficulties, and the resistance to which they sometimes lead, may be based on reality factors that have nothing to do with anyone's childhood experiences. Thus, a young female client may just happen to have an exceptionally bright, attractive, and kindly therapist who would be an ideal mate for her (or almost any other woman) if she met him socially; and she may quite realistically fall in love with him, even though he has virtually nothing in common with her father, her uncles, or her brothers. Similarly, her therapist may fall in love with her not because she resembles his mother but because, more than any other woman he has met and gotten close to in his entire life, she truly *is* charming, talented, and sexy to him.

When nontransference, reality-based feelings occur in therapy, and when they lead to intense warm or cold feelings on the part of the therapists and/or clients, they can easily foment resistance problems. Thus, a female client who intensely loves her therapist may resist improving in order to prolong the therapy; and a therapist who intensely loves his or her client may also (consciously or unconsciously) foment resistance to ensure that the therapy indefinitely continues.

These nontransference relationship feelings that encourage resistance are sometimes difficult to resolve, since they are reality-based and therefore both therapists and clients may derive special

gains (or pains) from them that may interfere with effective therapy. But they also may include iB's that can be disputed, such as:
"Because I love my therapist and it would be great to mate with
him. I *can't bear* giving up therapy. So I'll refuse to change!"
Or:"Because I really care for my client and enormously enjoy the
sessions with her, I *must* not help her improve and bring these
sessions to an end!" These iB's can be sought out and disputed,
until the client and/or therapist gives them up and thereby removes motivation for resistance.

Fear of Disclosure Resistance

One of the most common forms of resistance stems from clients'
fear of disclosure. They find it uncomfortable to talk about themselves freely (e.g., engage in free association) or to confess
thoughts, feelings, and actions that they view as "shameful" (e.g.,
lusting for their mothers or sisters). They therefore resist being
open in therapy and getting at the source of some of the things
they find most bothersome (Dewald, 1982; Freud, 1926/1965b;
Schlesinger, 1982).

Where psychoanalysis finds this kind of resistance exceptionally
common and attributes it to deeply unconscious and often repressed feelings of guilt, RET holds that clients who resist therapy
because they are afraid to reveal "shameful" thoughts about themselves usually do so because they are quite aware of these feelings
or else have them just below their level of consciousness (in what
Freud called their preconscious realm of experience). Thus, if a
male client resists talking about sex because of his incestuous feelings for his mother or sister, he usually (though not always) is
consciously aware of these feelings but deliberately suppresses
rather than expresses them. He resists talking about such feelings
in therapy because he is usually telling himself irrational beliefs
such as "It's wrong to lust after my mother, and I *must* not behave
that wrongly!" "If I told my therapist that I lust after my sister, he
would think I was a sex fiend and wouldn't like me. I *have to* be
liked by my therapist and would be a shit if even he didn't like
me!"

In RET, we help clients to reveal these iB's and, more important,
to dispute and surrender them. We help them to see that their
"shameful" feelings may not even be wrong (for to lust after your
mother is hardly to copulate with her!) and that even when they
are self-defeating (as having continual obsessive thoughts about
incest would be), human *behaviors* never make one a totally rotten
person. By helping clients to give up just about *all* shame and self-

downing, RET sees that they rid themselves of what Freud would call superego-instigated resistance and are considerably more open in therapy than they would otherwise be (Dryden, 1983; Ellis, 1957, 1962, 1971b, 1973; Ellis & Grieger, 1977; Ellis & Whiteley, 1979).

Resistance Created by Fear of Discomfort

Probably the most common and strongest kind of resistance in therapy is that motivated by low frustration tolerance or what RET calls discomfort anxiety (Ellis, 1979, 1980). Even psychoanalysis, albeit reluctantly, recognizes this form of resistance. Blatt and Erlich (1982) acknowledge it as broad and basic, a fundamental resistance to change and growth. They call it an expression of the basic wish to maintain familiar and predictable modes of adaptation, even though these are uncomfortable and painful in the long run. Dewald (1982) talks about strategic resistance, that is, clients' efforts to seek fulfilment of childhood wishes and to demand unrealistic or impossible goals.

In RET this important form of resistance is attributed to short-range hedonism—clients' shortsighted demands that they achieve the pleasure of the moment even though this may well defeat them in the long run. The main irrational beliefs that lead to low frustration tolerance (LFT) or discomfort anxiety are "It's *too hard* to change, and it *shouldn't be* that hard! How *awful* that I have to go through pain to get therapeutic gain!" "I *can't tolerate* the discomfort of doing my homework, even though I have agreed with my therapist that it is desirable for me to do it." "The world is a *horrible place* when it forces me to work so hard to change myself! Life *should be* easier than it is!"

RET shows clients how to dispute these grandiose ideas and to accept the realistic notion that no matter how hard it is for them to change in therapy, it's harder if they don't. It teaches them that there is rarely any gain without pain and that the philosophy of long-range hedonism—-the seeking of pleasure for today *and* for tomorrow—-is likely to result in therapeutic change. It shows them how to use their natural hedonistic tendencies by reinforcing themselves for therapeutic progress (e.g., overcoming procrastination) and penalizing themselves when they refuse to work at therapy (e. g., when they procrastinate) (Ellis & Knaus, 1977; Knaus, 1982). RET also stresses problem-solving skills that help clients to achieve more successful solutions to their problems with an expenditure of minimum unnecessary effort (D'Zurilla & Goldfried,

1971; Ellis, 1962, 1977a; Ellis & Harper, 1975; Ellis & Whiteley, 1979; Spivack & Shure, 1974).

Secondary Gain Resistance

Several nineteenth-century and early-twentieth-century therapists noted that many clients receive secondary gains or payoffs from their disturbances and that they therefore are very reluctant to give them up (Ellenberger, 1970). Thus, if a factory worker who hates his job develops hysterical paralysis of the hand, he may resist psychotherapy because if it succeeds he will have to return to the work he hates. Freud (1926/1965b) and some of his followers (Berne, 1964; Fenichel, 1945; A. Freud, 1936) emphasized the unconscious aspects of this defensive process and insisted that if clients have direct gains to make by improving but have important unconscious secondary gains to maintain by refusing to improve, they will stubbornly resist treatment for deeply unconscious, and often repressed, reasons. Thus, a woman will refuse to lose weight or to have good sex with her husband because of her underlying hatred of her mother and the strong unconscious payoff she is receiving by spiting this mother (who wants her to be thin or to have a good marriage).

Although Freudians usually exaggerate the deeply unconscious (and very dramatic) element in secondary gains, it seems clear that many clients do resist change because the payoffs they are getting from their disturbances are (or at least *seem* to be) considerable. Goldfried (1982) puts this kind of resistance in behavioral terms by pointing out that when clients change for the "better," they sometimes discover hidden penalties. Women may overcome their unassertiveness, for example, only to find that assertiveness is often ill-rewarded in our society. Hence, they may "logically" fall back again to being unassertively neurotic!

Using RET analysis, we often find that secondary gain resistance is spurred by several iB's, such as "Because my mother *must not* try to make me lose weight, and is a *rotten person* for criticizing me for being overweight, I'll fix her wagon by remaining a fat slob!" Or "Because macho men will put me down if I am an assertive woman, and I *can't stand* their put-downs, I'll give up my desire for assertiveness and remain fairly submissive for the rest of my life." Using RET, we show clients how to dispute and surrender these iB's and thereby to be able to achieve the *greater* payoff of losing weight rather than the neurotic one of spiting their mother. And we may encourage women to achieve the *primary gain* of being assertive rather than the *secondary gain* of winning the approval of macho men.

Resistance Stemming from Feelings of Hopelessness

A sizable number of clients seem to resist therapeutic change because they strongly feel that they are *unable* to modify their disturbed behavior, that they are *hopeless* and *can't* change (Ellis, 1957, 1962; Turkat & Meyer, 1982). Such clients sometimes at first make good progress; but as soon as they retrogress, even slightly, they irrationally tend to conclude, "My falling back like this proves that it's *hopeless* and that I'll *never* conquer my anxiety!" "Because I *must* not be as depressed and incompetent as I now am, and am therefore a *complete depressive*, what's the use of my trying any longer to conquer my depression? I might as well give in to it and perhaps kill myself!"

Thoughts and feelings about the hopelessness of one's disturbed state are part of what RET calls the *secondary symptoms of disturbance*. As I have noted elsewhere (Ellis, 1962, 1979, 1980) these secondary symptoms tend to validate the RET or cognitive–behavior theory of neurosis. For on the level of primary disturbance, people desire to achieve their goals (such as success and approval), fail to do so, and instead of sanely concluding, "It would have been nice to achieve what I wanted but since I didn't, too bad! I'll try again next time," they irrationally conclude, "I *should* have achieved success and approval, and since I didn't do what I *must* do, it's *awful* and I'm no damned good as a *person!*" They then become, or, in RET terms, *make* themselves, disturbed. But once emotionally upset, they *see* their upsetness and cognize about it in this vein: "I *shouldn't* disturb myself as I am now doing! How *awful!* I am a *total fool* for acting this foolishly, and a fool like me *can't* change. It's hopeless!"

RET, because of its theory of secondary disturbance, particularly shows clients how they falsely *invent* their thoughts and feelings of hopelessness and how they can dispute and give them up. It uses (as will be indicated later in this series of articles) many cognitive, emotive, and behavioral methods of dispelling feelings of hopelessness that lead to resistance (Ellis & Abrahms, 1978).

Resistance Motivated by Self-punishment

Freud (1926/1965b) held that one of the main forms of resistance originates in the superego or in our guilt-creating tendencies. Thus, a female client who is jealous of her more accomplished sister and who may become more conscious of her hatred during therapy may strongly feel that she deserves to be punished for her meanness and may therefore resist giving up her self-defeating neurotic behavior (such as overeating or compulsive handwashing). During my 40 years of clinical practice I have rarely found this kind of self-punishing resistance among neurotics (though I have found it a little more often in psychotics and severely borderline clients).

Assuming this kind of resistance does exist, it would seem to stem from irrational beliefs along these lines: "Because I have done such evil acts, which I absolutely *should not* have done, I am a thoroughly *worthless individual* who *deserves* to suffer. Therefore, I deserve to be continually disturbed and will make no real effort to use therapy to help myself." If clients actively have these ideas, RET would be most appropriate to show them how to combat their iB's. Psychodynamic therapies, on the other hand, might well be contraindicated, because, although they might show clients how self-punishing they are, they might not teach them how to eradicate the irrational beliefs behind this kind of masochism.

Resistance Motivated by Fear of Change or Fear of Success

Psychodynamic therapists, from Freud onward, have often held that resistance sometimes stems from fear of change, from fear of the future, or fear of success (Blatt & Erlich, 1982). This is probably true, since many disturbed people have a pronounced need for safety and certainty, and even though their symptoms are uncomfortable, at least they know and are familiar with their negative limits and may be afraid that if they lose them they may experience even *greater* discomfort. So they prefer to stick with the tried-and-true discomfort.

More important, perhaps, many symptoms (such as shyness and fear of public speaking) protect clients against possible failure (such as failing in love or giving a laughable speech). To surrender these symptoms would therefore mean to risk subsequent failure and disapproval, and many clients would find this much more "catastrophic" or "awful" than they find retaining their symptoms.

What has been labeled "the fear of success" is almost never really that, but a fear of *subsequent* failure. Thus, if a withdrawn teenage boy stops withdrawing and begins to succeed at school, at sports, and at social affairs, he may (1) lose the comfort and indulgence of his overprotective parents, (2) gain the enmity of his siblings, (3) risk later failure at the activities in which he has now

begun to succeed, and (4) be forced to take on much more responsibility and effort than he would like to assume. He may *view* his
academic, athletic, and social "gains," therefore, as actual "dangers" or "failures" and may resist or retreat from them. Does he,
then, really have a "fear of success"—or of failure?

When clients do resist psychotherapy because of fear of change
or fear of success, RET looks for their iB's, such as "I *must* not
give up my symptoms, since change would be *too* uncomfortable
and I *can't stand* such change!" "I cannot change my neurotic
behavior and do better in life because that would be too risky. I
might encounter greater failure later, as I *must* not; for that would
be *awful!*" These and similar iB's that underlie the fear of change
or fear of success are revealed and eliminated during rational–
emotive therapy, thus minimizing this kind of resistance to change.

Resistance Motivated by Reactance and Rebelliousness

A number of clinicians have observed that some clients react or
rebel against therapy because they see it as an impingement on
their freedom. Especially if it is active and directive, they perversely fight it, even when they have voluntarily asked for it
(Brehm, 1976; Goldfried, 1982). Noting this form of resistance, several therapists have invented or adopted various kinds of paradoxical or provocative therapy to try to trick these perversely
rebellious clients into giving up their resistance (Dunlap, 1928;
Erikson & Rossi, 1979; Farrelly & Brandsma, 1976; Fay, 1978;
Frankl, 1960; Haley, 1963; Watzlawick, Weakland, & Fisch, 1974).

When clients resist therapy because of reactance, RET looks for
their irrational beliefs, such as "I *have to* control my entire destiny; and even though my therapist is on my side and is working
hard to help me, I *must not* let him or her tell me what to do!"
"How *awful* if I am directed by my therapist! I *can't bear* it! I
should have perfect freedom to do what I like, even if my symptoms are killing me!" RET reveals and helps clients rip up their
iB's, but it also selectively (and not cavalierly!) makes use of paradoxical intention. For example, it gives some clients the homework
assignment of failing at a certain task, to show them that failure is
not world-shattering (Ellis & Abrahms, 1978; Ellis & Whiteley,
1979).

As can be seen by the foregoing survey of some of the common
kinds of resistance, clients frequently come to therapy because
they are plagued with symptoms of emotional disturbance, and yet
they stubbornly resist the best efforts of their therapists to relieve
their suffering. In many instances their "resistance" is partly at-

tributable to therapeutic fallibility—to the poor judgment, inept theories, and emotional rigidities of their therapists. But often (perhaps more often) they have their own reasons for resisting the therapist-directed procedures that they voluntarily seek. As noted, these reasons are varied and wide-ranging.

While some aspects of the rational–emotive approach to treating common resistances have already been briefly outlined, the next section will discuss RET's cognitive antiresistance techniques in considerably more detail.

DISPUTING CLIENTS' IRRATIONAL, RESISTANCE-CREATING BELIEFS

RET employs a number of cognitive methods to interrupt, challenge, dispute, and change the irrational beliefs (iB's) that are found to underlie clients self-sabotaging resistances. These include the following techniques.

Cognitions That Underlie Resistance

Virtually all RET clients are taught the ABC's of emotional disturbance and dysfunctional behavior. Thus, when clients have a neurotic symptom or self-defeating consequence (C), such as depression and self-hatred, following their experiencing an unfortunate activating event (A), such as rejection by a significant person, they are shown that while A (rejection) probably contributes to and influences C (depression), it does not directly (as they tend to falsely "see" or infer) *create* or *cause* C. Rather, the more direct (and usually more important) "cause" of C is B, their belief system, with which they mainly "create" or "cause" C. Although they mistakenly believe that their depression and self-hatred directly and inevitably follow from their being rejected (A), they actually have a *choice* of B's and C's, and they foolishly *choose* to make themselves inappropriately depressed and self-hating (neurotic) at C, when they theoretically could have *chosen* instead to make themselves feel only appropriately disappointed and frustrated (self-helping and unneurotic) (Ellis, 1957, 1962, 1973; Ellis & Harper, 1975).

According to the ABC theory of RET, when these clients want to be accepted and approved at A (activating event) and are unpleasantly, instead, rejected, they *can* choose to manufacture or resort to a set of sensible or rational beliefs (rB's) and *can* thereby conclude, "How unfortunate that so-and-so disapproved of some of my traits and therefore rejected my friendship or love. Too bad! But I can still find significant others to approve of and accept me. Now how do I go about finding them?" If they rigorously create and stay with these rB's, these clients would, as stated, feel appropriately disappointed and frustrated but *not* depressed and self-hating.

Where, then, do their inappropriate and disturbed feelings of depression and self-hatred come from? RET shows clients that these neurotic consequences (C's) mainly or largely (though not exclusively) stem from their iB's. These iB's almost invariably consist of absolutistic, dogmatic, illogical, unrealistic beliefs. Instead of being expressions of flexible desire and preference (as rB's seem to be), they are inflexible, rigid commands and demands—absolutistic and unconditional shoulds, oughts, musts, and necessities. Thus, feelings of depression and self-hatred (at C) that follow disapproval and rejection (at A) are largely the result of iB's like (1) "I *must* not be disapproved of and rejected by a person I deem significant"; (2) "If I am rejected, as I must not be, it's *awful* and *terrible*"; (3) "I *can't stand* being disapproved, as I *must* not be"; and (4) "If I am rejected by a significant other, as must *never* under *any* conditions, occur, there has to be something horribly rotten about me, and that rottenness makes me a thoroughly *despicable, undeserving person!*"

RET, using its cognitively oriented ABC theory of human disturbance, first tends to show depressed and self-hating clients how they (and not their parents, teachers, society, or culture) unwittingly (and largely unconsciously) *choose* to *disturb themselves;* how they can therefore *decide* to change their iB's and thereby undisturb themselves; and how they can mainly (though not completely) acquire a realistic philosophy of *preference* rather than an absolutistic philosophy of *demandingness* and consequently rarely seriously disturb themselves in the future.

In combatting clients' self-defeating resistances, RET puts them into the ABC model and shows them that when they promise themselves and their therapists that they will work at therapy at point A (activating event) and when they act dysfunctionally at point C and achieve the self-defeating consequence of resistance, they have both rational beliefs and irrational beliefs at point C. Their rB's tend to be "I don't like working at therapy. It's hard to change myself! But it's hard*er* if I don't; so I'd damned well better push myself and do this hard work right *now* to make my life easier and better later." If, says the theory of RET, they *only* believed and felt these rational beliefs at B, they would not be especially resistant at C.

No such luck! When clients seriously and self-injuriously resist, they usually *also* create and indulge in irrational beliefs such as these: (1) "It's not only hard for me to work at therapy and change myself, it's *too* hard! It *should not, must not* be that hard"; (2) "How *terrible* that I have to work so hard and persistently to change myself"; (3) "I *can't stand* working at therapy that is harder than it *should be";* and (4) "What a *rotten therapist* I have, who makes me work harder than I *should!* And what *crummy methods* he or she inflicts on me! I'm sure there is some easier, more enjoyable method of changing, and until I find it I'll be damned if I'll make myself so uncomfortable with this one!"

These iB's of resistant clients, which mainly consist of a devout philosophy of low frustration tolerance (LFT) or discomfort anxiety (DA) (Ellis, 1979, 1980), can also be supplemented with a philosophy of self-downing or ego anxiety (EA). Resistant clients' iB's then tend to run along these lines: (1) "I absolutely *must* work hard and succeed at therapy"; (2) "If I don't change as much and as quickly as I *must,* it's *awful* and *terrible";* (3) "When I don't make myself change as well as I *must,* I *can't* stand it and life is *intolerable";* and (4) "Unless I do as well as I *must* in therapy, I am an inadequate, hopeless, worthless person!" One might think that these self-blaming iB's would help spur on clients to work at therapy and to overcome their resistance. Occasionally, this may be true, but usually these iB's sabotage clients, lead them to feel that they *can't* change, and result in still greater resistances.

RET's primary cognitive technique of combatting resistance, therefore, consists of showing clients that they do not "just" resist and that they do not *merely* resist *because* they find it difficult to change, but that they *choose* to subscribe to a philosophy of low frustration tolerance and/or of self-deprecation which, in turn, largely "causes" their resistance. The main cognitive message of RET, of course, is that they can instead choose to *dis*believe and to *surrender* their iB's and can exchange them for rB's that will help them work at rather than resist therapeutic change.

Disputing Irrational Beliefs

The basic disputing techniques of RET can be employed to show clients that the iB's behind their absolutistic *shoulds, oughts,* and *musts,* and behind the inferences, attributions, overgeneralizations, non sequiturs, and other forms of crooked thinking that tend to stem from these *musts,* can be annihilated or ameliorated by vigorous scientific thinking (Ellis, 1958a, 1962, 1971a, 1973; Ellis & Becker, 1982; Ellis & Grieger, 1977; Ellis & Harper, 1975; Ellis & Whiteley, 1979). Thus resisters are challenged by the therapist and are induced to keep challenging themselves with scientific questions like "Where is the evidence that I *must* succeed at changing myself?" "Why is it *awful* and *horrible* that it is difficult for me to change?" "Prove that I *can't stand* my having to work long and hard at therapy." "Where it is written that it's *too hard* to change and that it *should not* be that hard?" This kind of scientific disputing is persisted at, by both therapists and clients, until resisters start changing.

After A (activating event), B (rational and irrational beliefs), and C (emotional and behavioral consequences), RET goes directly (and often quickly) on to D: disputing. As just noted, D is the scientific method. Science accepts beliefs as hypotheses, constructs, or theories, not as facts. Furthermore, scientific theories are not dogmatic, inflexible, absolutistic, or devout. Otherwise they are religious rather than scientific (Ellis, 1983a; Rorer & Widiger, 1983). RET not only tries to be scientific about its own theories and to set them up so that they are precise and falsifiable (Bartley, 1962; Mahoney, 1977; Popper, 1972) but it is one of the new forms of cognitive–behavioral therapy that attempts to teach clients how to think scientifically about themselves, others, and the world in which they live. If, RET contends, people were consistently scientific and nonabsolutistic, they would rarely invent or subscribe to dogmatic *shoulds* and *musts*, would stay with their flexible wishes and preferences, and would thereby minimize or eliminate their emotional disturbances.

RET, therefore, encourages all clients, and particularly resistant ones, actively and persistently to dispute (at point D) their iB's and to arrive at point E, which is a new effect or effective philosophy. Where D consists of clients' disputing their iB's, E consists of the logical and empirical answers they then give to this disputing. Thus, to perform D and to arrive at E, a client's internal dialogue in regard to her or his resistance would go something like this:

IB: "I *must* succeed at changing myself during therapy!"

D: "Where is the evidence that I *have* to succeed?"

E: "There is no such evidence! Succeeding at changing myself would have several distinct advantages and I'd definitely like to get these advantages. But I never *have* to get what I desire, no matter how much I desire it."

IB: "If I don't succeed in overcoming my resistance and working at therapy, I am an incompetent, hopeless person who can never stop resisting!"

D: "Prove that I am an incompetent, hopeless person who can never stop resisting."

E: "I can't prove this, I can only prove that I am a person who has *so far* failed to stop resisting but not that I have, or always will have, *no* ability to do so in the future. Only my *belief* in my total incompetence to change myself will make me *more* incompetent than I otherwise would probably be!"

IB: "It is *awful* and *horrible* that I have to work at therapy and to change myself."

D: "In what way is it *awful* and *horrible* to work at therapy and to change myself?"

E: "In no way! It is distinctly difficult and inconvenient for me to work at therapy, and I'd rather it be easy. But when I label this work *awful* or *horrible* I mean that (1) it *should not* be as inconvenient as it is, (2) it is *totally* or 100% inconvenient, and (3) it is *more than* (101%) inconvenient. All these conclusions are wrong, since (1) it should be as inconvenient as it is because that's the way it is, (2) it virtually never can be 100% inconvenient because it invariably could be worse, and (3) it obviously cannot be 101% inconvenient because nothing can be *that* bad! Nothing in the universe is *awful* or *terrible* or *horrible*, since these are magical terms that go beyond reality and have no empirical referents. If I invent such antiempirical "descriptions" of my experience, I will thereby make my life *seem* and *feel* "awful" when it is only highly disadvantageous and inconvenient; and I will then make myself suffer *more* than I would otherwise suffer."

IB: "I can't *stand* my having to work long and hard at therapy."

D: "Why can't I stand having to work long and hard at therapy?"

E: "I definitely *can* stand it! I don't *like* working that long and hard and wish that I could change myself easily and magically. But I *can* stand what I don't like, as long as (1) I don't die of it and (2) I can still in some ways enjoy myself and be happy. Fairly obviously I won't die because I work at therapy (though I may kill myself if I don't!). And even though this kind of work is often unenjoyable, it leaves me time and energy for other pleasures. In fact, in the long run, it helps me to achieve *greater* life enjoyment. So I clearly *can* stand, *can* tolerate the therapeutic work that I don't like."

IB: "Because there is no easy way for me to work at therapy and I'd better uncomfortably persist at it until I collaborate with my therapist and change myself, the world is a *horrible* place and life is hardly worth living. Maybe I'd better kill myself."

D: "Where is it written that the world is a horrible place and that life is hardly worth living because there is no easy way for me to work at therapy?"

E: "It is only written in my self-defeating philosophy! It seems evident that, because of the way I am and because of the way the world is, I will often have trouble changing myself through therapy. Too bad! Really unfortunate! But if that's the way it is and that's the way I am, I'd better accept (though still dislike and often try to change) the world's limitations and my own fallibility, and I'd better attempt to live and to enjoy myself as much as I can with these undesirable realities. I can teach myself, as St. Francis recommended, to have the courage to change the unpleasant things that I can change, to have the serenity to accept those that I can't change, and to have the wisdom to know the difference between the two."

RET's most famous and most popular technique is the one just outlined: that of teaching resistant clients to find their main irrational beliefs that significantly contribute to or "cause" their resistances; to actively dispute these iB's by rigorously using the logico-empirical tools of the scientific method; and to persist at this disputing until they arrive at E, an effective philosophy that is self-helping rather than irrational and self-downing. As Kelly (1955) brilliantly noted, humans are natural predictors and scientists. RET, along with other cognitive behavioral therapies, tries to help them be better and more productive scientists in their personal affairs (Ellis, 1962, 1973; Ellis & Becker, 1982; Ellis & Grieger, 1977; Ellis & Harper, 1975; Ellis & Whiteley, 1979; Friedman, 1975; Mahoney, 1974, 1977).

Rational and Coping Self-Statments

RET, following the leads of Bernheim, (1886/1947) and Coué (1922), teaches resistant clients to say to themselves, repetitively, rational or coping statements and to keep actively autosuggesting these statements until they truly believe them and feel their effect. Thus, they can strongly say to themselves rB's such as "Therapy doesn't *have* to be easy. I can, in fact, *enjoy* its difficulty and its challenge." "Sure it's hard to work at changing myself, but it's much harder if I don't." "Too bad if I am imperfect at changing myself. That only proves that I am still, and will continue to be, a highly fallible person. And I *can* accept myself as fallible!" Unlike positive thinking, however, RET encourages resisters to think through, and not merely parrot, rational and coping statements.

Referenting

RET uses the general semantics method of referenting (Danysh, 1974) and teaches resistant clients (1) to make a comprehensive list of the disadvantages of resisting and the advantages of working at therapy and (2) to keep regularly reviewing and thinking about this list (Ellis & Abrahms, 1978; Ellis & Becker, 1982; Ellis

& Harper, 1975). Thus, under disadvantages of resisting, clients can list: "(1) It will take me longer to change. (2) I will keep suffering as long as I resist changing. (3) My refusing to change will antagonize some of the people I care for and will sabotage my relationships with them. (4) My therapy will become more boring and more expensive the longer I take to change myself. (5) Continuing to afflict myself with my symptoms will make me lose much time and money. (6) If I continue to resist, I may well antagonize my therapist and encourage him or her to put less effort into helping me. (7) My refusing to work hard at therapy and thereby continuing to remain irrationally fearful and anxious will force me to forego many potential pleasures and adventures and make my life much duller." Similarly, using this referenting technique, clients are shown how to list the advantages of working harder at therapy and thereby abetting their own personality change. By reviewing and examining these disadvantages of resistance and these benefits of nonresistance, they are helped to resist considerably less.

RET often forcefully brings to clients' attention not only present but probable later disadvantages of resisting therapy. Thus, the RET practitioner can reward the client: "Yes, you don't have to work right now at overcoming your low frustration tolerance, since your parents are still around to help support you economically. But how are you going to earn a decent living after they are gone unless you prepare yourself to do so now?" "Of course, you may be able to get away with your drinking and staying up late at night at present, but won't it eventually sabotage your health? And do you really want to keep making yourself fat, tired, and physically ill?"

Challenge of Self-Change

RET tries to sell some resistant clients on the *adventure* and *challenge* of working at changing themselves. Thus, it gives clients the homework exercise of disputing irrational beliefs (DIBS) which helps them debate their iB's and to reframe some of the difficult things they do with therapy by asking themselves questions like, "What good things can I feel or make happen if I work hard at therapy and still don't succeed too well?" (Ellis, 1974a; Ellis & Harper, 1975). Rational–emotive therapists also prod resistant clients with questions like "Suppose you pick the wrong therapy technique and work hard at it with few good results. Why would that be great for you to do?" By these paradoxical questions they hope to help resisters see that (1) trying something and at first failing at it is usually better than not trying at all; (2) striving to change leads to important information about oneself that may result in later success and pleasure; (3) action can be pleasurable in its own right, even when it does not lead to fine results; (4) trying something and at first failing at it is usually better than not trying at all; (5) trying to change oneself and *accepting* delayed results increases one's frustration tolerance, and (6) the *challenge* of striving for therapeutic change (like the challenge of trying to climb Mount Everest) may be exciting and enjoyable in its own right.

Although ego-enhancing methods of therapy are seen by RET as having their distinct dangers (since if clients are led to think of themselves as good or worthy individuals when they succeed at therapy, they will also harmfully view themselves as bad or worthless individuals when they fail), some elements of verbal reinforcement can be used to combat resistance. Thus, therapists can show clients that *it* is good and desirable (and not that *they* are good or worthy) if they use their energy and intelligence to work at therapy. This technique can be combined with the challenging method. For example, the therapist can say to the client, "Yes, many people are prone to sitting on their asses and to stupidly resisting changing themselves. But anyone who fortunately has *your* intelligence, talent, and ability *can* overcome this kind of resistance and show how competent he or she is at changing. Not that you *have to* use your innate ability to change. But wouldn't you get much better results if you did?"

Proselytizing Others

One of the regular RET cognitive techniques that can be especially helpful with resistant and difficult clients consists of inducing them to use RET methods with others (Bard, 1980; Ellis, 1957; Ellis & Abrahms, 1978; Ellis & Harper, 1975; Ellis & Whiteley, (1979). If, using RET, you have clients who resist giving up anger, you can try to get them to talk others—relatives, friends, employees—out of *their* anger. If your clients refuse to do their RET homework, you can try to induce them to give homework assignments to others and to keep checking to see if these people actually do their homework.

Cognitive Distraction

Cognitive distraction frequently is used in RET to divert clients from anxiety and depression (Ellis, 1973; Ellis & Abrahms, 1978; Ellis & Whiteley, 1979). Thus, clients are shown how to relax, to meditate, to do yoga exercises, and to use other forms of distraction when they upset themselves. Distraction, however, is often not that useful with resistant clients, since it only temporarily diverts them from rebelliously and defensively persisting with their disturbed behavior and they therefore soon return to it. One form of distraction that works well if you can get these clients to use it is in the form of a vital, ongoing interest that really absorbs them. Thus, if you can help them get absorbed in writing a book, being an active member of a self-help group, or volunteering to help others, they can sometimes find such constructive enjoyment as to minimize their need for self-defeating behavior like alcoholism, drugs, or stealing.

Use of Humor

Many resistant clients have little sense of humor, and that is precisely why they find it so hard to see how they are defeating themselves and how absurd their thoughts and behaviors are. But some, in spite of their severe disturbance, do have a good sense of humor that can be used to interfere with their resistance. Thus, I kept showing one of my stubborn clients how ironic it was that she railed and ranted against cold weather and thereby made herself suffer *more* from the cold. I also frequently tell resistant clients, "If the Martians ever come to visit us and they're really sane, they'll die laughing at us. For they'll see bright people like you vainly insisting that they can do something they can't do—such as change your parents—while simultaneously saying they can't do something that they invariably can do, namely, change yourself. They won't be able to understand this and will probably fly back to Mars because we're so crazy!" RET frequently uses humor and rational humorous songs to combat therapeutic resistance (Ellis, 1977c, 1977d, 1981).

Paradoxical Intention

With highly resistant and negative clients, as Erikson (Erikson & Rossi, 1979), Frankl (1960), Haley (1963), and others have shown, paradoxical intention sometimes works and is therefore a cognitive method of RET (Ellis & Whiteley, 1979). Thus, you can tell depressed clients to loudly wail and moan about everything that occurs in their lives. Or you can have highly anxious people take the assignment of only allowing themselves to worry from 8:00 to 8:15 AM every day. Or you can insist that resistant clients refuse to do *anything* you tell them to do, such as refuse to come on time for their sessions and refuse to do any homework assignments. Perversely, resisters may then stop resisting. But don't count on this! Paradoxical intention is a shocking but limited method that tends to work only occasionally and under special conditions.

Suggestion and Hypnosis

You may deliberately use strong suggestion or hypnosis with some difficult clients, even though these are inelegant techniques that somewhat interfere with clients' independent thinking. Resistant clients who *think* hypnosis work may allow themselves to change with hypnotic methods when they would not allow this without hypnosis. RET has included hypnosis methods from its inception in 1955 (Ellis, 1958a, 1962). Stanton (1977), Tosi (Tosi & Marsella, 1977; Tosi & Reardon, 1976), and other researchers and clinicians have shown how it can sometimes be used effectively with resistant clients.

Philosophy of Effort

The usual practice of RET is to explain to all clients, right at the beginning of therapy, that they have enormous self-actualization powers (as well as self-defeating tendencies) and that only with hard work and practice will they be able to fulfill these powers (Ellis, 1962; Grieger & Boyd, 1980; Grieger & Grieger, 1982; Walen, DiGiuseppe, & Wessler, 1980; Wessler & Wessler, 1980). Clients are also shown that they can easily fall back to old dysfunctional patterns of behavior and that they therefore had better persistently keep monitoring themselves and working to change. With resistant clients this realistic message is often repeated with the aim of both prophylaxis and cure. A favorite RET slogan is "There's rarely any gain without pain!" This philosophy is steadily promulgated to combat the low frustration tolerance of resisters (Ellis, 1979, 1980).

Working with Clients' Expectations

As Meichenbaum and Gilmore (1982) have shown, clients bring cognitive expectations to therapy and may see what is helping in their sessions with the therapist as disconfirming these expectations. Consequently, they may resist changing themselves. If so, you can accurately and empathically perceive and share your clients' expectations, make sense out of their unproductive resistant behavior, and thereby help overcome resistance. Using RET, you might well go one step further and, as you help your clients explore and understand the reasons for their resistance (and the iB's that often underlie this resistance), you can actively push, encourage, and persuade them to surrender their resistant ideas and behaviors.

Irrational Beliefs Underlying Primary and Secondary Resistance

Clients frequently have both primary and secondary resistance. Primary resistance stems largely from their three main musts: (1) "I *must* change myself quickly and easily, and I'm an incompetent person if I don't"; (2) "You *must* not force me to change, and I'll fight you to death if you do;" and (3) "Conditions *must* make it easy for me to change, and I won't try to help myself if they don't!" Once humans resist changing themselves for any of these three (or a combination of these three) reasons, they *see* that they resist and have another set of irrational beliefs about this resistance, such as (1) "I *must* not incompetently resist change, and I'm a pretty worthless person if I do"; (2) "I *must* not resist change in a hostile or rebellious manner, and it's *awful* if I do"; and (3) I *must* not have low frustration tolerance that makes me resist change, and I can't stand it if I do!" Their secondary disturbance, that is, their guilt or shame *about* resisting, tends to tie up their time and energy and incite *increased* resistance. In RET, therefore, we look for and try to eliminate secondary as well as primary resistances, and we do so by showing clients their primary and secondary iB's and by disputing both these sets of iB's, just as we would dispute any other irrational beliefs. By helping them first to undo their disturbances *about* their resistance, we show them how to remove these secondary problems and then how to get back to changing the ideas and feelings that constitute the primary resistance.

Irrational Beliefs Underlying Avoidance of Responsibility

Resistance may sometimes stem from clients' trying to avoid responsibility for change and from their deliberately (though perhaps unconsciously) fighting the therapist's efforts to help them change. This form of childish rebelliousness can arise from ego irrationalities ("I must thwart my therapist and 'win out' over him to show what a strong, independent person I am!") or from low frustration tolerance irrationalities ("I must not have to work too hard at therapy, because if I assume full responsibility for changing myself life becomes too rough and unsatisfying!"). When avoid-

ance of responsibility and concomitant rebellion against the therapist or against working at therapy result in resistance, RET tries
to show clients the irrational beliefs (iB's) behind this kind of
avoidance and rebellion and teach them how to combat and surrender these iB's.

Use of Quick and Active Disputation

Although RET therapists may sometimes help create resistance
by actively and quickly disputing their clients' irrational beliefs,
they may also, by "poorly" employing this technique, promptly
smoke out clients' resistances, see exactly what kind of D.C.'s (difficult customers) these clients are, and promote more efficient and
effective therapy methods. Active disputing, though risky, may uncover resistances rapidly, save therapists and clients considerable
time and effort, lead to vigorous countermeasures by the therapist,
and sometimes lead to a suitable quick (and inexpensive!) end to
therapy.

Some cognitive behavioral therapists (e.g., Meichenbaum &
Gilmore, 1982) recommend that resistance be overcome by gradu-
ating the change process into manageable steps and by structuring
therapeutic intervention so that the therapist maximizes the likelihood of success at each stage. This will sometimes work but also
has its dangers with those who resist because of abysmal LFT.
With these individuals gradualism may easily *feed* their LFT and
help them believe that it is *too* hard for them to change and that
they *must* do so in a slow, gradual manner (Ellis, 1983c).

Disputing Impossibility of Changing

When clients contend that they *can't* change, RET can show
them that this is an unrealistic, antiempirical view not supported
by any facts (which merely show that *it is difficult* for them to
change). But RET therapists do not use only this realistic, scientific refutation but also employ the more elegant anti*must*urbatory
form of disputing. Clients usually tell themselves, "I *can't change*"
because they start with the basic proposition "I *must* have an
ability to change quickly and easily, and I'm incompetent and
pretty worthless if I don't do what I *must*." RET disputes this
*must*urbatory, absolutistic thinking by showing them that they
never have to change (though that would be highly desirable) and
that they are *people who act incompetently* rather than *incompetent
people*. This disputing of the idea "I can't change" is therefore
more profound and more elegant than the simple antiempirical

disputing of Meichenbaum (1977), Beck (1976), Maultsby (1975), and other proponents of CBT.

Helping Clients Gain Emotional Insight

RET often shows resistant clients that they falsely believe they are working hard to improve and to overcome their own resistance, when they really aren't. Thus they frequently say, "I see that I am telling myself that therapy should be easy, and I see that that is wrong." They then mistakenly think that because they have *seen* how they are resisting and have *seen* the error of their ways, they have worked at changing this error and thereby *overcome* their resistance. But they have usually done nothing of the sort. Their "insight" has not been used to help them *fight* the idea that therapy should be easy. They can now be shown that they'd better see and fight this idea, that is, dispute it by asking themselves, "*Why* should therapy be easy?" and by vigorously answering, "There's no damned reason why it should be! It often is—and should be— *hard!*"

RET tries to distinguish clearly between so-called intellectual and emotional insight (Ellis, 1963). Resistant clients often say, "I have intellectual insight into my hating myself but this does me no good, since I still can't stop this self-hatred. What I need is emotional insight." What these clients mean is that they hate themselves and may even see the irrational self-statements they make to bring about this feeling (e.g., "I must always succeed at important tasks and I am worthless when I don't!"), but they do not know how to change their iB's or they know how to change them but refuse to do the persistent and strong disputing that is required to give them up.

In RET we try to show clients, particularly resistant ones, three main kinds of insight:

1. People mainly disturb themselves rather than get upset by external conditions and events.

2. No matter when they first started to disturb themselves (usually in childhood) and no matter what events contributed to their early *disturbance*, people *now*, in the present, continue to make themselves upset by *still* strongly subscribing to irrational beliefs similar to those they held previously. They now keep their old disturbances alive by continually reindoctrinating themselves with these iB's.

3. Since people are born with the tendency to accept iB's from others and to create many of their own, and since they consciously

and unconsciously reinstill these iB's in themselves from early childhood onward, and since they easily, automatically, and habitually actualize these ideas in their feelings and actions and thereby powerfully reinforce them over long periods of time, there is usually no simple, fast, easy, and complete way to change them. Only considerable work and practice to challenge and dispute these irrational beliefs and only long, concerted *action* that contradicts the behavioral patterns that accompany them will be likely to minimize or extirpate them.

RET, then, teaches clients that insights #1 and #2 are important but not sufficient for profound philosophical and behavioral change and that they had better be accompanied by the most important insight of all—#3.

More specifically, RET shows resistant clients who say that they have intellectual insight into their symptoms (such as self-hating), but can't give it up because they don't have emotional insight, that they usually only have insight #1—and even that, often, partially. Thus, a young woman may say, "I see that I hate myself," but may not see what she is irrationally believing to create her self-hatred (e.g., "Because I am not as competent as I *must* be, I am a thoroughly *inadequate person*"). Even when she sees what she is believing to create her self-hatred, she only has achieved #1; and she may falsely believe that she obtained her self-hating belief from her parents and *that* is why she now hates herself.

In RET, we would therefore help her achieve insight #2: "No matter how I got the irrational belief that I *should* be more competent and am an *inadequate person* if I'm not, *I* now continue to indoctrinate myself with it so that *I* am fully responsible for believing it today; and therefore *I* had better give it up."

RET doesn't stop there, since she still might be left with only mild or "intellectual" insight, but pushes her on to insight #3: "Since *I* keep actively believing that I *should* be more competent and am an *inadequate person* if I'm not, and since I tend to keep recreating and newly inventing similar irrational beliefs (because it is my basic nature to do so), I had better keep steadily and forcefully *working and practicing* until I no longer believe this. For only by *continually* disputing and challenging this belief and only by *forcing myself* to keep acting against it will I be able *finally* to give it up and replace it with rational beliefs and effective behaviors."

Insight #3, plus the determination to act on this level of understanding, is what RET calls "emotional" insight or "willpower." It is this kind of cognitive restructuring or profound philosophical change that RET particularly employs with resistant clients.

Bibliotherapy and Audiotherapy

RET employs bibliotherapy with resistant clients and encourages them to read RET-oriented pamphlets and books, such as *Reason and Emotion in Psychotherapy* (Ellis, 1962), *A New Guide to Rational Living* (Ellis & Harper, 1975), *Humanistic Psychotherapy: The Rational–Emotive Approach* (Ellis, 1973), and *A Guide to Personal Happiness* (Ellis & Becker, 1982). RET practitioners also give a good many talks, courses, workshops, marathons, and intensives that help clients understand theory and use the techniques of rational–emotive therapy. I have especially found that some RET cassette recordings, films, and TV cassettes are useful with resistant clients, who are urged to listen to them many times until the presentations on these materials sink in. Notably useful in this respect are the cassette recordings *Conquering the Dire Need for Love* (Ellis, 1977b), *Conquering Low Frustration Tolerance* (Ellis, 1977a), *Overcoming Procrastination* (Knaus, 1974), *I'd like to Stop, But . . .* (Ellis, 1974b), *Self-Hypnosis: The Rational–Emotive Approach (Golden, 1982), Twenty-One Ways to Stop Worrying* (Ellis, 1972b), and *How to Stubbornly Refuse to Be Ashamed of Anything* (Ellis, 1972a).

Imaging Methods

One of the main modes of human cognition is imagery, and RET frequently employs imaging methods. These are sometimes especially useful with resistant clients, since some of them resist because they see and feel things more incisively through pictorial than through verbal means (Coué, 1922; Lazarus, 1978, 1981). Consequently, when they block on or find difficulty with verbal self-statements and philosophical disputing of irrational beliefs, they can sometimes be reached more effectively by imagery methods. To this end, RET, following Coué (1922) and a host of his disciples, can teach resisters to use positive imagery to imagine themselves doing things that they negatively contend that they can't do (e.g., successfully giving a public talk), and it can help them imagine bearing up under frustrating conditions when they normally think that they absolutely can't bear such conditions. Also, RET frequently employs Maultsby's technique of rational–emotive imagery (Maultsby, 1975); Maultsby & Ellis, 1974), by which resistant (and other) clients are shown how to imagine one of the worst things that could happen to them, to implode their disturbed feelings about this happening, and then to work at changing these to more appropriate negative feelings.

Modeling Techniques

Bandura (1969, 1977) has pioneered in showing how modeling methods can be used to help disturbed individuals, and RET has always used such methods (Ellis, 1962, 1971a, 1973; Ellis & Abrahms, 1978; Ellis & Whiteley, 1979). In the case of resistant and difficult clients, RET practitioners not only teach them how to accept themselves unconditionally and fully, no mater how badly or incompetently they behave, but they also model this kind of acceptance by displaying firm kindness to these clients and showing by their attitudes and demeanor (as well as their words) that they can fully accept such clients, even when they are nasty to the therapist, when they come late to sessions, when they fail to do their homework, and when they otherwise stubbornly resist the therapist's efforts (Ellis, 1962, 1973; Ellis & Whiteley, 1979). RET also sponsors public workshops, such as my famous Friday night workshops that are given regularly at the Institute for Rational–Emotive Therapy in New York, where live demonstrations of RET are given for large audiences, so that the members of the audience can see exactly how RET is done and can model their own self-help procedures after this model. Resistant clients who serve as volunteer demonstratees at these workshops are often particularly helped by the public session they have with me (or other RET therapists, when I am out of town) and by the feedback and the comments they receive from 15 or 20 members of the audience.

Recorded Playback of Therapy Sessions

Carl Rogers (1942) pioneered in using recordings of therapy sessions to help therapists understand exactly what they were doing and how to improve their techniques. RET, beginning in 1959, pioneered the use of audiotapes for two other purposes: (1) to show therapists throughout the world exactly how RET is done, so that they could model their own use of it after the practices of its originator and other RET practitioners (Elkin, Ellis, & Edelstein, 1971; Ellis, 1959, 1966a, 1966b; Wessler & Ellis, 1980), and (2) to give clients recordings of their own sessions so that they could listen to them several times and thereby hear and internalize some of the therapeutic messages that they would otherwise miss or forget. This second use of recordings, which also can be done with video equipment if this is available, has been found very useful with resistant clients. If they are given homework assignments of listening to their own taped sessions (and sometimes the taped session of others), they often get across to themselves some of the elements of RET that they otherwise easily miss (Ellis, 1979; Ellis & Abrahms, 1978; Ellis & Whiteley, 1979). One of my borderline clients, for example, who argued vigorously against almost every point I made about his needlessly upsetting himself, accepted these same points almost all the time when he listened to a cassette recording of each session several times during the week following this session.

CONCLUSION

As can be seen from the material just presented, RET cognitive methods, when carefully selected and employed with resistant and difficult clients, can often be effective. Also, RET often employs a variety of emotive and behavioral techniques, in addition to many cognitive methods, with resistant clients. Rarely, if ever, would it compulsively stick to one favored method. In fact, the more resistant a client is, the more cognitive, emotive, and behavioral methods are usually employed. RET is designed to be not only effective but efficient and therefore to solve clients' problems as quickly as feasible, utilizing minimal therapist time and effort (Ellis, 1980). With average clients who are not resistant, it can therefore often employ a relatively small number of techniques and can help these clients to improve significantly in a fairly short period of time. It invariably uses some cognitive, emotive, and behavioral modalities but doesn't have to utilize many of them compulsively, as is sometimes done in multimodal therapy (Lazarus, 1981) or in holistic psychotherapy. With resistant clients, however, RET is often done more comprehensively and intensively because that is what such clients may require.

REFERENCES

Bandura, A. (1969). *Principles of behavior modification.* New York: Holt, Rinehart and Winston.

Bandura, A. (1977). *Social learning theory.* Englewood Cliffs, NJ: Prentice-Hall.

Bard, J. (1980). *Rational–emotive therapy in practice.* Champaign, IL: Research Press.

Bartley, W. W. (1962). *The retreat to commitment.* New York: Knopf.

Basch, M. F. (1982). Dynamic psychotherapy and its frustrations. In P. L. Wachtel (Ed.), *Resistance.* New York: Plenum.

Beck, A. T. (1976). *Cognitive therapy and the emotional disorders.* New York: International Universities Press.

Berne, E. (1964). *Games people play.* New York: Grove.

Bernheim, H. (1947). *Suggestive therapeutics.* New York: London Book Company. (Originally published, 1886).

Blatt, S. J., & Erlich, H. S. (1982). Levels of resistance in the psychotherapeutic process. In P. L. Wachtel (Ed.), *Resistance.* New York: Plenum.

Brehm, S. S. (1976). *The application of social psychology to clinical practice.* Washington, DC: Hemisphere.

Coué, E. (1922). *My method.* New York: Doubleday, Page.

Danysh, J. (1974). *Stop without quitting.* San Francisco: International Society for General Semantics.

Dewald, P. A. (1982). Psychoanalytic perspectives on resistance. In P. L. Wachtel (Ed.), *Resistance,* New York: Plenum.

Dryden, W. (1982). The therapeutic alliance: Conceptual issues and some research findings. *Midland Journal of Psychotherapy,* June, *1,* 14–19.

Dryden, W. (1983). Vivid RET II: Disputing methods. *Rational Living. 1,* 9–14.

Dunlap, K. (1928). A revision of the fundamental law of habit formation. *Science, 67,* 360–362.

D'Zurilla, T. J., & Goldfried, M. R. (1971). Problem solving and behavior modification. *Journal of Abnormal Psychology, 78,* 107–126.

Elkin, A., Ellis, A., & Edelstein, M. (1971). *Recorded sessions with RET clients (C2025).* New York: Institute for Rational–Emotive Therapy.

Ellenberger, H. F. (1970). *The discovery of the unconscious.* New York: Basic Books.

Ellis, A. (1957). *How to live with a "neurotic."* New York: Crown.

Ellis, A. (1958a). Hypnotherapy with borderline psychotics. *Journal of General Psychology, 59,* 245–253.

Ellis, A. (1958b). Rational psychotherapy. *Journal of General Psychology, 59,* 35–49.

Ellis, A. (1959). *Recorded sessions with adolescent and child RET clients (C2011).* New York: Institute for Rational–Emotive Therapy.

Ellis, A. (1962). *Reason and emotion in psychotherapy.* New York: Lyle Stuart.

Ellis, A. (1963). Toward a more precise definition of "emotional" and "intellectual" insight. *Psychological Reports, 13,* 125–126.

Ellis, A. (1966a). *Recorded sessions with RET neurotic clients (C2004).* New York: Institute for Rational–Emotive Therapy.

Ellis, A. (1966b). *Recorded sessions with RET severely disturbed clients (C2004).* New York: Institute for Rational–Emotive Therapy.

Ellis, A. (1971a). *Growth through reason.* Palo Alto, CA: Science and Behavior Books; Hollywood, CA: Wilshire.

Ellis, A. (1971b). *How to stubbornly refuse to be ashamed of anything* [Cassette recording]. New York: Institute for Rational–Emotive Therapy.

Ellis, A. (1972a). *Psychotherapy and the value of a human being.* New York: Institute for Rational–Emotive Therapy.

Ellis, A. (1972b). *Twenty-one ways to stop worrying* [Cassette recording]. New York: Institute for Rational–Emotive Therapy.

Ellis, A. (1973). *Humanistic psychotherapy: The rational–emotive approach.* New York: Crown and McGraw-Hill Paperbacks.

Ellis, A. (1974a). *Disputing irrational beliefs (DIBS).* New York: Institute for Rational–Emotive Therapy.

Ellis, A. (1974b). *I'd like to stop, but...* [Cassette recording]. New York: Institute for Rational–Emotive Therapy.

Ellis, A. (1976). RET abolishes most of the human ego. *Psychotherapy, 13,* 343–348.

Ellis, A. (1977a). *Conquering low frustration tolerance* [Cassette recording]. New York: Institute for Rational–Emotive Therapy.

Ellis, A. (1977b). *Conquering the dire need for love* [Cassette recording]. New York: Institute for Rational–Emotive Therapy.

Ellis, A. (1977c). *Fun as psychotherapy* [Cassette recording]. New York: Institute for Rational–Emotive Therapy.

Ellis, A. (1977d). *A garland of rational songs* [Songbook and cassette recording]. New York: Institute for Rational–Emotive Therapy.

Ellis, A. (1977e). *How to live with—and without—anger.* New York: Reader's Digest Press.

Ellis, A. (1979). Discomfort anxiety: A new cognitive behavioral construct: 1 *Rational Living, 14*(2), 3–8.

Ellis, A. (1980). Discomfort anxiety: A new cognitive behavioral construct: 2 *Rational Living, 15*(1), 25–30.

Ellis, A. (1981). The use of rational humorous songs in psychotherapy. *Voices, 16*(4), 29–36.

Ellis, A. (1983a). *The case against religiosity.* New York: Institute for Rational–Emotive Therapy.

Ellis, A. (1983b). Failures in rational–emotive therapy. In E. Foa & P. M. Emmelkamp (Eds.), *Failures in behavior therapy.* New York: Wiley.

Ellis, A. (1983c). The philosophic implications and dangers of some popular behavior therapy techniques. In M. Rosenbaum & C. M. Franks (Eds.), *Perspectives on behavior therapy in the eighties.* New York: Springer Publishing Co.

Ellis, A., & Abrahms, E. (1978). *Brief psychotherapy in medical and health practice.* New York: Springer Publishing Co.

Ellis, A., & Becker, I. (1982). *A guide to personal happiness.* North Hollywood: Wilshire Books.

Ellis, A., & Grieger, R. (Eds.). (1977). *Handbook of rational–emotive therapy.* New York: Springer Publishing Co.

Ellis, A., & Harper, R. A. (1975). *A new guide to rational living.* Hollywood, CA: Wilshire; Englewood Cliffs, NJ: Prentice-Hall.

Ellis, A., & Knaus, W. (1977). *Overcoming procrastination.* New York: Institute for Rational–Emotive Therapy; New York: New American Library.

Ellis, A., & Whiteley, J. M. (Eds.). (1979). *Theoretical and empirical foundations of rational–emotive therapy.* Monterey, CA: Brooks/Cole.

Erikson, M. H., & Rossi, E. L. (1979). *Hypnotherapy: An exploratory casebook.* New York: Irvington.

Farrelly, F., & Brandsma, J. M. (1974). *Provocative therapy.* Fort Collins, CO: Shields.

Fay, A. (1978). *Making things better by making them worse.* New York: Hawthorn.

Fenichel, O. (1945). *Psychoanalytic theory of neurosis.* New York: Norton.

Frankl, V. (1960). Paradoxical intention: A logotherapeutic technique. *American Journal of Psychotherapy, 14,* 520–535.

Freud, A. (1936). *The ego and the mechanisms of defense.* New York: International Universities Press.

Freud, S. (1965a). The dynamics of transference. In J. Strachey (Ed. and Trans.), *The standard edition of the complete psychological works of Sigmund Freud.* New York: Basic Books. (Original work published 1912)

Freud, S. (1965b). Inhibitions, symptoms and anxiety. In J. Strachey (Ed. and Trans.), *The standard edition of the complete psychological works of Sigmund Freud.* New York: Basic Books. (Original work published 1926)

Freud, S. (1965c). The interpretation of dreams. In J. Strachey (Ed. and Trans.), *The standard edition of the complete psychological works of Sigmund Freud.* New York: Basic Books. (Original work published 1900).

Friedman, M. (1975). *Rational behavior.* Columbia, SC: University of South Carolina Press.

Goldfried, M. R. (1982). Resistance and clinical behavior therapy. In P. L. Wachtel (Ed.), *Resistance.* New York: Plenum.

Grieger, R., & Boyd, J. (1980). *Rational–emotive therapy: A skills-based approach.* New York: Van Nostrand Reinhold.

Grieger, R., & Grieger, I. Z. (Eds.). (1982). *Cognition and emotional disturbance.* New York: Human Sciences.

Haley, J. (1963). *Strategies of psychotherapy.* New York: Grune and Stratton.

Johnson, N. (1980). Must the rational–emotive therapist be like Albert Ellis? *Personnel and Guidance Journal, 59,* 49–51.

Kelly, G. (1955). *The psychology of personal constructs.* New York: Norton.

Knaus, W. (1974). *Rational–emotive education.* New York: Institute for Rational–Emotive Therapy.

Knaus, W. (1982). *How to get out of a rut.* Englewood Cliffs, NJ: Prentice-Hall.

Lazarus, A. A. (1978). *In the mind's eye.* New York: Rawson, Wade.

Lazarus, A. A. (1981). *The practice of multimodal therapy.* New York: McGraw-Hill.

Lazarus, A. A., & Fay, A. (1982). Resistance or rationalization? In P. L. Wachtel (Ed.), *Resistance.* New York: Plenum.

Mahoney, M. J. (1974). *Cognition and behavior modification.* Cambridge, MA: Ballinger.

Mahoney, M. J. (1977). Personal science: A cognitive learning therapy. In

A. Ellis & R. Grieger (Eds.), *Handbook of rational–emotive therapy*. New York: Springer Publishing Co.

Mahoney, M. J. (1980). Psychotherapy and the structure of personal revolution. In M. J. Mahoney (Ed.), *Psychotherapy process*. New York: Plenum.

Maultsby, M. C., Jr. (1975). *Help yourself to happiness*. New York: Institute for Rational–Emotive Therapy.

Maultsby, M. C., Jr., & Ellis, A. (1974). *Technique for using rational–emotive imagery*. New York: Institute for Rational–Emotive Therapy.

Meichenbaum, D. (1977). *Cognitive behavior modification*. New York: Plenum.

Meichenbaum, D., & Gilmore, J. B. (1982). Resistance from a cognitive–behavioral perspective. In P. L. Wachtel (Ed.), *Resistance*. New York: Plenum.

Popper, K. R. (1972). *Objective knowledge*. Oxford: Clarendon.

Rogers, C. R. (1942). *Counseling and psychotherapy*. Boston: Houghton Mifflin.

Rogers, C. (1961). *On becoming a person*. London: Constable.

Rorer, L., & Widiger, L. (1983). Personality assessment. *Annual Review of Psychology, 34*, 431–463.

Schlesinger, H. J. (1982). Resistance as process. In P. L. Wachtel (Ed.), *Resistance*. New York: Plenum.

Spivack, G., & Shure, M. (1974). *Social adjustment in young children*. San Francisco: Jossey-Bass.

Stanton, H. E. (1977). The utilisation of suggestions derived from rational emotive therapy. *Journal of Clinical and Experimental Hypnosis, 25*, 18–26.

Tosi, D., & Marzella, J. N. (1977). Rational stage directed therapy. In J. L. Wolfe & E. Brand (Eds.), *Twenty years of rational therapy*. New York: Institute for Rational–Emotive Therapy.

Tosi, D., & Reardon, J. P. (1976). The treatment of guilt through rational stage directed therapy. *Rational Living, 2*(1), 8–11.

Turkat, I. D., & Meyer, V. (1982). The behavior-analytic approach. In P. L. Wachtel (Ed.), *Resistance*. New York: Plenum.

Wachtel, P. (Ed.) (1982). *Resistance*. New York: Plenum.

Walen, S., DiGiuseppe, R., & Wessler, R. L. (1980). *A practitioner's guide to rational–emotive therapy*. New York: Oxford.

Watzlawick, P., Weakland, J., & Fisch, R. (1974). *Change*. New York: Norton.

Wessler, R. A., & Wessler, R. L. (1980). *The principles and practice of rational–emotive therapy*. San Francisco: Jossey-Bass.

Wessler, R. L. (1982, September). *Alternative conceptions of rational–emotive therapy: Towards a philosophically neutral psychotherapy*. Paper presented at the Twelfth European Congress on Behaviour Therapy, Rome.

Wessler, R. L., & Ellis, A (1980). Supervision in rational–emotive therapy. In A. K. Hess (Ed.), *Psychotherapy supervision*. New York: Wiley.

How To Deal with Your Most Difficult Client—You

14

INTRODUCTION

In 1983 the Division of Consulting Psychology of the American Psychological Association invited Ellis, as one of its former presidents and as a distinguished practitioner, to give an address, and because he would be mainly addressing practicing therapists, he picked this relevant topic. After publication of his article in both Psychotherapy in Private Practice *and the* Journal of Rational–Emotive Therapy, *Ellis received more requests for reprints than he has ever received for the great majority of his 600 published articles.*

Although innumerable articles on countertransference have been written by psychoanalytic writers, few of them have looked at the irrational beliefs that spark this kind of therapist reaction to clients. This paper takes a long, hard look at this iatrogenic phenomenon. As such, it is an important Ellis and RET article.

Reprinted from the *Journal of Rational–Emotive Therapy*, 1983, 1(1), 2–8, with permission of the author and the journal. This article also appeared in *Psychotherapy in Private Practice*, 1984, 2(1), 25–35.

Although the literature on difficult and resistant clients is extensive (Freud, 1912/1958a; Wachtel, 1982; Weiner, 1982), much less attention has been given to the difficult and resistant therapist. Psychoanalytic writers, to be sure, have emphasized the dangers of countertransference (Coltrera & Ross, 1967; Freud, 1912/1958c; Greenson, 1967; Wolstein, 1959), but they have often ignored other problems of the therapist. The present paper will attempt to address some of these problems and make a few hopefully educated guesses about how therapist difficulties arise and what may be done to alleviate them.

Before we can consider what are some of the main blocks to the therapist's effective functioning, it would be nice to have a picture of what a fully functioning therapist is. Unfortunately, we have as yet no real agreement on this point. Freudians, who tend to be relatively passive and who emphasize looking for unconscious determinants of clients' disturbances, stress therapists' listening with their third ear (Fenichel, 1953; Freud, 1904/1958b; Reik, 1948). Rogerians emphasize the therapist's genuineness, accurate empathy, and unconditional positive regard (Rogers, 1957) and nonpossessive warmth (Truax & Carkhuff, 1967; Truax & Mitchell, 1971). Behavior therapists and cognitive behavior therapists recommended that effective therapy also include several kinds of teaching and persuasive skills (Ellis, 1979a; Meichenbaum, 1977; Wessler & Ellis, 1980).

I still take the stand I took a quarter of a century ago when I objected to Rogers (1957) seminal paper, "The Necessary and Sufficient Conditions of Therapeutic Personality Change," and pointed out "that although basic constructive personality change—as opposed to symptom removal—seems to require fundamental modifications in the ideologies and value systems of the disturbed individual, there is probably *no* single condition which is absolutely necessary for the induction of such changed attitudes and behavior patterns" (Ellis, 1959; 1962, p. 119).

With some amount of temerity, however, let me hazard the guess that when the facts have been more diligently researched, we will find that the most effective therapists tend to practice somewhat as follows:

1. They are vitally interested in helping their clients and energetically work to fulfill this interest.
2. They unconditionally accept their clients as people, while opposing and trying to ameliorate some of their self-defeating ideas, feelings, and behaviors.
3. They are confident of their own therapeutic ability and with-

out being rigid or grandiose, strongly believe that their main techniques will work.

4. They have a wide knowledge of therapeutic theories and practices and are flexible, undogmatic, and scientific and consequently open to the acquiring of new skills and to experimenting with these skills.

5. They are effective at communicating and at teaching their clients new ways of thinking, emoting, and behaving.

6. They are able to cope with and ameliorate their own disturbances and consequently are not inordinately anxious, depressed, hostile, self-downing, self-pitying, or undisciplined.

7. They are patient, persistent, and hardworking in their therapeutic endeavors.

8. They are ethical and responsible and use therapy almost entirely for the benefit of the clients and not for personal indulgence.

9. They act professionally and appropriately in a therapeutic setting but are still able to maintain some degree of humanness, spontaneity, and personal enjoyment in what they are doing.

10. They are encouraging and optimistic and show clients that, however difficult it may be, they can appreciably change. At times, they forcefully urge and push clients to change.

11. They not only try to help clients feel better and surrender their presenting symptoms, but also try to help them make a profound attitudinal change that will enable them to maintain their improvement, continue to improve, and ward off future disturbances.

12. They are eager to help virtually all their clients, freely refer to other therapists those they think they can't help or are not interested in helping, and try to be neither underinvolved or overinvolved with those clients they retain. They sincerely try to overcome their strong biases for or against their clients that may interfere with their therapeutic effectiveness. They monitor their prejudices (countertransference feelings) that lead to their strongly favoring or disfavoring some of their clients and, if advisable, refer such clients to other therapists.

13. They possess sufficient observational ability, sensitivity to others, good intelligence, and sound judgment to discourage their clients from making rash and foolish decisions and from seriously harming themselves.

Assuming that effective therapists tend to behave as just described, which of you practitioners reading this consistently follow this ideal pathway? Very few, I would guess! I fully admit that in the forty years I have been practicing psychotherapy, I have by no means fully lived up to this ideal myself. Nor do I know any of the scores of therapists I have supervised who has done so. On the other hand, I have met and supervised many who have fallen far below this ideal.

Although therapeutic infallibility is hardly a realistic goal, we may still ask: How do therapists block their own effectiveness and what can they do to their resistances by seeing and eradicating their blocks? If you are a psychotherapist and are ignoring some of the best rules of the game—including several that you personally endorse and would prefer to follow—how can you understand your own blocks to good practice—and how can you unblock yourself? How can you decrease, if not quite annihilate, some of your therapeutic fallibility?

Ever since I threw off the shackles of psychoanalytic theory some thirty years ago and started to develop a new theory that soon blossomed out into rational–emotive therapy (RET), I have stubbornly insisted that human disturbance is contributed to by environmental pressures, including our childhood upbringing, but that its most important and vital source originates in our innate tendency to indulge in crooked thinking. People not only learn or take over unrealistic expectations, absolutistic ideas, illogical conclusions, and irrational beliefs from their parents and their culture; but they also have a positive genius for inventing and exacerbating these self-defeating cognitions themselves. They don't *have* to think exaggeratedly, perfectionistically, dogmatically and unscientifically, but they sooner or later do; and they thereby make themselves—yes, creatively make themselves—emotionally disturbed and behaviorally dysfunctional. Their parents, teachers, and peers appreciably help them in this respect. But, being talented screwballs in their own right, they scarcely need such help and can easily louse themselves up without it (Ellis, 1957, 1962, 1971, 1973, 1976).

Being, in spite of their aspirations to godliness, still human, psychotherapists often indulge in the same kind of irrational absolutistic beliefs that other people hold. After giving this matter some thought, reviewing my experiences with therapists I have supervised, and considering the therapeutic irrationalities that other writers have observed (Grieger & Boyd, 1980; Novaco, 1980; Tosi & Eshbaugh, 1978; Weinrach, 1977; Walen, DiGiuseppe, & Wessler, 1980; Wessler & Wessler, 1980), I have come up with several irrational beliefs that I hypothesize often lead to therapeutic inefficiency:

1. *"I have to be successful with all of my clients practically all of the time."* Although, as RET hypothesizes, strong wishes, desires, and preferences will rarely get you into serious emotional trouble, absolutistic necessities and demands frequently will. If you under all conditions *must* succeed with your clients, you will tend to be horrified and depressed when you don't—and be still anxious when you do. For how can you be sure that you will succeed again next time? You can't!

Your dire need to help virtually all your clients all of the time leads to several equally pernicious corollaries: (a) "I must continually make brilliant and profound interpretations." (b) "I must always have good judgment." (c) "I must help my clients *more* than I am now helping them." (d) "If I fail with any of my clients, it has to be my fault." (e) "When I fail, as I must not, I'm a thoroughly lousy therapist—and a rotten person!" (f) "My successes don't count if I have a *real* failure!"

When you place golden ideals like these on your therapeutic back, how can you fail to feel inadequate, to interfere with your work, and to make yourself a prime candidate for early burnout? Not very easily!

2. *"I must be an outstanding therapist, clearly better than other therapists I know or hear about."* This is another preferential goal which, when you escalate it to necessity, tends to incapacitate you. Some corollaries of this absolutistic demand include (a) "I must succeed even with impossible clients"; (b) "I must have *all* good sessions with clients"; (c) "I must use the greatest and most prestigious system of therapy and be outstanding at using it"; (d) "I must be famous as a therapist"; (e) "Because I am a therapist, I should have no emotional problems myself and am disgraced if I do."

Like the first irrational belief mentioned above, this second one leads to frantic endeavor and to the inefficiencies that accompany such franticness. Panic also results when it appears that this unrealistic goal may not be achieved—or may not be constantly reachieved.

3. *"I have to be greatly respected and loved by all my clients."* If and when you have this dire need—instead of preference—you again frequently have several perfectionistic corollaries: (a) "I must not dislike any of my clients and especially must not show that I dislike them." (b) "I must not push my clients too hard, lest they then hate me." (c) "I must avoid ticklish issues that might upset and antagonize my clients." (d) "The clients whom I like and who like me must remain in therapy practically forever." (e) "My clients must see that I am thoroughly devoted to them and that I

never make any mistakes." (f) "It's horrible to be disapproved by any of my clients because their disapproval makes me a bad therapist and a rotten person."

4. *"Since I am doing my best and working so hard as a therapist, my clients should be equally hardworking and responsible, should listen to me carefully, and should always push themselves to change."* This irrational belief displays your low frustration tolerance and anger—and leads you to damn your clients for being disturbed. It frequently has several unrealistic corollaries, such as (a) "My clients should not be difficult and resistant!" (b) "They should do exactly what I tell them to do!" (c) "They should work very hard in between sessions and always do their therapeutic homework!" (d) "I should only have young, bright, attractive, and not too difficult clients!"

5. *"Because I am a person in my own right, I must be able to enjoy myself during therapy sessions and to use these sessions to solve my personal problems as much as to help clients with their difficulties."* This irrational idea partly contradicts the nature of paid psychotherapy—which indeed may be of help to therapists but which ethically puts the interests of clients first. The philosophy of self-indulgence that underlies this belief often leads to several corollaries that also sabotage therapy: (a) "I must mainly use therapeutic techniques that I enjoy using, whether or not they are very helpful to clients." (b) "I must only use techniques that are easy and that do not wear me out." (c) "I must make considerable money doing therapy and must not have to work too hard to make it." (d) "If I exploit some of my clients amatively and sexually, that will do both them and me a lot of good." (e) "Because I am so helpful as a therapist, I should be able to get away with coming late to appointments, canceling them at the last minute, sleeping during sessions, and indulging myself in other ways."

Now I am not contending that all of you therapists reading this frequently and strongly hold many of the above irrational beliefs. Some of you—lucky souls—may hold none of them or may maintain the few that you do hold very lightly. What I am hypothesizing is that when you resolve to work at doing effective therapy but then sabotage your own efforts and wind up with strong feelings of anxiety, depression, hostility, guilt, or self-pity about your therapeutic endeavors, you then tend to subscribe to some of these irrationalities. And I am suggesting that you may be resistant to finding and surrendering them. Why? Because, first, you may be reluctant to admit that you, a psychotherapist, really have deep-seated emotional difficulties. Second, you may be so preoccupied with helping others that you rarely think about helping yourself. Third, you may wrongly assume that your authoritative knowledge of disturbance and your self-explorations during your training protect you from being disturbed about the therapeutic process. Fourth, you may have the same kind of low frustration tolerance—commonly known as laziness—that prevents so many of your own clients from working to change themselves. Fifth, you may be so involved with yourself that you myopically fail to see shortcomings and emotional difficulties that a more objective observer would observe.

For reasons such as these, you may well be your most difficult client. If so, don't despair, bolster your defenses, and run away from facing and dealing with the situation you are in. As a therapist, you often meet clients' resistance and do your best to overcome it. Why not similarly tackle your own?

I have been outlining, in a recent series of articles in the *British Journal of Cognitive Psychotherapy,* the RET theory and practice of resistance in regular and difficult clients (Ellis, 1983a, 1983b, 1984). Let me, to conclude this paper, apply some of these practices to resistant therapists. If you have been consciously or unconsciously subscribing to some of the irrational beliefs listed above, if you have consequently felt disturbed about yourself as a therapist, and if your effectiveness has consequently suffered, here are some of the cognitive, emotive, and behavioral techniques you can use to deal with your most difficut client—you.

1. Assume that some strong irrational beliefs lie closely behind your therapeutic upsets and that these include one or more absolutistic shoulds, oughts, or musts, such as those listed above.

2. Search diligently for those that specifically apply to you and your therapy. Don't give up until you find a few.

3. Consider these irrational beliefs as hypotheses, not facts, that you can dispute and surrender. Use the same scientific methods to challenge them as you would employ to question any other dubious hypothesis. For example: "Where is the evidence that I *have to be* successful with all of my clients practically all the time?" "Who says that I *must* be better than other therapists?" "Where is it written that *it is necessary* for me to be respected and loved by all my clients?"

4. Carefully think about these hypotheses until you come up with disconfirming evidence and therefore are really willing to give them up.

5. Create alternative rational, preferential statements to substitute for these unrealistic, unconfirmable hypotheses. For example:

"I clearly don't *have to be* successful with all of my clients, though that would be lovely! Because I would *like to* help most of them, let me work at that goal."

6. Convince yourself that you can unconditionally accept yourself as a person—that is, see yourself as deserving to continue to live and enjoy yourself—*whether or not* you succeed as a therapist and *whether or not* your clients (or other significant people) approve of you. Acknowledge some of your deeds and traits (such as your acting irresponsibly in therapy) as ineffective and deplorable, but refuse to lambaste your *self* or your *being* for this failing.

7. Refuse to awfulize about anything. See that it's most inconvenient and annoying when your clients refuse to do their agreed upon homework. But it's not awful, horrible, or terrible. *Just annoying!* (Ellis, 1979a, 1980).

8. Instead of mainly looking at the ease of staying the way you are and the discomfort of changing, make a comprehensive list of the pains of maintaining your disturbance and the advantages of giving them up. Review and think about this list every day until you are much more motivated to change.

9. Give yourself the strong challenge and excitement of doing one of the most difficult and most rewarding things you can do in life—pig-headedly refusing to make yourself needlessly misearable about anything.

10. Actively talk your clients (and friends and relatives!) out of their irrationalities and thereby encourage yourself to talk yourself out of your own.

11. Reduce some of your self-defeating ideas to absurdity and see the humor in some of the profound stupidities that you rigidly hold. Tell yourself, for example, "I really *should* do only what I enjoy doing during my therapy sessions. What do you think those blasted clients are paying me for, anyway—to get better?" Sing to yourself one of the rational humorous songs made famous by RET (Ellis, 1977). [See Chapter 9.]

12. Show yourself that so-called intellectual insight into your difficulties is not enough and that what is often called emotional insight consists of at least three major kinds of knowledge: (a) the realization that you, rather than external events, largely create your own disturbance; (b) the understanding that no matter how and when you originally started to think irrationally, you still stubbornly persist in thinking that way today; (c) the insight that only considerably work and practice—yes, *work and practice*—to challenge and dispute your irrational beliefs and only persistent *action* against the dysfunctional behaviors that accompany these beliefs will suffice to make and keep you undisturbed.

13. You can use rational–emotive imagery created by Maultsby (1975) and adopted by me (Maultsby & Ellis, 1974) to change your intensely disturbed feelings. Thus, you can vividly imagine yourself miserably failing as a therapist, let yourself feel very anxious or depressed as you imagine this, implode this feeling, then (while still imagining this gruesome scene) make yourself feel only disappointed and regretful (and *not* depressed), and finally practice this new appropriate feeling every day for at least 30 days until you automatically begin to feel regretful and disappointed instead of anxious or depressed whenever you think about failing.

14. You can publicly perform one or more of the RET shame-attacking exercises (Ellis, 1969, 1972). The purpose of these exercises is to do some act that you normally consider foolish and shameful—for example, sing at the top of your voice while walking down the street—and make yourself feel *un*ashamed while performing it. You thereby show yourself that you never *have to* denigrate yourself even when other people clearly disapprove of you, and you help convince yourself that you *prefer* but do not *need* your clients' (and other people's) approval.

15. Whenever you can do so, unequivocally, strongly, and persistently *act* against your irrational beliefs. If, for example, you abhor difficult clients and think that you *can't stand* them, deliberately take some on and show yourself that you *can* tolerate what you don't like and that you *can* accept (and learn from) clients who behave obnoxiously. If you find yourself using only the techniques you find easy and enjoyable, force yourself to try some of the more difficult ones and keep trying them until they become familiar—and probably rewarding.

As you can see from the foregoing suggestions, dealing with yourself and your problems as a therapist may involve some of the same techniques you would often employ with your own difficult clients. The difference is that they have you to monitor them in following these techniques, while who do you have to monitor yourself? Answer: You, of course! You can, if you deem it desirable, go back into therapy yourself and thereby acquire a paid monitor. But unless you are a unusually D.C. (difficult customer), it would be better if you go it alone. Why? Frankly, to make things a bit more troublesome for yourself. For if you try to change yourself, at first, without guidance and support from another therapist, you may be able to appreciate better the struggles of your own clients when they strive to effectuate self-change, and you may thereby come to accept them with their struggles and their setbacks. In any event, if you find that you do not satisfactorily change on your own, you can always later work with another therapist. And had better!

Therapists are human—and, believe it or not, fallible humans. Ideally, they are supremely well informed, highly confident, minimally disturbed, extremely ethical, and rarely under- or overinvolved with their clients. Actually, they are hardly ideal. If you, as a therapist, find yourself seriously blocked in your work, look for the same kind of irrational beliefs, inappropriate feelings, and dysfunctional behaviors that you would investigate in your underachieving clients. When you ferret out the absolutistic philosophies and perfectionist demands that seem to underlie your difficulties, ask yourself—yes, *strongly* ask yourself—these trenchant questions: (1) Why do I *have to be* an indubitably great and unconditionally loved therapist? (2) Where is it written that my clients *must* follow my teachings and absolutely *should* do what I advise? (3) Where is the evidence that therapy *must* be easy and that I *have to* enjoy every minute of it?

If you persist in asking important questions like these and insist on thinking them through to what are scientific and logical answers, you may still never become the most accomplished and sanest therapist in the world. But I wager that you will tend to be happier and more effective than many other therapists I could—but charitably will not—name. Try it and see!

REFERENCES

Coltrera, J. T., & Ross, N. (1967). Freud's psychoanalytic technique—from the beginnings to 1923. In B. J. Wolman (Ed.), *Psychoanalytic techniques.* New York: Basic Books.

Ellis, A. (1957). *How to live with a "neurotic."* New York: Crown.

Ellis, A. (1959). Requisite conditions for basic personality change. *Journal of Consulting Psychology, 23,* 538–540.

Ellis, A. (1962). *Reason and emotion in psychotherapy.* New York: Lyle Stuart.

Ellis, A. (1969). A weekend of rational encounter. In A. Burton (Ed.), *Encounter.* San Francisco: Jossey-Bass.

Ellis, A. (1971). *Growth through reason.* Palo Alto, CA: Science and Behavior Books; North Hollywood, CA: Wilshire Books.

Ellis, A. (1972). *How to stubbornly refuse to be ashamed of anything* [Cassette recording]. New York: Institute for Rational–Emotive Therapy.

Ellis, A. (1973). *Humanistic psychotherapy: The rational–emotive approach.* New York: Crown and McGraw-Hill.

Ellis, A. (1976). The biological basis of human irrationality. *Journal of Individual Psychology, 32,* 145–168.

Ellis, A. (1977). *A garland of rational songs* [Songbook and cassette recording]. New York: Institute for Rational–Emotive Therapy.

Ellis, A. (1979a). Discomfort anxiety: A new cognitive behavioral construct: Part 1. *Rational Living. 14*(2), 3–8.

Ellis, A. (1979b). The theory of rational–emotive therapy: The practice of rational–emotive therapy. In A. Ellis and J. M. Whiteley (Eds.), *Theoretical and empirical foundations of rational–emotive therapy.* Monterey, CA: Brooks/Cole.

Ellis, A. (1980). Discomfort anxiety: A new cognitive behavioral construct: Part 2. *Rational Living, 15*(1), 25–30.

Ellis, A. (1983a). Rational–emotive therapy (RET) approaches to overcoming resistance: 1. Common forms of resistance. *British Journal of Cognitive Psychotherapy, 1*(1), 28–38.

Ellis, A. (1983b). Rational–emotive therapy (RET) approaches to overcoming resistance: 2. How RET disputes clients' irrational, resistance-creating beliefs. *British Journal of Cognitive Psychotherapy, 1*(2), 1–16.

Ellis, A. (1984). Rational–emotive therapy (RET) approaches to overcoming resistance: 3. Using emotive and behavioral techniques of overcoming resistance. *British Journal of Cognitive Psychotherapy, 2*(1), 11–26.

Fenichel, O. (1953). *The collected papers of Otto Fenichel.* New York: Norton.

Freud, S. (1958a). The dynamics of transference. In J. Strachey (Ed. and Trans.), *The standard edition of the complete psychological works of Sigmund Freud.* London: Hogarth. (Original work published 1912).

Freud, S. (1958b). Freud's psycho-analytic procedure. In J. Strachey (Ed. and Trans.), *The standard edition of the complete psychological works of Sigmund Freud.* London: Hogarth. (Original work published 1904)

Freud, S. (1958c). Recommendations to physicians practicing psychoanalysis. In J. Strachey (Ed. and Trans.), *The standard edition of the complete psychological works of Sigmund Freud.* London: Hogarth. (Original work published 1912)

Greenson, R. R. (1967). *The technique and practice of psychoanalysis.* New York: International Universities Press.

Grieger, R., & Boyd, J. (1980). *Rational–emotive therapy: A skills based approach.* New York: Van Nostrand Reinhold.

Maultsby, M. C., Jr. (1975). *Help yourself to happiness.* New York: Institute for Rational–Emotive Therapy.

Maultsby, M. C., Jr., & Ellis, A. (1974). *Technique of using rational–emotive imagery.* New York: Institute for Rational–Emotive Therapy.

Meichenbaum, D. (1977). *Cognitive behavior modification.* New York: Plenum.

Novaco, R. (1980). Training of probation counselors for anger problems. *Journal of Counseling Psychology, 27,* 385–399.

Reik, T. (1948). *Listening with the third ear.* New York: Rinehart.

Rogers, C. (1957). The necessary and sufficient conditions of therapeutic personality change. *Journal of Consulting Psychology, 21,* 459–461.

Tosi, D., & Eshbaugh, D. (1978). A cognitive experiential approach to the interpersonal development of counselors and therapists. *Journal of Clinical Psychology, 34,* 494–500.

Truax, C. B., & Carkhuff, R. R. (1967). *Toward effective counseling and psychotherapy: Training and practice.* Chicago: Aldine.

Truax, C. B., & Mitchell, K. M. (1971). Research in certain therapist skills in relation to process and outcomes. In A. E. Bergin, & S. L. Garfield (Eds.), *Handbook of psychotherapy and behavior change.* New York: Wiley.

Wachtel, P. L. (Ed.). (1982). *Resistance: Psychodynamic and behavioral approaches.* New York: Plenum.

Walen, S. R., & DiGiuseppe, R., & Wessler, R. L. (1980). *A practitioner's guide to rational–emotive therapy.* New York: Oxford.

Weiner, M. F. (1982). *The psychotherapeutic impasse.* New York: Free Press.

Weinrach, S. (1977). Even counselors have irrational ideas. *Personnel and Guidance Journal, 52,* 245–247.

Appendix

AN ANNOTATED SELECTION OF ALBERT ELLIS'S MAJOR BOOKS ON PSYCHOTHERAPY

Ellis, A. (1962). *Reason and emotion in psychotherapy.* New York: Lyle Stuart. This was Ellis's first major work on RET and continues to be his most-cited book. Some chapters are still relevant today, but the book is mainly of historical value.

Ellis, A. (1985). *Overcoming resistance: Rational–emotive therapy with difficult clients.* New York: Springer Publishing Co. This book represents a complete statement of Ellis's views on understanding resistance in psychotherapy and what can be done to overcome it.

Ellis, A., & Abrahms, E. (1978). *Brief psychotherapy in medical and health practice.* New York: Springer Publishing Co. This book represents Ellis's major statement on brief therapy. Although written for medical and health practitioners, its application is much broader.

Ellis, A., & Dryden, W. (1987). *The practice of rational–emotive therapy.* New York: Springer Publishing Co. This book considers the practice of RET in the major therapeutic modalities (e.g., individual therapy, couples therapy, family therapy, group therapy, and sex therapy).

Ellis, A., McInerney, J. F., DiGiuseppe, R., & Yeager, R. J. (1988). *Rational–emotive therapy with alcoholics and substance abusers.* New York: Pergamon Press. This book is a clear, concise treatment guide to helping clients with problems of addictions.

Ellis, A., Sichel, J. L., Yeager, R. J., DiMattia, D. J., & DiGiuseppe, R. (1989). *Rational–emotive couples therapy.* New York: Pergamon Press. This book gives a clear account of how to use RET to help couples in trouble.

Ellis, A., & Yeager, R. J. (1989). *Why some therapies don't work: The dangers of transpersonal psychology.* Buffalo, NY: Prometheus Books. This is a stinging and controversial critique of approaches to psychotherapy associated with the fourth force of psychology: transpersonal psychology.

OTHER BOOKS OF INTEREST

Bernard, M. E., & DiGiuseppe, R. (1989). *Inside rational–emotive therapy: A critical appraisal of the theory and therapy of Albert Ellis.* San Diego, CA: Academic Press. This book contains critical appraisals of the theory and therapy of Albert Ellis written by leading authorities on psychotherapy who are *not* exponents of RET. In the final chapter Ellis responds to his critics.

Wiener, D. N. (1988). *Albert Ellis: Passionate skeptic.* New York: Praeger. The first bibliography on Albert Ellis to be published. The book contains much interesting material not previously available in published form. However, it has not met with unreserved approval from Albert Ellis and other RET therapists.

Yankura, J., & Dryden, W. (1990). *Force and energy in practice: The psychotherapy of Albert Ellis.* New York: Springer Publishing Co. This book is the first to present a critique of Albert Ellis's way of conducting psychotherapy based on tapes of his actual work with clients.

Index

ABCs of RET, 7–14, 40–41, 122
  in assessment of clients, 158
  in resistance, 179–280
Abelson, R. P., 220
Abramson, L. Y., 98
Absolutistic demands, 6, 7, 26
Absolutistic philosophy, 15, 42, 153,
    309
Acceptance, 18–19; *see also*
    Self-acceptance
  of uncertainty, 19
  unconditional, 136, 146, 147, 167,
    179, 192,197, 272, 301
Activating Event, 7, 40, 53
  changes in, 27, 28, 174
  in client assessment, 153
Active-directive style, in therapy, 148,
    149, 150, 198
Addictions, 58, 70, 103
Adler, A., 195
Affective theory, 46
Agoraphobia, 109
Ainslie, G., 74
Anger, 9; *see also* Hostility
  vs. annoyance, 22
  and discomfort disturbance, 95
  guilt about, 24
  as inappropriate emotion, 158, 179
Annoyance
  vs. anger, 22
  as appropriate emotion, 158, 179,
    307
Anorexia, 128
Antiprocrastination exercises, 173,
    211–213
Anxiety, 58
  about anxiety, 24, 47, 97, 98, 107,
    153, 161
  vs. concern, 21
  as inappropriate emotion, 158, 179
  kinds of, 96–98
  and low frustration tolerance, 94
  and relaxation therapy, 110–111
  and self-ratings, 39
  social, 25, 97
Assessment, of therapy clients, 151

components of, 152–153
  disputing process in, 160, 161
  importance of, 151
  incorrect, 176
  primary vs. secondary problems in,
    161, 176, 179
  RET sessions as, 151
Attachment process, 120–121, 127
Audiotherapy, 293
Audio/video playback, 294–295
Autism, 38, 73–74
Avoidance, 25, 60
"Awfulizing," 15–17, 161
  alternative to, 18, 214
  in therapists, 307
Axtelle, George, 85

Bandura, Albert, 48, 129, 219, 267
Bartley, W. W., 118
Beal, D., 150
"Beautiful Hang-Up," 210
Beck, Aaron, 36, 49, 98, 102, 115, 117,
    129, 219
Behavior modification, 35
Behavior therapy, 47; *see also*
    Cognitive–behavioral therapy
Behaviors
  biological basis of, 43, 257–258
  changes in, 28
  dysfunctional, 6, 8, 153, 159
  hereditary components in, 35, 37, 45,
    46, 118
  illogical thinking about, 34–35
  instinctive, 32, 41
  irrational; *see* Irrationalities
Beliefs
  in ABCs of RET, 7, 8, 10–12, 14, 41
  absolutistic, 23, 177, 230, 303
  changing, 224
  in client assessment, 153
  disputing, 228; *see also* Disputing
  invented, 73
  as mediators, 8
  in psychological disturbance, 15
  rational vs. irrational, 5–6, 8–9,
    11–12, 228–233; *see also* Irrational

315